THE EARLY FEMINISTS

STUDIES IN GENDER HISTORY

Recent years have shown that the study of gender has proved to be of too great an importance to be ignored. By challenging long-accepted approaches, categories and priorities, gender history has necessitated nothing less than a change in the historical terrain. This series seeks to publish the latest and best research, which not only continues to restore women to history and history to women, but also to encourage the development of a new channel of scholarship.

Alison Bashford
PURITY AND POLLUTION

Kathryn Gleadle
THE EARLY FEMINISTS

Elizabeth C. Sanderson
WOMEN AND WORK IN EIGHTEENTH-CENTURY EDINBURGH

Pamela Sharpe
ADAPTING TO CAPITALISM

Lilian Lewis Shiman
WOMEN AND LEADERSHIP IN NINETEENTH-CENTURY ENGLAND

Clare Taylor
WOMEN OF THE ANTI-SLAVERY MOVEMENT

The Early Feminists

Radical Unitarians and the Emergence of the Women's Rights Movement, 1831–51

Kathryn Gleadle
Department of History
University of Warwick
England

St. Martin's Press
New York

THE EARLY FEMINISTS
Copyright © 1995 by Kathryn Gleadle

First edition 1995
Reprinted (with alterations) 1998

St. Martin's Press, Scholarly and Reference Division,
175 Fifth Avenue, New York, N.Y. 10010

Published in the United States of America

This book is printed on paper suitable for recycling and made from fully managed and sustained forest sources.

Printed in Great Britain

ISBN 0–312–12861–4 (clothbound)
ISBN 0–312–21013–2 (paperback)

Library of Congress has cataloged the hardcover edition as follows
Gleadle, Kathryn.
The early feminists : radical Unitarians and the emergence of the women's rights movement, 1831–51 / Kathryn Gleadle.
p.   cm.
Includes bibliographical references (p.   ) and index.
ISBN 0–312–12861–4 (cloth)
1. Feminism—Great Britain—History.   2. Women's rights—Great Britain—History.   3. Unitarianism—Great Britain—History.
I. Title.
HQ1596.G54 1995
305.42'0941—dc20   95–17959
                                                                                        CIP

Contents

List of Pseudonyms and Initials Used in Contemporary Publications

ABR	Angus B. Reach
C	Caroline Southwood Hill
GEJ	Geraldine Endsor Jewsbury
GJH	George Jacob Holyoake
Edward Search	William Henry Ashurst (Junior and Senior)
JR	William Bridges Adams
Junius Redivivus	William Bridges Adams
Kate	Catherine Barmby
MLG	Mary Leman Grimstone
One of the People	William James Linton
Panthea	Sophia Dobson Collet
P	Bessie Rayner Parkes
PMV	Margaret Mylne
RHH	Richard Hengist Horne
Silverpen	Eliza Meteyard
Spartacus	William James Linton
SY	Sarah Flower Adams
WJF	William Johnson Fox
WJL	William James Linton
WT	William Thompson

Acknowledgements

This book could not have been written without the assistance of the librarians and archivists of a great number of libraries and record offices, both in this country and abroad. To them, I am extremely grateful. In particular, special thanks are due to the following institutions, which have allowed me to quote from manuscript material in their care: the Beinecke Rare Book and Manuscript Library, Yale University; Birmingham City Archives; Birmingham University Library; the British Library of Political and Economic Science; the Syndics of Cambridge University Library; the Rare Book and Manuscript Library, Columbia University; Dr Williams's Library; the Mistress and Fellows, Girton College, Cambridge; Houghton Library, Harvard University; the John Rylands University Library, Manchester; Leeds City Archives; Brotherton Collection, Leeds University Library; Liverpool Libraries and Information Services; Liverpool University Library; Manchester College, Oxford; The Trustees of the National Library of Scotland and the Wordsworth Trust, Dove Cottage, Grasmere.

I should also like to thank Dr Ruth Watts and Dr John Guy, who shared their knowledge and enthusiasm for Unitarian history with me. Professor R. K. Webb kindly sent me copies of his work, both published and unpublished, and I am also grateful for his encouragement during the early days of my research. I am extremely appreciative of the moral and practical support which Colin Rogerson, Ron and Wendy Gleadle and Jane Raistrick provided during the preparation of this book. I should also like to thank Giovanna Davitti of Macmillan for her much-needed assistance. I am grateful to both the British Academy, which funded me for three years of my research, and the History Department of the University of Warwick, which assisted with the financial costs of photocopying manuscript material from around the world.

Finally, my greatest debts are to Dr Fred Reid and David Rogerson whose encouragement, advice and inspiration proved invaluable.

Introduction

The nineteenth-century woman has been subject to exhaustive historical scrutiny over the past two decades. The dichotomy between the realities of her iniquitous legal and social standing on the one hand, and the cultural worship of the womanly nature by contemporaries on the other, has made her a fascinating object of study. Moreover, it was during that century that women first began to organise themselves into campaigns to demand reforms in their status. Indeed, historians have now delved beyond the suffragettes' battles to argue that from the 1850s onwards, a small, but vocal group of middle-class women started to agitate for better education, improved legal rights (especially within marriage), employment opportunities and the right to vote.[1]

This book seeks to highlight the weaknesses of the existing historiography of early Victorian feminism, by addressing itself to the origins of these campaigns. In particular, it questions the historical assumption that the women's rights movement began in the 1850s. The study of a particular group of reforming activists, whom I have termed the 'radical unitarians', demonstrates that it was during the 1830s and 1840s that the essential ideologies and personnel networks which were to determine the feminist movement of the succeeding decades were laid.

The existence of a feminist tradition dating back to the early 1830s has been woefully overlooked by previous histories of the women's rights movement. While the work of some of the more famous of these radicals is often alluded to, their vital role as the direct precursors of the women's rights movement has not been subject to analysis.[2] Biographies of some of the more prominent figures, such as Mary Howitt, W. J. Fox and W. J. Linton point to the existence of such a feminist circle, but fail to expand upon its nature or significance.[3] Jane Rendall's work on the origins of modern feminism has performed a great service in articulating the cultural forces shaping progressive debates on the woman question (she points in particular to the contribution of Evangelical and republican discourses). Moreover, Olive Banks has considered the role of Evangelical, Enlightenment and socialist influences on the development of feminist thought during the early stages of the movement.[4] While she refers to the radicalism of those such as W. J. Fox (a figure central to this work), neither of these valuable studies explores the existence of a widespread, nascent women's rights movement in the 1830s and 1840s.

A number of historians, pointing to the prevalence of literary figures in

1

the early days of the organised campaigns, have noted the existence of a 'literary feminism'. The activity of writing, it is suggested, enables 'power, self-assertion, active shaping rather than passive acceptance',[5] and thus provided an appropriate route to feminist awareness. This study relies heavily upon the activity and work of literary circles and accepts the important role which writing might play in the formation of a feminist consciousness. It also acknowledges the comparative unconventionality of literary coteries, which doubtless provided their female adherents with a freedom and opportunity for self-expression often denied them elsewhere. However, it is contended that an ignorance of the comprehensive reforming activity and ideological creeds of such groups has prohibited a full understanding of the role of the literary intelligentsia in the early women's rights movements.

Many other historians have tended to assume that between the great declamations of Mary Wollstonecraft in the 1790s and the beginnings of the organised campaign in the 1850s, feminism fell into something of a wasteland. Indeed, many histories present feminism during this period as little more than a series of isolated protests, by such figures as Sydney Smith or Lady Morgan.[6] This book argues that a specific feminist movement emerged during this period, based upon a network of writers and reformers, who supported and relied upon each others' work. It is to this precise group of activists, who were part of a self-conscious movement, that we must turn in order to understand the development of the Victorian feminist movement.

The notable exceptions to the portrayal of early feminist activity as isolated phenomena are the studies of communitarian and Owenite feminism during the 1830s and 1840s.[7] However, a concentration on this aspect of early feminism has exacerbated a tendency to consider feminism during these years as an extreme and minority movement. As such it is considered to have had little in common with the women's rights movement proper, which is thought to have begun many years later, at the instigation of a group of comfortably well-off women, many of whom came from the great dissenting Unitarian families. However, as will become apparent during the course of this book, the campaigners of the 1850s were the direct heirs of a particular feminist tradition, which was built upon an amalgamation of communitarian and Unitarian philosophies.

The essentially intellectual nature of this early feminism points to the second way in which this book dissents from much of the customary historiography. In searching for the roots of feminist activity, many historians have tended to focus upon the existence of collective female political action and the development of a specific female consciousness. In recent years such an approach has been exemplified by the work of feminist historians such as C. Smith-Rosenberg and L. Faderman who have evaluated the importance of friendship and sisterhood in women's experience.[8] These models have greatly influenced historians' conception of the nineteenth-century women's rights movement. This is clearly seen in the work of Jane Rendall, who adopts such a framework in her study of the two great Victorian feminists, Barbara Leigh Smith Bodichon and Bessie Rayner Parkes. Philippa Levine's *Victorian Feminism 1850–1900* is similarly informed by such an approach. This excellent monograph is very much concerned with the growth of female support networks as a vital accompaniment to the development of the women's rights movement.[9] Many other studies have pointed to the importance of female participation in such movements as the anti-Corn Law agitation and the anti-slavery campaign as a crucial precursor to feminist activity. This is especially true of those studies which emerged in the wake of the suffragette movement. Many feminist historians from this period tended to look back to a tradition of direct female political action in order to make sense of their own campaigns, rather than seeking to understand the intellectual origins of the movement.[10]

Certainly many of the women who were to become important figures in the Victorian feminist movement, such as Emilie Venturi and Priscilla Bright, appear to have played an active role in both these movements.[11] However, as this work will seek to demonstrate, such an approach is not always the most fruitful or accurate means of understanding the development of a specific feminist tradition. As Kenneth Corfield has shown, the relationship between anti-slavery campaigning and British feminism has often been greatly exaggerated. Certainly when the American feminist abolitionist, Lucretia Mott, visited Britain in 1840, she was greatly disappointed by the female anti-slavery campaigners, complaining that they had 'little confidence in women's action either separately or co-jointly with men, except as drudges'.[12] However, Mott and the other American activists found their feminist sympathies did strike chords with the particular radical intelligentsia with which this study is concerned and with whom they formed strong and lasting bonds.[13] Therefore, to understand the close relationship between the anti-slavery movement and feminism what we need to focus upon is not necessarily collective female action, but the existence of a particular reforming outlook – shared by men and women alike.

Analysing this progressive circle is vital in understanding the beginnings of Victorian feminism. However, in tracing the origins of the women's rights movement back to a specific group of radical reformers – the 'radical unitarians', this book also seeks to re-examine the traditional historiography concerning the relationship between the Unitarian and feminist movements. It is a connection which has often been commented upon by historians.[14] Although, as Olive Banks and Philippa Levine have shown, the majority of 'first wave' feminists hailed from an Anglican background,[15] Unitarian women did make a huge contribution to the women's rights movement. This fact is particularly striking as the Unitarian movement was numerically very small. Yet, despite this, it managed to produce many of the leading names in Victorian feminism, as well as a host of lesser-known activists. Barbara Leigh Smith, Bessie Parkes, Elizabeth Malleson, Elizabeth Reid, Eleanor Rathbone, Emmeline Pethick-Lawrence, the Biggs sisters, Emilie Venturi and Caroline Stansfeld, Eliza Fox, Helen Taylor and Clementia Taylor, all came from Unitarian backgrounds. The reasons why this should have been so are clearly vital in appreciating the nature of Victorian feminism.

The conventional historiography explains the widespread participation of Unitarian women in the campaign in terms of the superior education and liberal backgrounds which their Unitarian heritage bequeathed to them. Such is the approach pursued by Sheila Herstein in her biography of Barbara Leigh Smith, for example.[16] Nevertheless, recent studies of Unitarianism, such as those by Ruth Watts and John Seed have noted that Unitarians were often extremely conservative socially, persisting in patriarchal attitudes and relationships towards female members.[17] It is this paradox that needs to be investigated fully in order to truly understand the appeal of early Victorian feminism to many Unitarian women.

However, of even greater importance in tracing the origins of the women's rights movement, is the need to distinguish between Unitarianism proper, and the offshoot of progressive thinkers from the main body of the movement – the 'radical unitarians'.

The term 'radical unitarian', as it is used in the following chapters, should be seen as a fluid category. It is argued that it may be applied to the adherents of certain reforming circles who came to develop a distinctive ideological perspective. These writers and reformers entertained close links with the socialist, secularist, Unitarian and utilitarian movements of the day – to whose publications they often contributed. While the feminist slant of a couple of these journals, such as the *Monthly Repository* and the *New Moral World* has been acknowledged,[18] the feminism of the majority has not been explored. A handful of these publications, such as the *Star in the East* or the *Reasoner* have been studied in the context of the cooperative, secularist or Owenite movements of the day, but their progressive angle on the woman question has been neglected.[19] This is not least because of an ignorance of the network of radical unitarian feminist journalists who wrote for such papers. By the 1840s, these same journalists were playing a leading role in such publications as *Douglas Jerrold's Weekly Newspaper*, the *Howitt's Journal* and the *People's Journal*, the feminist aspect of which has been greatly overlooked. Catering for a wide audience, these journals did not always follow a feminist line. Their significance is that they offered a mouthpiece to the growing network of feminist writers to air their ideas. Indeed, by the late 1840s, these journals acted as a central forum for the developing feminist movement.

Certainly, all radical unitarians appear to have advocated progressive views on women and most (despite the anachronism of the term), were of 'feminist' views.[20] This work uses the terms 'feminism' and 'feminists' to apply to those who not only wished to improve women's position, but also had a cogent awareness of women's subordination in relation to men, and wished this anomaly to be revoked. The radical unitarians formulated just such an insight in their critiques of contemporary society.

The radical unitarian coterie was born from the Unitarian ministry of William Johnson Fox at South Place Chapel in Finsbury, London. As Olive Banks explains briefly in *Faces of Feminism*, Fox's extreme views on female suffrage, marriage and divorce, combined with his own personal problems, alienated him from the mainstream Unitarian body and caused him to resign from the Unitarian church.[21] In this book it is suggested that this breach was instrumental in precipitating the formation of the feminist movement. The willingness of the majority of the congregation to remain loyal to Fox effectively gave him a sanction to continue his feminist activities and unconventional lifestyle. From this point onwards, South Place Chapel became the breeding-ground for feminist ideas and discussions, with the *Monthly Repository* acting as a much-needed platform.

The origins of radical unitarianism thus lay within the mainstream Unitarian movement and radical unitarian circles continued to enjoy direct input from individuals who were either of direct Unitarian descent, or who were frequenters of Unitarian churches. Nevertheless, many of its adherents were not connected to Unitarianism itself. Indeed many do not appear to have ever made formal contact with the Unitarian denomination. Radical unitarian groups appear to have attracted those seeking a religion which sought to capture the heart of Christian ethics. Indeed it appealed to many from the liberal wing of the Anglican church, who exhibited a disillusionment with what they perceived as the ceremony, formality and pomp of establishment religion. Yet, despite this loose relationship with Unitarianism, the radical unitarians continued to be vitally informed by Unitarian thought. They shared, or took to greater extremes, many of its central premises – such as the emphasis on education and the need to search for truth; political radicalism; a tremendous faith in science and support for technology; a fascination with German Romanticism; and also the close relationship which Unitarians fostered with literary circles.

By the late 1840s, the radical unitarians had developed a powerful social, political and cultural critique of modern society, and women's role within it. Their proclivity to consider new modes of social organisation, and their willingness to use the imaginative arts to penetrate to both the truths and potential of society meant that the barriers to conventional ways of thinking about women might be lifted. This, combined with the environmentalist ideas they inherited from both the Owenite and Unitarian movements, made for a very comprehensive perception of women's oppression. Mary Leman Grimstone deftly encapsulated the need for such a broad approach to women's liberation in her declamation that, 'much has to be put from the literature, institutions, laws, customs, and manners to redeem man from the degrading marks of his own ignorant pride, as well as to raise her from her miserable vassalage'.[22]

The wide agenda for female emancipation which the early feminists thus formulated created an awareness that women might only be freed through a radical evolution in the existing culture. They perceived that true liberation would be achieved not merely by short-term measures, such as the abrogation of unjust laws. What was equally required was a far more profound revolution – one in which people were re-educated about their ideas concerning women; in which cultural representations and literary myths about women were replaced by the 'truth'; in which ancient conventions of behaviour were overturned; and in which women themselves learnt to adopt new modes of behaviour to break free of their 'slave' characters. Such goals could not be achieved overnight. They would have to be won by a long-term evolution in the country's culture.

This analysis of female emancipation was a product of the radical unitarian confidence that society was undergoing a gradual process of liberalisation, leading towards a state of perfect civilisation. The *Monthly Repository* spoke of 'a period like the present of mental activity and improving reason, when every ancient opinion is brought to the crucible'. The early feminists placed women's emancipation in precisely this context. Hence, *Eliza Cook's Journal* claimed that a march of civilisation was under way, in which religious disabilities had been removed; the serfs had been emancipated; and the condition of the working classes was improving. The liberation of women, it was claimed, would in time also be effected by this great movement.[23] Whereas later suffragettes were to stake their feminist claims upon a belief that female rights had been gradually eroded during the nineteenth century,[24] most of the early feminists were confident that they had already begun to detect signs of improvement in women's condition within this universal trend. 'Women are better off dear Barbara than they were', proclaimed the young Bessie Rayner Parkes in 1847.[25] Such declarations chimed in with the self-perception of the radical unitarians. They believed themselves to be at the forefront of modern improvement. Their ideas were not eccentric or fantastical propositions, but reflected, they opined, real developments at the cutting edge of cultural progress.

Originally a small and frequently maligned coterie, by the 1840s many radical unitarians were beginning to assume a more prominent position within contemporary culture. Their visionary agenda had led them to embark upon a number of specific campaigns to elevate women's position – including the reform of women's legal position; an attempt to secure female suffrage on the Chartist programme; efforts to tackle the problem of prostititution; and the launching of a unique experiment in adult education. It is these early feminists who were the pioneers of the Victorian women's rights movement.

It is my personal view that these neglected reformers developed a feminist vision which it is important for us to recapture today. Their thought and work remains a vital part of our women's rights heritage – and one that should be embraced. It may well be that the insights they developed have enduring significance for our situation, for the path modern feminism has taken remains alien to the lives and values of many women.

The radical unitarians articulated a feminism in which, although women's rights to equal treatment with men was essential, this was only half the battle. Indeed, they did not promote women purely in those areas where they might achieve like men, but were also keen to herald the particular contribution women might make to society in their capacity as mothers. Indeed, they celebrated the importance of the domestic situation, encouraging men to also embrace the caring values of the home and to reconsider their role within it. They wished women to advance in society not purely on men's terms, but hoped that the emancipation of women would form part of a wider cultural revolution, in which new values and priorities might triumph. Today, when society is increasingly geared to a work culture, in which the needs of children and working parents are often sacrificed, the early feminists' wish to truly abolish the dichotomy of separate-spheres ideology remains a valuable lesson. Indeed, to place feminism within a wider cultural focus, to see it not merely as securing the rights of women, but as advancing the wider needs of society and the health and happiness of the next generation; this is the early feminists' bequest.

1 Freedom and Patriarchy – The Unitarian Background

One of the most vital threads binding together the complex radical ideology of the early feminists was a close acquaintance with Unitarianism. The immense influence which this denomination exerted upon contemporary culture has rarely been fully acknowledged by historians. Yet, its shadow loomed large over many critical aspects of Victorian intellectual life. While a great number of early feminists were the direct product of the Unitarian heritage, many others engaged directly, if informally, with this rich source of reforming impetus. The Unitarian tradition is thus a crucial, yet underexplored intellectual and cultural context in which to understand the emergence of the women's rights movement.

Unitarian history, while not a widely excavated field, has long enjoyed fine treatment at the hands of such scholars as H. L. Short, H. McLachlan and H. Gow.[1] These historians have tended to focus upon the movement's esotericism. They have concentrated on such factors as the denomination's internal vicissitudes and its theological discourse. However, R. V. Holt's 1938 work, *The Unitarian Contribution to Social Progress in England*, although seriously flawed, pointed to the validity of a more catholic approach to Unitarianism.[2] In recent years, a handful of studies have pursued this angle, turning to the Unitarian engagement with contemporary culture. The most successful of these have considered such issues as the relationship between Unitarians and the anti-slavery movement; the ubiquitous Unitarian presence in pioneering educational endeavour; and the contribution which the denomination made to both provincial and national journalism.[3]

This chapter acknowledges the importance of the earlier scholarship, but remains committed to a perception of Unitarianism as a fruitful nexus of contemporary reforming and cultural concerns. This tradition is vital in understanding the development of the early feminist movement. However, this chapter further contends that a more sophisticated understanding of Unitarianism may be constructed by analysing the private writings of early-nineteenth-century Unitarians. Such a study reveals a tension between the urbane liberalism professed by Unitarians, and the conservative, patriarchal tenor which overshadowed their personal relationships and codes of etiquette. These findings have been corroborated by John Seed's consideration of the socio-economic dynamics of the movement.[4] Such contrariety demands dissection if we are to understand the close relationship which Unitarian women forged with the early feminist movement.

UNITARIANISM – ORIGINS AND FOUNDING PRINCIPLES

Unitarianism was a vital movement within nineteenth-century culture. While the denomination only crystallised towards the end of the eighteenth century, it rapidly emerged as a powerful force in the country's intellectual life. Numerically it was never a large denomination. The religious census of 1851 recorded only 229 Unitarian congregations in England, most of which were concentrated in the industrial North and the Midlands.[5] Ruth Watts has estimated that by this time there were approximately 50 000 Unitarians in Britain.[6] Reviled by many contemporaries as heretical, Unitarianism was nevertheless distinguished for the nationwide influence which belied its small membership.

Despite the denomination's self-confidence, perhaps the only aspect of theology common to all Unitarians was their insistence that Jesus was not the son of God (a position which was illegal until 1813). As one distinguished Unitarian was to remark, 'The name of Unitarian is usually confined to those who deny that there is a Trinity . . . it does not involve any doctrinal system.' This was certainly the experience of a contemporary preacher, Joseph Barker, who was bemused to discover that Unitarians 'differed from one another very much in their views'.[7]

The loose dogmatic nature of Unitarianism has caused considerable debate as to the movement's origins. The traditional historiography of the Unitarian movement tended to perceive a direct lineage between Presbyterianism and Unitarianism. Certainly many Unitarians fiercely supported the movement's role as the inheritor of the Presbyterian tradition. Nevertheless, as we shall see, by the 1840s, a new generation of Unitarians, who wished to inaugurate an era of non-denominational worship, began to stress the open, fluid nature of eighteenth-century Dissent, thus questioning theories which posited a straightforward connection between Unitarianism and Presbyterianism. This is a view which has gained considerable credence among modern historians.[8]

However, the germinal Unitarian movement was also contiguous to the Established Church. Indeed, it was Queen Anne's own chaplain, Samuel Clarke, who formulated the basis of Arian thought in his 1712 work, *The Scripture Doctrine of the Trinity*. This suggested that Jesus, although pre-existent and divine, was subordinate to God.[9] Such a view was a half-way house to the Unitarian belief that Jesus was actually human. As the century progressed most Arians appear to have become absorbed into the growing ferment of Unitarianism. Meanwhile, dissatisfaction was growing within the Anglican Church as to the necessity of subscribing to the Thirty-Nine Articles. This discontent culminated in the meeting at Salter's Hall of 1719, when the assembled ministers expressed their desire to adhere to the Protestant principle of the sufficiency of the Scriptures. During the 1770s, Joseph Priestley began to expound the basis of modern Unitarianism in a number of important publications; and, in 1774, the first avowedly Unitarian church was established at Essex Hall in London, by a seceder from the Anglican Church, Theolophus Lindsey.[10]

The fact that Lindsey was a product of the growing rationalist movement in Cambridge points to the need to consider demands for the individual interpretation of the scriptures in a wider context than merely that of Protestant dissent. Indeed, the great catalyst which lay behind such heterodoxy was the impact of Lockean philosophy. John Locke's faith in man's ability to reason led him to argue that it was the duty of each individual to use one's God-given powers of rational inquiry to arrive at one's own conclusions.[11]

If Unitarians were divided as to the precise denominational origins of their sect, they were unequivocal in claiming Locke as its founding philosopher. Locke's materialistic concept of knowledge, together with the theories of Locke's successor, Hartley, became the intellectual linchpins of Unitarian thought. Indeed, the great explicator of modern Unitarianism, Priestley, based his philosophy upon Locke and Hartley. As Lucy Aikin noted, 'It may be considered that his system of the origin of ideas was derived from Locke and enlarged upon by Hartley.' Consequently, the study of Locke and Hartley became embedded within the curriculum of Unitarian academies. Russell Carpenter recalled that at Northampton Academy, 'it was ordinarily the practise to read the works of Locke and Hartley with great care'.[12]

Such reverence for their philosophical forebears is symptomatic of the cerebral nature of Unitarianism. As one adherent admitted, Unitarianism was ill-equipped to attract popular appeal, for it was very much a religion for intellectuals.[13] This factor made for the formation of a very distinctive sect. It proved to be a denomination which cohered not so much through the adherence to a particular creed or dogma, but through the agency of a wider cultural perspective. Central to this outlook lay a rigorous commitment to public duty. As one Unitarian minister affirmed, 'it is the *duty* of every man to labour as much as he can for the relief of the destitute, the instruction of the ignorant and the redemption of the guilty'.[14]

As the denomination matured, its intellectual concerns became actively mediated through this sense of social responsibility. The result was that British Unitarianism (in distinction from its more conservative American counterpart) evolved as a powerful pressure group, championing the liberal and progressive causes of the day. As one Unitarian put it, 'it was hardly possible to find a Unitarian who was not a reformer'.[15]

The crowning precept in Unitarian reformative ideology was the primary importance of moral and intellectual education. This belief was derived from the adherence to Lockean philosophy. Firm believers in the power of the environment to shape the individual (and thus directly at variance with the emotive doctrines of original sin) Unitarians shared Locke's belief that the human mind at birth was a *tabula rasa*, but endowed with immense potential. Their consequent campaigns for the extension and improvement of existing educational provision came to play a crucial role in the formation of the Unitarians' distinctive culture.[16]

A distinguishing feature of Unitarian educational efforts was their progressive nature. In the Unitarian academies of the 1790s, groundbreaking studies were carried out in science, history, literature and bibilical exegesis.[17] Furthermore, in the first half of the nineteenth century, Unitarians piloted an innovative approach to secondary education. This is well seen in the prototypal schools established by the Hill family at Hazlewood and Bruce Castle. The Hills made a substantial break with traditional educational procedure both by focusing on subjects which might be of use to pupils in the commercial world and also in their experiments to allow the boys to govern the schools themselves. The Hills' projects earned a widespread reputation among liberal circles. Dickens (who engaged a Unitarian tutor for his eldest son), referred to Bruce Castle School as 'the only recognition of education as a broad system of moral and intellectual philosophy, that I have ever seen in practice'.[18]

The Unitarian commitment to the promotion of academic progress was further encouraged by their particular cosmology. Inspired by Priestley's necessarianism, Unitarians held that the universe was governed by laws, laid down by God. The object of a Unitarian life was to try and discover these laws so that one might better follow the Maker's divine plan. This had many implications for the denomination. In particular it encouraged a tremendous faith in science. It is fitting that Joseph Priestley, the guru of modern Unitarianism, was also a brilliant scientist, accredited with the discovery of oxygen. Indeed, Unitarians held that scientific investigation was a means of fulfilling their duty to apply their God-given powers of reason to discover the truth.[19] Thus, for Unitarians, the study of science was inextricably linked to the wider Unitarian ethos of freedom. As the Unitarian diplomat John Bowring wrote of his visit to Russia in 1819, 'I was much pleased with the conversation of Horch, the political economist, who complained of the impossibility of pursuing investigations into scientific questions under a despotic government.'[20]

The Unitarians' proclivity for supporting invention and science was further reflected in the number of Unitarians who became successful manufacturers. Many famous companies of the period were founded and managed by Unitarians – the Courtaulds, Strutts, Wedgewoods and Flowers to name but a few. In Sylvia Harrop's study of North Cheshire, it transpired that 66 per cent of the manufacturers in that area were established by Unitarians.[21] Needless to say, the great Unitarian shibboleths of individualism, self-advancement and hard work (as promoted by the Unitarian prophet of self-help, Samuel Smiles) helped to conduce such a successful business environment. One Unitarian spoke of the 'difficulty, I had almost said the impossibility, of good results being obtained by any help save self help'.[22]

Such an emphasis upon individualism, combined with the Unitarian concern to uncover the truth, had vital implications for Unitarians' political convictions. Unitarians supported fervently the right of the individual to use rational inquiry to arrive at one's own conclusions. It was, claimed Holbrook Gaskell, 'the golden rule'. Indeed, one Unitarian minister, H. W. Crosskey, stated that a chief aim of his life had been 'The maintenance and promotion of absolute freedom of thought on all conceivable questions'.[23] Consequently Unitarians proved to be staunch campaigners for the rights of minority groups, such as Jews, and were instrumental in securing Catholic Emancipation in 1829.[24] It is perhaps not surprising therefore to learn that Unitarians were frequently involved in campaigns to extend the franchise. Indeed, John Seed has pointed to the Unitarian thread which ran throughout popular radicalism.[25] This liberal political ideology was bolstered by Unitarian frustration that their social and professional prestige was not matched by political power. Therefore, in the late eighteenth century, many Unitarians participated in the radical societies which were then campaigning for reform. William Smith, for example, became an active member of the Society for Constitutional Information in 1782.[26]

Such political liberalism was matched by the Unitarians' adoption of the concept of fraternity. This was prompted by the environmental aspect of Unitarian thought, largely derived from Lockean philosophy. It encouraged Unitarians to think that people were separated not by any essential differences, but by upbringing and conditioning. Thus, one Unitarian spoke of 'the spiritual ties which connect them as brethren with the whole human race'.[27] In later years the twin concerns of environment and fraternity were to find expression in such projects as sanitary improvements for inner-city areas and their domestic mission movement, which hoped to reach out to the lower classes.[28] In the heady days of the 1790s, such ideas coalesced with the Unitarians' efforts to secure a more liberal and egalitarian political system. Thus, during this decade, many Unitarians openly embraced the doctrines of the French Revolution. As R. Brook Aspland wrote of the formation of the Unitarian Society, 'the absorbing interest of the French Revolution, then in its early glory, gave to the first public meeting of the Society, held in London, April, 1791, a very political tone'.[29]

These political activities, combined with the Unitarians' illegal doctrinal position, inevitably resulted in a great deal of hostility and distrust from other members of their communities. Such was the hatred which Joseph Priestley aroused in Birmingham that he was forced to flee to the United States. Similarly, Bowring recalled that his grandfather was 'deemed no better in those days than a Jacobin by politicians and a heretic by churchmen'.[30]

It was during this period that many Unitarians, almost, it would seem, as a defensive reaction against their persecution, began to assume an aggressive evangelising spirit – with missionary tours, and journalistic endeavours. Thus one Liverpudlian donated £100 to the Lancashire and Cheshire Unitarians to ensure 'a more general adoption of missionary preaching'.[31] A number of Unitarians, most notably Thomas Belsham, were bitterly opposed to such moves, perceiving them as a betrayal of the broad Presbyterian tradition.[32] Indeed, the leaders in this development, figures such as Robert Aspland and Joshua Toulmin, were actually of Baptist origin. Nevertheless, despite the dissenting voices, an era of greater national organisation among the Unitarian congregations was inaugurated. The founding of the Unitarian mouthpiece, the *Monthly Repository*, the establishment of the British and Foreign Unitarian Association and the foundation of the Unitarian Fund, all date from this period.[33]

The consolidation of organisational Unitarianism was matched by an intensification of Unitarian involvement in secular activities. In particular, Unitarians started to make an invaluable contribution to middle-class literary culture, at both a local and national level. As Charles Cowden Clarke was eager to point out, 'there is not a *really* fine literary institution in all England that has not been mainly promoted and sustained by some "little Unitarian Church"'.[34] Certainly a great many literary and philosophical societies had been established at Unitarian instigation. For example, the Liverpool Philosophical and Literary Club, established in 1793, was, as Allan Rushton has shown, ostensibly a Unitarian concern. Similarly, in many other towns, such as Nottingham, Leicester and Bristol, the town's prestigious literary clubs were predominantly Unitarian affairs. John Seed's discovery of the large proportion of Unitarians who were involved in printing, publishing or bookselling was doubtless an important contributary factor in this phenomenon.[35]

In addition to founding such notable institutions, the Unitarian movement also fostered a host of informal, but important literary circles. For example, Norwich, thanks to the activities of such Unitarians as the Opies, Taylors, Austins and Martineaus, became something of a literary capital during the last decade of the eighteenth century.[36] Stoke Newington is another prominent example, which further illustrates the way in which Unitarian literary communities often gave rise to political radicalism. The Aikin and Barbauld families resided at the heart of Stoke Newington's Unitarian community, along with the popular poet, Samuel Rogers. Rogers's progressive politics attracted other political radicals to the literary caucus at Stoke Newington. The prominent Unitarian William Frend and his family moved to the town in 1821. His presence, in turn, drew figures such as George Dyer and Charles Lamb to Stoke Newington in the 1820s. Mary Wollstonecraft also belonged to this community and worshipped with Rogers at the chapel of Richard Price.[37]

The Unitarians' engagement in temporal affairs was further facilitated by the growing relationship between Unitarians and utilitarians. Although few Unitarians were prepared to pursue to extremes the logic of the utilitarian position (George Armstrong, for example admitted, 'decided as I am in utilitarianism. . . . I am yet to learn how far the influence of his principles would carry a moral agent in the service of his fellow creatures'),[38] the connections between the movements were, on the whole, widespread and productive. Bentham himself confessed that he derived his central theory of the greatest happiness of the greatest number from Priestley's works.[39]

By the 1820s, many Unitarians were discovering that their denomination shared much broader sympathies with the utilitarians. Doubtless, the intellectual nature of utilitarian circles, combined with their enthusiasm for reform, made Unitarians and utilitarians likely bedfellows. Thus, as John Seed has noted, the inner core of the utilitarian circle came to be comprised almost entirely of Unitarians – W. J. Fox (who preached Bentham's funeral sermon), John Bowring, Thomas Southwood Smith and Edward Strutt. Mineka has pointed out that the Unitarian journal, the *Monthly Repository*, used a quotation from Bentham for its title-page from 1811 onwards and adhered closely to utilitarian arguments on such issues as Brougham's education bill, and poor relief.[40] As Margaret Parnaby explains, 'By the 1820s leading metropolitan *Unitarians* were becoming the natural companions of *utilitarians*. What drew them together was the vision of a sober, serious-minded and self-improving society.'[41] The relationship between these two movements was typified by such projects as the establishment of the *Westminster Review* and the foundation of London University. Both of these ventures were born from the marriage of Unitarian and utilitarian personnel and ideas.[42]

The Unitarians' involvement with London University exemplified the Unitarian concern to institute non-sectarian education. This was symptomatic of the politicisation of Unitarian endeavour. At a time when their more conservative contemporaries believed that literacy should be used as an instrument to educate the 'lower ranks' into accepting their social status, the Unitarians were campaigning for literature to be made ever more accessible to the people. Thus William Gaskell sought to introduce Mancunian workmen to literature, as a means not of reinforcing class barriers, but of attenuating them.[43] The lead the denomination took in the movement for public libraries may also be viewed in this light.[44] Furthermore, as Donald Read has indicated, Unitarians played a significant role in shaping the evolving nature of the provincial press. It was Unitarian editors who led the way in publishing political editorials and reports of local political meetings.[45]

Therefore, the Unitarian movement rapidly began to emerge as a powerful catalyst within contemporary culture. The growing social and economic status of its adherents, combined with their lively and prominent contributions to reforming activity and cultural endeavour, made for a muscular and highly influential sect. Nevertheless, the movement was also subject to the vicissitudes of complex internal dynamics which led to an increasingly heterogeneous movement. It was in this context that the reforming creed, which I have identified as 'radical unitarianism', began to emerge. This process, so vital to the origins of the women's rights movement, will be discussed at greater length in the next chapter. But first, it is necessary to set the scene for this development within the changing nature of mainstream Unitarianism during this period.

'NEW' UNITARIANISM

By the mid-1830s the position of the Unitarians was strikingly different to what it had been at the turn of the century. They now enjoyed both legal acceptance, and thanks to the 1833 Municipal and Corporations Act, increasing civic political power, with Unitarian mayors in a number of cities. In addition, the denomination benefited from substantial representation

in Parliament.[46] Now that they were no longer in such a defensive position, Unitarians appear to have turned inwards to question the bases of
their religion. As one minister recalled, 'a reaction was manifesting
itself in many minds against some of the distinguishing principles of the
philosophy of Locke and Hartley'.[47] Many began to feel that the harsh
necessarianism of Priestleyan Unitarianism had resulted in the neglect of
inner spirituality. Elizabeth Gaskell's reaction against 'the very worst style
of dogmatic hard Unitarianism, utilitarian to the backbone' represented the
sentiments of many. T. H. Ryland recalled the effect which the numinous
discourse of George Dawson had upon Unitarians such as himself: 'After
the dry bones and thrashed out chaff we had so long been fed on, it was
indeed a feast.'[48] In the wake of such discontent a positive response evolved,
led by James Martineau, J. H. Thom and J. J. Tayler. These divines established the basis of the 'new Unitarianism'. They emphasised the importance of the imagination in interpreting the Bible and were concerned to
establish a theory of action based on inner feelings. Most importantly, they
wished to search for the fundamental religious truths which might unite
Christianity.[49]

A number of factors contributed to this development. Ian Sellers has
considered such circumstances as the publication of Bentham's *Deonto-
logy*, with its extreme utilitarianism; the influence of the domestic mission
movement; and the effect of Owenite radicalism.[50] However, by far the
most significant influence was that of German culture and Romanticism.
The attraction of these ideas to English Unitarians was a trend to which
many of the old-school Unitarians reacted with disgust. The Unitarian
minister, George Armstrong, minced few words in his characterisation of
the new school as, 'the instinctive, transcendental and what-not German
school of moral and metaphysical philosophy – the spawn of Kant's mis-
understood speculations'.[51] Nevertheless, the accommodation of German
Romanticism into the movement acted as a safety-valve for those seeking
a medium by which they might transpose their religion into a richer, more
meaningful belief.

The Germanic influence was widespread and profound. Due to the
prejudice against Unitarians in British academic institutions, many young
Unitarians supplemented their education by studying in Germany. As Lucy
Aikin wrote to Dr Channing, 'To us Germany is of more importance [than
France]. It is a school in which numbers of our young men are learning
lessons.'[52] Germany's intellectual elite shared a common perspective with
the British Unitarians. As one German schoolmaster explained, 'The Ger-
mans have no name for Socinians and Deists [terms by which Unitarians
were often known], because . . . all our men of learning and talents are

so.'[53] The significance of German culture became apparent throughout the movement as Unitarians began to translate and promote German literature and philosophy in their journals and academies.[54] Indeed, the Unitarian William Taylor of Norwich has been largely accredited with introducing German literature into this country and Unitarians such as Henry Crabb Robinson and Thomas Beddoes played a key role in the propagation of German letters among English literati.[55]

The most critical impact of the German scholarship lay in its challenge to Unitarian attitudes towards the Bible. The old-school Unitarianism had based its authority entirely on the Bible. It claimed that the Bible must be capable of rational interpretation, as it was derived from God.[56] However, towards the end of the eighteenth century, Unitarians began to interest themselves in biblical exegesis. The 'higher criticism' which issued from Germany shed doubt on the authority of the Bible. Philological methodology enabled scholars such as Griesbach, Eichhorn and Wetstein to point to the discrepancies in biblical records. They questioned, for example, the authorship and dating of the gospels. This process revealed that the Bible, far from being an infallible text, was the work of a myriad of authors, all writing at different times and with different standpoints. This encouraged the adoption of an historicist approach to the Bible. Consequently, doubt was cast on the validity of biblical miracles – hitherto held by Unitarians to be verification of the Christian Revelation. It was now argued that miracles might only be understood within their cultural context – as a means by which a primitive people explained natural phenomena.[57]

This scholarship, which was widely disseminated throughout Unitarian culture, clearly struck at the heart of the Unitarian faith in the Bible's probative function. Therefore, Unitarians began to search for new sources of religious authority. For many, the answer lay in the idealist school of German philosophy. This constituted a direct challenge to Lockean empiricism. Henry Crabb Robinson, for one, came to be 'convinced of the failure of empirical philosophy as exemplified by Locke' by his attendance at Schelling's lectures. Thus, travelling to Germany in 1800 a good Priestleyan Unitarian, he returned five years later, 'acquainted with a totally new set of ideas . . . the transcendental view of things . . . Locke, Hartley, Priestley, . . . were entirely supplanted'.[58] Certainly Locke's claim that understanding was an essentially passive phenomenon came under attack as the German philosophers came to posit a definition of reason as the organ of spiritual and imaginative insight.

These assumptions enabled idealists to formulate a new perception of God. Rather than being separate from humanity, God could be seen as residing within the individual. This often led to a mystic individualism, with theologians such as Schleiermacher repudiating the institutionalised church, in favour of viewing religion as individual perception and feeling. Thus, Christianity had to be viewed not as a theological system, but as an integral part of humanity and life itself.[59]

Unitarians became cognisant of the work of thinkers such as Fichte, Schelling and Schiller not only through their own intellectual contacts with Germany: they also imbibed these sentiments, indirectly, through the likes of Coleridge (himself a Unitarian preacher at one time), and to a lesser extent, Carlyle, both of whom had themselves been influenced by the Unitarian scholarship.[60] Furthermore, these philosophies also found expression in the English Romantic poets, perhaps most notably in Wordsworth, whose work was widely discussed amongst the Unitarian literati. As M. H. Abrams has shown, biblical imagery and idioms became firmly enmeshed within Wordsworth's verse, as his poetry came to represent the secularised spirituality which German philosophy had foreshadowed.[61]

British Unitarians were further exposed to such ideas through the agency of American transcendentalism. This was born from a group of Boston Unitarian clergymen, who began to absorb the ideas of Carlyle, Coleridge and the German Romantics.[62] One contemporary Unitarian spoke of the 'via media opened up between the mere moralism of the English Unitarianism and the subjective transcendentalism of the American New School'.[63] Certainly adherents to the transcendentalist school received a ready welcome from their liberal Unitarian counterparts in England. Ralph Waldo Emerson, in particular, became intimate with such circles on his visits to Britain.[64] By the 1830s, the American divine W. E. Channing had also earned tremendous popularity among British Unitarians. Himself a Unitarian, he was profoundly influenced by the transcendentalist school. His tremendous faith in the goodness of human nature further refreshed the lagging Unitarian spirit, as he looked not to the authority of the Bible, but to a deeper, spiritual faith in God.[65]

As a consequence of these ideas, many began to question the Unitarian assumption concerning the exclusivity of its Presbyterian background. New voices focused upon the catholicity of the dissenting tradition. Those such as Martineau started to call for an end to denominational divisions and looked instead to the foundation of a national church. Martineau began to perceive Unitarianism not as an independent sect, but as a position which an individual might hold at any one time.[66] The loose nature of its theology certainly made Unitarianism accessible to many who were experiencing perhaps a temporary dissatisfaction with their usual denomination. Increasingly, liberal churchgoers were thus drawn to the Unitarian church.

Indeed, Unitarianism and the Broad Church movement were beginning to move ever closer.[67] Certainly, many 'Unitarians' never formally left the Anglican Church.

The appeal of Unitarianism to intellectuals from other denominations was strengthened by an increasing perception that the Unitarians' religious and philosophical principles predisposed them to a particular set of liberal cultural views which many found appealing. At Robert Aspland's chapel in Hackney, a large number of his congregants were not Unitarians, but found inspiration in shared political and social views. The Winkworth sisters discovered a similar situation in Manchester.[68] As we have seen, the Unitarian world-view was one in which God, the Creator, had laid down all-encompassing laws. Thus, they already had a perception of the way in which life was pervaded by the religious principle. The influence of German idealism, with Schelling's inspiring concept of the Absolute as the whole and only reality,[69] intensified such an apprehension. As William Crosskey put it, 'The religious life consists in the full harmony of God and man, and will be perfect when no discord exists between human desire and divine law.' A younger generation of Unitarians sought to apply this philosophy to their work, as literature, politics and social issues were brought within the compass of their religious discourse. In the process they often had to fight against a conservative element. Crosskey had to defend himself from the older members of his Glaswegian congregation who censured him for substituting Sunday's customary religious sermons with literary lectures. Crosskey's defence of this secularisation is revealing, 'The ... grave charge against this church is that it has become a mere secular hall, and not a house of prayer – devoted to literary purposes, and not to worship ... It seems to be heresy to-day to believe too thoroughly in God! I believe in an Infinite God pervading all things with his holy presence.'[70]

It was during this period that another powerful influence also began to make its mark upon Unitarianism. For, by the 1820s and 1830s, the Unitarian interest in radical politics led many into contact with contemporary left-wing movements. This relationship, while far from widespread, served to blur the boundaries between 'respectable' liberalism and the offbeat world of early socialist culture. This proved to be a provocative context in which the early feminists, as subsequent chapters will argue, might forge their own political ideologies.

While some Unitarians shied away from such radicalism,[71] many, such as Rowland Hill, earned themselves a reputation for progressivism in socialist circles.[72] The links between Owenism and Unitarianism were particularly pervasive, encompassing both personal and ideological connections. In the 1790s, while living in Manchester, Owen had become closely involved with the cultural aristocracy of the city, at that time dominated by the Unitarians, through their work at the Literary and Philosophical society and the newly formed Manchester College.[73] Many aspects of Owen's ideological position are suggestive of this Unitarian influence. Indeed, Harold Silver and J. F. C. Harrison have both pointed to the importance of Enlightenment rationalism in the formation of Owen's theories. Moreover, as the *Monthly Repository* reminded its readers, the doctrine of philosophical necessity meant that Unitarians accorded with one of Owen's fundamental ideas – 'that the character is formed *for* and not *by* the individual'.[74] Conversely, correspondents to the Owenite press often pointed to the common ground between themselves and the Unitarians.[75] Although most Unitarians rejected Owen's economic theories and others, such as Henry Crabb Robinson, remained sceptical as to their practical application,[76] across the country, Unitarians demonstrated their willingness to assist Owenite activities. Many Unitarian chapels lent their premises for Owenite lectures and in Huddersfield, the Unitarians even took over management of the Owenite Hall of Science.[77] Moreover, Unitarians such as Lady Byron, William Hawkes Smith, John Finch and John Ashton Yates actively participated in Owenite communitarian projects.[78]

Unitarians also displayed considerable interest in French communitarian theories. Henry Solly, for example, delivered sermons upon 'Fourier's Phalansterium'.[79] Other Unitarians were fascinated by the Saint-Simonians, who toured the country during the early 1830s. Unitarian journals such as the *Monthly Repository* and the *Unitarian Chronicle* often published articles on the sect.[80] Certain aspects of Saint-Simonian thought were completely at variance with Unitarian ideology – as Mazzini was quick to point out, its authoritarianism struck at the heart of liberal tenets.[81] Nevertheless, the Saint-Simonian aspiration to be a 'religion of humanity', its pacificism and its stress on duty; the great emphasis the movement placed upon science and industrial planning, all proved of interest to the Unitarians.[82]

The Unitarian involvement with such movements also brought them into contact with radical views on women. As Barbara Taylor and Gail Malmgreen have shown, contemporary left-wing ideology promised women a new era in which they would be liberated from sexual oppression and household drudgery.[83] However, as the remainder of this chapter will demonstrate, although the liberalism of the denomination made Unitarians willing to listen to progressive views on women, the majority invariably fell back upon traditional notions of domesticated womanhood. While a few historians of Unitarianism have acknowledged this point,[84] it is a phenomenon which has not been subject to detailed examination. Moreover, historians of Victorian feminism have proved reticent in incorporating this aspect of Unitarianism into their treatment of the Unitarian movement. However, as the following survey of Unitarian attitudes towards women will suggest, it was precisely this paradox within Unitarian ideology that led many Unitarian women to join the women's rights movement.

'FOR A WIFE TO BE HAPPY' – CIRCUMSCRIBING THE
FEMALE ROLE

Given the progressive nature of Unitarianism, it is perhaps not surprising that Unitarians were often sympathetic to advanced ideas of womanhood. As Watts explains, 'The stress on associationism led to the belief that inequalities once accepted as physiological and immutable were, in fact, social and modifiable.'[85] Consequently, Unitarian women were born into a denomination which encouraged a considerable amount of respect for their intellects and judgements. Indeed, one Unitarian minister, J. B. Estlin, pronounced Unitarianism to be 'the religion of females'.[86] Many on the fringes of Unitarian circles were prepared to go much further and advocated advanced feminist ideas. Mary Wollstonecraft was herself closely involved with Unitarianism.[87] Her radical views were shared by other contemporary Unitarians such as William Frend and Mary Hays.[88] A few Unitarians, William Shepherd, for example, had even advocated female enfranchisement as early as the 1790s.[89] While this progressive element remained but a minority voice within Unitarianism during these years, its existence, and the discussions it provoked within Unitarian circles, alerted many Unitarians to the possibility of radical concepts of women's rights. Furthermore, many key elements within the Unitarian culture helped to provide a sympathetic environment in which feminist awareness might grow – in particular the denomination's radical political activities, its educational progressivism and its emphasis upon individualism.

Nevertheless, the mainstream Unitarian movement remained subject to the complex contemporary processes by which women's subordination was woven into wider cultural and social developments. Leonore Davidoff and Catherine Hall have ably demonstrated how the growth of the mores and values of middle-class culture were inextricably linked to the florescence of specific ideologies concerning gender and the role of women.[90] Judy Lown's recent study of the Courtauld silk-mills has allowed for a close analysis of this process. She has shown how the self-perceptions and ideologies of the mill-owners in their capacity as employers were underpinned by the patriarchal attitudes they assumed in their domestic life.[91] As Catherine Hall indicated in an earlier study, once validated by Evangelical domestic ideologies, the patriarchal attitude towards women and its concomitant frame of reference for womanly behaviour, rapidly took hold of Victorian culture.[92] Certainly, as Lown's work has indicated, to keep a wife in supposed leisure at home, was, by the 1830s and 1840s, the ambition of all those aiming at 'respectablity'.[93]

Unitarian women were touched keenly by these processes. While Unitarians often hailed from the professional middle classes, many held very privileged positions in society as merchants, factory-owners, mayors and judges. In some cities (in particular, Liverpool and Norwich), they came to form something of a patriciate, where they functioned both as leaders of the cities and as civic patrons. Thus John Seed has detected in Mancunian Unitarianism, 'the language of organic ties and patriarchal authority, the gestures of paternalist philanthropy'.[94] Similarly, Unitarian William Taylor described the merchant class of Unitarians who resided in his home town Norwich as, 'proud and severe, impatient and authoritative, overbearing and dictatorial. Reverenced as patrons, they acquired the influence of Lords.' Within such a context patriarchal attitudes prevailed. Indeed, W. J. Fox acknowledged the existence of 'patriarchal presbyterian heads of families' within the Unitarian movement.[95] Certainly, such mentalities dictated relationships in the Taylor household. As William Taylor recalled of his mother, 'her first care was to promote the comforts of her husband and son: the whole management of her house was conducted with this view', and 'His acquirements were her pride, his fame was her glory.'[96]

A study of the Rathbone family, the great Unitarian dynasty which dominated Liverpudlian civic life, paints a similar picture. As is the case with many Unitarian families, the Rathbones appear at first sight to have supported progressive concepts of womanhood and female activity. However, a closer scrutiny of the sources reveals that both within their family relationships and in their civic commitments, professions of liberality often shielded their conservative treatment of women.

William Rathbone IV, in common with other members of his family, encouraged female education and intellectual endeavour. For example, he advised his close friend, Hannah Greg, who was depressed by the narrow routine of domestic life, to channel her energies into writing an educational book for children. His own wife appears to have been equally supportive of liberal ideas. Her son was later to maintain that his claim to be 'an advocate of freedom' was thanks to her influence upon him.[97] William Rathbone V appears to have taken his father's progressive attitudes one step further and to have become actively involved in feminist debate. On his visits to London, Rathbone attended the services of the radical unitarian feminist, W. J. Fox; and his wife, Elizabeth, was friendly with many feminist figures, such as Anna Jameson, Lady Byron and Mary Howitt.[98] During her stay in Britain, the American feminist, Lucretia Mott, visited Liverpool three times, where she became well acquainted with William and Elizabeth Rathbone. Her diary reveals that on each occasion the Rathbones were eager to discuss her views on women. Their interest in the issue appears to have been genuine and sustained. Mott recalled that they asked her to write and inform them 'how far we considered their minds [those of English women] fettered and crushed by public opinion and external restraints – also that we would give our opinion of the comparative situation of American and English Females'.[99]

One must question, however, how far this interest prompted the Rathbones to actively pursue improvements in women's position. In the late 1840s, William Rathbone joined other Liverpool Unitarians in establishing the Roscoe Club. This was modelled upon London's Whittington Club, which, in opening its doors to women, had been devised as a feminist experiment. However, the Liverpool club, despite its patronage by many of the city's leading Unitarians, including George Holt (a pioneer in female education), displayed no interest in female participation in the club. Moreover, at times it seems to have actively discouraged any connections with women at all.[100]

The correspondence of William Rathbone VI reveals further the Rathbones' limited commitment to the liberation of women. In 1861 he wrote a private letter to his daughter, Elizabeth, which she was to open on her marriage day, should he have died. The letter discloses Rathbone's true sentiments towards women's nature and position. He urges her to sacrifice everything in order to satisfy her spouse, and explains that her whole life must be conducted along this principle. He maintains, 'women are generally much more self-sacrificing and gentle and less expecting than men; they are so I believe naturally; but their life also is generally free from that struggle for existence which unless carefully watched hardens men's character. You must not expect to receive from your husband all that you give him, but must seek your happiness in loving and devoting yourself to him.' He further expostulates, 'for a wife to be happy she must not think of her own happiness'.[101]

The private correspondence of other prominent Unitarian families reveals a similar pattern. As noted in the previous chapter, the family of the Unitarian MP William Smith has often been considered to have fostered feminist awareness among its members, by dint of its educational ideas and tradition of liberal dissent. Smith's son, Benjamin, had a large family out of wedlock and educated his daughters equally with his sons. He also broke convention by settling an independent income upon all his children, regardless of their sex.[102] One of these children was, of course, the important mid-century feminist, Barbara Leigh Smith. However, the memoirs of Leigh Smith's aunt, Julia Smith, and the letters of Julia's sister, Patty, indicate that the reality was far more complicated than the customary historiography would have us believe. In 1845, Patty Smith confided to her friend, Fanny Allen, that considering how one of her brothers believed women should be treated as wives, it was just as well that he remained unmarried. And Julia Smith remembered how her brother used to express his opinion concerning the 'inferiority of women' and how he would claim that they had 'no reasoning power'.[103]

Therefore, even those Unitarians customarily attributed with progressive attitudes towards women perpetuated many of the conservative mores of contemporary culture. In particular, as William Rathbone indicated, there existed an assumption that women were relative creatures. They existed not for their own fulfilment, but for that of their menfolk. Moreover, as the Smith family records testify, even those of a liberal Unitarian background persisted in an underlying assumption of male superiority. Elizabeth Gaskell discovered on the publication of her novel, *Ruth*, that many Unitarian men were not only extremely hostile to progressive treatments of women's issues, but also assumed control of their wives' access to such material. As she wrote to Fox's daughter, Eliza, on the reaction of three members of her Unitarian congregation, 'Now *should* you have burnt the first vol. of Ruth as so *very* bad? Yet, *two* men have; and a third has forbidden his wife to read it.'[104]

These issues are further clarified by considering the Unitarian attitudes towards female education. Ruth Watts has provided an admirable account of the excellent education which many Unitarian girls received. In this they were indebted to Priestley's injunction that women, having the same moral duties, dispositions and passions as men, required a proper education. Some, such as Sophia Frend and Lucy Aikin, benefited from fine instruction at home; while others attended the reputable institutions run by figures such as Mary Carpenter in Bristol, Catherine Turner in Nottingham and Rachel Martineau in Liverpool. Certainly, individuals like Harriet Martineau and Mary Carpenter were highly fortunate in the excellent education they received at the hands of Unitarian notables Lant Carpenter and James Martineau.[105]

However, it should be pointed out that such education was not the experience of all Unitarian women. In his survey of Unitarian education in Mary Wollstonecraft's day, McLachlan was led to conclude, 'Mixed schools were the exception, and the number of schools for girls was inadequate.'[106] Moreover, Wollstonecraft's contemporary, the prominent Unitarian writer, Letitia Barbauld, berated against educating women too highly, arguing that the best way for women to acquire knowledge was through the intercourse of the family circle.[107] Even by the 1840s, attendance at Unitarian schools of the very highest reputation could not guarantee a very satisfactory standard of instruction. Certainly this was the experience of Elizabeth Malleson, who in 1842, began her studies at the Misses Woods school in Clapton. Although the school was then 'a Unitarian school of much repute', the level of teaching was evidently unimaginative and poor. 'Learning by rote from poor textbooks was the method employed, there was no explanation, no illustration, no attempt to awaken the mental faculties.'[108]

Even when Unitarian women did receive a good education, the ends to which Unitarians believed it should be put often belied the supposed radicalism of the denomination. Thus, prior to their marriage, John Austin required his future wife, Sarah – both of them moved in 'liberal' Unitarian circles – to embark upon a formidable course of reading. He wished her to be familiar with all the works he was then studying – Adam Smith, Matthews, Blackstone, Bacon and Locke, and, as Sarah Austin explained, 'he exhorts me to study Latin, and read Tacitus attentively'. While such a request reveals considerable respect for his fiancée's intellectual capacities, the purpose was merely to increase Sarah's desirability as a wife. As John Austin stated, 'I shall desire to talk with you on all subjects which engage my attention.'[109]

In the education which they provided for working-class women, Unitarians seem to have been genuinely concerned to help them improve both their skills and living standards. However, in this field also, they proved themselves to be as bound as their contemporaries by standard expectations of female roles. The publication of Sarah Austin's *Two Letters on Girls' Schools and on the Training of Working Women* in 1858 demonstrated her acquiescence in her husband's conservative view of the ultimate purpose of female education. She explained, 'we do earnestly desire that those to whom the training of working girls is entrusted, should keep steadily in view what are the qualities and attainments *indispensable* to the domestic servant or the working man's wife'. When Lucretia Mott visited Britain in 1840, she was disturbed by the nature of the instruction provided for girls in the Unitarian charity school she visited. She noted in her diary that it was 'designed to make good servants – not taught enough, – confined to sewing, reading, and writing and little figures'. The Unitarian charity school of Birmingham New Meeting Unitarian Chapel evidently practised similar conventions. In this case it was not until 1888 that their policies were challenged, when the Rev. Joseph Wood complained that too much emphasis had been laid on training girls for domestic service.[110]

Therefore, as Ruth Watts has acknowledged, while most Unitarians were concerned to improve the treatment and education of women, they did not necessarily assume a radical stance on the issue.[111] Indeed, the views of many Unitarians were remarkably similar to those of their Evangelical contemporaries. The Evangelical cynosure, Hannah More, urged that instead of women being treated as ornaments, they should be recognised as beings worthy of great respect and education, not least because of the enormous importance of their childrearing responsibilities.[112] As Unitarian Lucy Aikin appreciated, 'Hannah More had the merit of raising her voice against mere "finger accomplishments" in female education'.[113] Such an attitude, while encouraging a progression in social perspectives on women, nevertheless cocooned them within conventional expectations of their characters and roles.

The close parallels between the Evangelical and Unitarian attitudes towards women is captured in 'The Character and Mission of Woman', a sermon delivered by the Unitarian minister John Omer Squier in 1837. Squier used representations of women from the Bible to support his argument concerning the need to respect and reverence women.[114] However, despite his injunctions that women should not be merely ornaments within the home and his demand to 'Let Women, then, emerge from ignorance, degradation, and slavery', Squier was unable to perceive of self-defining roles for women. He envisaged for them not independence, but the subsidiary occupations of nursing and companionship. Lapsing frequently into flowery rhetoric, he argued that 'Woman be appointed by Providence to instruct the young and support the aged; to visit the sick and console the dying; to be "a help meet" for man, to make his home a blessed abode'. Moreover, Squier's view of the female character, while an attempt to present a positive image of women, hardly augured well for those wishing greater liberation. 'How deeply implanted is the sentiment of compassion and kindness in woman! How vast her capacity for self-sacrifice and patient endurance!'[115]

Fellow Unitarian minister Robert Aspland adhered to similar rhetoric in his sermons. While, as Chapter 2 will explain, many aspects of his argument were an important stepping-stone towards more radical attitudes towards women, he too, perceived woman in solely her domestic capacity. He eulogised the way in which she 'nourishes our infancy, instructs our childhood, polishes and refines our youth, is our most pleasing companion in adult years, dividing our cares and lightening our sorrows'. While Aspland praised Christianity for the advances it had meant for women, he, like Squier, conformed to conservative views of women's character. The New Testament, for example, was heralded for recommending to women, '*the ornament of a meek and quiet spirit*, and decreeing to them, in the event of misunderstanding and strife, the honour of a submissive temper'.[116]

It is important to remember that many of these Evangelical notions of womanhood must have provided middle-class Unitarian women with a positive evaluation of their role. Indeed, Mrs Stansfeld was sure that her friend, Mrs Turner (also a Unitarian), would enjoy the work of Mrs Ellis, who advanced such views.[117] However, for many women, especially those of the younger generation, such attitudes were becoming increasingly frustrating, not least because these Evangelical notions were at variance with many of the tenets of Unitarianism with which they lived. The Unitarian belief that the environment formed the character, rather than naturally determined differences; the denomination's profession to provide a far more advanced education for its women than other contemporaries; the Unitarian ethic of useful work; and the acquaintance of Unitarian circles with a more radical discourse on women, all conflicted with such conservative proscriptions on women.

The antinomies of Unitarian gender relations lie at the heart of the relationship between Unitarianism and feminism. Indeed, a vital catalyst in the formation of a feminist awareness was that the expectations of personal fulfilment, which the Unitarian movement encouraged in women, were not met. The realities of endless household chores and caring rubbed uneasily alongside a dogma which extolled equality for all, intellectual achievement and public service. It is little wonder, for example, that Elizabeth Malleson should have been drawn to feminism after years of domestic drudgery. Stinchcombe points out that her 'good fortune' at being born into an intellectually stimulating Unitarian household was 'only relative, because as the oldest child in an impecunious household she was expected to devote her young life to educating, nursing and entertaining her ten siblings'. For many women of this class, it was not so much the onerous nature of their domestic duties which irked them, but the boredom of a life dominated by petty household cares. As Francis Power Cobbe recalled, 'Like most women I was bound hand and foot by a fine web of little duties and attentions, which men never feel or brush aside remorselessly.' Susannah Taylor was also troubled by this, and talked of the 'stimulus which is so necessary to keep the active mind from weariness and lassitude'.[118]

Consequently, a constant *leitmotif* in the private writings of educated Unitarian women was the problem of trying to find satisfaction in a life dominated by the demands of domestic routine. For many, the intellectual stultification which resulted from such a life led to emotional cries of the need they had of a fulfilling job. Florence Nightingale, herself a product of Unitarian circles, articulated the problem with great force: 'A profession, a trade, a necessary occupation, something to fill and employ my faculties, I have always felt essential to me. . . . In my thirty-first year I see nothing but death.'[119]

These issues are clearly detailed in the early correspondence between Bessie Rayner Parkes and Barbara Leigh Smith. As seen above, Parkes and Leigh Smith are usually cited as the prime examples of how a liberal Unitarian background led women into feminism. However, the letters which the two women wrote to each other in their late teens, actually demonstrate the limitations of the Unitarian background and its ensuing frustrations. For, as Rendall has noted, even during this early period, both women were expressing their profound dissatisfaction with the existing condition and position of women.[120] Parkes confided to Leigh Smith, 'There is no *depth* in our domestic life, nothing beyond the *surface* of every day concerns, and sometimes when I pump I find too little water in my well of hope or Faith.' She went on to rue the circumscribed nature of women's lives. She talked of 'all kinds of demands [which] are made on time, temper and spirits in a small domestic life, and among a heterogeneous mixture of people, and this is the case of most girls and women, and what makes the hindrance to female improvement so infinitely great'. Parkes and Leigh Smith appreciated the dilemmas which the Unitarian insistence upon the work ethic could create for women. As Leigh Smith wrote, 'I have a great deal to say to you about *work* and *life* and the necessity of *yr* [sic] fixing yearly on a train of action, *you* I mean,' she continued, 'what is so sad, so utterly black as a wasted life, and how common! I believe there are thousands and tens of thousands who like you and I *intend doing*, – *intend working* – but live and die only intending.'[121]

Both Parkes and Leigh Smith had benefited from the unusually advanced education for which Unitarians were famed. As Parkes explained, 'I can understand some things better than girls perhaps because like you I have had a peculiar education.' However, she drew attention to the important point that education in itself was not sufficient to change women's position. Indeed, better education without improved opportunities could prove even more tantalising than no education at all. 'What', she asked her friend, 'shall I educate myself *for*? . . . I feel possessed of all sorts of faculties and constrained to put them to a use.'[122]

While Barbara Leigh Smith and Bessie Rayner Parkes evinced the frustrations and exasperations which the cultural prohibition against women working occasioned, the correspondence of Elizabeth Gaskell provides insights into how the domestic nature of women's lives affected them at a more subtle level, affecting not only their relationships, but their very sense of identity.

Gaskell's letters chronicle painfully the tensions many Unitarian women experienced. On the one hand, one finds her extolling the circumscribed roles of wife and mother. In a letter to the Evangelical, Lady Kay-Shuttleworth, she writes, 'I am always glad and thankful to Him that I am a wife and Mother and that I am happy in the performance of those dear and defined duties.' However, when writing to her radical unitarian feminist friends, such as Eliza Fox (the daughter of W. J. Fox) and Emily Shaen (the wife of radical unitarian feminist, William Shaen), Gaskell was freer to hint at the darker fears and frustrations which a life of cloistered domestication often entailed. She described to Emily Shaen how Parthenhope Nightingale had dedicated herself to performing the family's domestic duties so that her sister, Florence, would be free to pursue her activities: 'Parthe has annihilated herself, her own tastes, her own wishes in order to take all the little duties of home, to parents, to poor, to society, to servants – all the small things that fritter away time and life, all these Parthe does, for fear if anything was neglected people might blame F[lorence] as well as from feeling these duties imperative as if they were grand things.' Similarly, in confidence to her close friend Eliza Fox, Gaskell's confusion is evident as she tries to express the need for women to have a refuge in something such as art, 'to shelter themselves in when too much pressed upon by daily small Lilliputian arrows of peddling cares . . . it keeps them from being morbid as you say . . . assuredly a blending of the two is desirable (Home duties and the development of the individual I mean) . . . I have no doubt that the cultivation of each tends to keep the other in a healthy state.'[123]

It is when she is in the company of Emily Shaen, that Gaskell finds she can resolve these insecurities, and forge a positive image of herself. As she revealed to Shaen, 'I always feel raised higher when I am near you and *held up* in a calmer and truer atmosphere than my usual anxious, poor, impatient one.' Certainly, as she was able to confide to Eliza Fox, her domestic life often created considerable dilemmas for her own sense of identity, 'that's the haunting thought to me; or at least to one of my "Mes", for I have a great number, and that's the plague. . . . How am I to reconcile all these warring members? I try to drown myself (my *first* self) by saying it's Wm [William, her husband] who is to decide on all these things, and his feeling if right ought to be my rule. And so it is – only that does not quite do.'[124] Gaskell discovered that her own marriage, although seemingly successful on the whole, was nevertheless imbued with society's patriarchal dictates. Thus, her husband did not permit her to keep her own earnings, but took control of her income, only permitting her a small amount for her own use.[125]

Therefore, many Unitarian women experienced great feelings of unease concerning the narrow field of activity allotted to them. However, these limitations were not confined to the private sphere. Their interaction with the public world was also severely curtailed by the Unitarian code of manners. Perhaps because of the opprobrium Unitarians faced for their religious views, they appear to have been very concerned to adhere to conventional etiquette.[126] Notions of female propriety were often mediated by Unitarian congregations themselves. In Birmingham, the Unitarian New Meeting Chapel laid down strict guidelines for female behaviour. Girls were not permitted to sing in the choir, for fear that it would encourage an unbecoming 'love of display and an unfeminine feeling of assurance'.[127]

These perimeters to the acceptable limits of female social intercourse were absorbed by many Unitarian women. Harriet Martineau, for example, wrote of the Queen's coronation that it was 'an occasion (I believe the only one) on which a lady could be alone in public, without impropriety or inconvenience'. Or, as Elizabeth Gaskell wrote to an acquaintance in 1849, 'I should not like to go to Leslie's lectures unless they were commonly attended by ladies; so if there be any doubt about it, that is at once shut up.'[128]

During the course of the century, a number of women discovered that an appropriate way to unite their Unitarian heritage of intellectual achievement and public duty, was to engage in philanthropic work. The Unitarians' strong network of contacts in both political and intellectual circles greatly facilitated reforming endeavour. Thus, some of the period's most notable female social reformers came from Unitarian backgrounds: Florence Nightingale was a granddaughter of William Smith (and thus a first cousin to Barbara Leigh Smith); Octavia Hill was the daughter of Caroline Southwood Hill – a correspondent of the *Monthly Repository*, herself the daughter of Thomas Southwood Smith – a well-known Unitarian physician; and Mary Carpenter was the daughter of the esteemed Unitarian educationalist, Lant Carpenter. However, many such women experienced increasing problems as to how they might fulfil their philanthropic work, without transgressing conventional propriety. The social rules which demarcated the boundaries of acceptable female behaviour were being pushed to their limits.

These pressures are documented in the life of Mary Carpenter. Carpenter was well-known for her pioneering work with juvenile delinquents, yet she was extremely sensitive to the codes of convention which established the limits of the womanly sphere. When relating a meeting of the Executive Committee of an International Arbitration Association which she had attended, she explained to Dr Guillaume, 'I was asked to take the chair. This of course I declined, as I always keep within my womanly sphere.' However, this was a little disingenuous. In reality, Carpenter was prepared to push back the barriers of conventional female behaviour. Thus, her brother Phillip had many years earlier described to Professor Henry how, at a meeting of the British Association for the Advancement of Science, 'She stood up and read in her usual clear voice and expressive enunciation . . . I suppose the first time a woman's voice had read a lecture there before dignitaries of learning and the church.'[129]

The ambivalence which Mary Carpenter exhibited concerning the truth about her public work is also discernible in Sarah Austin. In 1839, Austin wrote to W. E. Gladstone, expressing her regret that she was unable to involve herself more fully with the campaign for state education, 'I think for the same cause I would bear martyrdom if it would do any good: but I am, after all, a woman, and I cannot bear, without a good reason, the coarse and disgusting hands of the daily press to be laid upon me.' However, whatever Austin may have written to a politician with whom she was not well-acquainted, in practice she was prepared to cross the Rubicon of conventional womanly behaviour. For example, when her husband was ill, Austin carried out aspects of his diplomatic work for him. As she wrote to Dr Sciortineo, 'I had to do strange things for a woman, *contro il nostro decoro*.' However, she excused her behaviour on the grounds that, 'a woman fighting for her husband is always in the right'.[130]

Clearly in this case, as with Carpenter, the societal conventions facing women were becoming out of step with the actuality of their lives. While Austin, Gaskell and Carpenter never fully embraced the feminist cause, the pressure upon them to espouse a greater conventionalism than was actually true of their actions or sentiments indicates the increasing inadequacy of contemporary mores to reflect the real needs of women. As the contemporary novelist, Geraldine Jewsbury, unabashedly proclaimed, 'We are an indication of a development of womanhood which is not yet recognised . . . the present rules for women will not hold us – that something better and stronger is needed.'[131]

Therefore, the relationship between Unitarianism and early feminism is far more complex than has traditionally been assumed. For, as we have seen, there existed no natural corollary between Unitarian liberalism and a commitment to feminist principles. If we are to obtain a clear understanding of the nexus between the two movements we need to pursue not merely the traditional approach of analysing how individual Unitarians came to fight feminist battles; but to consider the wider issue of Unitarianism's role as a rich cultural tradition which provided contemporary radicals with a wealth of liberal ideas and reforming networks. Therefore, while the dissatisfactions experienced by Unitarian women ultimately rendered them a most receptive audience of feminist ideas, it is to their intellectual cousins, the radical unitarians – who so ably exploited the Unitarian tradition – that we must turn in order to trace the emergent women's rights movement of the 1830s and 1840s.

2 'The Assemblage of the Just'[1] – the Radical Unitarians

From the early 1830s, the Unitarian congregation at South Place Chapel eagerly embraced the new developments within the Unitarian movement. The lure of German Romanticism; the move towards secularised spirituality; the relationship with members of other denominations; and the acquaintance with socialist philosophies were all eagerly promoted by their minister, William Johnson Fox. Fox's sympathy with the harsh doctrines of political economy, and his firm allegiance to Bentham and Priestley, illustrate his grounding in the old Unitarian school. However, he also absorbed the new philosophics of the modern Unitarianism (as his theories of imagination and promotion of German literature and philosophy demonstrate), and enjoyed close contact with its principal exponents.[2] Within the exciting milieu of political radicalism and religious free thought which Fox fostered, a distinctive reforming creed began to emerge. As W. J. Linton proudly declared, Fox was the 'virtual founder of that new school of English radicalism, which looked beyond the established traditions of the French Revolution, and more poetical, escaped the narrowness of Utilitarianism'.[3] Taking the Unitarian propensity for freedom of thought to new extremes, the progressive set which began to evolve at South Place derived strength from its sheer eclecticism. It was a loose, fluid coterie whose adherents were not formally attached to Unitarianism, but who embraced its central tenets and ethos.

As young, radical talent from the world of letters and politics became drawn to South Place, the Unitarian journal, the *Monthly Repository*, played an important role in the consolidation of the radical unitarian set. Fox, who bought the journal in 1831, hoped to transform it from a sectarian journal into a radical, non-denominational forum for literary and current affairs. Although its circulation remained small (Herstein estimates that it never rose above 1000), it reached an important and influential audience. J. A. Emerton wrote to Fox of the 'extensive circulation of your Repository amongst men of literature and science'. Other contemporary progressive publications drew incessantly from its articles, and frequently reprinted material from it. The Owenite publication, the *Crisis*, was fulsome in its praise, declaring it to be 'the best and most truly liberal periodical now published'.[4]

Fox's *Monthly Repository* revealed what was to most distinguish the radical unitarians from their mainstream Unitarian counterparts: their feminism. Under Fox's proprietorship the periodical began to mount a relentless and spirited campaign on behalf of the rights of women. Its attack on the conventional attitudes and social oppression of women was vehement and comprehensive. Mary Leman Grimstone's great battle cry in her article on female education is testament to the flavour of feminist writing supported by the journal: 'I should little wonder if I were to hear it said, that I was one who walked out with a pistol instead of a parasol, and a blunderbuss in place of a book, that I had eschewed the bodkin for the battleaxe, that I had forsworn the social smile for the aspect of the grimstone heads which, on prison doors, petrify the passers by, and that instead of loving "jest and song", I never spoke but to breathe "curses, not loud, but deep".'[5]

Most mainstream Unitarians proved hostile to this development from its very inception and soon sought to distance themselves from it. One article in particular, 'On the Condition of Women in England' by William Bridges Adams, outraged most Unitarians. Adams avowed, 'Whatever be the rank of our females, whether high or low, they are, with few exceptions, as much slaves as in the inmates of a Turkish haram [sic]'. He went on to argue for marriage to be made a civil contract, 'capable of being dissolved like any other contract'.[6] Lant Carpenter (known as a champion of equal education for girls) declared that this article would 'disgust the pure and reflective spirit' and claimed that it would not be possible to read such material to a female audience. Carpenter made it clear that the *Monthly Repository* could no longer be considered to be the 'bond of union' among Unitarians, and demanded that Fox should dissociate his views on the Woman Question from the Unitarian body. After this affair, Carpenter and Fox, previously close allies in the Unitarian cause, had no further communication with one another. Other prominent Unitarians joined in the affray. William Turner, for example, criticised Fox on the same grounds; and Robert Aspland endorsed Carpenter's sentiments that the *Monthly Repository* 'ceased to possess the confidence of the Unitarian body and was no longer regarded as a suitable channel for the expression of their religious views'.[7]

At the same time, rumours began to circulate concerning the state of Fox's marriage. Marital disharmony had certainly been rife in the Fox household for some time, as Eliza Flower's painful letters from this period testify. These problems were compounded by Fox's fondness for Flower, his ward. Matters came to a head when Fox left his wife and openly set up a new home with Flower (who became the sub-editor of the *Monthly Repository*).[8] When explaining these actions to his congregation, Fox placed his decision in the context of his feminist views concerning marriage, and referred them to specific articles in the *Monthly Repository*. Many Unitarians were disgusted by Fox's arguments and a minority of the congregation left his ministry. However, the rest of the congregation endorsed Fox's decisions and persuaded him not to resign his position.[9] South Place Chapel remained Unitarian in name and many mainstream Unitarians continued to frequent it. However, other Unitarian ministers in the capital formally disowned Fox's connection with them and the chapel became officially detached from the denomination.[10]

W. J. Fox's circle came to represent immorality and profligacy to many outside observers. Carlyle believed that 'Most of these people are very indignant at marriage and the like, and frequently indeed are obliged to divorce their wives, or be divorced.' Many mainstream Unitarians were of a similar opinion. James Martineau was clearly troubled by the 'questionable tone of their free thinking and free-living clique'. Harriet Martineau, (who had been very close to the South Place circle) was also shocked by Fox's behaviour, and concerned at the desire of Harriet Taylor to leave her husband, especially as it coincided with the break-up of Fox's marriage. It 'gives it a serious character and dangerous publicity which bodes nothing but evil', she believed, and remained distant to the coterie. The Unitarian minister, James Yates, was even more scathing in his representation of the group – views which were widely disseminated among the Unitarian community. P. A. Taylor described how he 'insinuated that their numbers have been recruited from the classes which fill the penitentiaries of the metropolis and having represented their mothers, wives, sisters and daughters as leagued to deceive the public and banded together to patronise indecency'.[11]

Therefore, it would appear that the progressive feminist views of the South Place congregants occasioned a rupture within the Unitarian denomination. As J. J. Tayler noted, Fox's feminist views caused a 'great division of feeling in the Unitarian body'. Indeed, for contemporary Unitarians the emergence of this discrete cadre was a source of considerable debate. In an interchange between the mainstream Unitarian minister, J. B. Estlin, and his radical unitarian colleague, William Shaen, the fundamental differences between the differing wings of the movement is made apparent. Estlin was in favour of 'encouraging and extending the *education* of women'. He was also happy to countenance more useful employment for 'well educated women', but seemed shocked at the universality of the reforms which the feminists perceived to be required. He confessed, 'I am very far from clearly seeing either that a radical change in the constitution of our female society is needed, or *what* any change ought to be.'[12]

Such a rift is also captured in the response of mainstream Unitarians to Thomas Southwood Smith's work, *The Philosophy of Health*. Southwood Smith had made his mark as a preacher within the mainstream Unitarian movement, but became closely involved with Fox's radical unitarian set on moving to London. He practised a wholly unconventional lifestyle, living in a radical household with his mistress, Margaret Gillies, along with Margaret's sister Mary and, for a time, with Mary's partner, Richard Hengist Horne.[13] *The Philosophy of Health* was ostensibly written to equip mothers with a better understanding of the development of their children. Yet, as contemporary Unitarians were quick to detect, it also contained a barely concealed feminist agenda. The Unitarian *Christian Reformer* published a review *The Philosophy of Health* in 1834. The reviewer agreed with Southwood Smith, 'as to the importance of the information which this book contains'. He went on to concede that there were many deficiencies 'and evils in the most perfect of existing systems of female education'. However, while the *Monthly Repository* was highly appreciative of the work's feminist slant, the *Christian Reformer* was offended by Smith's assertion that many of women's supposedly 'natural' qualities had actually been instilled by cultural conditioning. In particular, the reviewer was appalled, as Estlin had been, by the sweeping reforms which the radicals believed must lay the foundations of female emancipation. He decried, 'to maintain "the total inadequacy of any remedy, short of a modification of our domestic institutions", [as Southwood Smith had done] is a startling proposition'.[14]

Mainstream Unitarians were right to pinpoint the revolutionary nature of the radical unitarians' feminist solutions. It was an agenda which the feminists themselves proclaimed unashamedly. As the *People's Journal* declared, 'What can the remedy be, but an entire reorganisation of social life?'[15] For, as the previous chapter suggested, oppressive ideologies concerning women were enmeshed within contemporary culture. Even within the comparatively liberal environment of Unitarianism, women were condemned to a secondary existence. The need for a comprehensive programme which would encompass reform both in the private relationships between men and women, and also in women's relationship to and interaction with the public world of employment, education and legislation, thus set the agenda for the early feminists.

THE RADICAL UNITARIANS

Who then, were these early feminists? The best starting-point is an examination of Fox's South Place coterie itself. At the heart of this circle was a vibrant, stimulating caucus of talented writers, artists and musicians, many of whom enjoyed contacts with the radical politicians of the day. The chapel attracted not only Unitarians, but other intellectuals of a liberal caste of mind, many of whom retained their allegiance to the Anglican church. Margaret Parnaby has provided a comprehensive survey of both the ideologies and activities of this group, detailing carefully its socio-economic make-up. She points in particular to the prevalence of auto-didacts such as Rowland Detroisier, Ebenezer Elliott and Thomas Wade.[16] While Fox was of humble origins himself, those who were instrumental in developing the feminist ideology of the *Monthly Repository* (and whose views were often more radical than Fox himself) were actually of a higher class origin. The celebrated musician, Eliza Flower, and her sister, Sarah Flower Adams (a highly esteemed poet) had enjoyed a permissive upbringing under their father, Benjamin Flower, a radical Unitarian publisher. Adams's husband was the political writer, William Bridges Adams, from Staffordshire. He also came from a relatively prosperous family, being the son of a principal partner in a coach and carriage building business.[17]

Perhaps of greatest importance, however, was the novelist, Mary Leman Grimstone. Grimstone's mother hailed from the distinguished Romilly family and her father, himself a man of letters, was of the gentry class. Grimstone also had two eccentric brothers who circulated within the radical world of London's literary culture. While in recent years some historians have begun to acknowledge Grimstone's contribution to the early feminist debate, scholars have to date only scratched the surface of her large body of work and significance. The little-known studies of some Australian academics have added considerably to our knowledge of Grimstone. However, what has been missed by previous historians is the vital role which Grimstone played within the feminist debate. For many early feminists, she was *the* great figure in the movement. First coming to prominence with her feminist articles for Leigh Hunt's theatrical newspaper, the *Tatler*, Grimstone went on to become a leading proponent of contemporary feminism, in her many periodical contributions and in her novels. Contemporary radicals refer to her work again and again, and her work had an immense influence upon them. Journals as diverse as the *New Monthly Magazine*, *La Belle Assembleé*, the *Leeds Times* and the *New Moral World* all received her work warmly and she was extensively quoted from and reprinted in a host of other progressive publications, such as the *Star in the East* and the *Reasoner*.[18]

Another writer central to the Repository circle was the widely acclaimed poet, Richard Hengist Horne. Born in Edmonton, London, he too was from a wealthy family – his grandmother had married a rich merchant. In common with W. B. Adams, he had travelled extensively before coming to South Place. The successful artist, Margaret Gillies, 'the female pioneer', and her sister, Mary, a writer, also made valuable contributions to Fox's radical salon at Craven Hill. Like Grimstone, they came from a literary family – John Gillies and Robert Pearce Gillies were close relatives. Their Scottish father, William (whom Grimstone was to marry), was a merchant, but they were brought up by their uncle, the eminent judge, Lord Gillies, and his sisters.[19]

The progressive, eclectic nature of South Place Chapel meant that it soon came to function as an intellectual magnet to progressive young writers and thinkers. As a reporter for the *New Moral World* marvelled, here, 'more than at any other place . . . an audience as respectable as it is great, enters with the most intellectual sympathy into the whole course of the subject pourtrayed [*sic*] by the inexhaustible lecturer'.[20] Such important figures as Bulwer Lytton, the Unitarian John Forster, Charles Dickens and G. H. Lewes were attracted to Fox's entourage. Robert Browning's nascent poetical ability was fostered and supported by the group and early feminist figures such as Harriet Taylor and John Stuart Mill were also closely involved in this circle during the 1830s.[21] In addition, Fox's ministry attracted an older generation of literati, people such as William Godwin, Leigh Hunt and Charles Cowden Clarke, who provided a direct line to the radicalism of the Mary Wollstonecraft set.[22]

In the late 1830s, the Craven Hill salon began to break up. The *Monthly Repository* ground to a halt in 1837, despite desperate bids by Richard Hengist Horne and Mary Gillies and then Leigh Hunt to keep it going. In 1839 Fox and Flower moved to central London, where they lived for a short time with Sarah and William Bridges Adams. Fox continued to deliver popular lectures at South Place Chapel, but increasingly his poor health, and extensive commitments to the Anti-Corn Law League meant that his links with the chapel became ever looser.[23] Some, such as W. B. Adams, gravitated towards more radical religious positions, as his rationalist, idiosyncratic journal of 1841, *Common Sense* testifies. Harriet Taylor's frosty account of a visit Sarah Adams paid her in the 1840s, illustrates clearly the distance which had grown between the members of the original South Place circle by this time.[24]

Nevertheless during the late 1830s, the feminists of the Craven Hill circle continued to form a cohesive cadre and were increasingly joined by new personnel.[25] The celebrated feminist writer, Anna Jameson, who was herself closely acquainted with Unitarian circles, had also become involved with the radical unitarian coterie by this time – indeed Horne claimed that she was a contributor to the *Monthly Repository* during Hunt's editorship.[26] While these years were not rich in feminist activity, the progressive views of the radical unitarians did find expression in the *Star in the East* and the *National*. The *Star in the East* was the brainchild of James Hill, a fervent Owenite, and his wife, the radical unitarian, Caroline Southwood Hill. Caroline, a former contributor to the *Monthly Repository*, was the daughter of Thomas Southwood Smith. Hill and her husband, James, previously a struggling corn merchant, became prominent radicals in the Cambridgeshire town, Wisbech. Declaring that the publication would consider the rights of women equally with the rights of men, the *Star in the East* proved a useful vehicle for women's rights discussions.[27] The Hills were able to make fruitful use of their radical unitarian and socialist connections from London's journalistic circles to make the paper a considerable success. However, once their marriage began to crumble, the newspaper – now presumably lacking Caroline's input – started to follow a more dogmatic socialist line.

The *National* was an ambitious project launched by the redoubtable William James Linton. A close associate of the Fox circle and intimate with other Unitarian radicals, Linton, a wood-engraver, was a staunch defender of women's rights. Through the *National*, he hoped to provide working people with a library of good-quality reading. While the journal always struggled to make its own way, it functioned as an important focus of feminist debate. One issue was even devoted exclusively to the topic.[28]

From the late 1830s to the early 1840s, the feminist initiative among radical unitarians passed from the literary to the legal community as a number of radical lawyers took up the feminist cause. At the centre of this group lay the prosperous lawyer, William Ashurst. A well-known radical, Ashurst had frequently lent his support to progressive and socialist causes. Moreover, he was crucial in founding a number of radical publications, such as the *Spirit of the Age* and the *Reasoner*.[29] Both these journals provided an arena for women's rights discussions, a topic on which Ashurst himself held strong views. It seems it was Ashurst who organised the campaign to protest against women's exclusion from the 1840 World Anti-Slavery Convention (an occasion which acted as a catalyst in the formation of many radicals' feminist views). Ashurst maintained that the convention provided the perfect opportunity to raise the issue of women's oppression.[30] Moreover, he had brought up his four daughters (he also had one son) to be independent and liberal. As Eliza admitted to her American correspondent, Mrs Neall Gay, 'we are allowed, and have been accustomed to, more freedom of intercourse, than many other Parents allow their children'. Certainly Caroline, Emilie, Matilda and Elizabeth shocked much of the London literary and political community by their liberal manners and outspoken ways. Jane Carlyle was appalled at Eliza's behaviour, complaining she 'does strange things'.[31]

The marriages of the Ashurst daughters greatly extended the family's radical unitarian network. Matilda married the Leicester businessman, Joseph Biggs, himself a Unitarian.[32] Caroline married the son of an affluent Unitarian family, James Stansfeld (who later became a cabinet minister), and Emilie married Sidney Milnes Hawkes (with whom Stansfeld later went into business – although both the marriage and the business failed). Both Stansfeld and Hawkes were solicitors, as were William Henry Ashurst Junior and their close friend, William Case (who married Stansfeld's sister and also appears to have hailed from mainstream Unitarian circles). Two more lawyers, John Humphreys Parry and William Shaen (the son of a Unitarian magistrate) were intimately involved with the set. Case's sister, Gertrude, also appears to have been a close member of the Ashurst circle, as, it seems, was Bessie Ogle, the future wife of W. H. Ashurst Jr. Many of these people had been members of Fox's congregation, and some, such as Parry, shared Ashurst's and Linton's close acquaintance with radical secularists.[33]

The contribution of this circle to the later women's rights campaigns has often been noted. Robert Spears, for example, claimed that James Stansfeld, 'did more than any other man in Europe to promote the educational and political advancement of the female sex'.[34] However, their involvement with an earlier feminist movement has not been fully explored. Yet, as Mazzini explained at the time, 'These sisters and their husbands are all deeply interested in all social and especially the "Women's questions".' Indeed, Eliza Ashurst was delighted that this close-knit group all shared feminist views. For example, she said of Hawkes, 'he was quite of our opinion concerning the *perfect* equality of the sexes, morally, intellectually and politically'. And of Shaen and her other brothers-in-law she rejoiced that they 'all agree on many important points, such as the moral and intellectual equality of the sexes, and the utter necessity for moral purity in men as well as in women'.[35] Many other acolytes of the Ashurst circle shared these feminist sentiments. Dr John Epps, for example (who was also a close friend of the Biggs family in Leicester) delivered public lectures on issues pertaining to women's rights; and Frank Stone taught Emilie Ashurst painting, which, it was hoped, would enable her to become an independent woman.[36]

The Ashurst circle (or 'Muswell Hill Brigade', as it was sometimes known) has been detailed by Eugene Rasor, who has provided superb accounts of many of its protagonists. It has also been studied in greater depth by Lee Chambers-Schillers who has explained how the Ashursts' home came to function as a focus for reformers, writers and radicals of the day.[37] Indeed, they befriended such figures as Robert Owen, W. J. Linton and Peter and Clementia Taylor. The Taylors, of old Unitarian stock, were a pivotal radical family in London and enjoyed friendships with William Shaen and W. J. Fox, as well as with other important figures in the rising radical unitarian set – in particular, Eliza Lynn and Elizabeth Malleson (who also hailed from a Unitarian background). These radicals all shared the feminist proclivities of the Ashurst family. Indeed, Clementia Taylor went on to become a leading figure in the women's rights movement. The Taylors were also close to the publisher, John Chapman, who edited the *Westminster Review*. Chapman, if not a wholehearted convert to the cause, was sympathetic to feminist views. He and his wife, Susanna, frequently provided a centre for many of these radicals, as well as attracting Unitarians and intellectuals such as Herbert Spencer to their soirées, at which women's rights discussions often formed an important element.[38] Another vital figure in the Ashurst entourage was the Italian revolutionary Giuseppe Mazzini, who shared many of the radical unitarian views. Correspondingly, the group was particularly noted for its championing of the cause of Italian liberty, and it was from precisely this coterie that the People's International League was born.[39]

The somewhat eccentric Barmbys – Catherine and Goodwyn, who had played a significant role in the Owenite movement, also moved into the radical unitarian orbit during the 1840s. Catherine Barmby had penned a number of important feminist articles in the *New Moral World*, under the name 'Kate'. Her husband, a lawyer's son, was also of strong feminist views, and his visionary ideas appealed to many in the radical unitarian set. Emilie Ashurst, for example, was particularly drawn to him. While critical attention has hitherto focused on the Barmbys' more extreme activities, such as their establishment of the Communist Church, the contribution which they made to this more mainstream radical community has not been widely noted. Their importance to the radical unitarian milieu was symbolised when, in 1848, Goodwyn Barmby became minister of South Place Chapel. He later went on to become a Unitarian minister in Wakefield.[40]

By the mid-1840s, London's radical unitarian community had been consolidated by the input of important literary figures. In addition to Douglas Jerrold and Mary and William Howitt who began to contribute to the radical milieu in the late 1830s, a number of other young writers began to move within this feminist milieu – figures whose contribution to the early feminist movement has frequently been overlooked. These included the translator and actor Matilda Hays; Eliza Cook, a self-educated London poet; and Eliza Meteyard, the daughter of an army surgeon, whose work as a struggling author was desperately needed to assuage the problems of her difficult family.[41] The Howitts (who had also been close to the protagonists of the *Monthly Repository* circle) were later to fall out with the Ashursts, but Mary Howitt revealed to her protégée, Eliza Meteyard, just how close they had once been. 'There was a time when the Ashursts and we were the dearest friends in the world. Never did either Anna Mary or I love people as we loved them. We were like one family.'[42] The ties between the Ashurst circle and this rising group of radical unitarian writers were strengthened by the latter's dependence on their legal advice. Parry and Shaen, for example, acted as solicitors for Meteyard. Meanwhile, as the correspondence of Mary Leman Grimstone testifies, there remained enduring links between writers such as herself and Leigh Hunt, with the likes of W. J. Linton and Sidney Hawkes. Her letters indicate that their common reforming outlook encompassed not only feminism, but also such issues as infant education and European freedom.[43]

Although the radical unitarians in London dominated the feminist culture of the day, they did profit from many valuable contacts in the provinces. A number of these held progressive and inventive views on the position of women. While the marriage of Matilda Ashurst to Joseph Biggs provided a link with radicals in Leicester, the Chapman circle entertained important associations with Coventry – in particular with the Brays and Hennells. (Originally of Unitarian conviction, both these families came to adopt extremely progressive views.) In Birmingham, the radical unitarian ideas were to find able expression in the popular preacher, George Dawson – a great hero of the Coventry radicals. He lectured on such pertinent topics as Mary Wollstonecraft, German philosophy and literature, and social reformation. Dawson, a former Baptist preacher (although he married into a Unitarian family) was, like Fox, too progressive for the likes of his denomination. With the help of his supporters, he established his own chapel, the Church of the Saviour, at which he was soon joined by seceders from the local Unitarian churches. Indeed, while Dawson, a great advocate of W. J. Linton's ideas, had a considerable influence upon many contemporaries, Unitarians and Unitarian sympathisers appear to have been particularly drawn to his ideas.[44]

In Leeds also there existed a lively, progressive culture, as J. F. C. Harrison has discovered. Its chief protagonists, Frederick Richard Lees and George Searle Phillips, along with local projects such as the Leeds

Redemption Society, often profited from the journalistic influence of their fellow radicals in the capital. In nearby Wakefield, Daniel and Mary Gaskell – nominal members of the local Unitarian chapel – proved to be a stimulating focus for many of the radical unitarians, in particular, Mary Leman Grimstone.[45] *Tait's Edinburgh Magazine*, presided over by William Tait and the feminist, Christine Johnstone, provided the radical unitarians with another important contact and they frequently published work in this journal. At one time it was hoped that *Tait's Edinburgh Magazine* and *Howitt's Journal* would merge. As Mary Howitt wrote to Eliza Meteyard of the plan, 'you shall have a corner in it and we will all do glorious things'. Even in Ireland, as Chambers-Schiller has suggested, the London radicals found an important advocate for their ideas in the influential figure of James Haughton, a Unitarian minister in Dublin.[46]

By the mid-1840s, William and Mary Howitt had begun to assume centre-stage of the radical unitarian milieu. Formerly Quakers, they found themselves drawn to Unitarianism in the early 1840s, and soon embraced the ethos of the radical unitarian circles.[47] Although their bitter wranglings with their publisher, John Saunders, strained their relations with many radical unitarians, their publications, *Howitt's Journal* and the *People's Journal* (with which figures such as W. J. Fox and W. J. Linton were also involved), became crucial forums for radical ideas. Although *Howitt's Journal* failed after a couple of years, and the *People's Journal* lost its radicalism once Saunders had assumed control over it, both these journals reached a very wide audience, having a circulation of over 20 000.[48] Indeed, the Howitts were extremely popular and successful authors (they were later to receive civil-list pensions from the government).[49] As Bessie Parkes noted of Mary Howitt, 'her books are in every shop throughout the kingdom; if she had a shilling on every copy she would be rich'. The Howitts' public respect was of great significance for the standing of contemporary feminists. As W. H. Ashurst acknowledged, the Howitts' public reputation would lend great credence to the feminist case.[50] The Howitts' particular brand of moderate feminism was certainly well-suited to spreading the word to a wider audience, with its emphasis upon domestic happiness and womanly grace.

The Howitts typified the new position which radical unitarian writers came to occupy during the 1840s. They were no longer perceived as an eccentric minority, but were well-known, esteemed figures with a large mainstream audience. Eliza Cook provides another example of how a writer of firm feminist views could succeed as a popular and widely-read author. Fox's daughter was informed that 'a lecture on her [Cook's] poems would attract a larger audience of working men and women than a lecture on any other author'. A largely self-educated woman, Cook established a lively platform for discussions on the woman question in the late 1840s – *Eliza Cook's Journal*. In 1849, its circulation reached between fifty and sixty thousand.[51]

The well-known writer Douglas Jerrold was to be of equal importance. Jerrold's feminist views have been invariably overlooked by previous scholars. However, as one contemporary female journalist appreciated (and as the many feminist articles which appeared in his journals testified), 'He had considerable faith in woman's capacities for intellectual pursuits, while fully recognising the difficulties under which they laboured when struggling in the battle of life.'[52] By the 1840s he had formed strong connections with the writers at the heart of the radical unitarian cohort. His political radicalism, scathing attacks on the establishment, vehemently anticlerical opinions, and advanced views on women found a willing reception here.[53] During the 1840s, the *Reasoner* and the *People* consistently supported his work, as the *Star in the East* and the *National* had long done.

In the 1840s Jerrold, like the Howitts, began to appeal to a broader audience. Although his *Illuminated Magazine* did not do well (R. H. Horne confiding to Edgar Allan Poe that its considerable circulation was insufficient), Jerrold's other ventures proved more successful commercially, *Douglas Jerrold's Weekly Newspaper* and *Douglas Jerrold's Shilling Magazine* were both popular and progressive. As Blanchard Jerrold later noted, 'The *Shilling Magazine* achieved a great success, for the editor had become undoubtedly a powerful speaker on the Radical side, in the state.' Ashurst was pleased to report to the great American reformer, W. L. Garrison, that *Douglas Jerrold's Weekly Newspaper* was 'a paper which has a large circulation, and is doing an immensity of good in England'.[54]

The cluster of radical unitarian journals which appeared during the 1840s targeted a very different audience than had their predecessors. With the exception of the *National*, journals such as the *Monthly Repository* had been aimed at the narrow, radical circle of writers and intellectuals. Hence Parnaby's definition of the *Repository* as a 'club bulletin'.[55] However, partly in response to the changing nature of the literate audience, these later publications hoped to reach the lower middle classes and higher ranks of the working classes. This, plus the new public position which radical unitarian writers assumed in the 1840s, inevitably had implications for the tenor of their work. Mary Howitt was constantly having to remind Meteyard to tone down her work for public consumption. 'The public is not yet ready for such things', she urged.[56] As will become apparent, this gradual accommodation of feminist thought into mainstream public discourse was of considerable significance for the development and status of the women's rights movement.

Despite the feminists' increasing concern to forge a better relationship with the general public, they remained rooted within the radical culture of the day. For the radical unitarians continued to function as a network of feminist journalists, utilising the publications of their radical contemporaries, as well as finding a voice in the more mainstream press. Thus, as the following chapters will show, their work was published in a number of left-wing journals. These included the *Spirit of the Age*, to which Ashurst, Shaen and Stansfeld contributed and which publicised the work of Goodwyn Barmby. Holyoake's *Reasoner* sang the praises of William Howitt, frequently advertised Goodwyn Barmby, published articles by Linton, Ashurst and Sophia Dobson Collet (a former member of Fox's congregation) and provided detailed accounts of Fox's lectures and activities. Another example was the *Republican*, whose principal contributor was Linton and which frequently published pieces by Eliza Meteyard and the Howitts' close associate, Edward Youl. The *People's Press* also gave opportunities to feminist writers such as Catherine Barmby, and in common with the other journals mentioned, publicised feminist activity such as the George Sand translations and the Whittington Club.

In the midst of this feminist activity, which found expression in so many diverse journals, the early feminists proved to have a consistent and unique reforming ideology. The rest of this chapter will explore its precise nature and trace its origins in the Unitarian, communitarian and literary culture from which it sprang.

RADICAL UNITARIAN IDEOLOGY

At the heart of the radical unitarian ideology lay a profound commitment to the great Unitarian principle of freedom. Indeed, South Place Chapel eschewed creeds. In the place of sermons it encouraged discussions and lectures. Its congregants, as J. S. Mill put it, were 'unsectarianized'. This was certainly how Sophia de Morgan recalled them, remembering that the chapel was 'frequented by persons of all beliefs and of no particular beliefs'.[57] The one characteristic which united the diverse religious beliefs of Fox's coterie was the wish to abandon the forms and rituals of established religion. Fiercely anticlerical, some were drawn to the religious philosophies of such theologians as Schleiermacher, and others to the ideas of the American transcendentalists. However, all advocated a return to the fundamental ethics of Christianity, by emulating Christ's example.[58] The

Leader newspaper proclaimed that Unitarianism's greatest contribution had been 'that of providing *recipients* of the better and more Christian ideas which are demanding men's attention at the present day'. It was to this which Fox's ministry aspired. As J. S. Mill explained, Fox's religion was 'a religion of *spirit*, not of *dogma*'.[59]

A consequence of this outlook was that South Place proved sympathetic to radical views on religion. Many who passed through its doors went on to adopt the more extreme doctrines of secularism and pantheism (movements which also fostered progressive views on the woman question). Indeed, there were many productive links between the leader of the secularist movement, George Jacob Holyoake (who had himself been influenced by Unitarianism during his youth), and the South Place circle (as is evident from their collaboration on many contemporary journals). While frequenters of South Place constantly urged Holyoake to embrace a more God-centred faith, they had great respect for the humanism of his philosophy.[60]

The radical unitarians were not only united by a shared religious perspective. Their common political and ideological responses to the questions raised by industrialisation were perhaps the movement's most cohesive factors. Their proposals to alleviate the social and cultural adversities inflicted by industrialisation encompassed a number of strategies, of varying degrees of progressivism. At the least contentious level, the radicals shared with their revered Lake poets a faith in the recuperative powers of nature. Wordsworth, in particular, was a source of great inspiration to them. When Margaret Gillies stayed with the Wordsworths in 1839, in order to paint the poet's portrait, she referred to her trip as a 'pilgrimage'. The Howitts were particularly keen to popularise Wordsworthian ideas and poetry. As William Howitt wrote to James Hogg, 'in a great commercial country, where our manufacturing population are daily spreading over its face', there was a vital need to diffuse the 'animating and heart-preserving influence of nature'.[61]

Nevertheless, inspired by the Unitarians' more comprehensive understanding of nature, as the laws which governed the universe, the radical unitarians were critical of Wordsworth's naive response to mechanisation. For example, they were shocked by Wordsworth's 1844 sonnet, in which their cherished poet had protested against the proposed railway line which was to run through the Lake Distict. He wrote in anguish, 'Is then no nook of English ground secure / From rash assault?' Dickens wryly echoed these words in *Dombey and Son*, and they also prompted William Bridges to beseech in his poem for the *People's Journal*, 'Scorn not the Railway, Wordsworth'. It was an anxiety which Douglas Jerrold expanded upon at greater length: 'When Mr. Wordsworth wrote a Sonnet against the destruction of some piece of ground by a Railroad, we felt suspicious, not because we do not think the spoiling of a picturesque spot a very natural cause of lamentation, but because we thought it conveyed a regret at the advance of mankind, from that rude condition which approximates him most to unmodified nature.'[62]

The radical unitarians were sympathetic to the Unitarian insistence that it was the duty of mankind to discover the laws which governed nature and the Universe, and to use this knowledge for the benefit of mankind. As W. H. Ashurst explained. 'The discoveries of Science have opened the way to the unity of humanity.'[63] Indeed, true to their Unitarian roots, the radical unitarians were fascinated by science and the application of technology. Douglas Jerrold, for example, ran an inventors' column in his newspaper. One of the radical unitarians' leading protagonists, William Bridges Adams, was himself an important pioneer of railway technology. He also sought to use technology to improve living conditions, as his research into domestic heating systems testifies.[64]

The radical unitarian intelligentsia hoped that the country's scientific progress might improve the quality of people's lives – whether it was through more comfortable housing, better transport, or timesaving gadgets. Nevertheless, radical unitarians were equally concerned with the social problems industrialisation brought in its wake. They believed that the only way to truly harmonise technology with social progress was to inculcate new social values into those responsible for the spread of industrialisation. They advocated that the country's capitalists and manufacturers assume a sense of social responsibility. For example, they exerted constant pressure to ensure that the railways might be used to ameliorate social injustice. When Jerrold's *Illuminated Magazine* printed 'Some Points for a New People's Charter', cheap railway excursions were claimed as a right. Indeed, Dickens's *Household Words* maintained that it was the '*social duty*' of railway companies to provide cheap transport for the working classes. W. B. Adams and C. D. Collet continued to publicise similar ideas in the years to come.[65]

Furthermore, the radical unitarians called for new management practices which would cater for the wider needs of employees, and thus help to instil better class relationships. In this they were continuing the tradition of many mainstream Unitarian manufacturers, such as the Gregs and the Strutts.[66] The schemes implemented by W. B. Adams at his large railway-carriage manufactory in Bow were widely heralded. Adams's faith in the capitalist system was tempered by his socialist sympathies. He argued that workers should benefit, rather than suffer from industrial advance. He provided his work-force with schools, libraries and lecture halls, as well as setting up Provident Societies and a coal club.[67]

Therefore, while supporting the development of capitalism, radical unitarians wished its excesses to be assuaged by the adoption of caring managerial practices. However, they hoped that such policies would be but one reflection of a wider cultural evolution in which the humanity and equality of all was recognised. As Mary Leman Grimstone explained, they were advocating not a 'Utopian philanthropy', but wishing that a 'higher humanity may enter into commerce'.[68]

The radical unitarians' accommodating response to capitalism, and their visions of the role which women might play in social reformation made for interesting debates with contemporary left-wing movements. As seen in the previous chapter, mainstream Unitarians had already begun to engage with these philosophies. The South Place circle enlarged upon this development, providing a stimulating environment in which such cultural interchange might blossom. While the Owenites' views on women and the family were often at strict variance with their own, the radical unitarians did derive great inspiration from many socialist theories, including those of social organisation.

Evangelical ideals of womanhood were woven into the feminist philosophy of the Owenites and communitarians. Many of these radicals declared that were woman emancipated, her moral superiority would serve to redeem and beatify society. Indeed, their eulogy of woman's special powers often led followers of such movements to claim for women a unique religious role. The Saint-Simonians, for example, as John Bowring laughingly recalled, 'migrated to the Levant in the search of a female messiah'. Within the Owenite movement, Joanna Southcott's hierophantic claims also earned wide support.[69]

Radical unitarians were certainly informed by such ideas, particularly as their circles enjoyed constant input from Owenite figures. However, as the second part of the chapter will show, far from vaunting women's superiority, a central facet of the radical unitarian feminist agenda was to highlight the *inferiority* of women's character in the existing state of society. Some radical unitarians did at times refer to gender dissimilitudes. As later chapters will indicate, this was sometimes to appease a more conservative audience, sometimes the result of individual conviction. However, as staunch defenders of the power of the environment in forming character, they often argued that physical force was the only natural difference between the sexes.[70] But more importantly, they constructed a feminist vision in which female emancipation was part of a wider process than purely that of gender, whereby society might be ruled by reason and not by force; and true to their Christian ideals, whereby people were united by their common concern for one another. Within this context they campaigned not only for female liberation, but also for universal suffrage, national education, and new modes of social organisation.

These concerns shaped the radical unitarian response to communitarian ideology. Left-wing ideas on domestic organisation, in particular, they argued, held immense potential for initiating a cultural evolution. Indeed, the radical unitarians were greatly excited by communitarian ideas and consistently supported those who were trying to implement such philosophies. The *People's Journal* reported on the foundation of the Leeds Redemption Society with great interest. If it succeeded, it declared, the members would have the 'honour of carrying out for themselves the substantial portion of the plans of Owen, St. Simon or Fourier'.[71] However, utopian socialism did not fit neatly into radical unitarian ideology. Lady Byron's reservations concerning Owenism's dangerous tendencies typified the sentiments of many. The views of Leigh Hunt were representative of most radical unitarians, who, as the *New Moral World* acknowledged, wished not to uproot society, but to 'extract it [the millenium] out of the present combination of society'.[72] Indeed, radical unitarians adopted communitarian ideas but selectively, and always with an eye to temper their extremism. In so doing they sought to extend their appeal to a wider public.

The most palatable means by which radical unitarians could promote such ideas was to isolate the principle of cooperation from the complex communitarian philosophies. As W. J. Fox explained, 'Our social arrangements may stop far short of the forms contemplated by Mr. Owen, but there seems good reason to expect that they will be modified by the influences of his favourite co-operative principle.' They came to entertain a broad understanding of cooperation. They defined it as a system whereby individuals, by pooling their resources, overcame motives of self-interest, and thus looked to a principle of the common good. This concern accorded precisely with their Unitarian-inspired view that Christ's role was to unite humankind in brotherhood. As W. J. Fox declared in one of his public lectures, 'Christ was not a priest, nor were his apostles priests: their great and single-minded purpose was, to unite mankind in brotherly affection and in brotherly interest.'[73]

The ways in which the radical unitarians adapted the cooperative ideas of contemporary socialists to accord with their own ideological precepts is best seen in their promotion of associated housing schemes. This was a concept first clearly explicated by William Bridges Adams in 1834. He contended, in common with Fourier, that the present system of domestic organisation was clumsy and inefficient. As an engineer, Adams was particularly alert, as the Saint-Simonians had been, to the role that machinery and mechanical devices might play in increasing the efficiency of domestic management. Adams went into considerable detail as to how such a system might be arranged and managed. Each individual home was to be separate and complete in itself, but contained within a range of buildings. Families would then share such facilities as common kitchens, provisions, fires and libraries.[74] Adams's concept enjoyed considerable longevity among the radical unitarian intelligentsia. By the late 1840s radical journals were devoting long articles to the idea, openly acknowledging Adams's role as the originator of such schemes. It was commonly claimed that were they carried out correctly, the living expenses of a family might be cut by half.[75]

The feminist press was eager to encourage such projects as the Metropolitan Housing Association at St Giles which was established in the 1840s, and urged for other such schemes to be set up.[76] However, in keeping with their constant moderation of communitarian ideas, radical journalists advocated that projects for associated housing should only be undertaken on a small-scale basis. Richard Hengist Horne's serial novel *The Dreamer and the Worker* concerned a young woman, Mary, and her efforts to implement associated housing. The heroine soon reduced 'the original project of Associated Homes, which had failed from having been commenced upon a large building scale, instead of a *boarding scheme*'. She then began again, starting with one large house, which proved to be a great success.[77] This story was symptomatic of the extent to which radical unitarians departed from socialist thought. Essentially they wished not to abolish capitalism, but to reform it. They declared the community of property to be unnatural, being 'opposed to the principles of emulation and accumulation'. Radical unitarians recalled the words of R. W. Emerson – that Owen and Fourier were greatly deserving of praise, but that individualism should still be respected.[78]

The desire to restrict the size of associated housing projects also stemmed from the early feminist anxiety to preserve the sanctity of family life. Here again they clashed with the tenets of classic Owenism. Owen, believing the family to be a centre of despotism, had argued that the abolition of the family was crucial if the seeds of individualism and self-interest were to be demolished. Radical unitarians, on the other hand, with their firm grounding in the mores of mainstream Unitarianism, believed that 'No association can be perfect, which antagonises the natural, the sacred institution of family.'[79] Indeed, through their associated housing schemes, radical unitarians came to advocate a liberating concept of the family.

Individual families were to share their resources to create one larger family. Families were to act as stepping-stones to a new social vision in which co-operation made possible higher living standards, better education (through the release of resources due to cheaper housing) and consequently greater opportunities for all.

Furthermore, Owen had argued that established marital relationships would have to be dissolved before the new moral world might begin to rise.[80] However, the radical unitarians promoted associated housing schemes as a means of improving existing marriages – an issue which was to assume a vital point in their feminist agenda. *Eliza Cook's Journal's* article 'Associated Homes' argued that in the conventional mode of social organisation, 'He leads a life of money-making, she one of house-thrift and economical shifts. Thus the two natures very often grow more and more out of harmony, as life passes over their heads.' This was a line Mary Gillies pursued in her essay on 'Associated Homes for the Middle Classes'. She vividly depicted the sufferings of young women, who on marriage have to come to terms with the stressful demands of motherhood and household management. She regretted that, as a consequence, 'Many a marriage that began in love has ended in discord.' She went on to contend that, once married, while men continued to develop personally through their stimulating contact with the outside world, their wives' limited lives turned them into 'narrow-minded and unfit companions for their husbands and in these details we have the secret of many an unhappy marriage'.[81] As Chapter 3 will explore in greater depth, the early feminists hoped that associated housing would free women from such limited domesticity and thus enable them to pursue more fulfilling lives.

The appeal of cooperation was that it might be adopted by ordinary people without the upheaval, commitment and implacable conviction communitarian living demanded. Equally important, it provided the radical unitarians with the perfect entrance into the values of their target audience – the lower middle class and labour aristocracy. Although, as seen above, they hoped their message might reach the business and manufacturing classes, they believed a more profound reforming process might be set into action by appealing directly to those groups which formed such an important element in the new reading audience of the day. This comprised those new occupational groups which had mushroomed during the process of industrialisation – such as mechanics, shopkeepers and clerks.[82] During the 1830s, their professed desire to reach such people was largely theoretical, as their journals attracted chiefly middle-class intellectuals; however, by the mid-1840s, the radical unitarian publications were able to appeal directly to such an audience.

Many detailed analyses have traced the particular ideologies of these social groups. They suggest that the notions of independence, cooperation and respectability were central to their outlook. Indeed, it was from these classes that the culture of self-help and self-improvement, with its multifarious societies and institutions, drew its staunchest supporters.[83] The radical unitarians were keen enthusiasts of this world of mechanics' institutes, benefit societies and self-improvement clubs. They perceived in such activities the means to reform and improve industrial society. Radical unitarians began to support endless cooperative schemes and projects, which they envisaged would act as a panacea to society's ills. Their support for such projects was diverse and sustained. The Metropolitan Co-operative League, for example, was eagerly endorsed by the group. Both *Douglas Jerrold's Weekly Newspaper* and *Howitt's Journal* were keen to advertise its establishment and William Howitt was claimed as the 'original advocate of these leagues'. At the League's soirées the radical unitarians turned out in force, often addressing the meetings. They and their colleagues lent similar support to the Birmingham Co-operative League. In addition they gave constant publicity to cooperative ventures across the country, praising, for example, ventures to cheapen bread through the establishment of cooperative mills and bakeries. Their journals often functioned almost as newsletters for the activities of such projects and societies.[84]

For the radical unitarians, the adoption of cooperative principles by these classes was a vital prerequisite to the transformation of society. They deemed that if industrial society was to be transfigured, it was vital to inculcate new values into these strata. They believed the triumph of cooperative ideals among such people would engender a new age in which the harsh competitiveness of capitalism had been assuaged by a culture in which people shared and helped one another. On a more pragmatic level, as their many articles on the subject testify, it was hoped that cooperative schemes would contribute to the elevation of this sector of society, through helping to reduce their living costs, and also by providing greater opportunities for self-improvement and education.

The radical unitarian concern to aid the cooperative culture of these socio-economic groups was symptomatic of their wider concern to reform such classes. One primary reason lay in their wish to prepare them for responsible political power – for they trusted that before too long such people would be enfranchised. This was a belief which Grimstone captured vividly: 'Democracy, instead of creeping like a subterraneous stream, working its slow way suspicious of the light, is now leaping like a cataract from a precipice.'[85] Douglas Jerrold was also confident of the political future of these classes, rejoicing that 'political power [now] falls naturally and inevitably at their feet'. Moreover, the radical unitarians found the increasing educational power of these social groups immensely exciting. Adhering to the Unitarian belief in the importance of the intellect, they argued that society would only be redeemed through the triumph of the mind. For they dreamt of a new, enlightened age in which education for all ensured a land of opportunity, free from the prejudices of class and sex which contemporary ignorance fostered. If such a society was to germinate then, as the radical unitarians often pointed out, it was 'incumbent upon the toilers of society to become thinkers for society'.[86]

Such a process would necessitate achieving new educational standards among those traditionally deprived of such opportunities – women and the lower classes. As one reformer declared, 'The brain must liberate them. They must think themselves free.'[87] The radical unitarians believed that the edification of the working classes would best be achieved, not through the efforts of middle-class reformers, but through the influence of those who were on the brink between the working and middle classes. It was this group which would form the best teachers of the people. As William Bridges Adams explained, 'It is from amongst the ranks of the mechanics that the teachers must arise, who will gain the confidence of the working classes by their sympathy with their feelings, by knowledge of their wants, and their freedom from conventional prejudices, and slavery to customs, which so strongly beset the *middling* classes of the community.' Barbara Leigh Smith, a consumer of contemporary radical unitarian literature, agreed and reiterated such arguments in later campaigns: 'This class just above the labouring one which touches it, influences the latter more than the higher branches can do, and it is a very sure and sound way of helping the lower classes, to educate those who are richer than themselves, but in immediate contact with them.'[88] Thus, by targeting these potential educators, the radical unitarians hoped that they were initiating a vitally important process of education and elevation. Indeed, they thought the regeneration of society might lie within the hands of this social group.

Therefore, the radical unitarians were not merely passive promoters of cooperative activities. They sought to imbue such pursuits with a progressive philosophy. One of the most telling aspects of these efforts was their wish to persuade the consumers of the cooperative culture to adopt more radical views on women and women's position. This desire, as further chapters will indicate, dictated their feminist strategy on a number of issues – from advocating associated housing as a means of liberating women for full-time employment, to establishing their own feminist adult recreation institution, the Whittington Club.

This concern to inject a feminist perspective into these activities was particularly pressing, given the social mores of the lower middle and upper working classes whom they hoped to reach. The Radical unitarians proved sympathetic to the wider ethos of respectability, which permeated the world-view of these strata, and did not question the value of well-kept homes, hard work and sobriety. However, as Judy Lown has shown, a crucial facet of the doctrine of respectability was an adherence to conventional notions of gender roles and womanly behaviour. She argues that a key aspect of the aspirations of this class was to emulate their wealthier middle-class peers and earn a wage which would be sufficient to ensure that their wives did not need to work. Thus, to boast a wife of leisure, confined purely to the duties of home-making, was the zenith of respectability.[89] This factor provided the radical unitarians with their most difficult task – to persuade the lower middle classes and labour aristocracy that their true elevation might only be effected if they were prepared to acknowledge the oppression of contemporary women and adopt new and radical ideas concerning their roles.

Such an agenda involved not merely challenging patriarchal social structures, but, as the following section will demonstrate, necessitated enabling women themselves to assume new characters and aspirations. Barbara Leigh Smith, again writing in later years, captured clearly the radical unitarian argument,

> If we could make these women high-minded, intelligent, and simple in their tastes, instead of leaving them to be brought up to vanity, false ideas of what is lady-like, and every shallow showy accomplishment, it would indeed be a blessing! At present, their contact with those above them is just of that external character which causes them to imitate their dress, and the vanities and follies of those they call real ladies.[90]

In order to convince their readership of the egregious position of contemporary women, and to inspire their audience with neoteric images of female potential, the radical unitarians turned to literature.

THE USES OF LITERATURE

The influence of Romantic thought upon English literary culture had led to a tremendous elevation of the role of the writer. As Carlyle claimed, 'Intrinsically it is the same function which the old generations named a man Prophet, Priest, Divinity for doing.' Continuing both the emphasis which Unitarians placed upon the role of literature and the denomination's increasing tendency to secularise religious concepts, radical unitarian intellectuals embraced this idea. Indeed, they claimed that literature was as important as religious discourse. Sarah Flower Adams, for example, claimed that drama was a 'supplement to the pulpit'.[91] In tandem with their opinion that society would be transformed through the triumph of the mind, they claimed that writers possessed the capacity to express the wants and needs of the age and to envisage and make possible the formulation of new solutions. Therefore, as struggling writers, Fox's followers wished to achieve a universal respect for the value of the artist (not least through practical measures, such as a reform in the copyright laws), and to raise the literary world from what they perceived as its state of depression.[92]

The radical unitarians thus concurred with the concerns of their close associates, the utilitarians and the Chartists, that literature should not be purely decorative but might perform a social and political function.[93] Hence, reviewing the work of Mary Leman Grimstone, the *Monthly Repository* argued, 'We cannot treat Mrs Grimstone merely as a novelist.' It talked of the need to see her as a 'moralist' and recommended her volumes to 'the attention of all who are interested in that social reform and progress'. They were also keenly aware of literature's potential as a publicity vehicle. Thus *Douglas Jerrold's Shilling Magazine* was keen to stress, 'the advantage novels give to a cause'.[94]

However, the radical unitarians focused upon literature's potential function as a repository of truth. They argued that it might be used to capture accurately the state of society, and inform the reader of the hidden truths which lay beneath the layers of unreliable convention. This belief formed a vital facet of their reform agitation, acting as it did as a means of promoting awareness, and consequently protest against the existing society.

Nowhere was the radical unitarian concern to employ literature as a social and political instrument more clearly seen than in their attempts to use it as a tool for achieving female emancipation. The early feminists maintained that it was vital to alert their audience to the character of woman under the present social system. Only then might women begin to reform and claim the social status due to them. It was argued that literature and literary conventions had been particularly culpable in disseminating distortions of truth concerning the real nature of women. The reality, they suggested, was that women were so oppressed by existing customs, institutions and culture that their characters were vitiated and debased. Therefore, there was a need to promote a new literature which might expose the truths of society, enabling them to lay bare the hypocrisies and injustices which formed existing sexist assumptions. In addition, they hoped that literature might also perform a more visionary role. For, within literature, there lay the possibility of using creative imagination to release the public mind from the limitations of conventional attitudes towards women.

The feminists maintained that the most common lie which the existing culture perpetrated about women was their portrayal as perfect, angelic beings. It was an aspect of modern discourse which particularly infuriated Unitarian Lucy Aikin. She questioned the conventional wisdom which esteemed English women to be pure, accomplished and possessed of all the 'domestic virtues'. In reality, she believed, they were the 'slaves of so many stupid and debasing prejudices'.[95] The more radical believed that such representations formed part of an explicit strategy to subordinate women. Grimstone, as ever, couched the theme in emotive tones: 'For thousands of years, she has listened to flattery and falsehood, administered to reconcile her to wrong, and keep her in the trammels of the slave.' This was a common theme, which ran throughout the period in question. John Stores Smith (a Manchester feminist and close associate of Leigh Hunt and Geraldine Jewsbury) was typical, when in the early 1850s he observed that flattery and gallantry were a means of blinding women to the real nature of their oppression.[96]

Douglas Jerrold expressed clearly the feminists' conviction that literature was largely responsible for the propagation of these ideas, 'in poetry, in tales, in plays that profess to teach human passion and reflect back on our social state – we praise woman as a creature superior to man'. This, it was believed, was largely due to the legacy of the chivalric age, when the adulation of women became an integral facet of contemporary literature. This was the view taken by the *Spirit of the Age*, which argued that these chivalric attitudes were 'rather the creation of poetic minds than a genuine picture of social habits'.[97]

The radical unitarians were concerned that people had started to believe these literary images of women. A reviewer for *Tait's Edinburgh Magazine* asserted that false opinions of women had become so embedded into popular thinking, that they were no longer stated; nevertheless, they remained enshrined within the literary canon. Talking of society's oppression of women, it argued, 'No one longer says in words, though the opinion is insinuated in the charming creations found in much fiction and poetry.'[98] In the *New Moral World* Catherine Barmby attempted to address precisely this point, in her 'Conversations with Jane and Eliza'. Eliza initiates the debate by claiming that woman's character is far superior to that of man, 'and, therefore [I] consider improvement most essential in the other sex – in the oppressor rather than the oppressed'. Her companion, Jane, replied that such a view demonstrated the degree to which Eliza had been influenced by false conventions, 'How do your words breathe of the lessons the world has taught you; lessons which prove to every heart as a vulture. . . . The character of woman, in every respect, [is] inferior to what it should be.'[99] Grimstone raised a more worrying aspect of the debate in her novel, *Woman's Love*, where she suggested that the power of these conventions was such that women tried to shape their characters to fit the images of women which men desired.[100]

Therefore, the radical unitarians were eager to draw attention to literature which they believed captured instead the actual character of women and their true position in society. Shakespeare was often praised in this context. Feminist Anna Jameson, in her *Characteristics of Women*, reasoned, 'In Shakespeare the male and female characters bear precisely the same relation to each other that they do in nature and in society – they are not equal in prominence or in power, they are subordinate throughout.'[101] This aspect of feminist literary criticism was well exemplified in W. B. Adams's lengthy review of *Coriolanus*. Volumnia's admission that she would rather give birth to a son than a daughter arouses all of Adams's feminist fervour:

Why should a woman glory in giving birth to a man-child, more than a woman-child? Because Volumnia, like many other women, has the keenness, or rather the instinct, to perceive that the lot of woman is for the most part that of a slave, that she is generally linked to man as a necessary convenience, that is at best not a sympathising friend, but an amusing toy, to be thrown away when the owner is tired of it.[102]

In the explication of these theories, the feminist-minded intelligentsia did not rely solely on their reviews and critiques of well-known writers. An equally important element of their work was the composition of a literature of their own. At the forefront of such endeavours stands Mary Leman Grimstone. A common convention within feminist letters was to present lists of women's unattractive qualities in the present state of society. Dr Alexander, in a two-part series for the *Star in the East*, typified such an approach as he proceeded to describe contemporary women as, 'mentally inferior, gay, trifling, volatile and superficial'. Grimstone's skill was to capture these faults within an array of negative stereotypes. In one of her early essays she wrote of the 'vain, cruel, capricious coquette; the termagant, treacherous wife; the envious, illiberal associate; the extravagant, comfortless domestic manager; these are the rickety crippled produce of abused female nature'.[103] Grimstone's most significant contribution to feminist literature came when she developed these stereotypes in a series of short stories which she composed for the *Monthly Repository*. Her 'Sketches of Domestic Life' were designed to use literature as a means of drawing the relationship between women's negative character-traits and the cultural conditioning which had produced them. They also demonstrate the extent to which the radical unitarian feminist view was informed, as was the feminism of Mary Wollstonecraft (whose influence they rarely acknowledged publicly), by the Unitarian concerns of rationality, education, and the power of the environment in creating the individual.

The first of these stories concerns a young man, Cyril, who meets and falls in love with a distressed, vulnerable woman, Caroline. Their consequent marriage proves disastrous, resulting in the mental debilitation of Cyril and consumptive, retarded children. Grimstone initially appears to be following a well-worn literary path as she describes how Cyril meets Caroline, exhausted and rain-drenched on the streets. She is the damsel in distress *par excellence*, and conforms perfectly to conventional notions of womanly beauty, fragility, and humility. Grimstone indulges her reader with the excessive rhetoric of romantic fiction in her description of Caroline's tantalising effect upon Cyril: 'the murmur of her voice', for example, 'made music amid the din of battling winds'.

However, having lulled the reader into such reveries, Grimstone abruptly pulls her audience up short by subjecting the romance to rigorous scrutiny. She proceeds to completely undermine the conventions which the story originally followed by examining the reality behind such supposedly ideal women as Caroline. With ruthless candour, she begins, 'Little has hitherto been said of Caroline, because she is of a class of women who say little for themselves, and for whom little can be said.' She then proceeds to demonstrate that Cyril has been lured into accepting the literary conventions of women, to the extent that such ideas have come to dictate his responses to the actual women in his life. 'That she had won the love of such a man as Cyril, was partly owing to his imagination, which . . . had endowed his idol with supposititious gifts, and partly from the conventional and poetical notions which he entertained of women.' Grimstone enunciates the dangers of absorbing so passively cultural and particularly literary conventions: 'Experience was destined to awaken him to the truth, that it is art, not nature, which has made men and women so widely different.' The consequences of Cyril's acceptance of misleading cultural notions is that he 'looked on women . . . as things to be cared for and controlled – whose faults were to be forgiven for the sake of their weakness, – whose errors were pardonable on account of their ignorance'.

Having dissected Cyril's response to Caroline, Grimstone then proceeds to consider the conditioning factors in Caroline's own upbringing. In this process, Grimstone presented her own analysis of the real characters which lay behind such simpering, fragile beauties as Caroline Conway. Grimstone focused upon an aspect of women's education of which she particularly despaired – the emphasis that was placed on fostering beauty, rather than cultivating the intellect. Caroline's parents, she explained, had failed to bring her up according to the principles of reason. Consequently, Caroline 'devoted her life to maintaining an idea of physical beauty, at risk to her health'. In Caroline's case the consequences were dire. She 'sank into a debility which rendered any mental action, beyond a feeble irritableness, impossible'.

The true foundation of Caroline's character was discovered too late by Cyril. 'His ardent imagination had supplied to the averted eyes of Caroline language for which he now looked into them in vain. His heart thirsted to hear her sentiments and opinions, her hopes and expectations . . . to draw from her new inspiration.' Thus, Caroline's conditioning and Cyril's false expectations find their ultimate tragedy in the effect they have upon the marriage.[104]

The baneful effect of the failure to treat women rationally remained a persistent theme in the following stories. All too often, Grimstone illustrated, women were either spoilt like children, or required to respond with unquestioning submission. Grimstone and her fellow feminists suggested that one indication of this failure to treat women as intelligent beings was the pitiful education afforded to them. It was an education designed not to develop their minds and resources, but to fit them as ornamental objects, pleasing to men. This led to a common idiom in feminist circles – while among the working classes, women were used as drudges, their middle- and upper-class peers were treated as toys. As 'F J.' argued in *Eliza Cook's Journal*, 'In polished society . . . it has become customary to regard her as an agreeable toy, to be flattered and caressed, or neglected and despised, as the caprice of the opposite sex might dictate.'[105] In 'The Insipid', Grimstone illustrated how such shallow education and treatment of women led to the formation of female characters who were 'living concentrations of selfishness'. Similarly in her later tale about the Mortons, the failure to treat the family's daughters rationally led them to have but superficial characters, their only interests being 'the vulgar enjoyments of dress, display and dissipation'.[106]

These themes, which were to be developed by later feminists such as Emily Davies, reverberated throughout the progressive elements of the literary world.[107] As Geraldine Jewsbury wrote of her heroine, Agnes Worral, 'poor Agnes, a pretty, giddy young thing' – 'She is much to be pitied, it is not *her* fault that she is vain and frivolous. . . . she never had one sentence addressed to her capable of stirring the heart of a rational creature.' Dora in Dickens's *David Copperfield* also provided a perfect example of the immature, unreasoning character which feminists believed the cultural oppression of women induced. Dickens describes how she 'seemed by one consent to be regarded like a pretty toy or plaything'.[108] Dora is terrified by David's attempts to reason with her, and David's emotions concerning his 'child wife' appear to have been presaged in Grimstone's insight that, 'The existing mode of social intercourse between the sexes in its best form, is that of an adult and a child; in peculiar cases this is a happy and beautiful relation, but it is not the true one, and in its general effects produces the mischief incident to everything that is false.' As David himself admits, 'I did feel, sometimes, that I could have wished my wife had been my counsellor, had had more character and purpose to sustain me and improve me by, had been endowed with power to fill up the void which sometimes seemed to be about me.'[109]

Mary Leman Grimstone thus set the agenda for establishing literary strategies as a means of feminist protest. During the 1840s, these methodologies were developed through specific literary projects, as feminists sought to implement the vibrant debates of the 1830s through practical schemes. In particular, they were concerned to bring English women in touch with the pertinent writings of continental women. Mary Howitt, for example, embarked upon translating the works of the Swedish feminist, Frederika Bremer. Bremer, herself closely involved with London's radical literary community,[110] has been almost completely overlooked by both literary scholars and historians of nineteenth-century feminism alike. However, Howitt's translations were eagerly received, not only by the radical unitarian set, but also by a wider reading public. As *Tait's Edinburgh Magazine* commented enthusiastically, 'For once, an English translator of foreign novels has made a hit.'[111]

Mary Howitt was keen to draw attention to the feminism of Bremer's work. She explained, 'An intense desire animated her to aid in the liberation of every oppressed soul; above all, to rescue her country-women from the dark and narrow sphere allotted them.'[112] Certainly, Bremer's dissension from the female character-types so prevalent in contemporary British fiction was, as *Tait's Edinburgh Magazine* pointed out, extremely refreshing. In one tale, for example, the narrator's sister, Selam, at first appears to be an archetypal literary heroine. She is beautiful, dutiful and placid. Yet, the reader is soon to learn that even she is subject to unattractive moods of pique and malice.[113] This complex characterisation added considerably to the sensitivity of Bremer's treatment of the lives of her female characters. Furthermore, as the next chapter suggests, Bremer captured brilliantly the feelings of frustration which so many middle-class women experienced during this period.

A more ambitious literary scheme was piloted by Matilda Hays, who

with the assistance of Eliza Ashurst and Edmund Larken (a chief promoter
of the *Leader* newspaper and a staunch supporter of the Leeds Redemption
Society) undertook to translate all of George Sand's novels.[114] This was a
brave undertaking, for Sand had earned a scandalous reputation in Britain.
As the *People's Press* put it, her life and works had been 'scurrilously
condemned'. She was known as a 'woman of the most eccentric or even
debased habits'.[115] However, the radical unitarians believed Sand's work
fulfilled perfectly their own literary ideals. The *Republican* explained how
she had penetrated to the heart of society and 'with daring hand [had] torn
away the veil'. As the *Spirit of the Age* argued, she wrote the type of novel,
'which delineates the operation of social laws, conventions, and opinions,
and which develops, dramatically, the great working of ideas, the mutation
of societies, the growth of new and the action of old principles'.[116]

Sand's literary methods enabled her to explore two themes which were
of particular concern to the radical unitarians. The first of these was their
desire to reform social behaviour and mores by challenging the false conventions of society.

Sand created fictional worlds in which rigid societal conventions were
superseded by high moral principles. Thus, W. J. Linton, in a public address, praised Sand for her predication of 'the clear heaven of a morality
which shall displace the conventional foulness of our hypocritical and
brutal system'.[117] Secondly, and perhaps more importantly, Sand was concerned to detail the nature of women in existing society. She was, Eliza
Ashurst declared, the 'Mary Wolstonecraft [sic] of the age'.[118] Certainly
Sand was often scathing in her illumination of the double sexual stand
ard which operated in society, with its consequent oppression of women.
Moreover, like Grimstone, she was concerned to illustrate what she perceived as mistaken assumptions concerning the capabilities of women. In
Simon, for example, Bonne, the solicitor's daughter, has been conditioned
to imagine that 'in all stations of life, the cares of housewifery formed the
chief glory of woman'. Sand also detailed the vitiated character of women
in existing society. Hence, in *The Last Aldini*, we are told of Bianca, 'she
was a woman; that is to say, weak, enslaved, the object of remorseless
prejudices'.[119]

Of equal significance was Sand's ability to ideate new role-models
and character-types for women. As one feminist reviewer raved, 'She is
the prophetess of woman's future.' *Douglas Jerrold's Shilling Magazine*
eulogised the creation of 'Edmée, the female heroine, [in whom] we have
the embodiment of intellect and sensibility, perhaps indicative of the future
condition of humanity, when refined by juster laws, and circumstances'.[120]
Edmée, a protagonist of *Mauprat* (1837), was certainly a refreshing

departure in female characterisation, with her staunch views on sexual equality, strong intellect, and healthy appetite for physical exercise. She was joined by a gallery of other novel female characters – such as Marcelle Blanchemont (the heroine of *The Miller of Angibault* (1845)) with her shrewd business acumen, great heroism and physical strength; and the brilliant, individualistic Fiamma in *Simon* (1836).

The radical unitarians fervently believed that the translations would actually make a major contribution to the liberation of English women. The *People's Press* claimed that they were by 'good and brave English women, and destined to put down bigots, and help to work a revolution in the social position of women'. The *Spirit of the Age* echoed the belief that the works would precipitate such a feminist revolution. The *Republican* believed that the effects of English women reading Sand would be momentous; they would serve to raise women's awareness of their present condition and thus prove to be 'a revelation, a gospel of the woes, the wrongs, the duties, and the promised future of womanhood'.[121]

Consequently, the radical journals ceaselessly exhorted English women to read these novels. As Linton put it, 'In the hands of every English-woman should be the works of that greatest genius of our time – in the heart of every Englishwoman, the wisdom and beauty of their ennobling lessons.' The *Republican* concurred, adding, 'we believe no greater boon could be bestowed on the women of England (truly on the men also) than to enable them to learn by heart the lessons of George Sand'.[122] Despite the eulogies of the radical press, the translations proved to be a commercial flop and Hays was forced to terminate the project before its completion, Ashurst blaming the poor business publisher chosen by Hays.[123] Nevertheless, in the process, Hays and her colleagues had become feminist heroes. The *Spirit of the Age* eulogised the 'stainless characters of those brave women who have run the risk of odium to aid the holy cause of truth and right'.[124]

THE ORIGINS OF FEMALE SLAVERY

The radical unitarians' employment of literature indicated their comprehensive awareness of the cultural oppression of women. Their Unitarian heritage enabled them to posit an historical explanation for this tyranny. This revolved upon redefining the concepts of slavery prevalent within contemporary discourse. The resulting arguments provided feminists with the intellectual pabulum necessary to inform their women's rights campaigns.

The comparison of women's position with that of the slave was a common idiom among early feminists. One Owenite, 'Justitia', gave a full exposition on the theme, 'In what does the slavery of woman consist?' She asked, 'Does it not consist in being subjected to laws which she has been carefully excluded from all participation in forming? . . . Does not slavery consist in having been systematically excluded from an education, which, however miserably defective it may be, has been an additional weapon in the hands of her tyrant?'[125]

Many studies, noting the prevalence of such language among Victorian feminists, often relate this phenomenon to women's direct participation in anti-slavery campaigns.[126] However, the more subtle analyses of anti-slavery historians such as Betty Fladeland and Patricia Hollis enable the reconstruction of a more convincing explanation. Their studies have alerted us to the extensive use made of the lexicon of slavery within the radical culture at large. As the work of James Walvin has demonstrated, it is not surprising that British radicals should have appropriated such rhetoric, for during the early part of this period, the massive propaganda efforts of the anti-slavery movement ensured that the issue of slavery became steeped within the public consciousness. Thus, in a stimulating essay, Seymour Drescher argues, 'Between 1830 and 1833 the intrusion of "slavery" into political rhetoric became almost reflexive.'[127]

However, the metaphorical use of slavery also came to function as a contentious ideological arena. A range of discrete reforming groups manipulated its emotive power to prick the sensibilities of fellow campaigners in other fields. Thus, Hollis has shown that the adoption of such rhetoric could also be the vehicle by which working-class radicals expressed their hostility against the narrow vision of middle-class anti-slavery campaigners. Bronterre O'Brien, for one, claimed that the abolitionists 'financed their philanthropy abroad by increasing the exploitation of their white "slaves" at home'.[128] However, Hollis, in common with other anti-slavery historians, does not mention that in domino fashion, so did many working-class women react against the blinkered approach of their menfolk. They adopted Shelley's axiom as their slogan, arguing that 'Woman has been the slave of a slave.'[129]

Radical unitarians also used the concept of slavery to project their specific ideological grievances. Most strikingly, they rejected the manner in which slavery was evoked within working-class radicalism. A working-class political tradition stretched back to Paine, which identified slavery in terms of exclusion from the political system. However, within working-class radicalism, as seen above, there also existed a second, more literal interpretation of slavery as labour exploitation. This was an angle largely missing from radical unitarian critiques. Within the radical unitarian frame of reference, any peoples not granted the freedom of self-determination might be considered as enslaved – hence their support for the nationalist movements in Italy, Hungary and Poland. They tended to adhere to an intellectual definition of slavery, perceiving it as the denial of reason, and the rights of the individual.

The previous section illustrated that radical unitarians also applied such criteria in their analyses of women's treatment. However, their Unitarian heritage also endowed them with a more precise use of slavery as a metaphorical tool. A clue to the nature of this liberating rhetoric lies in the fact that when writing on female slavery, the radicals did not necessarily allude to the slavery of the American blacks. While reference to their position is often made, far more commonly writers described the plight of slaves in the Ancient world, or in those societies which they believed were still in a primitive state of civilisation, such as the Far East. Thus Linton's cry, 'Alas! the ancient slavery subsists!' finds echoes throughout feminist letters.[130]

As David Brion Davis has illustrated, it was not until the sugar boom of the fifteenth century that slaves were used as labourers for the manufacture of goods on a large scale. Hitherto, slaves had been defined more in terms of their relationship to the household in which they served. Davis explains, 'What distinguished slavery in much of the pre-modern world was not its antithesis to free labour, but its antithesis to the normal network of kinship ties of dependency, protection, obligation, and privilege.' Thus slavery was defined as the acceptance of loyalty to authorities who were not of the same kin.[131] To the feminists, more concerned with domestic and cultural oppression than purely capitalist exploitation, this was a powerful model to adopt. They focused upon the crucial concept that slavery was a cultural and not a purely economic phenomenon. In particular, they adopted the notion that slaves might be defined as those who joined a household in the need of a protector. Contemporary culture, they professed, pushed women into just such a position.

In formulating these ideas, radical unitarians relied upon their Enlightenment heritage, which was filtered to them via their mainstream Unitarian predecessors. Jane Rendall's survey of the work of late-eighteenth-century scholars is vital in understanding this legacy. She notes that during this period, intellectuals were becoming increasingly aware of the different cultures and societies then existing. Montesquieu, for example, employed a comparative analysis of customs and laws among different societies, to analyse the role of the family, and the condition of women in society. He was followed by a number of Scottish and French writers who, making much use of the contemporary anthropological work on American Indian cultures, sought to explicate 'universally applicable theories of history', based upon the different stages through which all societies passed. The summit in this evolution, it was maintained, was western, commercial society.[132] Rendall provides a fruitful and important disquisition on these ideas. However, she gives no clues as to how such ideas might have been specifically received or criticised by others. By contrast, a close study of the work of the radical unitarian intelligentsia reveals that their own thought and writing directly incorporated and expanded upon the studies of these earlier writers.

Enlightenment scholars were particularly interested in the treatment of women in what they perceived as 'savage' states. Adam Ferguson and William Robertson considered the position of women among Indian tribes, where they noted that women performed much of the work. The crucial observation was made that such women were the property of their men. Ferguson contended that although this did not constitute a formal slave system, and the women's condition was assuaged by affection, nonetheless, in these situations women suffered from a form of slavery.[133] Moreover, William Alexander's study of primitive societies led him to draw a critical conclusion which was to long influence feminist thinking: 'among the rudest savages and in the earliest ages of antiquity, . . . bodily strength was the only thing held in particular estimation; and women having rather a less portion of this than men, were on that account never so much esteemed'.[134]

A persistent theme within these studies was to chart the progression of women's condition as society evolved. Millar, for example, claimed that the invention of taming and pasturing cattle was the first breakthrough. Women's position continued to improve 'when men are acquainted with the cultivation of the ground, and have made some progress in the different branches of husbandry'. Moreover, Millar was typical in heralding the age of chivalry as a major breakthrough in the treatment of women, focusing upon the period's courtly and 'delicate' manners and its adulation of women.[135] Montesquieu was interested to learn how women's position was dictated by the different types of government – such as monarchies, republics or despotic regimes.[136]

The works of scholars such as Millar, Ferguson and Robertson were readily received amongst the Unitarian literati. Indeed, they were employed by the more latitudinarian as a vehicle with which to explore enlightened views of women's position. The promininent Unitarian minister Robert Aspland was one who made great use of this scholarship. This is evident from an oration which he delivered in Hackney in 1812, *The*

Beneficial Influence of Christianity on the Character and Condition of the Female Sex. This was eagerly received by Aspland's audience, and they urged him to publish it.[137] This erudite work followed precisely the scheme adopted by the writers above, as he proceeded to trace the position of women throughout the ages in a variety of cultures. Aspland, like earlier scholars, was keen to address the condition of women in the *savage* state. In this element of his analysis he openly acknowledged his debt to Robertson's work, referring to him warmly as that 'popular historian'.[138] Indeed, Aspland quoted at length from this author, drawing in particular upon his treatment of women in Indian communities.

However, despite the similarity of method, the central contention of Aspland's work was rather different from that of intellectuals such as Millar and Robertson. He moved the woman question to centre-stage, his argument being, 'Amongst whole nations, and for ages, we behold the sex degraded to an ignominious bondage, mere instruments of the convenience of man, victims of his tyranny, slave to his appetites and passions, or the sport of his caprice.'[139] For Aspland, women's position was not related to the economic development of society, or the evolution of political organisation. This is made apparent in his treatment of ancient classical civilisation. The majority of early anthropologists, detailed above, had a great faith in the culture of the Greek and Roman republics. While they recognised that the treatment of women in these societies was still far from civilised, they maintained that in these states women reached greater heights than in many other early societies.[140] By contrast, Aspland notes that even in 'civilised' Greek and Roman societies women's position was very low and they suffered from barbarity, although, 'in a different shape'. The root of the problem, he suggested, was that in these cultures also, 'woman was the property of man'. Aspland did believe that women's condition had improved through the centuries, but argued that this was due to the spread of Christianity. There were, he expostulated, a number of factors which accounted for this: Christianity had 'exploded' iniquitous practices, such as polygamy and divorce; fostered benevolence; and promoted morality. Moreover, it had 'cherished the spirit of freedom'.[141]

In a work long forgotten by modern scholars, *Epistles on Women* (1810), Aspland's contemporary, Unitarian Lucy Aikin, demonstrated the degree to which her thought was similarly informed by the work of intellectuals such as Robertson. Aikin also adopted the strategy of a comparative and historical analysis of woman's slave position. She openly acknowledged her debt to this earlier scholarship, criticising Rousseau for failing to 'consult the interests of the weaker sex in his preference of savage life to civilised'. She favoured the work of Robertson and Hearne on the American

Indians, who, she believed, captured accurately the true picture of the terrible life and condition of women in the northern tribes. Nevertheless, Aikin, like Aspland, did not passively absorb the intellectual tradition of the Enlightenment academics. In common with Aspland, she dissented from the orthodoxy of her source historians in the bleak picture she painted of the condition of women in the Greek republic, 'Thy wives, proud Athens! fettered and debased.'[142] But whereas Aspland was concerned to detail the ways in which women had gradually been granted a greater degree of respect, through the spread of Christianity, Aikin's poem had more overtly feminist aims. At times it appears to have drawn on a more radical tradition, as she evoked the imagery of William Blake's 'Daughters of Albion'. She later explained to Dr Channing that the poem was written with her youthful fervour for the 'Rights of Women'.[143] Indeed, as she states in her second epistle, 'the weaker sex [is] held by all in some kind of subjection'. She describes in vivid terms the fate of women throughout the many cultures she has considered, 'Scorned and caressed, a plaything and a slave,/ Yet taught with spaniel soul to kiss the rod'. Moreover, Aikin isolated William Alexander's critical insight in her explanation for this universal oppression of women, as the following, sardonic verse reveals,

Nature endows him with superior force,
Superior wisdom them I grant, of course
For who gainsays the despot in his might,
Or when was ever weakness in the right?
With passive reverence too I hail the law,
Formed to secure the strong the weak to awe.[144]

Aikin was less convinced than Aspland that women's condition had improved. Her poem adopts an exhortatory tone, urging men to grant women greater freedom, and encouraging women to learn from the lessons of history so that they might 'improve, excel, surmount, subdue, your fate!' For Aikin, this potential for women's liberation is made possible by the triumph of the intellect within the enlightened world.[145]

Both Aspland and Aikin were well-known to the radical unitarian community. W. J. Fox was a close associate of Aspland and had been a member of his congregation in Hackney, where the above sermon (*The Beneficial Influence of Christianity*) was delivered. Aikin also maintained close ties with the Unitarian literati, in particular, Harriet Martineau.[146] Consequently, the feminists enjoyed a direct intellectual heritage upon which to base their arguments concerning the enslaved nature of women's

condition. Thus, the work of Aspland and Aikin functioned as an interme-
diary stage between the arguments of the Enlightenment anthropologists,
and the radical unitarian feminists of the 1830s and 1840s.

Radical unitarians continued to be interested in relations between the
sexes in savage states, and in the notion that women were the property of
men in such situations. They accepted completely the proposition that the
underlying reason for this was that in such barbaric societies, women, as
the physically weaker sex, were dependent upon men for protection. While
they continued to be interested in the link between women's condition and
the state of society, they too, questioned the precise relationship. Aspland's
theory, that Christianity was the cause of women's improvement, was
hotly disputed by radicals of the 1830s and 1840s.[147] The radical unitarians' approach to the question of female improvement was closer to that
of Aikin. This involved the belief that it must be related to cerebral phenomena, and maintained that women might only be truly freed by the
liberalism of a new age.

However, the radical unitarians went much further than either Aikin or
Aspland when they rejected a fundamental assumption of the Enlightenment theorists. The central contention of the latter had been that society
had evolved from an age of barbarism into a modern world of commercial
sophistication. By contrast, the feminists argued that although civilisation had progressed, the relationships between men and women had not
advanced at the same pace. Women's condition might be progressing
slightly, but essentially, the feminists maintained, women remained enslaved because in the sphere of domestic relations, the ancient notions of
feudal protection, which privileged physical force over reason, still prevailed. Therefore, unlike the Enlightenment writers, they did not believe
that society had yet reached the peak of civilisation. It was at best but half-
civilised. Grimstone, for example, alluded to the 'semi-barbarism of the
present period', and Thornton Hunt (the son of Leigh Hunt) mourned the
fact that society was 'poisoned by half-civilisation'.[148]

Victorian feminists continued to employ such arguments throughout the
century.[149] As Lee Holcombe has shown, the feminist campaigners of the
1850s relied heavily upon Caroline Cornwallis's contributions to the *Westminster Review*. What Holcombe neglects is that Cornwallis's arguments
drew directly upon the feminist analysis of barbarity, as promulgated by
the radical unitarians.[150] Mill's *Subjection of Women* may also be placed
within this tradition. Indeed, the work was criticised by conservative contemporaries precisely because he rejected the notion that men should
enjoy power because of their physical superiority. Mary Shanley has ably

explained Mill's notion that the development of the species was held in check by a system of domestic slavery, and his subsequent conclusion that mankind could not progress unless the master–slave relationship within marriage was overthrown. She is clearly mistaken, though, in characterising Mill as a pioneer of this approach. For these ideas were but the culmination of a long debate within radical unitarian circles.[151]

Feminists of the 1830s and 1840s constantly promulgated these issues. Birmingham radical George Dawson proved an able exponent of the feminist case. In one of his public lectures upon National Education, he fumed, 'Barbarism still looks upon woman as a convenient drudge, a useful slave or an inferior helpmate.' W. J. Linton also published numerous declamations on the subject. 'Witness', for example, wrote eloquently on the issue, describing, 'the false position in which women have ever been placed, and in which they still linger by reason of those remains of barbarism which yet give to physical force the advantage over all kinds and degrees of moral and spiritual power'. Fox reiterated these concerns in a lecture he delivered at South Place Chapel. He argued that the importance of brute force had all but gone from society. The only place where it still remained was in the relationships between men and women. Indeed, he contended that among the sexes, 'the effect of the disparity of physical strength between man and women has not so vanished . . . is much more practically felt, and its results are deep and broad in the legislative and social wrongs which the weaker has still to endure'.[152]

As Fox's argument indicates, radical unitarians perceived that society's reliance upon the superiority of force had become ingrained into the culture. In particular, this led the feminists to campaign for reforms in the existing legislature. For, as the *People's Journal* explained, 'laws being made by man are made for man, and woman, as the weakest, must yield and suffer'. It was an idea which Grimstone often explored in her novels. In *Cleone*, Mrs Howell, explaining her anxieties for the position of women within marriage, notes that man, 'has a strong arm and savage laws on his side'. This argument persisted throughout the period, as John Stores Smith's 1850 work, *Social Aspects* testifies.[153]

Thus, the early feminists sought to initiate a new age of equality, in which laws were framed according to the precepts of reason, thus assuring justice for all. Nevertheless, as the most radical among them appreciated, this goal might only be achieved were women to have an equal say in the legislature, and thus were themselves enfranchised. However, the early feminists appreciated that of equal importance was the necessity to root out the vestiges of barbarism within male/female relations, by challenging traditional social customs and manners. In particular, they were concerned with the legacy of the protection mentality which men still practised towards women. This involved attacking the chivalric code of manners, and arguing instead for new, liberal customs, in which women might be freed from the shackles of conventional manners and participate equally with men in all spheres of life. The following chapters will demonstrate how these concerns fuelled the radical unitarians' feminist campaigns of the 1830s and 1840s.

3 'The Stream of Freedom' – Democracy and Domestic Mores

'HAVN'T I AS MUCH RIGHT AS A MAN?' – PRESENTING THE ARGUMENTS FOR FEMALE SUFFRAGE

Historians have assumed that the relationship between women's legal status and their inability to vote was not forged by feminists until the 1860s. Shanley's work, for example, is firmly in this tradition. She maintains that it was only in the 1860s and 1870s, when the movement to reform the legal status of married women was under way, that feminists made the connection between, 'women's legal subordination to their husbands in marriage and the lack of the vote'.[1] However, a study of radical literary circles demonstrates clearly the inaccuracy of such assertions. Women were slaves, Justitia affirmed, precisely because she was 'Subject to laws which she has been carefully excluded from all participation in forming'.[2] The *Leader* (a newspaper founded by Thornton Hunt, G. H. Lewes and Linton) was one of many radical publications which echoed such sentiments, proclaiming, 'we are not willing that laws should arbitrarily declare woman to be the mere slave of man without a voice of her own'.[3]

In 1832, radical Unitarian, Matthew Davenport Hill, demonstrated the strength of feeling on the suffrage issue within radical circles when he publicly endorsed female suffrage to enthusiastic mixed-sex audiences during his successful election campaign in Hull. This was also the year in which the first petition for female suffrage was presented to Parliament. It was at this time that James Silk Buckingham declared himself publicly on the issue, arguing in Parliament that women should be entitled to political autonomy.[4] From this period onwards a groundswell of feminist agitation emerged, demanding women's right to vote. In 1841, the *Westminster Review*, referring its readers to the *Monthly Repository*, noted that there was an 'extreme party among the agitators' who raised the issue of female political rights.[5]

A formative influence upon the early feminists' articulations for female suffrage was their belief that the legislature had been framed according to the precepts of physical power and so militated against the interests of the physically weaker sex. The radical unitarians argued that it was only by establishing equality at the heart of the legislature that a just and rational society might be effected. Otherwise, as Linton, with characteristic vehemence put it, 'If you deny that woman has the right to vote – go back to the ancient brutality, "Let the strong-armed savage dash out the brains of Christ." '[6]

Within the pages of journals such as the *Monthly Repository*, feminists argued consistently the case for female enfranchisement. This journal expressed clearly the feminist vision of a perfect society in which both male and female interests were blended. 'While human society is compounded of the two sexes so also should be human legislation', it declared.[7] Feminists were later to expand upon this theme, claiming that the legislature would remain imperfect without the input of female qualities. While those on the edge of radical unitarian circles, such as Anne Knight and Anna Jameson, did pursue such ideas, on the whole, the early agitators tended not to dwell upon such thoughts. They focused instead upon the more polemical issue of women's rights. For, as one Repositarian maintained, to deny women the vote was but 'one form of a far deeper and more extensive anomaly'.[8]

The arguments of the early feminists usually centred on two points. Firstly they pointed to the inconsistency that the head of the realm might be female, and yet women were not permitted even to choose members of parliament. Secondly, they railed against the injustice that propertied women were forced to pay taxes, but had no political representation.[9] These arguments were accompanied by attempts to urge people to reconsider their conventional notions of womanly abilities and interests. As Brian Harrison has shown, nineteenth-century opinion usually considered that women's political opinions were unstable and irrational. The feminists, by contrast, talked of the 'erroneous notion', 'That political knowledge and political interests are unsuited to the female mind'.[10]

The debates on female suffrage which raged within utilitarian circles served as a vehicle for the radical unitarians' feminist perspective. Bentham's ambivalent and often contradictory remarks on the subject of female enfranchisement had left a complex ideological legacy for his followers to untangle. Consequently, utilitarians entertained a wide spectrum of views on the subject. James Mill, for example, caused an uproar among feminist circles when, in his *Essay on Government*, he argued that women were already adequately represented through the vote of their male relatives. The translator of Bentham's works, Dumont, had expressed similarly reactionary views on the matter. It was these contentious statements which inspired William Thompson to write his *Appeal to One Half of the Human Race*, in which he attempted to establish that Bentham held feminist views on the question of female suffrage.[11]

However, during the course of the 1830s, many feminists came to question Bentham's feminist credentials. This debate centred upon his contention that while in theory women should be given the vote, in practice it might not be countenanced as 'no minds could be at present prepared for it'.[12] The utilitarian organ, the *London Review*, fully accepted Bentham's judgement on this issue and refused to be drawn into a discussion on the question of female suffrage. It claimed that it was not a subject which, '[in] the present state of the public mind, could be made a topic of popular discussion with any prospect of practical advantage'. The *Monthly Repository* reacted with outrage to this statement. One correspondent wrote haughtily of his/her surprise at hearing such views emanating from the *London Review* and declared, 'the condition of women, of which the exclusion from all political rights is a prominent feature, is a topic to which the public mind, may not only be usefully directed, but towards which it is turning itself'.[13]

The *Monthly Repository* was also able to direct its attack through its extensive treatment of Bailey's *Rationale of Political Representation*. Bailey, a staunch Benthamite, was keen to push the logic of the utilitarian position on women to extremes to which Bentham and many of his followers had not been prepared to go. As Bailey himself noted, 'Even Mr. Bentham, bold as he was in the free expression of his opinions, scarcely ventured to do more than hint his views on the subject of female electors.' Bailey believed that women should be granted the vote immediately. This opinion sprang from his wide-reaching feminist perspective: 'it may be doubted whether the relation of the sexes to each other will ever be placed on a proper footing, until they have both their share of control over the enactments of the legislature', Bailey argued. Discounting Mill's arguments completely, Bailey professed that, 'The interests of the female sex are so far from being identified with those of the male sex, that the latter half of the human species have almost universally used their power to oppress the former.'[14] The *Monthly Repository* was delighted by such sentiments, and quoted at length from the work.

Therefore, within the select pages of the *Monthly Repository*, feminists were able to address the issue of female suffrage directly. However, when seeking a more general readership, most were aware of the need to use more subtle methods. This is illustrated clearly in the works of Mary Leman Grimstone. While Grimstone pleaded unequivocally for female legislative power in the *Monthly Repository*,[15] when appealing to a less radical audience she was careful to temper her rhetoric. One method she employed was to attempt to accustom her readers to the language of women's political rights. In an article upon Harriet Martineau in the performing arts journal, the *Tatler*, she exclaimed, 'Society and her sex owe much to Miss Martineau, and in the ballot of universal applause, I cannot deny myself the proud pleasure of giving my vote, though it can add little to the suffrage in her favour.' She went on to employ the same device in her novels. In *Cleone* for example, one of the book's central female characters is introduced to the reader with the following description, 'She was twenty, and would have made a better representative of the borough for which her brother was about to become candidate than he was likely to do at forty.' Douglas Jerrold was also anxious to habituate his readers to such language. In an article concerning the forthcoming elections at the feminists' Whittington Club, he urged his readership, 'Do not forget, young Whittingtonians, to give plenty of votes to the ladies.'[16]

During the 1840s, radical unitarians continued to support the claim of female suffrage. Dickens's best friend, John Forster, for example, indicated his belief in the justice of giving women the vote in 1846[17] (a fact completely overlooked by scholars of Forster). Whilst this view was stated in a private letter to W. J. Fox, when reaching out to a wide readership, fellow journalists were concerned, as Grimstone had been, to use more delicate tactics. The short story, a method which was to be employed so successfully to air the subject of the marriage laws, was not used to the same degree in the suffrage issue. This is perhaps not surprising – tales of abused women and marriage breakdown make for better stories than do anecdotes of the disenfranchised. Nevertheless, some writers did attempt to present the topic in this form. Thus Edward Youl in his story 'The Breadfinder' told of a young man who had recently lost his teaching job because of his radical political views. His wife berates him with the words, 'it was only because you talked so stupidly about every man's having a vote as if every man wanted a vote, as if I wanted one; and if I'm only a woman, havn't I as much right as a man?'[18]

Editors of such widely-read journals as *Tait's Edinburgh Magazine* and *Douglas Jerrold's Weekly Newspaper* also raised the question of female suffrage by urging their audience to read contemporary works on the subject. For example, Marion Reid's lucid disquisition on the need for female enfranchisement, *A Plea for Woman*, was recommended by both publications as a book their female audience should buy and read. The review gave Jerrold's paper (less cautious in its treatment of the subject than *Tait's Edinbugh Magazine*) the opportunity to declare itself in favour of giving votes to those women who paid taxes.[19]

Therefore, within the radical unitarian coterie, those writers who were most popular among a general reading public, such as the Howitts and Jerrold, did raise the issue of female suffrage, but they tended to do so either indirectly, through book notices, or by suggestion. However, they had many colleagues who, being on the more radical side of the radical unitarian set, were less in the public eye. During the late 1830s and mid-1840s these feminists made the issue of female suffrage central to their agenda. The context in which they did so was the Chartist movement.

THE UNPARDONABLE FAULT: CHARTISM, THE FEMINISTS' CHALLENGE

The radical unitarian intelligentsia all endorsed the aims of the Chartists. Figures such as P. A. Taylor, John Epps, W. J. Fox, Samuel Courtauld and W. H. Ashurst belonged to the Radical Club in London, which supported the Charter; whilst others, for example, John Bowring, were active in the Metropolitan Parliamentary Reform Association.[20] However, two components of the radical unitarian set became directly involved with the movement: the young lawyers just beginning to engage in the feminist movement, such as W. Shaen, J. H. Parry, W. H. Ashurst, S. Hawkes, W. Case and J. Stansfeld; and those radical unitarians who were closest to the left-wing and Owenite movements – for example, the Hills, the Barmbys and W. J. Linton.

The radical unitarian relationship with the Chartist movement was, nevertheless, a complex and often uneasy one. They had little in common with the ideas and beliefs of many Chartist leaders. The anti-machinery stance of many Northern activists was as little to their taste as was O'Connor's anti-internationalism. Moreover, many Chartists were extremely hostile to any middle-class involvement in the movement.[21] However, in William Lovett, the radical unitarians found an appealing advocate for many of their own ideas. Indeed, Lovett emerged from his Chartist activity with strong personal ties with the radical unitarian community. He came to publish the *Howitt's Journal*; and, in addition to the Howitts, numbered such key figures as John Humphreys Parry, James Stansfeld and Eliza Meteyard as close friends.[22]

The appeal of Lovett's brand of Chartism to the radical unitarian intelligentsia is easily explained if one considers the 'bible' of 'knowledge' Chartism – Lovett and Collins' publication, *Chartism, a New Social Organisation of the People* (1840). The bulk of this work is concerned with the establishment of a comprehensive education service which considers the needs of all – from young children to adults. The work relied upon the educational theorists so beloved in progressive circles, such as Pestalozzi and Wilderspin. With its emphasis upon practical knowledge, moral education, the development of imagination, and the appeal to reason (rather than corporal punishment), the work accorded perfectly with the educational philosophies of the radical unitarians.[23] Education was the great shibboleth of the radical unitarians (as it was to their mainstream Unitarian counterparts); it thus accorded with their own ideas concerning the best way to achieve democracy. William Shaen, for one, was greatly excited by Lovett's publication. He wrote enthusiastically to his sister of the merits of the work and told her of his plans to implement it at the Unitarian Sunday School, at which he was Superintendent Elect.[24]

In addition to this focus upon education, there were many other elements of Lovett's Chartism which appealed to the radical unitarians. His internationalist approach and his desire to effect an alliance between the middle and working classes both enhanced his support among them.[25] For these ideas dovetailed neatly into their own political tradition in which fraternity (across both classes and nations) was perceived as a powerful and liberating social force. Grimstone's 'Social Melodies' on the theme of fraternity were used as anthems within the radical unitarian milieu and W. J. Fox had already proved his credentials as a mediator between the classes in his work for the National Political Union. This was a tradition continued by J. H. Parry, who was committed to Joseph Sturge's efforts to establish cross-class alliances in the struggle for the vote. Parry was chosen to represent local Chartists at the formation of the Complete Suffrage Union in 1842.[26]

Lovett's comprehensive definition of democracy as '*the power of the people mentally, morally, and politically directed, in promoting the happiness of the whole human family*'[27] was also particularly welcome to the radical unitarians. It allied with their own perception that political reform should be but one aspect of emancipation within a wider cultural programme of elevation. Hence Shaen wrote, perhaps somewhat condescendingly, that the Chartists were 'rapidly learning that calm discussion and orderly behaviour must be their friends and missionaries, and that their strength must arise from their self-improvement, temperance and education'. As F. B. Smith has remarked of W. J. Linton, he 'saw his duty in teaching fellow Chartists to lift their vision beyond the six points'.[28] For the radical unitarians, this broader approach to democracy also embraced their religious faith. This is most clearly borne out in the words of William Shaen, who revealed in letters to his sister (herself a Chartist), that his concept of democracy branched into 'religion, social progress and education'. He went on to pronounce what he declared to be the 'grand truth', that 'Chartism and Christianity are brothers, the soul of each being the common brotherhood of the human race'.[29]

Lovett's relationship with the radical unitarians was forged when he established the National Association for Promoting the Political and Social Improvement of the People in 1841. The society's wide rubric certainly had much to entice the radical unitarians. Its aims being to 'unite in one general body, persons of all creeds, classes and opinions, who are desirous of promoting the political and social improvements of the people', it was to 'prepare our oppressed countrymen for the proper exercise of that franchise' through establishing educational centres throughout the country. Indeed, Goodwyn Barmby was particularly impressed by its 'attention to social reforms'.[30] Furthermore, the association admitted women on the same terms as men, and they were entitled to vote in all the society's elections.[31]

Lovett relied substantially upon his contacts with the radical unitarian community in the formation of the society, and figures such as Linton, Parry, Stansfeld, Hawkes, Shaen, James Watson (an intimate friend of Linton's), W. H. Prideaux (a founding Whittingtonian and close associate of the Howitts'), Dobson Collet and Ashurst all played an active role. Its publication, the *National Association Gazette* (1842), which bore as its subtitle, 'The Rights of Men and the Rights of Women', was edited by Parry.[32] (It is possible that he may have been assisted by W. H. Ashurst Jnr, Stansfeld, Hawkes and Shaen. Eliza Ashurst refers to a publication with which these men were actively involved, the dates of which coincide with the short-lived *National Association Gazette*.)[33] In addition, Lovett was also able to rely upon both Parry and W. J. Fox to deliver long series of lectures in the society's National Hall. The strong ties between the radical unitarians and Lovett were made evident at a public meeting, held at the National Hall in 1848, to pay tribute to Lovett. Parry acted as Chairman for the occasion, whilst the tribute itself was written by W. J. Fox.[34]

The National Association and its feminist connections have received but scanty attention from Chartist historians. The two experts in the field of London Chartism, Prothero and Goodway, are extremely dismissive of the society (which admittedly failed to flourish), claiming that it played no significant role in the Chartist movement at large. While most historians of the Chartist movement note that Lovett's 'new move' Chartism was sympathetic to feminism, this has not been subject to any greater scrutiny.[35] Schwarzkopf's book, *Women in the Chartist Movement*, does devote one paragraph to the National Association, but only briefly alludes to its feminist leanings. Although historians have paid considerable attention to the role women played within Chartism, this work has tended to concentrate upon recovering the lives and experiences of neglected women.[36] Crucial though this is, such a focus has been at the expense of neglecting feminist traditions among male radicals.

Most historians do allude briefly to such a tradition, but it has not been subject to any detailed analysis. Malmgreen, for example, observes simply, 'Their failure to speak out for women's political rights caused the Chartists to be chided by W. J. Fox, Harriet Taylor and other middle class liberals.' Dorothy Thompson is even less specific, claiming that, 'Support for the idea of women's votes was always widespread among the Chartists' and going on to note that some 'young radicals of the dissenting middle class' were drawn to the feminist elements in the Chartist movement.[37] David Jones has considered the issue at more length. Despite a lack of familiarity with the feminist press at this time, Jones does allude, if tentatively, to the efforts of middle-class radicals to input feminism into Chartism. This initiative, as Jones indicates, evoked a furious protest from other wings of the movement. The influential *Northern Star* was foremost in the counterattack, claiming that female suffrage would 'LEAD TO FAMILY DISSENSIONS, while it would not advance or serve the cause of democracy one single bit'. The paper's editor, O'Connor, fumed, 'When it was discovered we could not be broken up, Dr. Bowring and his party sought to outbid us for popularity, by declaring for what they called Woman Franchise.' Certainly John Bowring (a leading Unitarian figure who became closely involved with Fox's circle) had done his utmost to raise the issue in both the Chartist movement and in Joseph Sturge's Complete Suffrage Union. Jones also points to the efforts of such people as John Humphreys Parry and W. J. Fox to secure woman's suffrage, O'Connor referring to them scornfully as 'Pussy foot Chartists'.[38]

However, the attempts to place female suffrage on the Chartist agenda have been considered only through the eyes of Chartist historians. The result has been to diminish the importance of this feminist tradition because of the comparatively minor role which its protagonists played within the Chartist movement. Little attempt has been made to study such radicals on their own terms. Malmgreen's work is an exception here, but she does not draw out the connections between those feminists whom she notes contributed to the Chartist movement.[39] Thus, her study continues the conventional pattern of seeing feminist protests as isolated phenomena, rather than understanding them as part of an organised network. Hence it is completely overlooked, for example, that many of the radicals attached to the National Association were key figures in the developing women's rights movement. If one considers the work of the National Association and the radical unitarians connected to it from the point of view of the feminist movement, rather than from the perspective of the history of Chartism, a very different pattern emerges of its work and significance.

Indeed, contrary to the claims of many historians,[40] from the late 1830s, the Chartist movement was actually used as a vehicle to attract attention to the feminist cause. During the course of this initiative, which so enraged O'Connor and his associates, the feminists utilised a variety of contacts in the sphere of journalism to ensure publicity. Hence, articles criticising the Chartists on the issue of women's rights appeared not only in the feminists' own journals, but also in newspapers and journals run by close associates, such as the *Morning Chronicle*, the *Reasoner* and the *Westminster Review*. Harriet Taylor, for example, wrote an article on 'The Enfranchisement of Women' for the latter. This lent her the opportunity to publicly vent her fury upon the 'grossly selfish' Chartist petition, as she had privately dubbed it. 'The Chartist who denies the suffrage to women, is a Chartist only because he is not a lord: he is one of those levellers who would level only down to themselves', she decried.[41] The issue also reared its head in the provinces. The Hills, for example, publicised the debate in their newspaper in Wisbech. As they declared angrily in one of their numbers, 'amidst all the clamour which is now raging for the "rights of man" – the Charter – repeal of the Corn Laws . . . woman is entirely omitted – her power is scoffed at and her worth underestimated'.[42] In Cheltenham, Goodwyn Barmby was able to make use of the journals of close associates and in Leicester, William Biggs wrote an open letter to the Chartists, protesting at female exclusion from the Charter.[43]

W. J. Linton proved to be one of the most assiduous campaigners. As he explained to Thornton Hunt in 1849, his 'definition of equality' was 'Universal suffrage – complete equality for both sexes'. Linton, in common with his colleagues, used a variety of methods to attack the Chartists. Sometimes he targeted a specific publication, or group. For example, in his work for Holyoake's *Reasoner*, he used the Finsbury Tract Society's publication of *What is a Chartist?* to press his point. He expressed his disgust that, 'it has the fault, unpardonable in Finsbury Radicals, of passing by the Enfranchisement of Women as though the right were not'.[44] Edward Bulwer Lytton also favoured such a direct approach and made a personal attack upon the prominent Chartist, Henry Vincent, for his failure to include women within the term 'universal suffrage'.[45]

However, perhaps the most common strategy was the polemical disquisition. Thus, in Linton's translation of Lammenais's *On Slavery* (an author of great interest to Chartists and Unitarians alike[46]), he included a lengthy appendix explaining why women should be included in the suffrage. This was eagerly received by Linton's feminist colleagues, and the appendix was later reprinted in the *National Association Gazette*.[47] Linton's discourse appeared again in the *Republican* under the title, 'Universal Suffrage: The Principle of the People's Charter'. The essay began with the sardonic comment, 'But your Universal Suffrage includes women, too? There can be no doubt of it. Has not woman the same right as man?' The argument then proceeds, 'There is no golden mean, no mid-resting place for a principle. Either God or hell, either the truth or a lie.' All the prevalent arguments customarily advanced to deny female suffrage are carefully and lucidly destroyed; including such points as the assertion that women are not fit for exercising political rights; that women have no use for such rights, and do not desire them.[48]

The *National* also devoted much coverage to the topic. For example, in an article entitled 'Political Suggestions', a long list of 'remedial measures' to ease the condition of the working people was set forth. The second of these was 'the legal establishment of the *principles* of the PEOPLE'S CHARTER'. It was explained that the word 'principles' had been italicised for the following reason, 'We say principles – thinking some of the provisions of the Charter open to improvement. The suffrage should be extended to every adult (whether male or female) of the community. Now the unmarried woman has no political existence . . . surely she has a right to be heard. And though the interest of the married woman may be that of her husband – what then? Shall the voice of the couple have no more weight than that of the single person?'[49]

Joseph Barker, who was closely involved with Unitarian circles for a short period (the Howitts were particularly impressed by him) also proved willing to promote the cause.[50] Barker was not always as progressive on the woman question as some of his associates in the feminist milieu might have liked.[51] Nevertheless, after the radical unitarian minister James Haughton criticised Barker for failing to consider women's rights, he included the issue in his paper, the *People*. This was quite a coup for the feminists, as the *People* was a popular paper with a circulation of over twenty thousand.[52] Haughton's declaration that he 'should like to see the right of suffrage given to every man and woman arrived at the age of twenty one years, and who could read, write and cipher', was followed by supportive statements from Barker. In one of his numbers, for example, he declared that 'political rights and franchises should not be held as the exclusive possession of one sex'.[53]

In 1841 Catherine and Goodwyn Barmby printed a specific tract to publicise the issue, their 'Declaration of Electoral Reform', which they encouraged their associates to sign. This demanded that the People's Charter be amended to include female suffrage, 'in the names of Mary Wollstonecraft and Charlotte Corday'. This formed a supplement to Barmby's calls in the *Promethean* for the Chartists to redact the Charter, with female suffrage added. He complained that in its existing state the

People's Charter was 'nothing but General Masculine Suffrage'. He went on to proclaim, 'Every argument that the Chartist brings against Whig and Tory for not admitting the working-man to the right of voting, can we bring against the Chartist for not advocating the right of the woman to the franchise.'[54]

The abolitionist Quaker Anne Knight (who, it has been suggested, was herself influenced by the feminism of the Fox circle)[55] mounted a similar campaign, issuing a pamphlet on women's suffrage in 1847.[56] Knight based her arguments, as had Grimstone and Jerrold before her, on women's right to vote as taxpayers. She was frustrated that while, in private, prominent men had agreed with her demands, they would not urge the matter in public. As she wrote in frustration to fellow feminist, Matilda Ashurst Biggs, 'I wish that talented philanthropists in England would come forward in this critical juncture of our nation's affairs and insist on the right of suffrage for all men and women unstained with crime.' She, like the Barmbys, urged for genuine 'Universal Adult Suffrage' and, in a piece for the *People*, claimed that every human being, irrespective of sex, had an 'indubitable right' to the vote.[57]

Another method which the radical unitarians used to exert pressure upon the Chartist movement was through direct confrontation at Chartist conferences and meetings. At a Chartist conference in Birmingham in 1843, for example, John Humphreys Parry rose to bring the matter to the assembly's attention. Parry was certainly well-qualified to undertake such a problematic mission, for he was famed for his oratorical skills.[58] He declared, 'they had recognised in this document, the rights of man, but they had said nothing about the rights of woman'. This was greeted with laughter by the assembly. Parry continued undaunted, explaining that 'he had come to the conference, impressed with this conviction, that every adult woman, as well as every adult man, ought to possess the franchise'. He wished it to be officially recorded that he believed, 'it was as injust to deprive woman of her rights, as it was to deprive man of his rights'. Bowring attempted a similar tactic at a meeting of the Complete Suffrage Union later that year. There he expressed his dissatisfaction that they were not going far enough in their demands, for he, Bowring claimed, would, 'unhesitatingly enfranchise women'.[59]

In 1846, it is clear that Parry was still persisting in placing the woman's issue at the top of the agenda at radical conferences. At the anniversary of the National Association, Parry hotly contested Beggs's views on the political rights of women. Indeed, W. J. Fox was forced to try and smooth the ruffled waters between them.[60] This altercation may well have been symptomatic of deeper tensions within the association. The correspondents to the *National Association Gazette* demonstrated the extent to which conservative views regarding women prevailed within the association.[61]

Another tactic often employed by the group was the lecture. At the radical unitarians' centre, South Place Chapel, they commissioned Frances Wright to deliver a series of lectures to the congregation. During her orations she expressed the view that women's slave status was due to their exclusion from government.[62] John Stuart Mill informed Harriet Taylor that Fox, in his lectures to the working classes, was urging them to place female suffrage on their political agenda. Certainly, in his address to the Working Man's Association, Fox tackled the issues head-on. Wallas notes that Fox praised the 'respectful way in which women were mentioned in the introductory address which was published in the People's Charter'. However, Fox was keen to refute one argument, often put forward by Chartists hostile to female suffrage, asserting, 'in many cases the interests of men and women are not the same'.[63] Goodwyn Barmby also aired the topic in public speeches. At an address to the Workingmen's Hall in Marylebone, he argued for 'universal adult suffrage, or the franchise for man and woman, in contradistinction to the general male suffrage of the People's Charter'. According to the *Promethean*, the lecture was enthusiastically received by a large audience.[64]

'SEE WHAT SLAVERY WILL DO FOR THE SLAVE' – THE CASE AGAINST FEMALE ACTION

The efforts of radical unitarians to reform the Chartist movement on feminist lines was a campaign dominated by men. To a certain extent, such a policy was dictated by the conservatism of the Chartists. None of the major Chartist conferences sanctioned female speakers. At Chartist meetings, women were separated from the men and were often confined to galleries.[65] By the late 1840s, the more radical element within the feminist circle was beginning to encourage female political activity, as their policies within both the Whittington Club and Friends of Italy society demonstrate, in which women were permitted as equal members.[66] However, when it came to women fighting for their own freedom, feminists adopted a more circumspect approach. While radical unitarian women did occasionally join their partners on the platform at political events, they did not make a contribution in their own right (unless it was to assist with the entertainments).[67]

One reason for such diffidence may have been that popular writers such as Meteyard were wary of jeopardising their own public acceptance by breaching social convention in this way. Certainly, feminists made much capital out of the propriety and womanliness of women such as Mary Howitt.[68] They were eager to persuade the public that progressive views on women might coexist with such gentle, feminine figures. The lengthy extant correspondence between Meteyard and Howitt is packed with references to the difficulty they experienced in trying to advocate progressive ideas, without alienating the large conservative element in their audience.[69] Nevertheless, a more complex ideological reason must also be sought. For radical unitarian writers of both sexes actively supported the policy of male radicals fighting for female suffrage. It was a strategy which evoked heated controversy in radical circles and the ensuing debate provided a vehicle for the radical unitarians to promote their unique and idealistic scheme for female emancipation.

In the late 1840s, Holyoake launched an attack upon the feminist strategies adopted by the literary world. In common with the Chartists, Cooper and Harney[70] he did not believe that male activists should campaign for female suffrage, unless women themselves demonstrated that they too, wished to fight for these rights. 'They are taxed, and therefore they claim a right to vote', he exclaimed, 'But where are women's political unions – self-originated and self-sustained? If they want political rights, why do they not themselves ask for them?' He then urged, 'Let them take their own affairs into their own hands.' 'Let them have societies and public meetings of their own.'[71]

Holyoake's challenge brought to fruition a debate that had been rumbling within radical circles for many years. The Owenite Unitarian, John Finch had long urged, 'Women of England! arouse yourselves "they that would be free, have only to will it!"' and Catherine Barmby, among others, expressed similar views.[72] Nevertheless, many feminists did not agree. Certainly, as modern historians have noted, there were many factors which expressly hampered female organisation. The very nature of much female work made political union extremely difficult. Sally Alexander has considered this point in relation to the fragmented nature of slop work. Moreover, as Rendall has pointed out, the reality of working women's lives, with their double burden of employment and domestic responsibilities, meant that the chances of them having the time, resources or energy to embark upon any other activities were extremely slight.[73] However, what is striking is that contemporary feminists ignored such factors. They based their arguments on the concept of female slavery.

In the *People's Press* a lively debate arose directly from Holyoake's challenge. Some correspondents did accept his point, declaring, 'we call upon our sisters to vindicate their rights'. However, a more typical response was evoked from the paper's Parisian correspondent who argued, 'it is a cause too mighty to be entrusted to women in their present state of bondage'. She pleaded, 'Leave it not to poor women' and urged male radicals to include the cause of women in their political demands. Holyoake's arguments also met with an earnest response from Anne Knight. She wrote to the editor of the *People's Press*, expressing her approval that the paper was airing the issue of women's rights. However, she disagreed with the ploy of 'throwing blame on woman for not avenging the insults she receives'. She delineated the reasons for women's failure to unite: 'She has been so habitually down-trodden, and has been so habitually treated thus, that she is not conscious that it is insult [*sic*] and if her mind should chance to consider it, she regards it with the quiet resignation of the overloaded camel.' Knight went on to argue, 'it is not by any associated efforts of hers redress should be expected: because she has been so long nurtured in bondage, and her mother and grandmother before her pariahs and helotes, that the fetters have cramped her mind'. Knight thus argued that it was the duty of men to claim political suffrage for women.[74]

This argument was one with which most radical unitarians sympathised. Harriet Taylor represented the views of many in her bitter reaction to the Charter. Her belief that the emancipation of women might only be effected through a cultural transformation in which progressive theories and concepts would be infused into society was typical of most radical unitarians. As she avowed to a contemporary MP, 'ideas are just that needful stock in trade in which our legislators are as lamentably deficient as our Chartists, who with their one idea of universal suffrage are too purblind to perceive . . . or to proclaim that half the race are excluded'. Taylor maintained that the argument, 'who would be free themselves must strike the blow' was 'even less appropriate to the case of women than it would have been to that of the negroes'. She suggested that women's slave status was a unique one, for 'Domestic slaves cannot organise themselves – each one owns a master, and this mastery which is usually passive would assert itself if they attempted it.'[75]

These interchanges demonstrate the degree to which feminists had appropriated the symbolism of slavery. For, within feminist letters, the analogy of the slave was pressed so closely that feminists argued that the female character had been warped just as that of the slave. As Anna Wheeler remarked in a lecture at Finsbury chapel, 'The vices of women [are] always those of the slave'.[76] This insight into the effects of 'slavery' upon the female character had vital implications for the feminist strategies favoured by radical unitarians. For the feminist use of the imagery departed sharply from its use in working-class radical circles: slavery was not perceived purely as a means of economic or political subjection which could be addressed by the oppressed class, women, rising up to claim their rights. Women would only be freed by a profound and far-reaching cultural evolution in which legislative and social change might provide the environment for individual awareness and regeneration.

While some, as we have seen, manifested a faith in the ability of women to liberate themselves, such confidence was invariably overshadowed by the feminist concept of woman's slave character. This led most to conclude that it was completely unrealistic to ask women to associate together and demand their rights. A vital element of their analysis of the female slave character was that women bitterly resented any attempts to change their position. As Bulwer Lytton wrote, 'they are reduced so far as to prefer remaining creatures of frivolity'. Grimstone fully concurred, adding, 'and to see what slavery will do for the slave – to *this* system women have not only submitted, *this* system they have assisted to uphold'. Catherine Barmby also had to acknowledge that this proved a barrier to female political action, writing, 'according to the practice of *all slaves*, [they] denounce those amongst themselves who raise their heads, and demand for the sex a social position'.[77]

The fullest exposition on this theme issued from the pen of W. J. Linton. In 1848, the *Republican* reprinted the arguments Linton had developed in his special appendix to the translation of Lammenais's *On Slavery*, discussing the reasons why women should be granted, and yet often did not wish for political freedom. His perspicuous essay answered all the criticisms of Holyoake and his colleagues. He exclaimed that if women did not desire this emancipation, then 'so much the wretchedness of their condition', it was man's duty to teach her to want freedom. Men too, he pointed out, used to be content in their slavery. He concluded, 'It is because the woman-slave has not yet learned to think; because she is too fallen to feel her wrongs; because she wants self-respect.' These were arguments later developed by J. S. Mill who postulated that enslaved classes never asked for liberation.[78]

There was another aspect of contemporary female characters which the radical unitarians believed expressly militated against the possibility of concerted feminist action: they asserted that the debilitating effects of their education and treatment caused great antagonism and hostility among women. For example, Paul Bell noted the severity with which women treated other women who had broken the codes of convention; and Catherine Barmby was concerned that, 'in the spirit and forbearance and mercy towards her own sex, the great bond which should unite women together in a mutual determination to support and defend each other, she is entirely deficient'.[79] Grimstone explained this in terms of man's divide-and-rule policy towards women. Women were taught to seek admiration from men, she argued. This encouraged a fearful vanity, encouraging distrust and jealousy among women. Similarly, Ida lamented the 'frivolous chit-chat and bitter scandal' which so often demarcated female company. It was caused, she thought, by the lack of 'active duties' open to women.[80]

Consequently, it was often suggested that the onus fell upon men to recognise the extent to which women had been degraded, and thus to initiate their emancipation for them. Douglas Jerrold found it 'fearful to see how much depends on the voluntary zeal of those who will step aside to right wrongs that do not touch themselves'. As John Cowrie announced in his address to the Edinburgh Mechanics' Institute, '*It is* in the power of man to arise and exalt her . . . if she is degraded man is her tyrant.'[81] Thus, most radical unitarian feminists maintained that a vital precondition to such action was to raise men's consciousness of women's oppression. As Grimstone explained, 'the sources of female enslavement must be laid bare, that men may see and hate them'. This was a view reiterated in the work of Geraldine Jewsbury, who proclaimed in one of her short stories for *Douglas Jerrold's Shilling Magazine*, 'men it is who must begin to have higher and nobler aspirations for women, before women can break through'.[82]

The use of such arguments might be construed as an indication of the immaturity of radical unitarian feminism. It could be argued that it demonstrates the extent to which they remained coloured by conventional anxieties concerning the proper status of women and womanly action. Certainly in terms of twentieth-century pressure-group politics, the reluctance of female radical unitarians to engage in more direct political action appears circumspect and conservative. There is, of course, no shame in this – they were the *early* feminists. Moreover, as we have seen, they were fearful of antagonising a potential audience by adopting too avant-garde a stance. But we also need to respect the radical unitarians' own justifications for their position. Indeed, to penetrate a little deeper into their own discourse reveals that the radical unitarians constructed a visionary and wholly radical ideology which encompassed these tentative facets.

Within this progressive schema, it was advocated that the most fruitful means by which to attain female emancipation was for both sexes to pursue a broad, cultural initiative. Within this ideology, unilateral female political action was eschewed as inappropriate and deleterious. Even the political activity of male feminists was accompanied by some degree of ambiguity. Indeed, despite their vociferous efforts to inject feminism into the Chartist movement, activists such as Fox did at times admit that they did not expect female suffrage to be achieved for many years.[83] Thus, their Chartist campaign was not embarked upon as a true attempt to gain the vote for women. Rather, they were using the Chartist movement as part of a wider strategy to challenge the sexist mechanisms of contemporary culture.

The radical unitarian position needs to be understood within the framework of their wider, utopian aspirations. The feminists hoped that when men and women were granted the suffrage, a new age would dawn in which educated and freed woman would combine with man to inaugurate an epoch of peace, harmony and love. Only then, as Ashurst maintained in a letter to his anti-slavery contact, Sidney Gay, would 'The benevolence taught by Jesus' be 'brought into the legislature and social action'.[84] However, were women granted the vote before their egregious contemporary characters had been reformed, these grand millenial dreams would be jeopardised. These ideas encouraged the radical unitarians to argue that it was vital that the appropriate means of achieving female enfranchisement were practised. They hoped that women's liberation would be achieved through the triumph of reason and love; in such circumstances the new age might commence, unshackled by memories of a bitter struggle between the sexes. Were women, in their existing condition, to organise themselves into unilateral activity and wage war against male institutions, such hopes would be crushed.

Although Grimstone's frustration at woman's position did at times erupt into more hawkish rhetoric, these ideas remained central to many of her works. In *Character, Jew or Gentile*, the two central female characters, Agnes and Mrs Melburn, discuss whether women should rise up to assert their rights. The view of Agnes, the heroine, is that were women to pursue such a militant strategy they would themselves become tyrants. Grimstone was also fearful that too bellicose a movement on women's part would create a conservative backlash against them – 'No change has been made that has not been gradual', she proclaimed; 'Sudden revulsions throw forth that which they reject; with such force as to create a rebound.'[85] These were themes which also preoccupied radical reception to Tennyson's *The Princess*. This poem, which Tennyson wrote following consultation with the Howitts on the women's rights debate, assumed a high standing among feminist circles, as the many articles on it in the feminist press testify. The young Bessie Parkes was clearly alert to the issues it raised, writing of Ida, the poem's heroine, 'I heartily love her for her enthusiasm for her sex but she went to the other extreme and *put the men below* instead of *equal . . .* as she nobly confessed at the end there was mixed up with her truth and earnestness a *little* "Love of power, not rights".'[86]

Therefore, the radical unitarians trusted that their trenchant attack against the Chartists' sexist assumptions would make a major contribution to their own efforts to challenge the way in which people perceived the body politic. Furthermore, their dialogue with the Chartist movement provided the radical unitarians with the opportunity to urge that the wider issues pertaining to women's oppression might be considered. They wished that the extent of women's existing degradation be understood, and that consideration might be given to the ultimate aims of female suffrage. Their insistence that granting women the vote was but one measure within a gradual transformation of society was vital. Female enfranchisement had to come hand in hand with a number of other cultural and social reforms. Only then would a new era in social harmony and justice be effected.

FEMALE SLAVERY AND FEMALE EMPLOYMENT

The radical unitarian debate with the Chartist movement made apparent the feminists' broad concept of democracy. It demonstrated that their notion of female liberation encompassed a visionary image of the future state in which male and female interests would be harmonised. These two issues – female emancipation and democracy – were vitally connected within radical unitarian ideology. Their potent critique of the existence of 'domestic slavery' within marital relationships alerted them to the fact that freedom for all might not be achieved until equality had been secured in the personal, as well as the social sphere. Only then, they maintained, might the truly democratic state flourish. The feminist perception of the relationship between female emancipation and democracy led them to posit radical alternatives to conventional views of male and female roles in society. While this critique was aimed as much at 'radicals' such as the Chartists, as it was at the more conservative, the Chartist movement provides a useful focus with which to understand the radicalism of the early feminists.

Both the radical unitarians and the Chartists were concerned about the oppression of contemporary women. However, they entertained vastly disparate concepts of oppression. This stemmed chiefly from their differing class experiences and their divergent analyses of what consituted slavery. The contemporary working class tended to perceive female slavery in terms of the drudgery and hardship of women's labour. A female speaker addressing her socialist audience at Charlotte Street was representative in lamenting, 'a great deal was said of the slavery of the working classes and inadequate wages of the men, but never a word of the slavery of poor women, who were obliged to toil from dawn to midnight for seven or eight shillings'.[87] Such a sentiment is wholly understandable given the problems confronting female labour during this period. As the mechanisation of industry increased, women employed in industries such as textiles found themselves increasingly limited to low-status jobs, with poor renumeration and little hope of promotion. These developments have been subject to close scrutiny in recent years, with detailed studies focusing on specific industries. Judy Lown, for example, has demonstrated how women in the silk industry were barred from the promotion ladder of their male peers, and confined to poorly paid, monotonous tasks. Angela John's research has revealed a similar pattern operating against female mine workers.[88]

Within working-class radicalism, the notion of female slavery was invariably related to conservative ideas of womanhood. It is perhaps not surprising, therefore, to discover that a common response to such suffering from Chartist circles was to argue that women should have the right to stay at home. The authority on Chartism and women, Jutta Schwarzkopf, maintains, 'all Chartists were opposed to female waged labour'. She notes that in Chartist novels, labour was presented as incompatible with the female nature. For Schwarzkopf, the motivating force behind much Chartist thought was the belief that the existing political and economic situation prevented women from performing their natural maternal duties. Her central thesis is that Chartists were campaigning for the re-establishment of traditional home life.[89] Feargus O'Connor stated that one of his principle aims was to 'insure happy homes and protection for all – the release of women from slave labour'.[90]

Even the more progressive Chartists proved extremely ambivalent on the dual issues of female slavery and female roles. For example, although William Lovett regretted that he had had to drop the call for female suffrage from the original Charter,[91] he too acquiesced in existing gender roles. Lovett was saddened that his own daughter chose to follow a career rather than stay at home – sentiments which were given full expression in his poem, 'Woman's Mission', written during the 1840s. In the poem Lovett decried the numbers of women working in factories and mines, claiming that woman, 'man's property, his pet, his slave', had been driven from her home, where her true mission lay.[92] Such conservatism was reflected in Lovett's plans for a national education system. He insisted, 'While the male teachers should pass through all the schools in rotation, the female teachers might be limited to the *infant* department of education.' Furthermore, Lovett's concern to improve women's education, with his emphasis on dressmaking skills,[93] often derived purely from a desire to equip women to be better wives and mothers. Indeed, he spoke publicly on 'the connection between public improvement and the influence of mothers'.[94]

This philosophy met with sympathy from many feminists (perhaps most notably from W. J. Fox), and did augur a new age of womanly influence and responsibility.[95] Nevertheless, contemporary feminists were constantly battling to extend the perimeters of such an argument, for, as George Dawson avowed, 'Women are not made for man at all, but are made for themselves.'[96]

Lovett was not the only Chartist, who, while championing women's right to vote, still eulogised the domestic hearth and the customary sexual politics within it. Even when participants in the Chartist movement indicated a sympathy for women's political rights, this rarely overrode the inherent conservatism which characterised the movement as a whole. The London Chartist John Watkins urged that single women and widows should be enfranchised, but not married women, as they would have a voice through their husband's vote.[97] This was a common view. Indeed, the most oft-quoted 'feminist' tract of the Chartist movement, R. J. Richardson's 'The Rights of Women', was similarly steeped in domestic conservatism. Richardson proudly recounted his advice to the female calico-printers of Dumbartonshire, 'your places are in your homes: your labours are your domestic duties: your interests in the welfare of your families, and not slaving thus for the accumulation of the wealth of others, whose slaves you seem willing to be'.[98] There were other radicals, outside the Chartist tradition and well-known to radical unitarian circles, who demonstrated a similar ambivalence. Edward Vansittart Neale (a fellow promoter of the cooperative cause) argued for female enfranchisement while continuing to advocate the importance of woman's domestic sphere. The radical paper, the *Leader*, also advanced such an opinion, suggesting that women might have the vote, but they should still devote themselves to the home, and permit men to exercise 'supreme direction in matters of state'.[99]

The desire to see women return to the home sphere was, of course, a concern which equally occupied mainstream public opinion. During the early 1830s, both the Poor Law Amendment Act and the 1833 Factory Act revealed the extent to which the concept that women should be non-wage-earning dependants was becoming enshrined within the legislature; the latter especially serving to galvanise public opinion on the issue. The Evangelical movement in particular, spearheaded by Lord Ashley, was enraged by the employment of women in mines and factories.[100] Thus, the *Manchester Guardian* (a mainstream Unitarian newspaper) spoke for many when it declared the employment of married women in factories to be 'an evil of great magnitude'.[101]

Therefore, the concern over women (and especially married women) working in mines and factories united a broad spectrum of public opinion, from the politically radical, to the extremely conservative. However, radical unitarian feminists responded very differently to this question. For the early feminists, as the previous chapter highlighted, woman's slavery derived not from their labour, but on the contrary, from a historically distorted culture. The debate on female employment enabled feminists to expand upon this thesis. They lived in a society, they argued, in which man's superior physical force had granted to him the domain of power, while woman had been restricted to a subservient function within the home. These roles, they suggested, had become instilled within society, being supported both by public opinion and the legislature. While they paid lip-service to the drudgery and 'slave labour' of working-class women,[102] they believed women's real oppression lay in the societal prohibition against women working, and their lack of opportunities. The point was well made in an essay which appeared in the *People's Journal* in 1847, 'The Rights and Wrongs of Women'. This recognised that whenever 'male and female labour are brought into competition, the woman has scarcely ever an equal chance of that grand desideratum – "a fair day's wage for a fair day's work"'. However, it claimed that this was a minor consideration when compared to the need for 'enlarging the field of exertion'.[103]

Some figures in the radical coterie, for example Samuel Smiles (a Unitarian reformer who was an important figure in the establishment of both the Howitts' and Eliza Cook's journals), W. J. Fox and Thomas Southwood Smith, did support legislation to prevent women from working in mines and factories. Nevertheless, even they did so, not out of a desire to see women return to their homes, but purely in the belief that such work was unhealthy and dangerous for women. Indeed, they urged with equal vehemence that alternative job opportunities should be found for women.[104] Others argued that any moves to restrict women's employment would prove detrimental, as it would further reinforce the ideology of the separate spheres. They drew upon the Enlightenment heritage inherent within Unitarian thought, arguing that woman was enslaved because she had been denied the use of her reason to make her own rational judgements. Thus, as George Dawson proclaimed in one of his popular lectures, woman's wrongs would only be rectified by allowing woman 'freedom to be let alone'. Catherine Barmby pursued the theme with passion, threatening that unless such freedom was granted and women were allowed to participate equally with men in the industrial sphere, 'the clanging sounds and heaving groans of an oppressed slave class will ring and hiss around us'.[105] Emilie Ashurst persisted in the use of such arguments through to the 1870s.[106]

In the radical unitarians' response to this debate, one further case was articulated. The customary view of factory work was that it led to gross immorality among the female workforce and the breakdown of family life (not least because of the supposedly slovenly domestic habits of the female workforce) – a view shared by most mainstream Unitarians.[107] Radical unitarians, on the other hand, praised the characters of factory women. Dickens's *Daily News* (in which journalists such as W. J. Fox, John Forster, R. H. Horne and Eliza Cook played a key role) talked of factory women's 'free and graceful step, blended with the sense of independence so often denied to the sex and an honest pride in the business of the day'. This was an image also supported by *Eliza Cook's Journal*.[108]

The feminist position derived from the experience of a very different aspect of women's employment trends. As the nineteenth century progressed and new cultural attitudes began to crystallise, the range of jobs performed by women became ever smaller. Contemporary feminist Mary Gillies protested that the role of middle-class women as money-makers was usually forgotten and certainly women continued to play a vital role in the economy through home-centred and part-time work (both of which often eluded the census).[109] However, this factor did not override the broader pattern, in which traditional areas of women's work, such as millinery, bookbinding, brewing and hairdressing were being eroded. As Barbara Taylor has illustrated in the case of contemporary female tailors, this was a development which might affect women from any class.[110] Nevertheless, this reduction in opportunities for women plagued those of the professional and manufacturing middle classes in particular. An indication of the transformation in social attitudes is to be found in the Courtauld silk mills. Whereas in the earlier years of the nineteenth century, the women of the Courtauld family were engaged in the supervision of female mill-workers, by the middle of the century it was no longer thought suitable that middle-class women should be working in the mills.[111] As seen in Chapter 1, the limited avenues permitted to women plagued the lives of many Unitarian women, and certainly, as seen in the previous chapter, most of the early feminists hailed from professional or privileged backgrounds.

Consequently, the early feminists recognised that a great proportion of women were failing to achieve proper living standards, or self-fulfilment because of the *dearth* of employment opportunities available to them. This was a subject which captured the hearts of most contemporary feminists. The *Star in the East* believed that 'every woman should have her business or profession as well as every man'. Similarly, J. S. Mill was to be found calling for 'the opening of industrial occupations freely to both sexes'.[112] Other feminists suggested a vast panoply of possible jobs which females might perform – from female overseers and police officers to medical practitioners. Grimstone called for the professionalisation of nursing, a view publicised by the *Monthly Repository*.[113] It was argued constantly that only by opening up the job market to women might their real liberation be secured. For, as the *Monthly Repository* pointed out, women would remain in their state of slavery and servility while the means of providing their own support was denied to them. *Tait's Edinburgh Magazine* elaborated further, 'A revolution of opinion which would make female labour as profitable and honourable as that of men; the exercise of female talents, ingenuity and mechanical skill, commercial enterprise, or professional ability, a source of emolument and credit, and a recognised part of the social systems, contains the only true principle of female emancipation.'[114]

Nevertheless, radical unitarians appreciated that it was not enough merely to open up greater fields of employment for women. What was equally required was a cultural revolution in which the social pressures which militated against female work might be lifted. They tackled this problem using a variety of tactics. One strategy was to project a more positive image of working women, as seen above. Another was to publicise any further areas in which women's employment had already proved success-ful – in the arts, for example, or by women in the more liberal France.[115] A third, albeit rarer path was to implement practical steps to promote female employment. Hence, female waiters were encouraged at the feminists' literary club in London.[116] However, radical unitarians also wished to strike at the heart of the contemporary culture by challenging the very ideology of domesticated womanhood. As Anna Jameson had illustrated, such assumptions prevented society from recognising the truth concerning women's lives and capabilities.[117] Indeed, the wider feminist objective was to encourage the public to think of women not purely in terms of their domestic capacity, but as independent, capable and active beings. As a correspondent for *Douglas Jerrold's Shilling Magazine* put it, 'To manage household affairs well are most becoming duties in woman, but is this management the 'be all' and 'end all' of her existence? Is her mind to rise no higher than is required for the fulfilment of such labours?' This was a view shared by a reader of the *National Association Gazette* who com-plained, 'There is a very erroneous and without doubt vulgar impression on many minds that women were created only for domestic purposes.'[118] Furthermore, the *People's Journal* and the *People's Press* drew attention to the fact that extolling women's role as mothers and homemakers offered nothing to the many women destined never to be wives or mothers.[119]

The short story and novel proved popular vehicles for exploring such ideas. In 'The Orphan Milliner', which appeared in the *Illuminated*

Magazine, despite the narrator's assurances that Henrietta could have made a good wife, the story closes with her managing her own business.[120] Such concerns were also central to much of Grimstone's work. In 'The Merchant Bridegroom', Grimstone depicts a devoted wife who, while happy to commit herself to the 'exclusive duties of her domestic life', can, when the circumstances require it, manage her husband's affairs and act with independence and great resourcefulness. In a more radical tale, 'The First and Second Marriage', the protagonists learn 'that the domestic *ménage* is not the sole field for female intellect'. In this instance the heroine only finds happiness in married life when both herself and her partner go out to work.[121]

This last story illustrates the extent to which the radical unitarian arguments concerning women's work formed an important component of their wider feminist philosophy. In particular, for most early feminists the issue of female work was related to their concern to improve the contemporary marriage system. Herein lay the crucial difference between radical unitarian feminism and the philosophies of contemporary socialist movements. Whereas Fourier had advocated avant-garde notions of sexual liberation,[122] and Owen, the abolition of existing marriages, the radical unitarians sought to consolidate and improve monogamous marriage. As the *Monthly Repository* repeatedly asserted, if women were able to earn their own living they would not need to marry purely for economic reasons.[123] Hence, marriage would become the union of two equal, self-supporting individuals – a concept that later feminists were to continue to advocate.[124] Such a perception of marriage was radically different to that posited by the Chartist movement, which was striving to reassert the masculine position as the breadwinner and head of the family.

However, the subject of female employment was also crucial to another aspect of radical unitarian debate – the question of female character. This was partly an offshoot of their views on marriage, for as one radical writer explained, 'servile they must be, while they are trained to look to marriage as furnishing them with the means of support in idleness'.[125] More typically, however, the question was related to the feminists' concern with the lack of opportunities for women's talents and energies. It was feared that when women were denied the exercise of their influence through positive outlets, they asserted themselves through negative means. Women thus frequently became devious and cunning in their efforts to achieve recognition and status. As the *Spirit of the Age* argued, 'woman . . . restored to her rights and dignity, will no longer have recourse to the cunning and duplicity by which she now frequently regains the influence of which she has been so unjustly deprived'.[126] Ida of the *People's Press* drew attention to the bad temper for which contemporary women were often censured. She asked if it was any wonder that woman, educated to be a 'servile slave' should sometimes, 'turn upon her master and vent her ill-humour, a worm will when trod on'. The solution, Ida maintained, was to 'allow her field for the exercise of her powers and when this is granted, she will lose much of that self-will and stubborness'.[127] This was a view shared by Sarah Flower Adams who, following Wollstonecraft, argued, 'their fine energies in being denied full scope, are misdirected. In consequence, they too often become domestic tyrants, or suffer from ill health, the consequence of unemployed power.'[128]

Although one of the prominent doctors in the feminist entourage, John Epps, discussed these points in his public lectures,[129] literary representation remained one of the most accessible means of pressing the point. Geraldine Jewsbury, who proved sympathetic to the feminist strategies of the radical unitarians, tackled this issue in an early work, 'How Agnes Worral was Taught to be Respectable', published by Douglas Jerrold. She comments of the heroine's aunt (a malicious gossiper), 'Still she was not a bad woman, she only had more energy than she knew what to do with, and had an absolute need of some sort of excitement.'[130] Frederika Bremer, the novelist so beloved by the radical unitarians, pursued similar themes in her novel, *The Home*. She describes how the stifled life Petrea is constrained to lead at home results in her committing indiscretions with her brother-in-law, Jacobi, and becoming something of a flirt. As Petrea explains to her mother and sister, 'you cannot believe how dangerous it is to be idle, when one has an active spirit within one'. It is a problem which also vexes the family friend, Evelina. She confides how, 'the unemployed and uninterested life which I led' resulted in 'a desire for gossip, an inclination to malice and scandal'. Consequently, 'an increasing irritability of temper, began to get possession of a mind which nature had endowed with too great a desire for action for it blamelessly to vegetate through a passive life'. She maintains it was not until she came to lead an active life though employment, that 'I became more throroughly in harmony with myself'.[131]

Grimstone also tackled this problem in many of her short stories – although in her hands the consequences were usually more dire! In one, she told the story of a rich young woman, Isabella. The narrowness of the sphere permitted to her (which comprised solely of 'vanity and wedlock'), led Grimstone to compare her to a 'young Arab barb put upon a millwheel, who would circle it again and again like wildfire, till he destroyed himself and the dull instrument of his torture'. As a means of enlivening the torpor of her life, Isabella begins to flirt with a house-guest, Hubert

Walton. She drives him to such a state of distraction that he eventually collapses from mental exhaustion! Isabella's mother is alert to the circumstances which have produced such suffering. As she tells her son, '"Waste power *will* employ itself – if not for the purposes of good, for those of evil."' In 'The Notable', Grimstone pursued her point to an even more extreme conclusion, describing how a woman was led to poisoning her husband as a consequence of the narrowness of her life.[132]

FEMALE ROLES AND FAMILY LIFE

The feminists' campaign to persuade the public of the need women had for occupations posed one obvious problem. If women left the home each day, who was to ensure the smooth running of family life? For many writers this issue proved something of a Gordian knot. Even in the *Monthly Repository*, where writers were able to proclaim unabashedly their desires for equal rights, they were constrained to be more circumspect when discussing gender roles.[133] Certainly the question of female domesticity was the occasion of considerable vacillation and ambivalence among some of the early feminists. For example, William Shaen's brother-in-law, Henry Solly, reacted with indignation to moves to restrict women's employment, yet he still clung to the ideals of female domesticity.[134]

In some cases, such as the work which appeared in *Eliza Cook's Journal*, such ambiguity is readily explained in terms of the growing radicalism of the publication. That is, in the early volumes of the journal, when Cook was struggling to gain a readership, she often published comparatively conservative pieces on the woman question. As she explained to one contributor, she had to 'give them a popular interest' as the journal was gradually acquiring a 'good character'. When she grew in confidence, and the journal's circulation settled down, Cook began to include increasingly radical articles.[135] Publications such as *Howitt's Journal* and *Douglas Jerrold's Shilling Magazine* often tempered the extreme progressivism of many of their articles with more conservative stories of conventional married life. They were evidently eager to cater for a broad audience, and thus published pieces which might suit a variety of tastes. Even their radical contributors produced less progressive material from time to time, although their motives might differ. Eliza Meteyard, for example, was frequently having pieces returned, the editors complaining they were too radical. Meteyard, desperate for income, apparently acquiesced in penning conventional stories of married life.[136] Grimstone, on the other hand, seems to have actually modified her own views. Whereas in the 1830s Grimstone had argued that were no inherent differences between women and men, as people were shaped entirely by environment; by the 1840s, when she was writing for a far wider audience, she seems to have been happy to write some comparatively conservative stories which extolled women's special moral qualities, in order to urge for greater respect to be shown to women.[137]

Nevertheless, individual writers showed themselves to be capable of sheer inconsistency. During 1847–8, Catherine Barmby oscillated from exhorting woman that the home was her only true sphere, to declaring that 'industrial independence is, at least, as necessary for woman as for man'.[138] While Barmby's apostasy is partly explicable in terms of the differing audiences for which she wrote, such an explanation cannot solve the great tergiversations which beset the work of Ida, also a contributor to the *People's Press*. At times Ida complained that women were trained merely to be 'domestic animals'. In other articles she recognised the need for women to have domestic training, but maintained that this did not mean that women should spend all their time in the kitchen. Why should they not train to be mechanics or book-keepers, she asked. Yet in the following volume she was proclaiming, 'the domestic circle is her proper sphere'.[139]

One can only conjecture as to why some feminists found it so difficult to shake off ideas concerning women's domestic role. Was it a bid to appease a potentially hostile audience by suggesting that their feminism would not threaten the harmony of family life? One thinks of William Howitt's assurances that despite his wife's literary endeavours, her domestic management was second to none.[140] Or, does it demonstrate the extent to which some of these writers were themselves conditioned into accepting notions of female domesticity? Harriet Martineau dissented from many of her feminist associates with her declaration that, 'No true woman, married or single *can* be happy without some sort of domestic life – without having somebody's happiness dependent on her'.[141] Another possibility is that they were reluctant to reject the one area in which contemporary women were respected and valued. Certainly, some writers believed that the sanctified role women might fulfil as wives and mothers was, given the existing state of female employment, preferable to a life of drudgery in appalling working conditions.[142]

Nevertheless, among the hard core of accomplished feminist writers, there was a concerted attempt to redefine discussions concerning women and domesticity. Some of their suggestions appear contradictory and, to modern sensibilities, conservative. They persisted in eulogising woman's maternal role and continued to support her massive contribution to the home sphere, even offering advice as to how women might improve their domestic performance. Nevertheless, their work shared a common and progressive perspective. This was a desire to challenge contemporary assumptions of natural gender roles and affinities. Whereas contemporary ideology decreed that the home was woman's natural sphere, radical unitarians such as Grimstone, as well as other contemporary feminists such as Jameson and Reid, consistently argued that given the limiting education and narrow cultural horizons permitted to women, it was impossible to know what was their natural sphere.[143]

To ensure that in winning for women the freedom to pursue an occupation, domestic obligations did not suffer, one possibility aired by the early feminists was the adoption of associated housing schemes. As Grimstone was to comment, women would greatly benefit from such ventures, for in the existing system of domestic organisation, 'men realise more of social happiness than women'.[144] The idea that women would profit from schemes of communal living, by being liberated from domestic drudgery, had been much mooted by the radical communal movements of the 1820s and 1830s.[145] Writing in the 1830s, W. B. Adams followed in this tradition when he expressed his hope that associated housing would liberate women from 'drudgery in cooking, scrubbing, cleaning, watercarrying'.[146] Radical unitarians of the 1840s continued to herald the 'decrease of domestic drudgery'[147] which associated housing would entail. However, they also came to posit more sophisticated arguments which cut incisively into the prevalent domestic ideology of separate spheres. Grimstone and Gillies regretted that the husband should enjoy a life 'outside', thus 'leaving her to the narrow scope of the kitchen and the closet, which move little, if any intellectual power at all'.[148] Associated housing, they promised, would set women free from such circumscribed and frustrating lives. Indeed, Gillies argued it would produce effects 'so great and beneficial that we cannot see where they would end'. Middle-class women, she maintained, were in any case accustomed to hard work. Therefore, they would have a 'clear field before them, if the evils of their circumstances could be removed. . . . When the time comes, may women see and take advantage of their golden opportunity', she proclaimed. Grimstone was equally excited by the potential which such schemes harboured for female occupation. In her essay, 'Homes for the People', she articulated these ideas in Lockean terms. 'We are born with faculties and powers capable of almost anything', she enunciated, 'but it is only the exercise of these powers which gives us ability or skill in anything, and leads us towards perfection.'[149]

Within the feminists' discourse on associated housing there very occasionally arose a secondary theme – that were such schemes promoted in tandem with the provision of infant education, women, freed from the demands of childcare might be granted even greater opportunities to pursue an occupation. Anna Wheeler had long identified the immense potential for female emancipation which a national system of '*equal education for the Infants of both sexes*' would herald. Catherine Barmby also dreamed of the 'associative household, with its common nursery'. William Blanchard Jerrold shared an interest in such plans, as his work for Charles Dickens testifies; and William Bridges Adams similarly urged for the implementation of both schemes in order to emancipate women from their domestic ties.[150]

Mary Leman Grimstone led the way in championing another, equally radical concept. She urged people to consider the possibility that women might earn the family wage, while their husbands assumed responsibility for the home sphere. Grimstone had long suggested that both sexes might be trained to independence so that 'men and women would marry, not because one wanted a home and another a housekeeper, but because each required a shrine and a sanctuary for the superabundant affections flowering in the heart'.[151] This would necessitate a realignment in existing gender roles. Women should learn to work for a living, men should cultivate domestic skills. Grimstone admitted that many women had been taken out of their home sphere to labour in the factories. However, she maintained that women coped far better than men with the rigours of factory employment. She acknowledged that female labour was preferred by factory employers, and that male unemployment was often the result. She further recognised that, as a consequence, most women performed a double burden of work as they were also expected to carry out all the domestic chores. However, rather than demand woman's 'right' to stay at home, as the Chartists did, Grimstone's answer was to query, 'Are there not other duties for man, as well as woman, besides that of the manual industry by which he earns his bread?' She suggests that men should be encouraged to assume the role of homemaker, claiming that 'I think man might there, in some degree, supply her place.' She explained that the present convention against men performing domestic work was merely a question of fashion and that such attitudes could be changed in time.[152]

Grimstone's proposal certainly challenges the existing historiography, which maintains that Victorian feminists adhered to conventional gender roles within the household. Shanley, for example, claims, 'they did not ask that women be relieved of some of their domestic responsibilities nor that men participate actively in the home'. This is a view shared by J. A. Banks who argues, 'There was no question . . . of the feminists working to make Victorian marriage so much of a partnership that the wife could become a breadwinner while the husband stayed at home to take care of the household chores, or indeed that both would so share in the care of home and children.'[153]

Nevertheless, the feminists' hopes for associated housing and the swapping of gender roles should be seen as the visionary, experimental aspect of their work. The feminists appreciated that women would probably continue to function as the chief homemakers in the family. Despite the early feminists' close contact with the secularist movement (which advocated birth control) they rarely promulgated such views themselves – such a stance would have completely jeopardised the image of respectability they were working so hard to foster. In any case, the idea of liberating women through universally available contraceptives is very much a modern concept and one which would have been quite alien to the radicals of the 1830s and 1840s. Although Patricia Branca has demonstrated that by 1850 three contraceptive methods were (in theory) available, she cannot prove that people had access to this information or that they were widely used.[154] Certainly, among those contemporaries who did advocate contraception (and when they did so, it was rarely on feminist grounds),[155] the advice usually given (the withdrawal method – or even the female coughing after ejaculation)[156] was unlikely to ensure very good protection against pregnancy. Contraception during this period could not change the basic biological fact that most sexually active women would conceive – at best it could perhaps space some births apart. Motherhood – frequent motherhood – was the destiny of most women.

Therefore, the early feminists, writing before the great debate on single women burst on to the scene, had to address a situation in which they believed most women faced the prospect of many years of constant childbearing and rearing. This was the practical reality of women' lives – and so feminist ideology had to embrace the maternal role. Their celebration of maternity gathered apace during the 1840s, when it could also be used as a viable means of tapping into more mainstream debates, which were also seeking to redefine the maternal role. *Howitt's Journal*, for example, publicised those views which presented the praise of motherhood as an advance from valuing women purely as the 'companion and soother of man'. In this capacity, it was argued, she is 'weak and gentle', while as a mother she is 'the source of all human power and dignity'.[157] Yet, the feminists could ensure that as they sought to extend their credibility in this way, they might also discountenance the limiting ideology which surrounded motherhood within contemporary discourse.

Whereas the Chartists had urged that women be returned to their 'rightful' place in their home, where they might perform their 'natural duties', many radical unitarians suggested that women did not have any predeter-mined instincts or abilities which naturally disposed them for such work. These skills, they insisted, had to be learned. Mary Gillies put the point bluntly when she reasoned that society should not take for granted the sexual division of labour and thus women needed to be trained as housemakers. Emily Shaen was of a similar opinion, claiming that it was 'absurd to go on talking of the house being the proper sphere of woman, while we neglect to teach her the very rudiments of a *Housefrau*'s du-ties'.[158] The perceived decline in the domestic abilities of young women was a subject of much contemporary concern.[159] The radical unitarians were able to tap into this debate to offer their own solutions.

The radical unitarians believed fervently in the importance of a happy home life. Indeed, the establishment of true harmony and happiness at the domestic level was considered by them to be essential for the promotion of a healthy and successful society. Therefore, alongside more traditional advice concerning domestic management and marital relationships which even those such as Meteyard and Grimstone published, a more radical suggestion was also made. For as Ruth Watts and Margaret Parnaby have noted, 'liberal Unitarians' also sought to elevate domestic chores and maternal duties to the status of a proper science – they were considered to be matters for serious study, for which women required thorough training. Watts notes that the inspiration to 'professionalise' housework may be traced back to ideas aired by Unitarians such as John Aikin in the eight-eenth century.[160]

While, in practice, such schemes must have perpetuated conventional notions of womanly responsibilities, the early feminists hoped that by challenging public attitudes towards housework and motherhood in this way, women would be respected as rational, intelligent beings. Therefore, they gave public support to schemes which trained women in domestic science and economy. For example, *Eliza Cook's Journal*, recognised, as Grimstone had done, that the prevalence of female employment meant that households were not always run properly. Its response was to argue not that women should return to the home, as so many of their contemporaries believed, but that special institutes might be established to educate women in domestic skills and domestic economy.[161] However, it was hoped that such instruction would form but an accompaniment to an academic edu-cation. This was to encourage the development of women's rational and cerebral skills for their own independence and worth. Hence, in R. H. Horne's serial, 'The Dreamer and the Worker', Mary, the heroine, studies chemistry and geology, as well as dressmaking during her engagement.[162]

A vital element of this debate was the attempt to realign existing

perceptions of parenthood. While they often eulogised the importance of
the maternal role, the feminists wished to persuade their public that they
should not take for granted the natural propensity of women to make good
mothers. Samuel Smiles, in a contemporary book on childrearing, captured
the sentiments of many feminists when he pondered why 'qualifications
are needed for the garden or for the stable, but none are asked for the
nursery'. The Hills were eager to publicise this work, which argued that
child-management should be based upon a thorough understanding of
children's 'nature and constitution'.[163] One of the most limpid expositions
on these themes emerged in Thomas Southwood Smith's highly successful
publication, *The Philosophy of Health*. He wrote the book with the belief
that women did not instinctively know how best to rear their children. 'All
would be well', he explained, 'if the marriage ceremony, which transforms
the girl into the wife, conferred upon the wife the qualities which should
be possessed by the mother.' The book provoked heated discussion. The
Unitarian publication, the *Christian Reformer*, was particularly shocked
by the work. Its reviewer indicated clearly the distance between Smith's
view, and that held by most mainstream Unitarians, when he explained
how his opinions differed from those held by Smith, 'I maintain that the
Great Author of nature has implanted in the bosom of every mother, '*the*
DISPOSITION *which Society presumes her to possess'*.[164]

The Evangelicals argued that women should receive a better general
education so that they might make good wives and mothers.[165] The radical
unitarians, by contrast, entertained a far more rigorous and theoretical
approach. They stipulated that women needed training in the actual
pyschology of childrearing. For, as Grimstone declared, the education of
one's infant should begin even before their first smile. In their journals
they devoted series, most notably by Southwood Smith's daughter, Caroline,
on how to cope with young children, and considered such topics as beha-
vioural problems.[166] They believed that the proper education of young
children was essential for the promotion of a moral and intellectually vital
culture. This was reflected in their significant contribution to Samuel
Wilderspin's attempts to establish infant schools during the 1830s and
1840s. Mary Gaskell and Mary Leman Grimstone were particularly prominent crusaders in this campaign, the latter circulating petitions and
testimonials to further the cause.[167]

The campaign to establish infant schools should not be seen from the
uniquely feminist perspective of freeing women from childcare. For apart
from a few isolated calls for nursery education in connection with the
associated homes scheme, as mentioned above, their promotion of infant
schools was not publicly linked to the issue of female emancipation. Rather,

this specific campaign was part of a wider call for the better education of young children and was the result of the radical unitarians' pressing desire to germinate a new, enlightened society through liberating the mind. Within this agenda, they also wished to redefine the maternal role by urging mothers to learn for themselves the progressive educational techniques professed by the infant educationalists, Wilderspin and Pestalozzi, and apply them in their own childrearing practices. They consequently gave considerable publicity to both these men in a host of reviews, articles and poems. Pestalozzi's pedagogical innovations, it should be pointed out, did in any case place considerable emphasis upon the importance of mothers' interaction with their children.[168]

Therefore, whereas the Evangelical proscriptions on education perceived women as passively absorbing their instruction, then inculcating the precepts they had learnt in their children, the radical unitarians encouraged a dynamic model of motherhood. Women were to make good the shortcomings in the educational system by studying the most advanced educational psychologies of the day, and adapting them to their own situations. Women were asked to consider such advanced concepts as 'how do children actually learn?' It was typical of the radical unitarian development of mainstream Unitarian thought; in particular, the desire that women should be perceived as sophisticated, intellectual thinkers in their own right.[169]

In their efforts to promote new ideas of parenthood, the radical unitarians also posited progressive notions of fatherhood. At a time when many middle-class men seemed increasingly to foster an emotional and spatial distance from their children, the feminists projected a vision of paternity whereby men shared with women the caring familial role. As William Shaen confided to his sister, 'There are such things as domestic men . . . I am one myself.' He believed that a tender relationship between a father and his child ought to be the 'educating motive of a moral and intellectual man'.[170] Just as radical writers had used literature to explore different roles for women, so too, they discovered, could the novel adumbrate new perceptions of men. Frederika Bremer presented caring models of fatherhood in her novel, *The Home*, in which Judge Frank believes strongly in the concept of not just maternal, but paternal love. It is in his arms that his newly-born daughter, Eva, first opens her eyes.[171]

Therefore, the radical unitarians' challenge to contemporary domestic ideology involved both arguing for women's right to work, and urging for a reorientation of the family, and the roles and culture they felt it to perpetuate. However, these radical critiques spread ideological waves far beyond merely the debate on domesticity. For their attacks upon conventional domestic arrangements formed an integral facet of the radical unitarians' holistic concept of democracy. Democracy, they believed, was not merely a question of granting equal rights before the law. The feminists wished to overturn the idea that the home and the outside world were isolated phenomena – to be ruled by different values and sexes. They were convinced that true liberation might only be effected if liberty were practised throughout society, and the divisive separate-spheres ideology abolished. They wished for a new model of the family – liberal, caring and egalitarian – a democratic union in which force played no part. Such a family, they believed would form the wellspring for society at large.

Central to the radical unitarian case was their conception of the relationship between the family and the state. William Shaen proved uncompromising on this point. 'The rules of morality are uniform for the individual, the Family and the Nation', he declared. Hence for Shaen, as for the other members of his circle, democratic principles could not be confined to the state, but had to be extended to the family hearth. A recognition of this fact, would, Shaen wrote, effect far more good for the Chartists than 'any physical force propagandism'.[172]

This argument fuelled the radical unitarian frustration with those Chartists who campaigned for liberal principles to be effected in the state, yet persisted in a tyrannous patriarchy within their own homes. This was an issue which James and Caroline Hill were keen to address in their journal, the *Star in the East*. In an article entitled, 'The Rights and Wrongs of Women', their correspondent lambasted those such as the Chartists who publicly fought against unjust laws and preached progressive principles, yet, in their domestic life practised despotism towards their womenfolk.[173]

In challenging the domestic conservatism of the mainstream Chartist movement, radical unitarians drew once again upon their concept of domestic slavery. W. J. Linton expressed this clearly in a letter to the *Reasoner*: 'We may establish republican forms of government, we may harmonise and organise the different grades of society – and yet little will be done for social peace or national growth, so long as we leave unremedied that fearful household slavery, that wrong at the bottom of all tyranny, as the family is at the base of all society and government.' In other journals, too, Linton continued to launch his attack upon the Chartist who fought for freedom in the public sphere, while he 'pertinaciously maintains a despotic authority at home'.[174] The continuing importance of the feminist concept of domestic slavery in this debate is well-illustrated in an article which appeared in *Eliza Cook's Journal* in 1851, which proclaimed, 'The slavery of woman in her household is always the exact counterpart of the governmental slavery of a people.'[175]

Hence, the radical intelligentsia came to assert that the remnants of barbarity which existed within the private sphere actually retarded the progress of the democratic state. As Goodwyn Barmby was to fervently declare, 'We must have unsexual Chartism. How can the stream of freedom flow clearly when slavery is at its foundations?' Herbert Spencer also took up the point in one of his earlier works, well received among his radical unitarian associates, *Social Statics*, in which he claimed, 'The same extent that the triumph of might over right is seen in a nation's political institutions, it is seen in its domestic ones. Despotism in the state is necessarily associated with depotism in the family.' These arguments persisted within Victorian feminist thought over the coming decades. J. S. Mill, for example, claimed that with conventional marital relations in their existing state, the family was a 'school of despotism', whereas it should have been a 'school for the virtues of freedom'.[176]

In the same way, radical unitarian pleas for Italian freedom were not merely couched in terms of individual rights and self-determination. Their critique of oppressive regimes hinged upon a concern with the close relationship between the family and the nation. As Linton explained at a public meeting to establish the People's International League, 'we believe that nations . . . bear the same relation to that whole which individuals bear to a family' (a view Linton developed further in his correspondence with Thornton Hunt). Sophia Dobson Collet, in an essay upon Italian liberty, lamented that within authoritarian regimes, 'The wife becomes a meek slave; the children must not ask questions.' Thus, it was argued that tyranny had to be tackled within the family. For if the family, the core of the nation could be reformed, it would send the shoots of liberty throughout the state.[177]

The feminists' belief that the health of the state depended upon a new egalitarian model of the family was a subversion of contemporary Evangelical ideologies, so prevalent within nineteenth-century discourse. Catherine Hall has traced the way in which the Evangelical perception of the family and home became ingrained into Victorian culture.[178] The notion of the home as a tranquil, halcyon refuge from the commercial world, presided over by the passive, womanly woman was a ubiquitous theme during this period. While historians of Evangelicalism freely admit to the enormous contribution other religious and political creeds made to what is referred to as the 'Victorian frame of mind',[179] these interpretations still lack one crucial element: that is, how reformers of a different ideological persuasion interposed a perception of the family very different to that predicated by the Evangelicals.

The radical unitarians concurred with the Evangelicals in perceiving the home as a spiritual fount and shared in their eulogies of its essential peaceful and loving properties. Dawson typified such views in a lecture to the radical unitarians' brainchild, the Whittington Club, in 1849, 'We can correct much socialist nonsense by showing how deep in thought lies the sanctity of the household, the peculiarity of home.'[180] In this, they were continuing the tradition of mainstream Unitarians who frequently perpetuated such an ideology – for as one Unitarian minister proclaimed in a marriage address, 'Home is a sacred word.'[181] However, the radical unitarians rejected Evangelical attempts to use the family as a bulwark to prop up the conservative doctrines of the status quo.[182] They wished it to perform an emancipatory function and thus pave the way for a new egalitarian order. Thus, the radical unitarians sympathised with the Owenite perception of the family as a centre of despotism. However, unlike the Owenites, they wished not to eradicate the family, but to reform it. An important means by which this might be achieved was to extirpate the ideology of the separate spheres. They believed that the tendency among Chartists to profess liberalism politically, yet practise tyranny domestically was a consequence of the adherence to the Evangelical notion of separate spheres with separate values.

Grimstone's essay 'A Happy New Year to the People' was based upon these premises. She attacked vehemently the conventional arrangement, whereby men enjoyed a fulfilling life outside the home, while women were confined to stultifying domesticity. What was required, Grimstone indicated, was a reorganisation of social and cultural life so that women's true qualities might shine forth, and a genuine marriage of minds be made possible. As Grimstone explained, 'It is not "monster meetings," but fireside virtues that will best show and establish the people's power.'[183]

Therefore, the entry of the feminists into the Chartist debate provided the stimulus for wide-reaching debates concerning democracy and domesticity. The feminists consistently argued that true democracy would only be achieved by extending campaigns for the suffrage to include a comprehensive reformation of cultural mores. Within these discussions their analysis of domestic slavery provided the intellectual basis for their desire to revolutionise relationships and roles between husband and wife. Nevertheless, what they perceived as the needs of children and the family remained central within this ideology. Indeed, while the early feminists were quite content to advocate employment for married women, they rarely argued explicitly for the employment of married women with children. For the radical unitarians' feminist agenda always formed part of a wider reforming vision, in which what they took to be the needs of society, and not the rights of the individual, were paramount.

4 'Merely a Question of Bargain and Sale': Law Reform and the Union of the Sexes

The radical unitarian debate with the Chartist movement illustrated the former's desire to create a just legislature and also highlighted the emphasis they placed upon the marital relationship in establishing an equal and harmonious society. These dual concerns were given full expression in the early feminists' discourse on the unjust laws facing women. The law, they believed, was the cultural reflection of privileging physical power over reason or intellect. The consequence was a system of 'legal barbarism'.[1] This was most clearly expressed, they maintained, in the laws relating to women and marriage. While a minority in the feminist camp, such as Eliza Meteyard and R. H. Horne, were sceptical of placing too much emphasis on legislative change (preferring to emphasise more profound cultural factors),[2] for the vast majority, the desire to reform iniquitous laws formed a central element in their struggle to redefine the bases of both the marital relationship and women's position in society.

During the 1830s radical unitarian debates on the laws affecting women were strongly influenced by their acquaintance with Owenite circles and focused upon the taboo subject of divorce. This necessarily condemned the feminists to a minority audience, for as Horstman notes, 'Divorce was so unrespectable that talking about it tainted the speaker.'[3] However, as the chapter goes on to demonstrate, by the mid-1840s their analysis had been considerably tempered. Indeed, their agitation against the unjust laws concerning women proved to be an appropriate means of bringing feminist issues before the public eye. Despite this accommodation of their ideas, the radical unitarian perspective on law and women remained rooted within a specific feminist culture. For, in order to mitigate the worst excesses of women's egregious legal position, radicals forged their own customs dictating sexual union. As a consequence, the feminist debate on the law became inextricably linked with their perspectives on sexual relations. The nexus between these two issues proved to be a vibrant critique of marriage and what feminists declared to be its sordid underside – prostitution.

An analysis of this radical unitarian debate serves to overturn two specific traditions in the historiography. Firstly, the standard view of the origins of the women's rights movements, as Shanley explains in her recent work, *Feminism, Marriage and the Law*, is that preceding the debates of 1856, 'the issues of married women's property and divorce law reform were regarded not only as quite separate issues, but as having very little to do with women's rights'. She traces the 'emergence of specifically feminist demands for married women's property and divorce law reforms in the mid-1850s'.[4] Similarly, Phillip Mallet has lately claimed, 'By the middle of the century the laws relating to women had a number of critics, but these were for the most part more concerned to find remedies for particular injustices than to estimate the effect of less tangible themes, such as the dignity of being denied a legal existence.'[5] However, contrary to these claims, the radical unitarians' sophisticated discourse on law during the 1830s and 1840s amounted to the growth of a powerful feminist tradition, without which the campaigns of the 1850s cannot fully be understood.

Secondly, historians have long assumed that it was not until the 1870s that prostitution became a feminist issue. The conclusion of Professor Banks is representative, 'Not until Josephine Butler's campaign against the Contagious Diseases Act in the 1870s was concern for the prostitute linked specfically to feminist arguments about the relationship between men and women.' Indeed, Mallett even declares that Mona Caird's analysis of the relationship between marriage and prostitution in 1888 marked 'a watershed in the history of the women's movement'.[6] The glare of historical attention on these highspots of Victorian feminist argument has obfuscated the lively debate on prostitution which had been coursing through radical channels for many decades. For, contrary to the assumption that it was not until the 1860s that feminists made a connection between marriage and prostitution, it was during the 1830s that radical discourse came to focus upon prostitution as the most damning example of the baneful effect which the existing marriage laws had upon women. As one contemporary journalist remarked, the existing marriage system created two castes of women, 'those *called* pure and virtuous and those *called* dishonest and vicious'.[7] Moreover, it should be recognised that many of the chief participants in the struggle to rescind the Contagious Diseases Acts, for example William Shaen, James Stansfeld and Emilie Venturi (née Ashurst), were closely involved in the radical debates on the prostitution issue in the 1840s (a fact that has been completely overlooked by historians of the movement).[8]

ESTABLISHING THE TRUE MARRIAGE

During the 1830s Owen's argument that the laws of human nature conflicted with man-made laws evoked considerable interest among radical unitarian circles. Owen had claimed that sexual attraction was an essential law of nature. However, Owen, in common with Godwin and Shelley, believed it was nonsensical and unnatural to suggest that all married couples might remain emotionally and physically satisfied with one another, until death. Consequently, Owen argued that society should recognise that the present laws (curtailing divorce) were at variance with the natural laws of sexual attraction. Hence, divorce should be made freely available to all.[9] Within English radical culture there was a long tradition supporting divorce. The Barebones Parliament of 1653 had declared marriage to be a civil contract. Radical unitarians evoked this heritage by reminding their readers that divorce had long been advocated by John Milton (a great favourite in Unitarian circles).[10] Consequently, many fully endorsed Owen's calls to facilitate divorce. The Unitarian belief in the need for harmony between human desire and divine law made such theories most acceptable to them.[11] In a review of Owen's book in the *New Moral World*, Caroline Southwood Hill praised its, 'clear and true account of some of the fundamental laws of human nature'.[12] During the 1830s, therefore, radical unitarians made repeated attacks upon the oppressive nature of the existing marriage laws. This censure was inextricably linked to their concerns for the position of women.

The *Star in the East* took up the issue with vigour. In 1839 a series of articles on the rights of women focused upon the marriage law. The correspondent, G. S., berated, 'Nothing but the most lamentable ignorance of the constitution of human beings, and the greatest outstretch of priestly despotism, could have induced the interference with what is essentially beyond the power of human law.' Moreover, of all the evils in the present condition of women, G. S. claimed, 'the contemporary marriage laws were by far the worst'. W. J. Linton's paper corroborated the point, arguing, 'This *institution of marriage* was the cause of the false position in which women have ever been placed.' The journal went on to claim that marriage was a 'rash and unauthorised interference of man with the strongest passion of universal human nature'.[13]

The radical unitarians also brought their own tradition of biblical scholarship to bear on the issue, declaring that crucial texts in the Bible had been mistranslated. W. J. Fox, commenting on the Caroline Norton case, fumed that her suffering was 'all because the clergy have not sense and

learning enough to discover, or not honesty enough to tell, the true meaning of a text in the New Testament, which has just as much to do with the
morality of a public law of divorce, on reasonable grounds, as it has with
the commutation of tithes for hop-gardens, or with the adoption of poor-
laws for Ireland'.[14]

Furthermore, the radical unitarians fully concurred with the way in which
Owen yoked the issue of divorce to that of prostitution. Owen postulated
that the prohibition of divorce to all except the extremely wealthy was the
chief cause of prostitution. His premise was that the restrictions on divorce
prevented unhappy spouses from uniting respectably with other partners.
Therefore, the male partner would turn to prostitutes for sexual solace,
and sexually frustrated female spouses, might indulge in illicit relationships. The prevailing double standard of the day would intervene to condemn such women as 'fallen', and prostitution would often provide their
only recourse, thus perpetuating the problem.[15] Hence, as W. J. Linton
remarked with characteristic venom, 'Some thousands of these playthings
are annually sacrificed, with most horrible torture, for the amusement of
the males: this game is called *prostitution*, and is carefully provided for
by the marriage-laws.'[16] Such vehement language was also employed by
W. J. Fox in the *Monthly Repository*. In 1833, in an article highlighting
Unitarian efforts to secure the Dissenters' Marriage Bill, Fox argued that
the solution to the prostitution problem lay in making marriage a civil
contract. He urged that the high incidence of unhappy marriages, which
ensued from not allowing the termination of the contract, meant that men
were bound to involve themselves in extra-marital liaisons. Fox declared
that 'even a temporary toleration of polygamy would be better, infinitely
better than this eternal flood of prostitution'.[17]

A crucial source in this debate is an early novel of Eliza Lynn – *Realities*
(1851). The apparent conservatism of the later works of Lynn Linton (she
went on to marry W. J. Linton) has earned her a damning reputation as the
arch-antifeminist of the Victorian age.[18] However, as her autobiography
reveals, during the late 1840s and early 1850s, Eliza Lynn worked and
lived in the thick of radical unitarian circles.[19] At this time, she was, as she
herself later admitted, 'one of the most ardent and enthusiastic of the
advanced guard. I thought that the lives of women should be as free as
those of men.'[20] While *Realities*'s unabashed socialism prohibited its success among the general public, it found a ready audience in this feminist
milieu – as its reception by the Chapman circle and Geraldine Jewsbury
testifies.[21] Published in 1851, the work is remarkable for its attempt to
elucidate the major feminist theories concerning the prostitution problem which had been developing during the previous twenty years. Lynn

included such arguments as the egregious consequences of the false conventions of chivalric protection, the plight of needlewomen, and also explored the more general point that were relationships between the sexes more equal, prostitution would become a thing of the past. This in itself makes it one of the most important and neglected feminist novels of the period.

The novel is particularly clear in its treatment of the feminist arguments concerning the relationship between the circumscription of divorce and prostitution. Indeed, the marriage between Emma and Vasty Vaughan is used as a vehicle to explore this theme. Their marriage follows a classic course, predicted by many feminists. As W. B. Adams had prophesied in his infamous article, 'On the Condition of Women' (which had so enraged many Unitarians), middle- and upper-class women received but a pitiful education, geared to the attainment of superficial accomplishments with which to attract a prospective husband. The result of such baseless marriages would be that the husband would soon tire of his 'new toy', and in time, the wife may well be seduced by a lover.[22] Certainly, Vasty is quickly bored by Emma. 'Sated with her beauty in less time than a pretty bird would have wearied a child.' While Vasty indulges in a series of 'gross infidelities', Emma's patience wears thin, and she too takes a lover. The Vaughans do attempt a reconciliation, but it fails in a month. However, that Vasty took his wife back now means they cannot seek a divorce, for under English law, Vasty has condoned his wife's behaviour. As the narrator laments, 'Our wise laws were against them both; offering no relief to him, and no way of repentance to her.' When Emma's lover deserts her, she becomes a prostitute. Lynn argues that under a different legal system, where divorce were granted, 'Emma Vaughan might have been sacred.' However, the operation of a double standard causes Emma to lament bitterly to Glynn, her theatrical tutor, that Vasty 'held a higher position in society: that his vice, the same as hers, only increased the interest of that society in him: that where she was covered with shame and disgrace something like a glory clothed him'. Glynn's response (himself a socialist and feminist) is to wonder what Emma might have been, 'were laws more consistent with human nature'. Glynn maintains throughout that 'we ought to reconstruct our social relations on a basis broad enough for the whole of human nature'.[23]

During the 1840s, however, the debates concerning divorce and prostitution underwent a gradual modification within most radical unitarian discourse. Improving the basis of marriage (even common law marriage), and not divorce, was increasingly articulated as the panacea to the Great Social Evil of prostitution. One indication of the new emphasis on marriage was that many writers came to link these issues to the Malthusian debate. Both Jerrold and Dickens insisted, *contra* Malthus, that to delay marriage exacerbated the prostitution problem. Both these writers took up the banner of early marriages, presenting them as a preventative against prostitution. Dickens delineated this case in *The Chimes*, a work which contemporary reviewers acknowledged was 'alarmingly radical' and 'anti-Malthusian'.[24] While this was not an issue on which the early feminists were completely united, many being sceptical of the feminist value in promoting early marriages,[25] *The Chimes* may have gone some way in persuading the doubters. (Dickens was relieved by the tremendous effect this work had upon a private audience, which included figures such as W. J. Fox, who had previously inclined towards Malthusian views.)[26] Other radical journals joined in the debate. The *People's Press*, for example, published articles advising young couples not to delay marriage. Meanwhile, *Douglas Jerrold's Shilling Magazine* demonstrated that the concept of natural laws still informed the debate. In one of its fictional sketches, a cobbler objecting to his companion's assertion that legislation should prevent marriage, except in the case of the rich, declaims, '*In God's works there is no flaw. . . .* Nature's true laws co-exist not with Evil, for Nature is God.'[27]

A number of interrelating factors help to explain this shift in emphasis from divorce to marriage. Firstly, it is useful to consider this evolution in the light of the personal changes occuring within the radical coterie itself. During the 1830s, many key members of the set were suffering from the prohibition against divorce. W. J. Fox, T. Southwood Smith and Harriet Taylor were all facing the traumas of an unsatisfactory marriage; and W. J. Linton had faced another aspect of the restrictive nature of existing marital laws. By the mid-forties, however, Smith had settled down into a common-law partnership with Margaret Gillies; Fox's set-up with Eliza Flower had become well-established, and Taylor and Mill appear to have become reconciled to their situation.[28] Thus, it is perhaps not surprising if something of the urgency had gone from their desire to change the marriage laws. With the discovery that non-marital love-matches could work came renewed pressure from these quarters to convince others that it was not the form of a couple's union that was important, but the feeling which lay behind it.

There was a long tradition of unusual liaisons within radical unitarian circles. These were forged as an alternative to conventional marriage practice. At the most radical end of the spectrum, some have suggested that Thornton Hunt, along with the painter, Samuel Laurence and his wife and the Gliddons, adopted a Fourierist model of communal marriage.[29] Equally unconventional, Matilda Hays and Charlotte Cushman embarked upon a 'female marriage'. Their close friend, Eliza Cook, had a horror of marriage and remained single as a matter of principle.[30] More common, however, was the heterosexual non-marital partnership. Indeed, on this issue the radical unitarians were often more radical than their Owenite associates.[31] The most fervent advocate of such unions was W. J. Linton. In his own publication he considered the issue at length. As one of his correspondents put it, 'It is not decent to make a public exhibition of actions which in high natures result from the most sacred and private feelings.' The radical publication, the *Leader*, also treated the issue, detailing the sentiments of a fictional woman, whom they described as a 'Mary Wollstonecraft, a St. Simonian'. The *Leader* explained, 'She feels that the union of the sexes must be that of *lovers*, must have a moral foundation in the concord of the *affections*.'[32] These were views fully endorsed by the radical unitarians' favourite novelist, George Sand. Indeed, Eliza Ashurst was in awe of the relationship between Sand and Chopin – as she explained to her American correspondent, 'In the last twelve years she has been in all except the ceremony, the wife of *Chopin*.'[33]

The feminist suspicion of formal marriages derived from a hostility towards the subordinate legal position facing women once they became wives. The radical unitarians sought to promote marriage as a triumph of dual responsibility and commitment, rather than the domination of one sex over the other. Thus, one of the heroines in Grimstone's novel, *Cleone*, 'abjured', we are told, 'the ceremony by which it is pretended that woman is merged in man'. Grimstone goes on to explain to her reader that Rosina, 'never meant, if she married, to kneel at the altar and call God to witness an oath which her very nature told her she must violate, without entering a protest to declare that she acted in obedience to the law, not to her reason – that she came to give and to take the supporting hand of a sincere and sacred esteem, confidence, and love, not to vow a blind trust, dependence and obedience'. Rosina later informs her aunt that she considers herself to be already married to Connor – 'that I have done which *I* deem makes me his wife – the giving him my heart, and confessing as much to him'.[34]

In *Eliza Cook's Journal* a highly symbolic format was used to suggest the limitations of conventional, formal marriages. In a short story entitled, 'Light out of the Cloud', the protagonist, Thomas, spends all his earnings on drink and gambling, leaving his wife and child with no money to buy food. His wife Jane decides to pawn her wedding ring in order to buy something to eat. The psychological consequences of this action are dramatic, 'up to the night when she parted with her wedding-ring, Jane had been submissive and uncomplaining. She had met her husband's repinings with patience – had answered his reproaches and curses only by tears, and endured his wrongs almost tenderly and lovingly, but this evening a different spirit came over her – it seemed as though, with her ring, she lost her submissive character.'[35]

While many radical unitarians did live together unmarried, such a solution was not possible for all members of the circle. As we have seen, by the mid-1840s, the radical unitarians were coming to assume a more central place within the country's intellectual life. For those seeking to make a public career as solicitors, reformers and the like, public respectability was essential. Nevertheless, those who did marry did all they could to limit the effects of legislation and convention upon their relationship. Indeed, by the 1840s the feminists had developed their own distinctive culture of personal relationships and marriage traditions which accorded with their ideological concerns.

The desire to make marital arrangements which would abrogate the effects of the law, did have precedence within mainstream Unitarian culture. Unitarians such as Priestley and Elizabeth Reid, demonstrated their suspicion of existing marriage laws by leaving money to women with the proviso that their husbands were to have no control over it. Moreover, prior to the 1833 Dissenters Marriage Act Unitarians had, as Dissenters, challenged the existing marriage ceremony.[36] It should also be remembered that in contrast to other denominations, the Unitarians were very lax in their attitude towards the sacraments. This is clear in their baptismal practices, for example.[37]

The radical unitarians further developed these traditions, adding to them a distinctive feminist element. This was symbolised in the wedding of James Stansfeld and Caroline Ashurst. W. J. Fox, who presided over the service, explained 'the part he took in the ceremony not to be that of a priest who came to marry them for they married themselves but that he was simply asked as a friend to give as appropriate expression as he could to the feelings of the parties on the occasion'. The only conventional element of the service came when James and Caroline repeated, 'the two sentences rendered necessary by the Act'. Fox explained as they exchanged rings that they did so with the intention of overcoming convention and 'to express your views of the mutual nature of the engagement of which it is the type'.[38] This last sentiment was of particular importance to the early feminists. They believed that the standard marriage service perpetuated the notion of a relationship in which one partner could demand total submission from the other. Harriet Martineau, for one, had long displayed her antagonism to the contemporary marriage vows and her radical unitarian associates were among the first to advocate omitting the 'I obey' response in their wedding services. (This was in contrast to Chartist rhetoric which urged for a strengthening of traditional vows.)[39] Thus in one of Grimstone's early works, *Woman's Love*, the hero and the heroine shun the polished materialistic society in which they move to enjoy a simple, quiet wedding. At the ceremony Ida vows to 'love him, to honour him, to keep him in sickness and in health; to forsake all others, and cleave unto him alone'. She does not vow to obey him. Elizabeth Malleson, who moved closely in radical unitarian circles during the late 1840s, was clearly influenced by these ideas. As she recalled of her own wedding (at which Fox was a witness), 'The word *obey* was omitted from the marriage service by mutual consent.' She went on to explain that her marriage, 'brought me the completest individual freedom. This, of course lay at the basis of our conception of marriage.'[40]

Therefore, when the early feminists did decide to marry it was only with a critical eye to the existing marital conventions and laws. Indeed, Anna Wheeler had long drawn attention to the call of French feminists who urged women to '*reject as a husband any man* who is not sufficiently generous to consent to share with us all the rights he himself enjoys'.[41] John Stuart Mill's declamation to equalise his position with his wife, Harriet Taylor, is well-known; but many other couples made similar attempts to forge egalitarian arrangements within their marriages. Henry Solly, for example, (Shaen's brother-in-law) recalled his sister's admiration at the 'independent way in which we had carried out our critical experiment of matrimonial life and plans'.[42]

Central to the radical unitarian perception of marriage, then, was their insistence that it should be the union of two equal, and, just as important, *loving* partners. They continued in the radical Miltonic tradition in their belief that to marry without love was a sin before God. Indeed, their feminist perception of marriage was directly related to their religious concerns to capture the true spirit of Christianity. As Matilda Hays explained, 'the *form* of marriage where the *spirit* is not, is the law of man; unrecognised, and therefore unhallowed by Him who is the essence of Truth and Love!'[43]

The notion of the love match was not necessarily progressive. For example, as Walkowitz has noted of Evangelicals during the 1830s and 1840s, 'Like the radical sexual reformers of the time, they condemned the arranged marriages of convenience among the upper class.'[44] What made the radicals' position so striking was that they compared the love-less marriage so unequivocally with prostitution. As the *Star in the East* asserted in 1839, 'Wherever man and woman are bound together for filthy lucre's sake, without regard to love, there is prostitution.' In 1851, John Stores Smith rehearsed the same idea: 'these sale-marriages, these bought brides, are but legalised seduction and society-tolerated harlots'.[45] Therefore, the radicals sought to deconstruct the meaning of marriage, by asserting that loveless sexual union was always prostitution. Hence it was claimed that the words 'marriage' and 'prostitution', 'commonly mean the same thing'. From the late 1830s to the early 1850s, this equation enjoyed constant use among radical circles.[46]

By the middle of the 1840s even the more moderate members of the radical unitarian literary milieu articulated this issue unequivocally. Dickens, for example, made extensive use of the metaphor in *Dombey and Son* (1846–8). This, despite the fact that in 1841 Owen had caused a near-riot when he claimed at a public meeting, 'all couples married without affection are living in prostitution'.[47] Dickens's willingness to use such rhetoric demonstrates the extent to which feminist arguments were making headway among a wider reading public. Indeed, the novel illustrates the way in which liberal-minded writers were beginning to present feminist ideas to their audience.

In *Dombey and Son*, Alice Marwood, the 'fallen woman' of the piece and Edith Dombey, a 'commercial bride', both draw upon the feminist rhetoric which pronounced the commercial marriage as synonymous with prostitution. Edith considers her marriage but the sordid culmination of ten years of being 'hawked and vended' and acknowledges that her own mother was responsible for training her for such a fate. As she bemoans to Carker, 'I have not had an accomplishment or grace that might have been a resource to me, but it has been paraded and vended to enhance my value.'[48] The belief that women were educated into such 'bargain marriages' was a long-standing motif in radical circles. As W. B. Adams wrote in 1833 in a much-publicised article, higher-class women were 'studiously instructed that marriage is not an affair of love, or affection, or judgement, but merely a matter of bargain and sale'. They were consequently given the most superficial education, even being taught how to sit and to walk so as to best attract the eyes of prospective husbands. Thus, during their youth they were, 'trained to undergo . . . a species of prostitution'.[49] The prostitute, Alice, presents her history in identical terms to that of Edith. She explains how her mother, appreciating her good looks, 'thought to make a sort of property of me'. When the two pairs of women meet in Brighton, they illustrate their keen awareness of the sordid nexus which links them. Edith 'could not but compare the younger woman with herself . . . she felt a chill creep over her'. Alice is more explicit. She later claims that the only difference between herself and Edith is social class. She maintains

'Wretched marriages don't come of such things, in our degree; only wretchedness and ruin.' Alice then goes on to deliver the classic early feminist cliché of women's exploitation, 'I was made a short-lived toy, and flung aside more cruelly and carelessly than even such things are.'[50]

The way in which these two characters articulate their position using the unequivocal language employed by contemporary feminists is a point which has been muddied by previous critics. While some, such as Sally Mitchell, draw attention to the parallel the novel makes between marriage and prostitution, an ignorance of contemporary feminist debate has prohibited a proper understanding of Edith's and Alice's declamations. Roger Sell, for example, comments on Dickens's refusal to explore a 'more fully "feminist" reaction' in Edith. Sell is representative in seeing only the melodrama and not the ideology in Edith's words.[51] Of course, the forthright expressions of Edith and Alice are in keeping with Dickens's portrayal of two angry and bitter women, with whom we are never permitted to engage our sympathies too closely. The narrator, on the other hand relies upon insinuation, assuming a rhetorical, rather than a proscriptive tone. He delicately suggests the immorality of the commercial marriage, without alienating the audience with polemic.[52] In employing such a device, the way was left clear for the feminist conscious in Dickens's audience to identify with the elegies of the fallen women, without offending his general readership.

Other novelists, such as George Sand and Matilda Hays, were developing similar arguments in their own work at this time.[53] Jerrold's publications also made use of this imagery. In an article, the 'Wrongs of Women', based upon the legal wranglings between Angela Burdett-Coutts and her defrauder, Dun, it was claimed that the chief problem with women's present position in society was that a price had been set upon them, as if they had been in a slave market. Thus, 'seduction and adultery' had become 'purchaseable vices'. The correspondent fulminated, 'Woman, whether maid or wife, is considered by the libertine as a purchaseable toy.'[54]

WOMEN'S LEGAL POSITION – THE BATTLE BEGINS

The identification of the loveless marriage with prostitution coincided, in the mid-to-late 1840s, with a resurgence of feminist arguments concerning the egregious nature of the existing marriage laws. This is not surprising, given that within contemporary feminist ideology the two issues were closely linked. The feminists' claim that marriage was often synonymous with prostitution derived from a belief that the true purpose of marriage had been degraded. The laws dictating women's position within marriage were, they argued, a crucial factor to blame for this degeneracy. Within common law, women were subsumed in the personality of their husbands, as much as if they were his property or chattel. The feminists lamented that instead of recognising women as rational, independent beings, the law encouraged men to think of them as a commodity. While there was division on some aspects of contemporary marriage law, such as the prohibition against marrying one's deceased wife's sister,[55] the feminists were united in their belief that women should be entitled to their own property and earnings, and responsible for their own actions. Their treatment of these issues was strongly influenced by the debates of the previous decades. Indeed, during the 1830s, the subject had formed a continuous undercurrent in radical circles. The feminists of the 1840s continued to employ both the strategies employed by their predecessors, as well as developing the arguments and rhetoric they used. Thus, a radical tradition began to emerge, a tradition which was to feed directly into the women's rights campaigns of the 1850s.

During the early 1830s, Owenite women, prompted by the *Crisis*, attempted to militate opinion on the male laws which they believed accounted for the enslaved position of women. In 1833, a committee was formed for the establishment of a 'Practical Moral Union of the Women of Great Britain and Ireland, for the purpose of enabling them to attain a superior physical, moral and intellectual character'. Its object was to raise awareness of the laws regarding women, 'which, having been formed upon a false estimate of their nature, are, consequently, all unjust and unnatural'. There ensued a lively debate in the pages of the *Crisis* concerning the desirability of such female exclusive action. This discussion turned into a wider argument over an unlikely proposal that women should have a unique place within the legislature, legislating only for women.[56] While this plan seems naive and lacking in intellectual scope, the *Crisis* continued to pursue concomitant issues in a more fruitful fashion. In 1834, their correspondent Concordia penned a two-issue serial aiming to raise women's awareness of their legal position. Such an approach came to form a staple ingredient of feminist strategy. Concordia was typical of many feminists in her belief that, 'if women were more aware of their insignificance in the eye of the law, some of the decrees which disgrace our statute book would not only be dead letters, but absolutely repealed'. She then proceeded to give succinct disquisitions concerning the present inequalities facing women in jurisprudence.[57] This was a method which also appealed to journalists of the *New Moral World*, and such work was also bolstered by Anna Wheeler's rousing public lectures, in which she denounced the existing marriage laws for forming the basis of women's slavery.[58]

The desire to raise women's awareness of their legal position was an avenue pursued by another feminist closely acquainted with radical unitarian circles – Anna Jameson. Jameson, a woman so important to the campaigns of Leigh Smith Bodichon, Howitt and Parkes during the 1850s, had long been concerned to publicise women's legal position. This was a task to which she addressed herself in her 1833 work, *Winter Studies and Summer Rambles.* As she explained to Ottilie van Goethe, 'I write for Englishwomen and to tell them things they do not know.' The widely-read *Tait's Edinburgh Magazine* explained to its readers that the sum of Jameson's argument was that women should be 'left, in all cases, responsible for their own actions, their own debts'.[59]

However, periodicals such as the *Monthly Repository*, with its limited audience, adopted a polemical, rather than a didactic approach. It concentrated its efforts on developing the second important element in feminist treatment of the marriage laws – the relationship between women's legal position and their state of 'slavery'. This was a refinement upon the radical unitarian formulation of women's domestic slavery, as discussed in Chapter 2. In 1836, in an essay upon Channing's *Slavery*, reprinted in much of the feminist press, the reviewer argued that Channing ought to have considered the state of the marriage laws which rendered women as much slaves as the American blacks. The writer asked, 'Did the Doctor never see a marriage contract? What is the condition of woman, but that she *is* property, while she cannot possess property?'[60] Similarly a review of Campbell's *Life of Mrs. Siddons* was used as a vehicle for a discussion of married women's legal position. The writer protested, 'Quite enough is woman debarred from the opportunity of honourably earning her means of support; when she can and does earn them, it is barbarous to treat her like a Russian slave whose titled master pockets the pence.' In his lectures to the Working Men's Association in 1846, W. J. Fox continued to make use of the case of Mrs Siddons in his discussions upon the unjust nature of the marriage laws.[61]

The work of Fox and the *Monthly Repository*, and their analysis of women's legal position as slavery remained an important source of inspiration for feminist letters in the years to come. In the 1839 journal, the *National*, Linton frequently printed extracts from them.[62] His journal also demanded that women should be allowed to possess their own property, and exercise self-control for themselves. Women, in their existing state, were described as 'crippled, caged and chained'. The *National* condemned marriage, as had the *Monthly Repository*, for imposing 'the restrictions which impede her acquisition of a fair share either of the property or the poor freedom which the world affords'.[63] These were views endorsed by the radical unitarian community at large. Leigh Hunt, for example, wrote to Linton, informing him that he shared the ideas on marriage promulgated by the *National* and lamenting the injustice which women faced on such issues.[64] Moreover, the depiction of women's legal position as a form of slavery echoed persistently throughout feminist discourse in the years which followed. As *Eliza Cook's Journal* testified, it continued to inform feminist discussion in the 1850s. In 1851 it published a powerful essay which lambasted the established legal system, in which woman 'has no legal rights'. Complaining that 'the laws are wholly devised with an eye to the man's advantage', the journal insisted that there was a strong need to 'obtain some extensive modification of the law which still recognized the woman as a *slave* in all that respects her person, her property'.[65]

Therefore, the marriage laws were considered to condemn women as slaves by denying them their rights to both property and self-determination. However, the relationship was also considered to operate in a broader cultural sense. Just as later feminists were to understand the law to be the expression and exercise of power in society,[66] so the radical unitarians perceived the law as a vital educating force within society. As such they held it to be guilty of perpetuating the slave character of contemporary women. W. B. Adams made the point in 1833, by drawing attention to the legal responsibility which husbands must assume for their wives' debts. Such a practice, he argued, turned women into irresponsible slaves. This view also informed Bernard's *Theory of the Constitution*, in which the author traced the more general effect of the marriage laws, which, he declared, exacerbated the tendency to 'convert man into a domestic tyrant, woman into a cunning slave'.[67] These sentiments were echoed in the 1840s. Joseph Barker, for example, maintained, 'I would no more allow a man to take possession of the property of the wife against her will, than I would allow the wife to take possession of the property of her husband against his will.' Such a system, he claimed, 'makes the wife a slave, and the husband a despot'.[68] In the early 1850s, Harriet Taylor Mill followed this tradition as she continued to analyse the negative effects which women's legal position had upon the female character.[69]

Feminist arguments concerning the relationship between contemporary marriage laws and the debasement of marriage also remained constant from one decade to the next. In 1839, 'Witness', a writer for the *National*, was concerned that granting men the right to their wives' property resulted in 'changing the nature of love from an affection highly sympathetic, into a most selfish one. "I give all" is altered into "I will have all"'.[70] In the 1840s, Dawson proved equally keen to address the consequences of such laws upon individual relationships. In a public lecture, he argued that marital union had become 'a mercenary means of getting a living – a coming together of ill-assorted folks, regarding a home and a house as a safe-to-keep affair, or as a joint-stock'.[71] Such sentiments accorded with the feminists' argument that the existing marriage laws relegated women to mere objects. Here, the radical unitarians revealed their debt to the influence of left-wing thought. In Owenite circles, women's debasement to the status of property was seen as an inevitable consequence of the capitalist practice of individual property-owning. They posited the complete trans-formation of the social system as the only solution.[72] The radical unitarians called for more modest solutions – the reform of the law, and a change in cultural attitudes. Grimstone, for example, located the problem within the wider cultural context in which 'The love of property has usurped the place of the love of human nature.'[73] Despite this moderation of Owenite logic, the argument that under existing circumstances, women were property, became one of the most forceful and ubiquitous arguments in radical unit-arian disquisitions upon the marriage laws. It also fitted neatly into their thesis concerning the slave status of women.

W. J. Fox, for one, made frequent and emotive use of this rhetoric in the 1830s. He wrote, for example, of the way in which poor Mehetabel Wesley had it 'scourged' into her that she was 'a property and not a being'. These ideas gained in currency during the 1840s. W. J. Linton put them to scathing effect in his 1846 essay, 'Love and Marriage', arguing that the marriage laws had been framed 'to regulate the *possession* of women'.[74] Even those papers appealing to a wider audience made defiant use of such rhetoric. Such arguments appeared frequently in *Douglas Jerrold's Weekly Newspaper*. As one correspondent protested, 'Men make laws . . . with a fine calculating magnanimity, always the very best advantage of their own handiwork'; '. . . woman is man's *goods*, says the arithimetic of law', s/he continued. In other articles the paper made explicit attempts to alert women to the change in their legal situation, once married. In 'The Wrongs of Women – Hypocrisy of Man', the writer pondered that, 'It might, possibly, somewhat shock a bride upon her marriage-morning, were she told that the peal of bridal bells, duly inter-preted, told that she had become not, in symbolic truth merely the bone of bone and flesh of flesh of her husband, – but his goods, his chattel'.[75] A similar convention was employed in a story which appeared in the more conservative *Wade's London Review*. Once again, as soon as the young woman is married, she discovers that she is 'in all essential points a slave' and has surrendered her independence and will.[76]

From the mid-1840s, as the feminists' concern with contemporary mar-riage practice mounted, radical literary publishers appear to have launched a sustained campaign to inform their readers of women's legal position within marriage. This served to unite the tradition of feminist polemic, detailed above, with the more informative approach, favoured earlier by the *Crisis* and Jameson. A number of methods were employed by radical unitarian journalists to keep the question of women's legal position before the public eye. Some, such as Eliza Cook, took the straightforward approach of devoting articles to the explication of existing injustices in women's legal position. Cook's journal acknowledged the need to advance public opinion on this issue 'by such methods as we can'. Thus, it was explained, how legally, a woman's personality was merged with that of her husband. Consequently, married women were not entitled to keep their wages. Furthermore, it was urged that despite the Infants' Custody Act there were still many legal advances desperately needed by women.[77] The *Spirit of the Age* used a review of George Sand as a vehicle to discuss the way in which married women were 'robbed' of their property. This publication drew further attention to the issue by explaining how communitarian philosophies handled the problem. Under the Fourierist system, it was claimed, married women would be entitled to their own property and earnings.[78] Barker's paper, the *People*, used dramatic rhetoric, reviling those laws which legalised the 'plundering of the weak', as it saw it. It explained to its readers that 'The law of England declares that the goods of the wife do instantly, on marriage, become the property, and right of the husband.' Barker proclaimed that he would 'simplify the marriage laws of the empire, and give to woman her rights'.[79]

During the 1840s, two publications appeared which explored a feminist perspective on the existing legal system. The radical unitarian journalists took the opportunity to publicise these works, using them to air the subject of women's lack of legal rights. The first of these was Marion Reid's influential publication of 1843, *A Plea for Woman*. An 'excellent book', according to Harriet Martineau, it was primarily concerned with the necessity of enfranchising women, but devoted a whole chapter to exposing the injustice of laws relating to women. Reviewers in the progressive journals supported Reid's arguments wholeheartedly, one of them arguing that 'all must benefit by the ideas it develops'.[80] While Jerrold's paper criticised Reid for her moderation on some points, it agreed with her assessment of English law, that, 'even in matters of property, [she is made] the mere chattel of the man'. The review was then used by the paper as an opportunity to explain various aspects of women's legal position. It harshly criticised the law for forcing women to pay taxes whilst denying them the vote and lambasted the prohibition against married women holding property.[81]

The other influential work in this field was *Essays on Human Rights and their Political Guarantees* (1847) by the American judge, E. P. Hurlbut. Hurlbut delivered a stinging account of English common law, claiming, 'It is the law of the male sex gathering unto themselves dominion and power at the expense of the female. It took its origin in an age of ignorance and barbarism, when the condition of woman was depressed.' *Douglas Jerrold's Weekly Newspaper* praised the work for its protest 'against the injustice which deprives a wife of those natural rights which she possessed before matrimony' and reprinted Hurlbut's chapter on 'The legal consequences of wedlock'.[82] Hurlbut's work also had a considerable influence upon Barbara Leigh Smith at this time. She was introduced to the book by Bessie Parkes, who informed her that it contained a 'chapter on the political and *property* rights of woman which I am sure you would like'. She certainly did, for she quoted directly from the book in her seminal essay of 1854, *A Brief Summary, In Plain Language, of the most Important Laws Concerning Women: Together with a Few Observations Thereon.*[83]

Another means by which radical publications sought to keep their readerships alert to the matter was to publicise the reforms carried out in the United States. Some praised the reform in marital law which was passed in New York in 1848 which entitled married women to own property. 'This', remarked one commentator, 'seems to make marriage a very civil contract indeed.' The Women's Rights Convention which was held in the United States in 1851, and included the demand for equal property rights for wives, provided a similar opportunity.[84]

The other chief method of raising the awareness of their reading public to the legal injustices faced by women was through literature. Douglas Jerrold was concerned with the relationship between legal injustices and conventional literary representations of women. He was angered that, 'Conventional flattery is cheap. It is easy to call women angels because it makes them easier to render slaves. Sugar-plum phrases for the sex, as many as you will – but no equalising statutes.'[85] Consequently, through their own literature, radical unitarians attempted to present what they considered to be the truth of women's character and position. This is seen in the work of Leigh Hunt who had long considered literature to be an appropriate means of explicating women's legal position. His 1839 play, *A Legend of Florence*, was concerned with the plight of women within appalling domestic situations. He declined suggestions to moderate the work, explaining to Alexander Ireland, 'my conscience would not allow me . . . I felt that I had a piece of legislation in my hands, the duty of which I could not give up'.[86] In the 1840s, radical unitarians used *Douglas Jerrold's Shilling Magazine* as a forum in which to present complex legal issues within the accessible format of the short story. In 'My Opposite

Neighbours', 'C. W.' told of a paragon of a wife, tempted into borrowing by a disreputable neighbour. When the wife becomes embroiled in debt, due to the logic of married women's legal position, it is her husband who is thrown into jail – for a crime of which he knew nothing. In the following volume of the journal, William Howitt presented a tale entitled, 'English Scenes and Characters', in which a young woman marries a man who wishes only to live off her earnings. The exploited wife works scandalously long hours, but her husband immediately pockets and spends all her earnings, as would have been his legal right. Even once she has left her husband, and is living with an aunt, he still seeks her out to take her wages.[87]

Goodwyn Barmby used poetry to emphasise the point. The feminist-minded were sensitive to the irony of the marriage service, in which the husband proclaimed 'with all my worldly goods I thee endow', while in reality the wife was forced to hand over all her goods and assets.[88] Thus in his poem, 'Mine is thine', Barmby envisaged a world in which married couples genuinely shared all – not just their love for each other, but labour and material goods too. Poetry was a medium also employed by Dickens in his paper, the *Daily News*. In 1846 Dickens wrote to W. J. Fox, confirming that he would insert 'M. Michelet' in the newspaper – a sonnet which challenged the notion that woman was the property of man.[89]

MAKING HEADWAY: PUBLIC OPINION AND THE LEGAL ESTABLISHMENT

Therefore, it can be seen that during the 1840s, radical unitarians drew upon a rich feminist tradition of discussion on women's legal position. Moreover, they succeeded in developing a variety of methods with which to publicise the issue to a wider audience. Indeed, the ability of the radical unitarians to use progressive ideas in such a way that they might appeal to the more conservative proved to be a vital factor in the development of the nascent women's rights movement. For the desire of feminists to focus upon the subject of married women's legal position in the 1840s was not purely the result of the growth of feminist ideologies in themselves. This process was crystallised by two important factors. One factor, as will be discussed below, was the close relationship the radical unitarians had come to entertain with the legal establishment by this point. But of equal significance was the changing nature of the feminists' relationship with the wider public. The question of married women's legal rights transpired as the one feminist concern which met with sustained (and sympathetic) publicity among a broader reading public. As Anna Jameson later made apparent, while for feminists this issue was but the symbol of the wider oppression of women, the general public tended to perceive it as a specific, isolated abuse.[90] For the activists of the 1840s, who increasingly had their eyes upon accommodating, rather than alienating public opinion, this was no minor consideration. This factor both influenced feminists' presentation of the matter and determined legal reform as their most plausible target.

That the reform of the marriage laws was a question with which even those not prepared to condone the concept of women's rights *per se*, might have sympathy is evident from the treatment of the topic in contemporary journals. *Wade's London Review*, for example, rejected the notion of 'universal rights for women', while accepting that they should be granted greater conjugal rights. Similarly, the *Examiner*, a liberal, but in no sense a feminist newspaper, was prepared to reprint articles from the *Monthly Repository* on this very subject. In its preface to the reprint of Fox's work on Mehetabel Wesley, the *Examiner* spoke of, 'a marriage law, which as at present constituted, is one of the worst of our social institutions'.[91] The esoteric *Westminster Review* admitted that there were 'many faults and defects in the laws which concern women' yet was concerned that feminists were exaggerating their complaints. While it remained critical of those who demanded women's rights, it nevertheless acknowledged their claim that women became 'chattel' upon marriage. In a similar vein, the *Leader* was another publication which called for changes in the marriage law, while often adhering to conservative notions of women.[92]

The ground was set for such a shift in public opinion during the 1830s when a number of successful feminist publications appeared concerning the position of women in other countries. These works achieved considerable success among a wider reading public. The efforts of the Brahmin divine, Rammohun Roy, for one, to alleviate the deleterious legal position of women in India, had alerted many (particularly Unitarians) to consider the legal rights of women at home.[93] In 1837, Harriet Martineau's *Society in America* publicised the subject to an even wider audience. Martineau herself admitted that the work owed much to Anna Jameson's observations on the position of Canadian women.[94] Martineau, who wrote her book at a time when she was becoming increasingly concerned to 'obtain a revision in parliament of all laws regarding Woman', had been instructed to make the book, '*moderate* and *popular*'. However, this did not preclude her from delivering a scathing attack upon English marriage laws, in comparison to those of America. 'In no country', she declared, 'are the marriage laws so iniquitous as in England, and the conjugal relation, in consequence so impaired.' Despite this polemic, the work was a great success among the British public.[95] Martineau herself was thrilled by what she called the 'ridiculous' success of the work. Indeed, Martineau's frank evaluation appears to have touched a nerve among her female readership in England and she was deluged with moving letters from women telling of their oppression under English laws.[96]

More spectacularly, the legal action which Caroline Norton took against her husband, and the resulting Infants' Custody Act in 1839 succeeded once and for all in putting the topic of women's legal rights in the public domain. Norton's tyrannical husband, from whom she was estranged, forbade her contact with her two sons. Moreover, he continued to appropriate her literary earnings. Norton was a celebrated beauty and a well-known figure in London society. That her husband responded to her legal action by suing Lord Melbourne for relations with her, made the story headline news. Meanwhile, Talfourd's bill put the issue of women's legal position on the public agenda for the first time.[97] When the House of Lords debated the bill, Lord Brougham objected to the measure. His extraordinary reasoning for doing so constituted a recognition of the unjust legal situation which women faced. His refusal to vote for the bill was based on a fear that by touching a mass of laws so cruel and indefensible 'all must come down if any part were brought into question'. His speech served to broadcast feminist arguments as he explained that women were, 'but goods and chattel at their husband's mercy' and few were able to escape from marriage through divorce. Furthermore, 'She was excluded from Westminster Hall; and behind her back, by the principles of our jurisprudence.'[98]

In the 1840s, the plight of married women caught the public imagination once more when a number of cases of horrific domestic violence came to public attention.[99] The accessibility of this issue to the less progressive is demonstrated within the radical unitarian circle itself. For it was this aspect of women's legal position which aroused the more conservative members of the set, and they consequently urged their more radically feminist associates to act upon the matter. For example, Dickens's anxieties concerning the ill-protection afforded to wives of violent husbands (in *The Old Curiosity Shop* (1841), Dickens had detailed the suffering of Mrs Quilp at the hands of her brutal husband) came to the fore in 1846, when he wrote to John Forster, 'I hope you will follow up your ideas about the defective state of the law in reference to women.' John Chapman tackled Harriet Martineau in a similar manner, 'Can you propose any remedy for the wife-beating except divorce? The question is pressing for solutions.'[100] While the feminist response to the problem remained limited, it certainly proved to be a public anxiety which feminist journalists could easily tap into. Hence J. S. Mill and Harriet Taylor wrote a series of articles on the subject of male brutality within marriage for the *Morning Chronicle* during the period 1851–2.[101] Journalists on Douglas Jerrold's publications explained the phenomenon using the feminist analysis of the law. They maintained that the effect of men controlling the legislative process had been that women had been made the chattels of men, and a whole array of unjust laws were now arraigned against them. This resulted in the shocking cases of domestic violence which had lately been brought to the public's attention. The paper thundered, 'A man throws a woman, out of a window and though the human chattel, the immortal *goods* sustain a grievous injury, the ruffian escapes with a few weeks solitude from the vanities of the world.'[102]

If the relationship between the radical unitarians and the general public was instrumental in turning feminists' attention towards women's legal rights, so too was the changing nature of the radical unitarian coterie itself – in particular its relationship to the legal establishment. Historians of the women's rights movement have long acknowledged the important role played by certain Unitarian lawyers. Indeed, the first significant piece of legislation to improve women's rights, the Infants Custody Act of 1839, was passed largely thanks to the efforts of the Unitarian lawyer, Thomas Noon Talfourd. It has also been noted that both Talfourd and another important Unitarian lawyer, M. D. Hill, assisted Bodichon with the final draft of her *Brief Summary*. Also, as Shanley argues, crucial to the success of Bodichon's campaign for a change in the married women's property laws was her ability to secure the support of the Law Amendment Society.[103]

However, this historiography is weak on two points. Firstly, it is misleading as to the role played by the Law Amendment Society. In keeping with the tendency of feminist historiography to date the women's rights movement from the 1850s, it assumes that this body only manifested interest in the issue during this decade, and then at the instigation of Bodichon.[104] However, as will be seen below, the Law Amendment Society had begun to make its contribution to the debate on women's legal rights from the mid-1840s. Secondly, these accounts focus exclusively upon the role played by such prominent lawyers as Talfourd and Hill. They ignore the contribution of the lesser-known group of radical unitarian lawyers. As Chapter 3 indicated, during the 1840s, radical unitarian circles profited enormously from the enthusiasm and commitment of reformers such as W. H. Ashurst and his son, William Shaen, William Case, Sidney Hawkes, James Stansfeld and John Humphreys Parry. All of these men were practising lawyers, often acting for progressive or left-wing causes. Stansfeld and Case had earlier revealed an interest in the laws concerning women[105] and certainly as active feminists, the group was able to lend their judicial expertise to the campaigns to reform the legal position of women. This relationship remained a fruitful one in the decades which followed. In 1857, for example, Parry, himself a subscriber to the *English Woman's Journal*, gave Bessie Rayner Parkes vital assistance in her work relating to the Divorce Act. In similar fashion, William Shaen provided legal advice and assistance to feminist campaigns and projects, such as Bedford College, throughout his career.[106] However, as the following discussion will indicate, their important contributions to the efforts to reform women's legal status actually originated in the 1840s.

In London during the 1840s, a circle of utilitarian-influenced politicians and lawyers began to concern themselves increasingly with the issue of law reform. For the radical unitarian lawyers, these utilitarians formed part of a wider network of radical reformers with whom they had much in common. The utilitarian approach to reform was one area which seems to have gained in its appeal for many radical unitarians at this time (as the work of W. B. Adams and T. Southwood Smith testifies).[107] In particular, the utilitarian desire to effect a 'clear and rational' legal system accorded with the reform aims of the early feminists. They argued that if the complex legal position of women was rationalised so that all cases followed the precepts of equity, and not common law, then justice might be effected.[108] Indeed, while the utilitarians were interested in the reform of a whole variety of legal issues, such as the vast complexities of the existing legal system and the treatment of offenders, they also revealed themselves to be sympathetic to feminist concerns. Thus, in 1844, Roebuck raised the need for a 'law which would protect a woman's right to her own earnings, beyond the control of a vicious husband' in the House of Commons.[109] The radical unitarians' links with these radical lawyers and politicians was of considerable significance, for it meant that feminist-minded activists were moving closer to the channels of power, through their contacts with prominent voices in both the law courts and the House of Commons. This was of great importance, for as Mary Shanley has observed, 'The parliamentary history suggests that married women's property measures passed when they received the sponsorship of influential members of the legal profession, and not the account of petitions of lay-people.' It was a point also recognised by contemporary campaigners. As Caroline Norton (quoting from Dickens) exclaimed in her *English Laws for Women of the Nineteenth Century*, '"It won't do to have Truth and Justice on our side: we must have Laws and Lawyers".'[110]

The Law Amendment Society, established in 1844 by the prominent utilitarian, Lord Henry Brougham, functioned as a rallying-point for the interests of the utilitarian reformers. It attracted the support not only of prominent lawyers such as M. D. Hill, but also of many MPs, for example, Joseph Hume, C. P. Villiers, James Heywood, Henry Drummond and Richard Cobden. The society focused upon a range of legal iniquities, being particularly concerned with such topics as land rights, and bankruptcy.[111] However, it also considered the issues of women's legal rights and the necessity of reforming the existing divorce law. While it did not always adopt a feminist perspective,[112] it is clear that there was a radical element within the body which succeeded in putting women's rights issues on their agenda. Certainly the society's proceedings indicate that some important radical unitarians were closely involved with the society, in particular George Dawson, and more significantly, William Shaen, who was the leading figure in this set of radical unitarian lawyers. In addition, many of their close associates, such as E. V. Neale, Frederic Hill (the brother of Matthew Davenport Hill) and Charles Lushington (a president of the feminists' Whittington Club) were prominent.[113] It should also be noted that William Shaen was, in addition, secretary to the Metropolitan and Provincial Law Association which, like the Law Amendment Society, (which strongly supported its work), was beginning to advocate reform of women's legal position during the late 1840s.[114]

The Law Amendment Society took a progressive line on the divorce issue, strongly supporting claims for its reform. Arguing (contrary to the received wisdom) that 'the imposition of spurious offspring is not always a correct test of injury', it also proclaimed that 'The wife's happiness is no less an object of social concern than the husband's.' Furthermore, it recognised that 'public sentiment in this country has become at last favourable to the wife's claim of absolute release from her fetters'. The society also considered such topics as the legal rights of women who survived their husbands, recommending that 'the wife's rights [should] revive in full'.[115] Moreover, towards the end of the 1840s, some members were acknowledging the need for more radical reform of the laws concerning women. For example, in 1849 the society's journal gave a glowing review of John Fraser Macqueen's radical legal treatise on *The Rights and Liabilities of Husband and Wife*. Macqueen questioned whether the present situation, whereby women were alienated from their property on marriage, was 'a fit rule for an enlightened people to adopt'. He went on to argue that the power which the law gave husbands over their wives' 'property and person' was 'one of the most unsatisfactory and inexplicable in modern legislation'. The Law Amendment Society duly applauded the 'sterling merits' of the work.[116]

Therefore, by the mid-1840s, a powerful feminist lobby had evolved which called for a change in the laws regarding marriage. This was a departure noted by contemporaries. In a lecture delivered in 1847, 'On Social Reformation', George Dawson recognised the work of this campaign and declared his wish to join it. He explained that he was a 'firm holder of the equality of women with men', and revealed his exasperation that 'married women still have no claim to property'. He proclaimed that he too wished to protest 'against the system which merges the property of a married woman into that of her husband'.[117] The *Westminster Review* was also keenly aware of the existence of this movement. It acknowledged the feminists' arguments concerning the perpetuation of 'brute force' within male/female relations and referred to those 'agitators' who believed that the laws affecting women should be changed.[118]

Thus, the early feminists succeeded in laying both the intellectual foundations and personnel networks which were to determine the married women's property campaigns of the 1850s. Furthermore, they had played a vital role in encouraging public opinion to look sympathetically upon the matter. By 1856, feminists had gained sufficient public support to gather a petition with over 26 000 signatures, urging for reform.[119] Moreover, when the Matrimonial Causes Bill was debated in Parliament in 1856, Brougham was able to plead that the entire bill might be sent to committee, to consider the property and legal rights of married women in separation, as 'there was much interest in society in the plight of married women'.[120] Perhaps of greater importance was that by the late 1840s, feminist arguments concerning the nature of existing laws were influencing prominent members of the legal profession.

THE ASSOCIATE INSTITUTION

The campaign to alter women's legal position may not have coalesced into major, nationwide activity until the 1850s, but feminist activists of the 1840s did embark upon a sustained effort to reform one particular aspect of the law affecting women: the laws regarding the prostitution trade, and what the reformers perceived as the related issue of the penalties incurred by rapists or seducers. Their endeavours centred around the work of the Associate Institution. This was a crusade which provided feminists with vital experience and confidence for the battles of the 1850s. Moreover, it proved to be an issue that was to persist in feminist debate through to the 1870s. (James Stansfeld, in particular remained active in the cause.)[121] Despite this, this early campaign has never before been fully explored.

The laws concerning prostitution and rape had troubled those interested in women's issues for some time. For example, the Unitarian MP William Smith had sought to change the law in this regard many years earlier. Lucy Aikin had also demonstrated her concern with the subject during the 1830s.[122] However, the radicals' interest in the laws concerning prostitution had intensified by the 1840s, due in part to their own changing ideology. The transition from arguing that the marriage laws caused prostitution, to the idea that often marriage *was* prostitution had had a number of implications. In particular, it necessitated a reappraisal of the position of the prostitute herself. The feminist arguments of the 1830s implied that once the marriage laws had been reformed, the prostitution problem would not persist. Indeed, Owen had commented that the availability of divorce was all that was required to eradicate 'promiscuous intercourse' and sexual crime.[123] However, the later position posed no simple solution. Prostitution was woven into the culture, and the existence of an intransigent prostitution problem had to be faced.

During the 1840s, therefore, radical unitarians came to aid two initiatives to ease the suffering of prostitutes and diminish the scale of prostitution. This development coincided with a growing public awareness of the issue. Sigsworth and Wyke emphasise the point, referring to the fact that 'Victorians in the 1840s and 1850s thought that *both* prostitution and venereal disease were increasing', and Walkowitz has drawn attention to the growing involvement of Evangelicals in the question.[124] Contemporary feminists distanced themselves from any suggestion that their increasing interest in the plight of the prostitute was a product of this development. They stressed instead, at times a little condescendingly, that it was this advance in public opinion which now permitted them to broach the subject.[125] Nevertheless, clearly their projects involving prostitution must be seen within this broader framework. As the nature of these programmes illustrates, it was a testament to their growing relationship with the general public.

In the 1850s, the penitentiary movement exploded on to the scene, with a dramatic rise in the establishment of such institutions. Bristow has noted a new degree of clemency in many of the penitentiaries founded at this time.[126] Certainly, the preceding decade had been a critical period in the formation of public opinion concerning the use and nature of rescue homes. During the 1840s, the radical literati had helped to fuel this debate through their promotion of and association with the more enlightened penitentiaries. Most Evangelical penitentiaries fostered harsh, prison-like environments, many of them imposing a rule of silence. The Evangelical belief in the universality of sin and the need to battle constantly against it, helps to explain the nature of these regimes. They were, claims Fraser Harrison, 'little purgatories'.[127] Unitarians, on the other hand, maintained a Romantic belief in the innate purity of the individual, while recognising that the environment and circumstance might vitiate one's character into evil. The obvious implication was that, if the prostitute's circumstance were changed to a pleasant and conducive setting, she might have a chance to reform herself.

In the ventures which radical unitarians supported, they worked closely with conservative, Evangelical and often illustrious patrons. The result was a new kind of penitentiary, in which the harshest excesses of Evangelical zeal were assuaged by the more humanistic Unitarian approach. Urania Cottage, for example, was established by Dickens, then closely connected with radical unitarians and mainstream Unitarians alike and Angela Burdett-Coutts, a staunch Evangelical. Tensions inevitably arose between them owing to their disparate standpoints. But while Dickens often had to make concessions in order to appease his patron, he persisted in his arrangements to ensure that a home-like environment was created for the inhabitants.[128] In Leicester a similar venture was mounted. The Biggs and Ashurst families supported a largely Episcopalian effort which boasted the Earl and Countess of Howe and the Lord Bishop of Peterborough among its patrons. Eliza Ashurst stressed, like Dickens, that it was to be a home. Meanwhile, in Lincoln another such institution had as its president the Earl of Yarborough, and its secretary was Eliza Ashurst's colleague in the George Sand translations, Edmund R. Larken. Once more the hope was voiced that the women should look upon their new environment as a family.[129]

In their contribution to the penitentiary movement, radical unitarians thus revealed their desire to help 'fallen women'. In so doing they demonstrated a willingness to work with Evangelical and conservative reformers, while consistently positing their own ideological position. This pattern was repeated in their work for the Associate Institution. In the process they were forced to confront the very different assumptions and outlook of their associates. This friction appears to have acted as a catalyst as the radical unitarians came to develop their own uniquely feminist perspective on the role of the law in modern society. Moreover, their alliance with Evangelical thinkers encouraged the feminists to consider alternative means by which women might exert their influence in society.

The Associate Institution for Improving and Enforcing the Laws for the Protection of Women was born of a number of societies which had sprung up during the late 1830s and 1840s to promote female protection.[130] These amalgamated into the Associate Institution in 1844 under whose aegis they sought to legislate against brothels, and those who profiteered from the earnings of 'fallen women'. It boasted many prominent names, including a host of aristocratic vice-presidents, and Lord Robert Grosvenor as chairman. Robert Spooner was a conspicuous member, and they were able to secure the services of the Bishop of Exeter to advance the cause in Parliament. In addition to this powerful caucus of support, the organisation depended upon a network of affiliated institutions, which was set up thanks to the society's considerable propaganda efforts. These provincial organisations were designed to be an opportunity for the country's women to exert themselves on the part of their fallen sisters. It was intended that women should run the societies, although under the directorship of male patrons. They appear to have enjoyed considerable success in raising funds; and the Institution's scions proved active in compiling large petitions, the Liverpool committee producing as many as 60. One of the society's petitions was presented to the Queen in 1846.[131]

For such a large-scale operation, the Associate Institution has received but scanty attention from historians, never attracting more than a few, often caustic lines. Those interested in the issue of philanthropic endeavour have judged it solely in terms of what it achieved, which, in concrete terms was little – they succeeded only in securing the passage of a moderate bill in 1849. Thus Bristow claims, it 'fell flat on its face', and the Institution fares even worse under the hands of Sally Mitchell.[132] Feminist historians have deemed it unworthy of more serious attention, because of its apparent male-dominated and establishment composition. Walkowitz categorises it as an essentially conservative body which adhered to evangelical concepts of prostitution. She claims, 'As conservative reformers, members of the institute were concerned with redressing obvious inequities in order to legitimise male bourgeois supremacy.'[133]

To damn the efforts of the philanthropic male to help women as an inevitably self-centred ploy is perhaps not the most fruitful avenue. This becomes clear if one considers the wide scope and rhetoric which the Institute employed. The opening address of the organisation's journal, the *Female's Friend*, declared 'That deep and serious WRONGS are inflicted upon WOMAN may be proved to demonstration.' The Institution explained its wish that its own work would be 'only the commencement of a more general improvement in the laws for the benefit of women'. Moreover, the *Female's Friend* expressed its desire that 'The rights of woman will be duly regarded.'[134] There was no clear line of demarcation between the language of contemporary feminists and that of the men attempting to bolster their 'male bourgeois supremacy'. Indeed one of the most fascinating aspects of the Institution is that it proved to be a joint collaboration between radical unitarian feminists and conservative churchmen and statesmen – a fact which has been completely overlooked in the previous literature.

The correspondence of William Shaen sheds considerable light on the organisation's affiliation with feminist reformers. He explained to his sister how, 'We mean to work with them as long as we can or they will let us.'[135] Inevitably the partnership could often result in friction. Many feminists appear to have been uneasy about identifying themselves too closely with such a group. Eliza Meteyard complained that the Institution pandered to the wishes of its parliamentary sponsors: 'The main point of the bill already introduced into parliament seems directed against the traders in seduction; but why not against the seducers themselves? Did the framers fear, that it would curtail, too much aristocratic license?' Shaen was also chary of the Institution's make-up. It was, he regretted, 'the right thing by the wrong party'. Nevertheless, he manifested a genuine desire to put the expertise of himself and his friends at their disposal.[136] The legal training of this feminist group proved particularly helpful to the society. In the April issue of the society's journal, James Stansfeld wrote an article explaining the legal issues surrounding the proposed bill.[137]

While the work of feminists such as Shaen and Stansfeld was not publicised by either the society or themselves, other activists played a more public role in promoting the Institution's aims. This was especially true of the Leicester businessman William Biggs (Matilda Ashurst's brother-in-law), who proved a tireless campaigner for the cause. He wrote frequently on the issue and brought the subject to public notice in Leicester on several occasions, even bringing the matter before the town council.[138] Biggs was also an instrumental figure at the Institution's public meetings, where he was often joined on these occasions by a fellow radical, James Silk Buckingham.[139] Biggs was not the only product of radical unitarian circles to lend support to the campaign. As well as enjoying the aid of such reformers as Caroline Stansfeld and James Haughton,[140] the Institution was given considerable publicity by the *Leicestershire Mercury* (which had long been sympathetic to feminist issues),[141] the *People's Journal* and *Douglas Jerrold's Weekly Newspaper*.

With such an amalgam of influences supporting the work of the Associate Institution, it was inevitable that conflicting ideas often arose. At times the radicals had to fight to keep the more enlightened aspects of the question on the agenda. For example, many of the Evangelical members often blamed the moral laxity of the women themselves for becoming prostitutes. Hence, one member urged women to keep a close scrutiny over the personal lives of their servants, to prevent their moral lapse.[142] By contrast, the radicals were anxious to stress the environmental and social pressures which often drove women to such measures. They therefore considered the more disturbing facts of prostitution, such as the collusion of other women and the family in encouraging girls into prostitution.[143]

The Associate Institution also brought to a head the feminists' debate on the issue of protection. The promotional work of the Associate Institution was known as the 'Protection of Woman question'. To modern sensibilities the notion of protecting women strikes uneasily on the ear, as it seems to ring with conservative connotations. However, most radicals of the 1840s drew a distinction between the kinds of protection woman might be afforded. The first, which they deprecated, was the code of chivalric manners. They believed this harkened back to the practices of a more violent age, when women were subject to men because of their superior physical force and the consequent individual protection they could offer. However, in the 'modern age', feminists believed this had evolved into the influential, but patronising mode of chivalric behaviour. The feminists argued that the chivalric rhetoric concerning the need for men to protect women was laughable. As Grimstone, her barbed pen ever at the ready, berated in her 1835 essay, 'The Protective System of Morals', 'From what is she to be protected? Wolves and tigers do not prowl upon the highways. . . . From what then has man to protect woman? From his own violence, injustice and rapacity.' Catherine Barmby proved equally vociferous on the issue, suggesting that men's self-appointed role as the protectors of women further exacerbated women's poor social and cultural position, 'He has declared himself fully and entirely her protector; and from hence he has inferred, that it was needless to allow her to form any decided opinions as to what would be the most beneficial for her sex.'[144] Moreover, as fellow radical J. B. Syme appreciated, there was an ugly undercurrent which lay beneath men acting as protectors, for it revealed the prevalence of a violent mentality, 'There was something of force, of physical force behind it.' And, as John Stuart Mill had pointed out in the 1830s, 'the time has come when women may aspire to something more than merely to find a protector'.[145]

However, the feminists proposed two ways in which women might be protected. The first was to give women the means to protect themselves. This, they believed, might be secured by instructing women in sexual matters so that they would be more alert to potentially dangerous situations. Within the Associate Institution this discussion formed part of a wider debate which raged over the issue of female education. The Evangelicals believed that society would be cured of prostitution by better educating women for their childrearing roles. This, they suggested, would act as a great social panacea.[146] However, the feminists argued much more specifically that the sort of education required was sex education. As one supporter of the Associate Institution put it, 'certain physical laws and the consequences of certain physical acts, should be early and properly explained to youth'. Another sympathiser urged that the 'rising female generation' should be fully acquainted 'with all the trials and temptations which await their entrance into the world'.[147] Adhering to the Unitarian faith in the purity of the soul, the feminists maintained that it was female ignorance of sexual matters and the motives which often lay behind male attentions, that made them easy prey for men with dishonourable intentions. Indeed, it is interesting to note that within contemporary discourse, the concepts of 'seduction' and 'rape' were often used synonymously,[148] a convention the early feminists did not challenge.

They thus perpetuated the idea that prostitutes were seduced innocents. By the 1850s this stereotype had become a common image – even though, as modern historians have shown, it by no means accorded with the reality.[149] Professor Cominos has asserted that the representation of the prostitute as a fallen innocent was the product of a conservative ideology which denied that women might experience sexual passion.[150] However, the study of radical unitarian writing in the 1840s suggests that the stereotype was most relentlessly publicised initially by writers who not only acknowledged female passion,[151] but who deprecated sexual ignorance and so urged for sex education. Indeed, many feminists gave active support to the cause of female sexual education. The Ashurst family, for example, strongly supported Mrs Martin's course of women-only lectures on 'The Physiology of Women'.[152]

The second, and more fundamental proposal which feminists made for ensuring women's protection, was to grant them legislative protection. The Evangelicals tended to perceive the concept of women's legal protection in a narrow, paternalistic sense, with their concern to protect potential, defenceless victims. Such a view had been instilled into the judiciary by Blackstone, who considered that the common law, which so militated against the rights of women, was for their own protection.[153] In contrast, while, as we saw in Chapter 3, feminists were distrustful of those laws which 'overlegislated' for women and served to limit their opportunities (for example, factory legislation), they did campaign for laws which might ensure women greater independence by liberating them from oppressive social customs. This particular notion of protection came to inform many of the chief areas of feminist concerns, including employment, marriage and property.[154]

For the radical unitarians these ideas were inextricably related to their views on the role of the state. They dreamed of a world where the old feudal notion of the strong arm of the law had been superseded by the emergence of a truly liberal state. Goodwyn Barmby had declared his satisfaction that, 'While the Barbarian held the law in his own hands, the civilizationist or the civilian has given it up to society.'[155] Yet as his colleagues went on to argue, the ideal state had not been inaugurated as the relationship between society and the law had not yet reached its full potential. It was to be a state which, far from being merely *laissez-faire*, formulated laws under which every citizen was protected. W. J. Linton explained this concept in terms of the 'organised state' in which politics, art and literature were harmonised to this aim.[156] The protection given to the individual citizen would be buttressed by the state provision of education for all, so that individuals might exercise their own judgement and educated reasoning. (They were tireless campaigners in the cause of national education, for example.)[157] The evolution of such a concept was a vital moment in the development of feminist thought. It meant that feminists were not only campaigning to repeal abuses, they were fighting for the very function of the law to be changed.

The work of the Associate Institution also marked another departure in the growth of the women's rights movement. For the first time, feminists in widely-read journals were urging women to rise up and free their fellow women. Whereas the radical unitarian campaign to reform the Chartist movement in the late 1830s and early 1840s had not encouraged female involvement, by targeting the issue of prostitution in later years, feminists isolated a viable means by which women might extend their experience and influence. In so doing, they began to appeal to a sense of female solidarity. From the mid-1840s there had been a growing tendency among even conservative circles to elicit female support for various philanthropic causes by drawing upon a notion of womanly concern for their fellow women. This had been at the heart of much of the rhetoric which urged women to join the anti-slavery movement.[158] The Associate Institution followed in this path, appealing directly to women. Their meetings were often attended by large numbers of women, and the Institution looked especially to female help in the formation of its auxiliary societies. Moreover, the *Female's Friend* targeted a female audience, and printed many pleas exhorting the country's women to take up the cause of the Associate Institution.[159]

However, in the hands of the radical unitarians, the society's rhetoric concerning female involvement assumed a revolutionary tone, urging for concerted female action to lift the chains of oppression by which women were bound: 'If women once threw themselves heartily into the business of emancipating those of their own sex who are slaves to a worse set of masters than any negro slaveowners, the day would not be distant when the object of the Associate Institution would be gained.'[160]

If this rhetoric is compared to the early feminists' stance on female political action, an interesting pattern emerges. They eschewed direct female involvement in the traditionally male-dominated sphere of political action. But they did condone female initiatives when they derived from extending traditional bounds of female concern – such as philanthropy. It was hoped that encouraging women to undertake such work would not only prove beneficial to the rescued – it would also be a vital means of raising the characters and abilities of those women who acted as rescuers. The radical unitarians evidently felt that such a policy might prove a more acceptable means of advocating female action to a mainstream audience. (Certainly they did not challenge the strict rules surrounding female involvement which the society instituted to ensure respectability.)[161]

However, the radicalism of these ideas is made apparent when the feminists' call for women to plunge themselves into relieving the plight of the prostitute is seen in the context of existing philanthropic efforts on the part of women. As Prochaska and Summers have demonstrated, middle-class women made a vital contribution to social welfare throughout the nineteenth century, by dint of their philanthropic endeavours.[162] Moreover, Olive Banks and Jane Rendall have recognised that the evangelical notion of womanly philanthropy often fed into feminist ideas concerning the need for women to extend their sphere. Nevertheless, to rescue the prostitute was a rather different matter. Olive Banks explains that 'at this time virtually all rescue workers were men'.[163] As Prochaska has admitted, even 'some of the keenest supporters of charitable work drew the line at female volunteers visiting brothels and roaming the streets in search for abandoned sinners'. Bristow corroborates the point by quoting W. R. Greg's article from the *Westminster Review* of 1850, 'It is discreditable to a woman even to be supposed to know their [prostitutes'] existence.'[164] It was not until the 1860s that women undertook such work in any great numbers.[165]

The call of the radicals was, then, a progressive move. They wanted to push aside the barriers which had hitherto circumscribed women's charitable ventures and to encourage women to undertake work which would stretch their capabilities. Certainly, Stansfeld placed women's involvement with the Associate Institution in the context of the need to widen their 'confined sphere'.[166] The radicals envisaged that as a consequence of their work for the Institution, women would be inspired to plunge themselves into the ghetto haunts of the prostitutes and offer them new lives. For Eliza Lynn, to embrace such activity could indicate a new stage in woman's development. Clara's ultimate triumph in *Realities* comes when she uses

her new-found courage and independence (which her egalitarian relationship with Glynn has given her) to visit the wretched Emma Vaughan in the
slums. On her way there, Clara is informed that even the police refuse to
venture into that area of the city. For a single, unprotected young woman
to undertake such a mission is portrayed as a triumph of real Christian
values over societal conventionalism and prejudice.[167] Such a concern
lay at the heart of radical unitarian ethics. As Shaen wrote of the work
of the Associate Institution, 'the only real help is the practice of Christ's
doctrine'.[168]

The radical unitarian publicity on this issue appears to have met with
success among the more progressive of their audience. The young Bessie
Rayner Parkes was one who did decide to involve herself in missionary
work among the prostitutes of the Westminster slums. Parkes referred
enthusiastically to the influence of 'Unitarian and liberal women in London' in encouraging her to take this line of action.[169]

Clearly, by the late 1840s, thought and strategy within feminist circles
had progressed considerably. The progressive tenor of the early feminists
was increasingly modulated by their desire to present their ideas in a form
which would prove palatable to the general public. By targeting the issue
of women's legal position they were able to present a more acceptable
face of feminism, while their vibrant debates of the concomitant issues
provided the intellectual foundation for the more sophisticated and ambitious campaigns which were to follow in the next decade. Moreover, their
emphasis on the need to reform marriage (rather than merely advocating
divorce) as a means of emancipating women was especially shrewd. Earlier feminists had been lambasted for their supposed antipathy to marriage
and the espousal of 'free love' doctrines. This public image, set into motion
by the instability and unconventionalism of Wollstonecraft's private life,
and the connection in the public mind between feminism and the French
Revolution, had been fostered by the radical sexual doctrines of some
early Owenites.[170] In contrast, the radical unitarian feminists sought to
project a message which would prove meaningful to a mainstream audience. Certainly, the feminists were increasingly successful in their bids to
influence public opinion. By the early 1850s many of the radical ideas
perpetrated by these circles had become assimilated into mainstream public
opinion. (Their insistence on perceiving prostitutes as seduced innocents,
for example, greatly contributed to the realignment in public perceptions
of the prostitute.)[171] By the end of the decade, women's rights advocates
were no longer perceived as merely an extreme and eccentric minority.
They were serious social reformers, with whom even the conservative and
famous were prepared to collaborate.

5 The Whittington Clubs

In their campaigns for female suffrage and women's legal rights, radical unitarian feminists demonstrated their belief that in order to fully liberate women, legislative change had to come hand-in-hand with a freeing of the cultural shackles which cramped their minds and characters. As ever, this led the radical unitarians to focus upon education, as the only true guarantor of lasting and profound change.

During the 1840s, the vibrant debates on education which had preoccupied feminist circles over the previous years began to crystallise into action. The late 1840s were a fertile period for the development of female education, with the establishment of both Queen's College and Bedford College. The latter was a largely Unitarian project, instigated by Elizabeth Jesser Reid. A familiar figure to many of the circles discussed in this book, Reid was, as R. K. Webb puts it, 'an enthusiastic Unitarian who had followed W. J. Fox out of the faith'.[1] While some, such as Grimstone and Lady Byron, dreamed of an even more radical establishment,[2] Reid enlisted support from many literary feminists, and also from the younger generation of feminists who were beginning to emerge from their midst.[3]

These ventures have been well-documented in other histories.[4] However, one aspect of educational history notably absent from accounts of the women's rights movement is that of adult education. Such an analysis proves immensely valuable. The customary historiography of women during the nineteenth century has tended to focus upon the limiting culture they faced. This has often had the effect of delivering a monolithic and static view of the contemporary ideologies regarding women. However, as the history of adult education indicates, in reality, public opinion on the question was ever-shifting. This constant discussion and realignment provided a fertile ground in which feminists' ideas could often prosper. Although June Purvis has recently provided an excellent study of women in adult education institutes, she does not focus in any depth on the role they played in the emerging women's rights movement. Nor does Purvis consider the radical unitarians' unique, feminist experiment in adult education – the Whittington Club and Metropolitan Athenæum.[5] It is this project which forms the subject of this chapter.

The club was launched in 1846. Its eponymous hero, Dick Whittington, was extolled for providing a role model of self-improvement and honest exertion. The club was to furnish a cordial, home-like environment, in which working people might follow Whittington's example, through seeking rational recreation and amusement. It was equipped with libraries, reading rooms, lecture halls, and dining rooms and it was later to boast drawing rooms to host the club's soirées.[6] In addition, the club provided a venue for many progressive causes, such as the vegetarian society.[7] However, the club's most radical facet was its desire to inaugurate a new cultural and educational dawn for women. Indeed, this ambitious project gave feminists the opportunity to put their new-found relationship with the public to the test.

Despite the Whittington Club's grand feminist ambitions, its place within the development of the British women's rights movement has been completely ignored. Given the prominence of feminist campaigners within both its establishment and its running, this is somewhat surprising. Radical unitarian reformers were the very linchpin of the organisation. Douglas Jerrold was the club's president and William Shaen its chairman. W. H. Ashurst and his son acted as the club's solicitors, and the club's vice-presidents included John Bowring, the Cowden Clarkes, Charles Dickens, R. H. Horne, the Howitts, Giuseppe Mazzini, Dr Southwood Smith and Frank Stone; as well as figures closely connected to them such as R. Monckton Milnes, W. C. Macready and T. P. Thompson. On the club's council sat Matilda Hays, Eliza Meteyard, the Humphrey Parrys, the Prideauxs, the Stansfelds and Clementia Taylor; as well as close associates the Novellos, for example.[8]

The only existing monograph on the Whittington Club has come from Christopher Kent, who has proffered a thorough and wide-ranging analysis of the club.[9] Kent does pay tribute to the radical policy of the club regarding women. However, when the club is considered in the context of the radical unitarian feminists, the significance of its feminist policies becomes striking. Furthermore, in common with other historians, Kent does not give serious attention to the existence of the Whittington Club's sister institutions, which were established in Birmingham and Liverpool (a fourth was planned for Paisley). While these institutes were not so exclusively the brain-child of radical unitarian feminists, as was the case in London, they nevertheless followed the Whittington Club in propounding liberal practices towards women. Of the three, the London institute was by far the most successful. It thrived during its early years, and then managed to continue until 1873, albeit in a modified form. The other clubs were beset by major financial problems. The Birmingham Whittington Club appears to have disbanded in 1848 and the Roscoe Club in Liverpool failed in 1850 – never succeeding in fulfilling the cooperative principles of the radical unitarians.[10]

However, despite the long-term failure of these institutions, the extensive feminist propaganda which surrounded the clubs in their infancy has not before been exploited and, as this chapter reveals, provides a rich source of untapped material for gauging the state of feminist ideologies at this time. Also, the extant sources provide the opportunity to trace the reception of feminist ideas within the club. Indeed, the club's members provide a useful, and hitherto neglected sample audience for the reception of feminist thought.

AWAKENING MINDS – ADULT EDUCATION AND THE ADMISSION OF WOMEN

By the 1840s, the cultural map of England was punctuated by a myriad of self-improvement societies, mechanics' institutes and literary institutions. Such societies were heralded by Unitarians of all shades as a triumph of rational recreation. Both mainstream Unitarians and their radical counter-parts shared a belief in the need for cultural provision for the people and consistently supported schemes for public parks, libraries, museums and galleries.[11] For the Unitarians, adult educational institutes were the stars in this cultural firmament. Their belief in the importance of education and the emphasis which such institutions placed upon the mores of self-improve-ment, inclined them to look most favourably upon such projects. In par-ticular, Unitarians proved active in establishing and patronising mechanics' institutes. Indeed, the first of these was established in Birmingham in 1789, in connection with Joseph Priestley's church. These institutions were designed to provide mechanics with a forum where they could further their knowledge of their craft.[12]

However, the mechanics' institutes came under frequent pressure from many radical contemporaries, who envisaged a far more liberal and polit-ically informed model for educational institutes. Within progressive polit-ical culture an alternative to the mechanics' institutes soon began to emerge. The Owenite movement posited its own blueprint for educational en-deavour with the establishment of their Halls of Science. These sought to function as family cultural centres, where not only men, but women and children too might enjoy rational recreation and education. In cities such as Birmingham, Sheffield and Manchester, these Halls were frequently established as radical alternatives to local mechanics' institutes, many of which excluded women.[13] The Owenite example appears to have inspired other left-wing initiatives. William Lovett's National Association placed great stock in the formation of its People's Halls. Although Lovett's pol-icies on female education were far from egalitarian, these organisations, similar in conception to the Owenite institutes, promised education and recreation to adults and children alike.[14] The political radicals thus shared a vision of the extensive role which educational institutes might play. They were community centres which might foster closer family ties through enjoyable recreation and socialising. Yet they would maintain their political edge through insisting upon extending the education of working people, as a means of endowing them with greater power.

Within this debate, radical unitarians concentrated upon pursuing a specifically feminist line. They followed William Thompson's lead in calling for mechanics' institutes to open their doors to women.[15] They concentrated their attention upon the benefits which female admission might accrue to the marital relationship. They believed it would further their desire for marriage to be thought of as a bond of mutual benefit which would endow both partners with intellectual and moral pabulum. Mary Leman Grimstone, as ever, led the way. In the *Tatler* in 1832, she published a poem entitled 'The Poor Woman's Appeal to her Husband', in which the crux of the protagonist's plea was, 'I would ask some share of hours that you at clubs bestow – Of knowledge that *you* prize so much, might I, not something know?'[16] Grimstone confessed that the poem was 'not written without tears, and it flowed from the master-motive of my mind, the elevation of my own sex in the social scale'. This poem evoked a powerful response from the readership, and in particular from those literary feminists who were to play such a crucial role in the formation of the Whittington Club. Charles Cowden Clarke was so struck by it that he wrote to Grimstone (whom he did not then know), claiming it had awakened his mind. This evidently delighted Grimstone, who rejoiced that someone 'thinks so perfectly with me'.[17] The poem went on to become an important text in feminist circles, and was often reprinted.[18] Meanwhile, the *Tatler* continued to foster debate on the issue. The following month it declared its willingness to encourage discussions as to whether women should be permitted entrance to coffee houses.[19]

In the radical unitarian journals of the 1840s, the issue of women's right to participate in adult education was a persistent theme. In particular, as will be seen below, the establishment of the Whittington Club provided the opportunity for constant publicity and propaganda on the subject. This sympathetic environment enabled Grimstone to continue to press for the admission of women to self-improvement clubs. Thus, in a story for the *People's Journal*, she detailed the marriage of a young couple, Philip and Susan. Philip went out every night to self-improvement organisations, but 'it never occurred to him it was her equal right'. Susan becomes nervous and delicate due to the 'dull unvarying round of her domestic duties, with her spirit full of capabilities unexplored and unexpanded'. Susan enters a spiral of atrophy, and eventually dies. In a secret diary, found after her death, Susan urges her husband, should he remarry, to spend time with his wife and to ensure she is stimulated and educated.[20]

By the 1840s, the feminist lobby appears to have been winning the argument for women's right to access to adult education. As Herstein notes, by the mid-1840s, there was a perceptible change in public attitudes towards women's education.[21] While mechanics' institutes had begun to admit women from the 1830s, this trend accelerated markedly during the following decade. Nationally, female members formed but 9.4 per cent of the total membership of mechanics' institutes. However, in individual institutes, in Glasgow and Plymouth, for example, women comprised a sizeable proportion of the membership, thus proving that female membership could often prove to be an extremely popular policy.[22]

The radical unitarian journalists eagerly promoted and advertised the new trend for admitting women. Ida, of the *People's Press*, 'rejoiced' in the 'various societies springing up on every hand' which promoted and encouraged women.[23] The radical unitarians particularly praised the efforts of such bodies as the Edinburgh Mechanics' Institute, the Bolton Essay and Discussion Class and the Winlaton Literary and Mechanics' Institution, all of which put the woman question high on their agendas, holding regular debates and lectures on the topic. Eliza Cook, the Howitts and George Dawson all supported institutes such as the Kentish Town literary institution, which opened its doors to women.[24] Figures closely associated with the radical unitarians, Edward Bulwer Lytton and Matthew Davenport Hill, for example, also made public pronouncements on the admission of women to adult education. Charles Dickens proved particularly active on this front, heralding the policy of Leeds and Liverpool mechanics' institutes for providing female education.[25] Dickens also praised the athenæums for their policy towards female admission. It was an issue to which he had drawn particular attention in his address to the Glasgow Athenæum in 1847. Similarly, when presiding at the first soirée of the Manchester Athenæum in 1843, he had also celebrated the admission of women to the club's proceedings.[26] The policy of the Manchester Athenæum towards female admission had certainly attracted considerable publicity. Disraeli, addressing the Athenæum in 1844, claimed that female members were largely responsible for the Athenæum's success.[27]

The manner in which female admission was treated at the Manchester Athenæum suggests that from the mid-1840s, such policies were seen by participants as a natural corollary to new liberal attitudes towards women. Lord Morpeth, speaking at one of the Athenæum's great soirées, placed the admission of women within the context of the need to make female education 'Sound, substantial and enlightened'. This he related to the position women might assume within society, as civilisation progressed. Others connected with the Athenæum, including its secretary, Edward Worthington, were also active in promoting adult education for women within the city.[28] The Birmingham Whittington Club was even more explicit, explaining its wish to admit women in the context of 'the now-recognised educational wants of woman'. The Edinburgh Mechanics' Institute similarly welcomed the growing trend for female participation in adult education, claiming 'we shall ever esteem it as one of the most promising and hopeful signs of the times that the women of our class are beginning to take as lively an interest in educational institutions as the men'.[29]

By the 1840s, to be seen to admit women to an educational society could even be used as a publicity tactic. It demonstrated that the institute was open, liberal and 'modern'. Hence, the Roscoe Club in Liverpool actually advertised its policies towards female members as far more liberal than they really were. While its original advertisements promised women access to the 'Lectures, Concerts and Soirées as the other members enjoy', in private session, the club's council agreed that women should only be permitted admission to the library and lecture hall; and even this failed to be implemented.[30] Certainly, many societies claimed that female admission was vital to the success of their institute, even though the actual number of women members may have been very low.[31] This suggests that the policy of female admission was in itself an attractive and 'sellable' aspect of their policy.

Female admission to adult education in the 1840s, therefore, suggests a considerable advance in public attitudes towards women. Nevertheless, the picture is complicated further by the fact that the facilities on offer to women in these educational establishments varied tremendously. The terms and assumptions which dictated female admission to the different institutes testify to the wide spectrum of cultural values and ideologies which operated even within this comparatively liberal environment. In order to tease out such disparities, it is necessary to consider the social status and cultural functions which differentiated the various types of institutes.

Those institutions which catered for the lower ranks of the working class tended to provide a basic non-gendered education. This was the policy instituted in the lyceums of Manchester in the early 1840s. Founded by the Unitarian, James Heywood, these clubs were distinguishable by their low subscription rates, which, it was hoped, would make them more accessible than many of the mechanics' institutes. They were established to 'facilitate and promote the moral and intellectual improvement of both sexes by means of a newsroom, library, reading-room, classes, concerts, discussion, and literary recreative purposes'. Workers' wives were encouraged to attend and a home-from-home environment was sought. At the Ancoats Lyceum in 1842, 133 males, and 55 females were recorded to have attended the reading, writing and arithmetic classes.[32] A similar project was launched in Birmingham – the People's Institution. This too was characterised by low subscriptions – one shilling per quarter or one penny per week. In addition, it offered free classes and lectures to children and adults alike. During 1847–8 at its free evening classes for the instruction of both sexes, 20 per cent of the participants were women.[33]

A very different educational policy prevailed in many of the mechanics' institutes. This must be seen within the context of the changing nature of these institutes themselves. In the course of the 1820s, it had become increasingly clear that the mechanics' institutes were appealing to a very different audience than that for which they were intended. Contrary to expectations, they were usually patronised by the lower middle classes, and in particular, by shop workers and clerks. This audience tended to demand recreational facilities and entertainments as much as scientific instruction. Thus, the mechanics' institutes soon came to serve a very different cultural and social function. J. F. C. Harrison notes that 'the majority of clerks and shopkeepers who frequented the institutes wanted not science and the discipline of study, but the opportunity of acquiring a little of the cultural elegance which they had noted as a peculiar adornment of their social superiors'.[34] Certainly, Anderson's study of Victorian clerks suggests that an underlying feature of their mentality was a desire to emulate their employers.[35]

The desire of the lower middle classes to acquire the manners and culture of their social betters encroached equally upon their aspirations for their womenfolk. Thus, as the social composition of mechanics' institutes' membership changed, so did the sorts of facilities which they came to offer to their female members. While many institutes did continue to cater for working-class needs,[36] Manchester Mechanics' Institute, which attracted a middle-class and artisanal membership, was typical of the trend to appeal to middle-class tastes. In 1845, it launched a scheme of female education which it hailed as 'liberal and comprehensive'. This instruction transpired to be not a 'useful' or intellectual training, but one which might endow its students with the superficial polish and graces demanded by middle-class convention. It trained women in the accomplishments of French, drawing, music, dancing, millinery and dressmaking. It thus turned out women who might function as the perfect social accessories to up-and-coming young men. The classes proved very popular among the female members – boasting an average annual attendance of 120.[37]

During the 1840s a different type of adult education institute, the athenæum, began to enjoy a renaissance. The first athenæums had sprung up in the 1790s, again largely under Unitarian auspices.[38] They aimed to cater for precisely those social classes which the mechanics' institutes had come to attract. Thus the Manchester Athenæum was promoted as 'an institution for the benefit of the tradesmen, commercial assistants and apprentices, professional students, clerks, of this very populous and flourishing town'.[39] Despite the input of progressive thinkers such as Morpeth, Alexander Ireland[40] and Worthington, the Manchester Athenæum, in common with others of its type, was often chararacterised by a conservative view of women's propensities. This tended to assume that the female sex should be equipped, not for useful endeavour in their own right, but to enhance and uplift social intercourse. The Glasgow Athenæum was typical in offering 'French and Italian lessons for the ladies'. Thus, Disraeli, addressing the Manchester Athenæum in 1844, celebrated the 'refining graces of the softer sex' within the institution.[41] Furthermore, despite the glowing publicity which surrounded the admission of women to the Manchester Athenæum, they were not actually granted full membership. They were permitted only to subscribe to a reduced form of membership (also open to men), which allowed them the use of the library and admission to the lectures only. It was not until 1844 that women were also entitled to attend the Essay and Discussion Society. Female 'members' were not entitled to sit on any of the Athenæum's committees, and thus were denied a voice in the management and policy of the institution. Instead, they were permitted merely to sit on a ladies' council.[42]

'MEETING THE GREAT SEXUAL QUESTION'

Therefore, when the radical unitarian feminists launched the Whittington Club, they were entering a field which was already rife with conflicting ideas concerning the role of women. Behind them lay a heterogeneous and often discrepant tradition: the Owenite Halls of Science which advocated equal gender participation and stressed the importance of their institutes as a basis for familial recreation; the Chartist People's Halls, which welcomed men and women alike in their endeavour to educate the people in preparation for political responsibility, but where women did not achieve equal educational status. Then there was the example of the lyceums – with their non-gendered education; the mechanics' insitutes whose policy towards women tended to vacillate according to the sociological make-up of their members; and finally, the athenæums which admitted women for their supposedly refining influence.

In name, the Whittington Club and Metropolitan Athenæum placed itself within the tradition of such bodies as the Glasgow and Manchester Athenæums. Certainly in their publicity for the Whittington Club, its promoters claimed that they were adopting the plan of the Manchester Athenæum.[43] However, the Whittington Club's policy on female membership far extended the perameters of most athenæums. In contrast to the practice adopted by the Manchester Athenæum, the ladies' council at the Whittington Club was formed in addition to the 'admission of women to every privilege of the institution'.[44] In this, the Whittington Club was extremely progressive; it was not until the 1860s that such a policy became widespread.[45]

In reality, the Whittington's feminists seem to have derived inspiration not from the athenæums, but from the more progressive educational projects. Indeed, many of the club's founding members drew directly upon their radical roots. Perhaps most noticeably, many of the Whittington Club's originators had been closely involved with Owenite culture during the 1830s,[46] which, as we have seen, offered a radical alternative to the customary male elitism of mechanics' institutes. Robert Owen was himself at the founding meeting of the Whittington Club and attended some of its subsequent soirées. Southwood Smith's daughter and son-in-law, Caroline and James Hill, had entertained important links with Owenite culture and had eagerly promoted the Owenite Halls of Science.[47] In addition, such prominent club members as Goodwyn and Catherine Barmby and William Ashurst had all been prominent in Owenite activities during the late 1830s and early 1840s. Catherine Barmby had long praised the new social customs which the Owenites often adopted, such as mixed-sex public dining. Such practices, she believed, augured a new age for female emancipation. For Goodwyn Barmby, the concept of the club had an even more profound significance. He believed it to be an essential prerequisite for engendering the consummation of society. In a speech to the Communist Temple at Marylebone in 1841, he stated that the club and lodging house formed the first of four stages which would inaugurate the coming of the perfect communist state.[48]

A second tradition which club members drew upon was that of 'New Move' Chartism. The group of young radical unitarian lawyers who played such an important part in the formation of the National Association came (in some cases with their wives) to be instrumental members of the Whittington Club. William Shaen, for example, became one of the club's leading activists. The National Association, 'with its library, coffee house, high subscription',[49] bore many resemblances to the Whittington Club. Yet the Whittington Club gave the feminists the opportunity to effect the more liberal policies towards women which had not triumphed within the National Association.[50]

The input of these 'Education Chartists' into the Whittington Club movement was perfectly in keeping with its political tenor. In the public mind the Chartist and Whittington Club movements seem to have been closely linked. Some observers in Birmingham were anxious that the Whittington Club there might serve to spread Chartist principles. Such fears were not unfounded. At the London club's discussion class, the majority accepted the motion, 'Is the adoption of the People's Charter Desirable?'[51] Moreover, despite the club's protestations that it was not a political institution,[52] the progressive political ideas of its founders permeated the club's structure and running. This was of course implicit in their adoption of the Dick Whittington legend. The example of an ordinary man raising himself to political power was a potent message. Jerrold had himself urged his readers to consider the 'second and more hidden meaning' in the Whittington tale.[53] The hope that the lower classes might elevate themselves was the first step in the founders' agenda of universal suffrage. Dr Raphall, a founder member of the Birmingham Whittington Club, was explicit on this point when addressing a public meeting at the town hall. 'Who, the most humble among them', he asked, 'might not, some day or other, by the force of talent, and the power of education, hope to take his place in the Senate House?' A subsequent speaker, T. Ragg echoed this call, as he stressed the interdependency of education and suffrage.[54]

There were two levels at which it was hoped the Whittington Club might contribute to the political education of its members. Firstly, it was hoped that people might utilise the club's facilities to improve their education. This would enable them to exercise their franchise wisely and eventually, fit them to rule. Secondly, it sought to promote political awareness more directly, through the establishment of a quasi-parliament within the club. This introduced club members to the way in which parliament functioned. They performed their own sessions of parliament at which contemporary issues were debated.[55] This injection of politics into the club was the culmination of a long struggle on the part of middle-class radicals to persuade mechanics' institutes to become more politically conscious.[56] More crucially, in the Whittington Club, women were permitted to participate equally in such politically conscious activities. They were expected to share in the responsibility of governing the club and were exhorted to sit on its councils and management committees.[57]

The club revealed its originators' close connections with left-wing ideologies in another important way. Within radical unitarian ideology the club played a crucial role as an experiment in cooperation. The club's own gazette declared that 'The Whittington Club is essentially a co-operative institution' and the club was often discussed at events such as the Co-operative League soirées. Indeed, 'active members of the Whittington Club' were prominent on the platform on these occasions.[58] Through adopting cooperative principles, the club hoped it might succeed in being self-supporting.[59] It was seen in Chapter 2 that, in their plans for associated housing, the radical unitarians entertained a vision of a new moral society built upon the extension of the family from its sanctified hearth into the public sphere. However, these schemes had not met with the success that they had wished for. Therefore, in the Whittington Club they sought to illustrate how such principles might operate on a limited scale. It formed part of their efforts to demonstrate that, far from being a communist threat, cooperative principles might enhance family life, and help considerably with living costs. As *Douglas Jerrold's Shilling Magazine* was to point out, the so-called 'sanctity of home' and its 'strong yet tender ties', often amounted in reality to 'the smell of ill-cooked food – the steam of wet linen – the loaded atmosphere of small chambers perpetually inhabited'. By contrast, the Whittington Club, an example of 'co-operation judiciously administered', was to provide a 'home from home' where well-cooked food, and good company would furnish the backcloth for intellectual improvement.[60]

It was suggested that a further advantage of cooperative principles would be that the club might provide women some relief from the domestic drudgery of individual family life.[61] However, the treatment of cooperative ideologies by the club's promoters illustrates that ambivalence on the position of women was built into the club's position from its inception. While for some, the ideology of the cooperative home which the club represented was the opportunity for female liberation, others entertained far more traditional assumptions of the role women were to play in the club. As one writer urged, 'female ingenuity might take its part in the genial scheme [the Whittington Club], of beautifying the Home of much comfort. . . . The beautification of a resting-place for the weary – of a refuge for those narrow fortunes . . . would be no selfish nor frivolous occupation for Woman's leisure'.[62]

Therefore, conflicting ideologies beset the club from the start. It was not only the multifarious tradition upon which the club was built that was to blame for this. The problematic relationship between radical unitarian feminist thought and the mores of their target audience also created difficulties. The founders of the Whittington Club hoped to reach a lower middle-class audience. Douglas Jerrold's paper had stated this explicitly: 'We write to the clerks, the shopmen, the young and intelligent operatives of London', it explained. In Birmingham, the initiative for the club's establishment actually came from a group of shop assistants.[63] Feminists shared with the more cautious a central desire that the club should be an instrument for the elevation of this sector of society. The Birmingham establishment had talked of the 'elevating and humanising influence' which it was hoped the club would impart to its members. For the radical unitarians this formed a crucial facet of their social ideology. They sought to regenerate and reform society through liberating the country's intellect. They believed this might be facilitated through clubs such as the Whittington, which offered education and stimulating recreation.[64]

However, a problem arose because, as Chapter 2 indicated, conventional views of womanhood usually formed an important component of the aspirations and ideology of this social group. Other institutes which attracted such membership tended, as we have seen, towards a conservative treatment of the women in their establishments. However, for the feminists, women's role was not the ephemeral one of refining and polishing men as they rose in social stature and political power. They argued that society might only be truly reformed if female minds were emancipated equally. In the feminist agenda, women were instrumental and not incidental in effecting change.

The initial articles concerning the formation of the Whittington Club, which appeared in publications such as *Douglas Jerrold's Weekly Newspaper*, appear to have been aimed at a purely male audience.[65] However, the club's pronouncement of its intention to allow female admission soon widened the debate. The decision originally invoked praise for the benefits which female membership would bring to the club's men. Thus, at the club's founding meeting, the chairman claimed that the admission of women would serve to refine their male counterparts.[66] Such rhetoric resounded with the conservative pronouncements which had dictated the policy of other athenæums towards female members. These sentiments seem to have struck immediate alarm bells in the ears of feminist commentators. The feminists had hoped that the Whittington Club would provide a radical alternative to such practices. From this point onwards, therefore, they lost no opportunity to proclaim the club's radical policy towards women as the great issue which would herald the Whittington Club's place in the ever-rising sun of societal regeneration. Consequently female admission was made central to the treatment of the club within the feminist-minded press. Some, such as William Howitt, were concerned that the Whittington Club should not be seen as an end it itself for achieving female liberation. He was anxious that the public should be reminded that the Whittington Club was but a starting point, and should be accompanied by such measures as the implementation of associated housing schemes.[67] Nevertheless, he was unable to dampen the ardour of many of his colleagues, who saw the Whittington Club as the great feminist panacea of the age. Eliza Meteyard, for example, declared the club was, 'meeting the great sexual question of society', while William Shaen pronounced the club's policy towards women as illustrative of 'one of the most important social movements of the day'.[68]

It was this image of the club which Douglas Jerrold sought to project. His newspaper stressed that the first resolution to be passed at the public meeting held to establish the club was that the admission of women was held to be a fundamental principle. Three weeks later, when the first general meeting of enrolled members took place, the chairman, William Howitt, was praised by the paper for focusing his speech upon the club's cornerstone of female membership.[69] Indeed, in his treatment of the Whittington Club, Douglas Jerrold composed an image of an avid discipleship, which readily embraced the *avant-garde* notions of its bohemian sponsors. In reality, the promoters of the club were far from preaching to the converted. Within the broad spectrum of liberal opinion which comprised the membership, there lay a minority, which could embrace only gingerly the progressivism of their peers. Mary Howitt's correspondence with her protégée, Eliza Meteyard, illustrates that among the club's early membership there were many who were fearful of the radicalism of the club's original rubric.[70] William Howitt was also sensitive to the feelings of the more circumspect. In his panegyric upon the club's policy of admitting women to management positions, he was careful to add, 'To those who may fear that such a position for ladies may in any degree unwoman them, we need only point to the ladies of the Society of Friends'. This concern was again apparent when the *People's Journal* reported on the first public meeting held to establish the club. Appreciating that the admission of women might harm the image of the club's respectability which the Howitts sought to project, the journal was anxious to stress that the club had been sanctioned by highly respected and well-known literary women, such as Mary Howitt, Harriet Martineau and Mary Leman Grimstone.[71]

The existence of a conservative element within the club was exemplified by the establishment of a women's committee. Jerrold's treatment of this topic tends to minimise its conservative connotations. He mentions that the admission of women will proceed 'under the regulation of a committee of ladies'. He does not, however, dwell upon the reasons for the establishment of this committee. Indeed, the reference comes in the midst of a paragraph extolling the benefits which will accrue to Whittington women by means of their membership.[72] However, Mary Howitt, in a private letter, revealed the real motives behind this move. It was, she confessed, 'a sort of sanction to the timid ones'. Indeed, the club's council explained that the 'unceasing attention' of this body was 'directed to the enforcement of every regulation necessary to ensure propriety of manners and correctness of conduct, at our social meetings'.[73]

Therefore, despite the great feminist proclamations of many of the club's founders, the initial conservatism of its pronouncements and the existence of more tentative club members, illustrate the complex assumptions and values which beset the Whittington from the outset. The picture is further complicated by the ambivalent rhetoric which even the club's feminists employed at times. This is most clearly illustrated in their treatment of the language of womanly influence. The radical unitarian lawyer, J. Humphreys Parry, alluded to this theme when he addressed the Whittington Club in October 1847. The presence of women at the club, he believed, 'would tend to refine and exalt the institution'.[74] The reasons why feminists should have employed rhetoric more associated with the conservative athenæums are, of course, complex and open to speculation. Parry may well have been expressing a personal view that was not typical of his fellow feminists, or he may have been tempering his own views to pander to the sentiments of his audience. As Rosemary Billington notes, it is often difficult to assess whether Victorian feminists were actually subscribing to the dominant ideology, or using it to their own ends.[75]

However, it is also important to appreciate that many concepts within contemporary discourse did not have rigidly defined, static meanings. Rather, their semantic ambiguity might be exploited by those such as the feminists, to further a particular ideological end. This was so of the concept of womanly influence. Indeed, the majority of the early feminists tried to draw a distinction between conservative and progressive understandings of the term. The conservative approach was perceived as one in which woman's influence was seen as an essentially passive property. It might be infused, almost unwittingly, for it was seen as some sort of refining balm, which gently emanated from her.

As historians have now shown, for the more radically minded, such notions of female influence might be put to use within a feminist agenda.[76] Contemporary Owenites, for example, employed conventional ideas of womens' purity to argue for an extension of their sphere. Kate Barmby, in her Owenite days had talked of 'She only, who can purify the moral atmposphere of society'.[77] Radical unitarians often made use of such ideas.

They too believed that women might be the regenerators of society.[78] However, the radical unitarians also put a more progressive slant on the argument by maintaining that women could not perform such a role in their present state. As previous chapters have illustrated, radical unitarians argued that contemporary women were perverted by negative character traits, induced by social conditioning. Hence, they argued that women's true potential as the redeemers of society might only be effected if they were first emancipated. Projects such as the Whittington Club were to play a central role in this revolution. For example, Ida of the *People's Press* maintained that frivolity and a relish for malicious scandal presently demarcated women. This was due to the fact that they were in 'dire need' of recreation and improvement. She believed that, were women actively engaged and provided with stimulating recreation and education, such as the Whittington Club might afford, the negative aspects of women's characters would be reformed.[79]

Consequently, the early feminists came to formulate a concept of active female influence. They stressed that it should be a wholly dynamic property, brought into practice by woman's active participation in the world around her. Ideally, it would be the fruit of worldly experience and thorough education. This was an idea which had long been gathering within feminist circles. In the mid-1830s, Fox had lectured on the need to transform women's existing 'indirect influence' into 'a fair and direct influence'.[80]

The attempt to redefine the concept of womanly influence was closely related to the feminists' exasperation that women were more valued as ornaments than for their worth as rational beings.[81] Sarah Flower Adams had addressed these issues in 1834 in her short story, 'The Three Visits'. Here, she refuted the conventional notion that female influence resulted purely from 'her grace and gentleness, and feminine delicacy'. She sought to illustrate that the only reason why women were unable to exercise the dynamic and active influence exerted by men was the 'hitherto prescribed system for the education of women'.[82] Harriet Martineau proved equally eloquent on the issue, explaining that, 'The true humanising influence of woman will never be fully experienced until she becomes wise in thought, independent in action, and able to build up the charities of life on the foundation of principles ascertained by herself, instead of being taken upon trust.'[83] By the 1850s, the issue was increasingly connected to that of female employment. Hence, *Eliza Cook's Journal* acknowledged woman's passive, unseen influence in such areas as government and justice. The journal went on to imply that such indirect influence should be made active by permitting women to properly engage in these professions in their own right.[84]

Eliza Meteyard was a persistent advocate of such ideas. This had emerged clearly in her writing on the Associate Institution. For her, the role women might play in the rescue of prostitutes revolved precisely upon differentiating between these concepts of influence. She, like the conservative members of the Institution, played upon the identification of women with their fallen sisters. However, whereas the official rubric of the Institution tended to develop its arguments in terms of women's mission of redeeming society, Meteyard was more concerned to place their participation in the context of woman's increasingly powerful role in society: 'We conceive woman can best raise her fallen sister woman; and her advanced social condition in society is becoming such that she will have the power.'[85] Meteyard appreciated that it was not enough to hope that womens' supposedly curative powers would affect any real change in the position of fallen women. Women would only be able to make a substantial difference to the world once they had been endowed with proper education and access to the channels of power.

For Meteyard, as for many of her colleagues, the Whittington Club was seen as a means of effecting the transition between these two types of influence. Hence in her essay, 'The Whittington Club and the Ladies', she encouraged women to consider the increasing independence they might exert, pointing out that women were now able to earn their living by pen, pencil or voice, just as men could. She argued that the Whittington Club would help to facilitate this process. She envisaged women playing an active role in the club, participating on the councils, and fostering their feminist awareness through lectures delivered by the more able among them.[86] These concepts were at the heart of William Howitt's hopes for the Whittington Club. He warned against identifying the Whittington Club with the conservative view of the question, by explaining that women were not admitted to the club merely to cast the 'charm of their presence' over the proceedings. Howitt expatiated upon the radicalism of the club's decision to recognise that there was 'no sex in souls', and thus men and women were equally welcome on its governing councils. Howitt maintained that this opportunity for women to participate in the club's management would help to elevate women to their proper place in the social scale, where they would be able to impart their refining influence.[87]

The feminists maintained that in the current, imperfect state of society, the real potential of neither sex had been realised, as their more noble traits had been warped and repressed. Once given the opportunity to release and explore these characteristics, a new and better society might begin to emerge through the harmonisation of male and female natures. This was a view expressed by *Eliza Cook's Journal*: 'the social intercourse of the two sexes draws forth and invigorates all the purifying, delightful qualities of our common nature', it postulated.[88] The Whittington Club was to provide the ideal cultural situation in which such a process might begin. It was only by permitting women action in the public sphere and thus enabling them to mix freely with men, that they might reach their potential, and society be truly improved. Meteyard explained, 'In the better unity of her characteristics with that of man, seems to lie the real secret of the question as to woman as a moral and social agent.'[89] While these ideas did, at times, tend to reinforce conventional gender differences (the Eliza Cook article, for example, suggested that while women needed mental corroboration, men required softening and refinement) – something the feminists often refuted elsewhere, this was to urge for a more active concept of female influence.

Goodwyn Barmby, a prominent Whittingtonian, presented the issue in more transcendent terminology. In *Howitt's Journal* he lamented the fact that women had hitherto been excluded from club life: 'The feminine element – the soft refining influence of the woman-power – has been eschewed in them.' At first sight there does not appear to be anything particularly radical in this statement. The clue, however, lies in the phrase, 'woman-power'. In the Owenite paper, the *New Moral World*, Barmby (with the aid of some complicated tables and terminology) had argued that during various stages of civilisation either the woman-power or the man-power had been predominant, thus creating an imbalance which rendered society imperfect. Barmby believed that in the perfect communist state, the woman- and man-power would be 'equilibrated'. In Barmby's eyes, woman-power does not necessarily reside in women, nor man-power in men. These gender-orientated qualities are seen more as free-floating essences.[90]

The need to forge a new, feminist concept of female influence was thus high on the agenda for the radical Whittingtonians. However, others stressed a rather different aspect of the problem. The successful unity of male and female characteristics might only be effected, many feminists believed, if social manners were revolutionised. As Catherine Barmby appreciated, in effecting female emancipation it was as important to change customs as laws. Meteyard pursued these ideas in the context of the Whittington Club. She believed that the immense social impact of such clubs would have far greater significance than legislative advance.[91] Conventional manners, the feminists declared, were prohibiting women from going forth into the world and achieving their potential. As Parry explained, 'Conventional propriety has hitherto cramped her faculties and limited her aspirations.'[92]

This was an avenue which Douglas Jerrold pursued in his journals. One of his correspondents, drawing upon the prevalent feminist concept of the distorted nature of woman's character, argued that the solution lay as much in re-educating men, as in women – 'Were our courtesies to the other sex more simple and dignified – less contemptuously exclusive in being addressed only to Youth and Beauty, we should hear of less exaction among women in their spring and early summer, less sourness and selfishness in their autumn.' Thus, the argument continued, if women were to frequent the club, men would need to learn to respect their independence. The feminist battle against chivalry was perpetuated as the writer railed against the empty compliments of chivalric manners – 'as much civility as you please – but no sycophancy', s/he pleaded.[93] The feminists' aim, therefore, was that the Whittington Club should provide a place where women could dine alone without fear of impropriety. (It thus demonstrated that the club sought to address the problems of single, as well as married women.) William Howitt rejoiced that in 'admitting women to the *table d'hôte* as well as to the saloons of music and instruction, the committee of the Whittington Club have broken the ice of a most dreary custom in this country'.[94]

A similar approach was advocated by George Dawson. When presiding at a meeting to found the Whittington Club in Birmingham, he made clear his 'common-sense' approach to the issue of female admission: 'a great deal of nonsense had been uttered. It was either the right or the reverse. Nature did not seem to fear that under the same roof there should be gathered together boys and girls.' These sentiments echoed those put forward in *Douglas Jerrold's Shilling Magazine*, which maintained that the admission of women, if treated as a case of 'simple rights, simply administered' would mean that 'the mixture of sexes will cause little more disturbance than in a church or a market'.[95]

Therefore, the feminist propaganda surrounding the establishment of the Whittington Club highlighted two important facets of contemporary feminist ideology. The first concerned women's need to become active, independent beings, capable of making a real contribution to the needs of society. This might be achieved through the reception of proper education and experience with the world beyond the hearth. It would serve to counteract the debasing effects which social convention had upon the female character. Secondly, they perceived that greater female participation in society might succeed only if men helped to overturn old modes of social behaviour.

Most feminists recognised the necessity of wedding these two approaches. The way in which these two ideas could be melded to form a powerful feminist critique emerges in the primary plot of Eliza Lynn's *Realities*. Eliza

Lynn used the imaginative world of the novel to postulate an image of how women might be, were these principles allowed to triumph. The novel's heroine, Clara, is entirely duped by Vasty Vaughan's polished manners and assumed air of respectability. Vaughan, who adheres to the old-fashioned notion of personal protection and represents the shallow and limiting world of conventional etiquette, demands complete obedience from Clara. He increasingly circumvents her actions, until he forbids her to even leave the apartment without him. Nevertheless, Clara continues to meet her friend, Glynn, a socialist drama tutor who, by contrast, treats her as an equal, intelligent being. This creates a considerable personal dilemma for Clara, 'She had always heard that obedience was the first duty of a woman, and she hoped that she did well in paying it to Vaughan. Then again, the sense of independent judgement, and the virtue of honest action, somewhat counteracted this educated idea of womanly duty.'[96]

Clara eventually finds the strength to end her relationship with Vaughan. He tries to humiliate her in revenge, but he is to be surprised at her reactions to his insults. Clara demonstrates that individuals behave and develop according to the way in which they are treated and the expectations which others place upon them. Her egalitarian relationship with Glynn, based upon genuine respect, has drawn out the graceful, rational aspects of her character. In rejecting Vaughan and acknowledging her love for Glynn, Clara is not merely embracing the progressive treatment towards women. She is also seen to have learnt that inner moral sense is more important than the outward show of conventional manners. The replacement of conventional manners by essential Christian values, is the very factor which brings Clara and Glynn together. Clara, learning that Glynn is dangerously ill, goes to him, alone and comforts him in his room. All these actions, it is stressed, utterly transgress convention. Nevertheless, she remains as pure 'as an angel'. Clara later demonstrates the degree to which she has been liberated from the needless protection of Vaughan, when she visits the most violent and deprived areas of the city, once more, alone. Clara thus emerges as role model for the new, emancipated woman, 'as I would to Heaven we had thick among us'.[97]

It was this ideal of the pure and charitable, yet brave, rational and active woman which the feminists hoped the Whittington Club might foster.

WHITTINGTONIANS AND THE 'MIGHTY IDEA'

Therefore, it is evident that the Whittington Club was launched under the auspices of a diverse feminist campaign. To analyse how readily the club members appropriated these ideals is obviously more difficult to ascertain. The sources are, admittedly, flawed. Extant manuscript letters between club members are rare, and one is forced to rely heavily upon the testament of the *People's Journal* and *Douglas Jerrold's Weekly Newspaper*. Obviously this information, coming as it does from the quarters of the club's originators, has to be treated with caution. Fortunately, the club left its own record in the form of the *Whittington Club Gazette and Metropolitan Athenæum*. By examining these sources in conjunction, it is possible to arrive at a reasonably detailed assessment as to the efficacy and endurance of feminist ideology within the club.

The most prominent issue in the *Whittington Club Gazette* was, by far, the issue of female membership and its concomitant debates. The primacy of this topic demonstrated that the feminism which the founders hoped to inject into the club did not sink naturally into the club's consciousness. It remained a persistent and often discordant *leitmotif* throughout the club's proceedings. The articles and quotations within the journal are striking for the sheer diversity of viewpoints concerning women. No doubt this was due to the laudable editorial policy pursued by the journal. The editor stipulated that the journal had a responsibility to represent fairly the views of all its readers.[98] The editor often contrived to make a virtue out of this difficult situation by arranging texts so that they formed an implicit debate in themselves. Hence, whenever more conservative excerpts were published, they were countered by at least one article to refute their suppositions. For example, one piece, the 'Parallel of the Sexes', delivered a classic encomium upon innate gender dissimilitudes. One of these axioms in particular, 'man is great in action, woman in suffering', was subverted in consequent texts. 'Courage in Women' acknowledged the differences between the sexes in existing relationships, but demonstrated that this was due not to an inherent characteristic in women, but to their present conditioning.[99]

The sharp differences of opinion regarding the Woman Question among Whittingtonians were brought to the fore in a bitter altercation over Mary Wollstonecraft, which raged in the *Gazette*. The debate began when a correspondent wrote to the editor, in an apparent attempt to rehabilitate Wollstonecraft as a respectable forerunner of the women's rights movement. This was met with a furious rebuttal from the pen of 'Homo'. Shocked at the inclusion of these sentiments in the journal, he referred to such 'strong-minded females', as Wollstonecraft, as a 'disgrace to their sex'. In reply to this, another member, Anna H, explained 'the teachings which I have gathered from that authoress are, that virtue, truth, and justice know no distinction of sex – that the voices of man and woman should alike be raised in defence of these'. She also praised Wollstonecraft for her 'excellent precepts for the education of her sex' (although she was anxious to distance herself from Wollstonecraft's views on the political rights of women).[100]

Given the wide divergence of opinion concerning women among the readership of the *Whittington Club Gazette*, one must question how successful the club's founding feminists were in implementing their progressive policies. The sources hint that there were indeed initial obstacles in carrying out the feminist principles which hailed its establishment. In particular, the many debates on the fixing of subscription rates provide useful insights into the attitudes of club members towards female admission.

In the first years of the club, women's subscription rates, in line with contemporary practice, were half that paid by men.[101] However, there were frequent petitions within the club to revise this rule. The debate was set alight in 1848 by J. T., who argued that female subscriptions should be raised as women now had the use of greater facilities within the club (thus implying that initially, women did not have access to all aspects of club life). This declaration provoked a series of letters to the Gazette's editor. Many of these correspondents were fearful that such a move would make women members unable to continue with their subscriptions. S. W., for example, was wary of doubling their fee, 'because I am anxious that the ladies should be continuous subscribers'. Nevertheless, this correspondent implied that it was the women themselves who ought to make the decision.[102]

The matter was later debated formally at the club's Quarterly General Meeting. A Mr Richardson raised the issue by proposing that women's subscriptions should be raised, as a matter of basic justice. He stated that it was 'the worst compliment that could be paid to the ladies, to fix their subscription at so low a rate'. Mr Dowson agreed, although his reasoning was less sympathetic to the position of female members: 'We must look the matter fairly in the face. The ladies' subscriptions were not in proportion to those of the gentlemen; the subscriptions should be equally levied upon all.' However, others demonstrated an awareness that a blanket policy of sexual equality was perhaps not the most effective means of furthering the women's cause. Pavey (who accused some members of the meeting of wishing to drive women out of the institution), drew attention to the fact that lady members did not have the same financial resources as men. Druce agreed, arguing that Richardson's proposal went too far, and declared that it was 'oppressive' upon lady members. A Mr Maguire also expressed reservations about adhering to a policy of rigid equality, with no positive discrimination towards women. He believed it would prove more effective to call for 'improved exertions' on the part of the committee, in order to implement a fairer working of the present system. The meeting as a whole, however, concurred with Richardson's presentation of the argument, and the proposal was passed.[103]

When this debate is contrasted with the policies instituted in other societies, the comparatively advanced position of the Whittington Club is highlighted. In 1844, the Manchester Athenæum took an opposite course to that followed by the Whittingtonians. Rather than raise women's subscriptions, so that they were on equal terms with men, they lowered them. This move was in no sense an auspicious departure for the female members. It was, as the management of the Athenæum openly admitted, a recognition of the reduced facilities to which women were granted access. In particular, we learn that, 'ladies cannot avail themselves of the Newsroom'.[104] Thus, instead of altering their rules so that women might have greater opportunities within the club, the Athenæum reinforced their sexist attitude by justifying their stance financially. This was in marked contrast to the Whittington Club, where, if women's subscriptions were increased, it was to reflect their equal status within the club.

The fate of women within the Roscoe Club reiterates the comparative success of feminist propaganda within the London club. The Roscoe Club was established as a sister institution to the Whittington Club. With a strong input from local Unitarians (including William Rathbone, George Holt, William Sandbach and William Potter, among others)[105] it did not, however, advocate the progressive policies towards women favoured by the radical unitarians. Indeed, the Unitarians with whom it was associated came from the city's patriciate elite, whom, as we have seen in Chapter 1, proved extremely ambivalent on the question of woman's position. When a group of members tried to urge the adoption of a more progressive path on the issue of female membership, they were suppressed by the reactionary majority. In 1849, a proposal to institute concerts, 'to which the ladies should be admitted', was rebuffed. The proposal had initially been put to the Executive Committee who refused to deal directly with the suggestion, but referred the matter to the club's council. When the council next met, a motion was passed to delay consideration of the issue until the following session. The proposal was not heard of again. A similar fate befell an attempt to appoint lady patronesses to the club. Once again, the council refused to discuss the matter and declared it should be brought up at the next meeting, 'special or general of the Council'.[106] As before, this sounded the death-knell of any progressive policies.

However, while in comparison, female members of the Whittington Club were granted a respected status, one must question whether this

implied an acceptance of feminist ideology. This issue was brought to
a head when in November 1850 a member, calling himself 'E. P. R.'
declared, 'I think the admission of ladies *at all* objectionable, and trust
some day or other the doors will be closed against them.' This caused
an absolute furore among club members. One member, calling himself,
'Shenstone Short' argued that 'In the early part of this club's existence,
such sentiments as E. P. R.'s might have been tolerated; because then we
had an experiment to try', but now that 'the experiment has been tried and
found to answer beyond the most sanguine expectation of its promoters'
such notions were 'sheer folly'.[107] Douglas Jerrold was similarly uncompromising in his statement that, 'This admission of women to every privilege of the institution, so wisely made a fundamental principle at the very
outset, is almost the grandest feature in this society; and it has met with
complete success.'[108]

Shenstone Short and Jerrold were clearly making bold assertions concerning the Whittington's success. If the club really did fulfil the hopes of
its founders it was evidently a landmark in the acceptance of feminist
principles. While their rebuttals may well be tinged with exaggeration, the
E. P. R. debate did effectively put the feminist propensities of club members
on trial. Perhaps the most striking aspect of the issue was that E. P. R.'s
announcements seem to have hit upon a raw nerve among the majority of
members. The *Whittington Club Gazette* was deluged with protests. Most
members appeared to believe that the admission of women was integral to
the club's existence. In a letter to the editor fulminating against E. P. R.,
Timbuctoo (a regular correspondent) alleged female membership was a
major reason for the club's numbers being 'six times as many as most
institutions possess'. W. Batley also maintained that the admission of women
was responsible for the club's success. He argued, 'were the doors closed
against the ladies, and consequently those entertainments abolished in which
they take a prominent part, we should very soon be compelled to close the
doors of the institution, as the falling-off in members would be so great,
that we should be unable to pay our way'.[109] These arguments were not
merely pointing to the reduced membership and revenue which would
ensue were women themselves ejected from the club. Numerically, women
never formed a high percentage of the club – indeed in 1850, only 400
of the club's 1900 members were female. Financially they were of even
less consequence. The club's accounts for the year 1849–50 establish
that female members contributed less than 10 per cent of the club's
income.[110] The arguments were actually testifying to the enormous weight
which club members placed on women's participation.

Therefore, the denial of female membership was seen to strike at the very roots of the club's being. However, this should not be interpreted simply as the acceptance of the feminist ideals of the club's founders. Batley's letter would seem to suggest that it was the wider opportunities for social activities which were one of the most appealing aspects of female membership and not the implementation of feminist ideals in themselves. It should be remembered that other contemporary societies which admitted women, often instituted a policy of sexual segregation, through separate entrances and different hours.[111] Clearly, the congeniality of mixed-sex socialising was the deciding factor for many. Adolphus Quiet spoke of 'the enjoyment have I had from contemplating their engaging smiles; listening to the hum of their most sweet voices; and inwardly participating in their joyful and mirth-exciting laughter'. Similiarly, L. N. admitted that he regarded, 'their presence among us, by far, the most charming feature of its attractions'.[112]

Such sentiments indicate that on one level, the admission of women to the club had worked. It had, as the *Whittington Club Gazette* put it, 'broke[n] through the stereotyped rules of society'. It went on to proclaim, 'A mighty idea has been begun, is being carried out, the commingling together under one roof persons of either sex.'[113] Hence women were given greater opportunities for socialising, a fact which was greatly appreciated by many members. Others, however, took a more sober view of the question. In a stiff letter to the editor, 'A Lady Member' indicated that the feminists' ideals concerning the role of women in the club had far from won the day. She stated that the original purpose of the Whittington was 'to elevate and polish the minds and manners of the young gentlemen of the present day, by bringing them more into the society of *ladies*'.[114] This was, of course, an argument which had prevailed in many other adult education institutes, where women were admitted not for their own advancement but for the elevation of male members.

Nevertheless, the opinions of 'A Lady Member' were far from universal. 'Timbuctoo', for one, fiercely contested such an approach. In a letter to the club's gazette, he began on a conservative note, stating that the Whittington Club was intended to provide a home-like environment. 'And where', he asked, 'was the word home ever truly exemplified without the ladies' presence?' However, while Timbuctoo insisted that women had an important role to play in maintaining the etiquette of the club, he argued that this did not mean that they were admitted to the club merely so that men might benefit from the charm of their presence. Indeed, he digressed upon more feminist lines with his avowal that the club was intended as much for the development of women, as for the refinement of men. He declared that women had the right to participate and enjoy equal social advantages with men. (This was a point which the Birmingham Whittington Club had also been keen to keep high on its agenda, paying particular concern to the educational needs of its female members.) Timbuctoo noted that the Whittington Club was the first institution in the country to solve the problem of how to break through England's 'frigid and unsociable manners', which were so detrimental to women's opportunities.[115]

An equally progressive stance was taken by the author of a sketch which appeared in the *Whittington Club Gazette* – 'Extract from an un-published drama'. This depicted the reception of E. P. R.'s comments among the club's female membership. Initially, E. P. R.'s ideas are met with hysterical horror. The women are portrayed as flustering and fainting feather-brains. But gradually, they adopt the voice of reason and their rationalism begins to triumph over these stereotypical representations. By the end of the scene, the women have decided to emulate serious political action by forming themselves into a committee of inquiry. This, as one of the women observes, is to behave, 'As in Parliament they do'. This drama needs to be seen in the context of the political education of club members which the Whittington was to effect.[116] In this case, the need to instruct the disenfranchised in the means of asserting their rights politically is seen to apply equally to women.

It is evident that the eddy excited by E. P. R. brought to the surface a plethora of dearly-held opinions concerning the existence of women within the club. The debate was so fearsome that at one point it threatened to permanently disrupt the harmony of club life. Thus, an official response from the club's council attempted to smooth the club's ruffled waters by encompassing as many of the divergent views as it was logically able. Nevertheless, it finally came down on the conservative side of the question. It urged that women had a duty to 'refine and elevate the masculine character', and that in attending the club, women were fulfilling this mission.[117] This was a great blow to the feminist principles which had heralded the club's establishment. It was undoubtedly policy statements such as these which exasperated the club's founding feminists, such as William Shaen. Relating the council's decisions to the social class of its members, he fumed that it was, 'poisoned by the conservative shopkeeping spirit: the pennyweight caution of the back parlour'. Shaen's disillusionment was further illustrated during his adjudication of an essay competition on 'Woman's Mission' which was aimed chiefly at club members. He refused to appoint a winner, claiming, 'not one of them treats the subject in a complete or satisfactory manner'.[118]

Therefore, it would seem that while women were permitted equal rights within the club, among club members tensions persisted concerning the reasons for their presence. Nevertheless, these debates tell us little about how the female members themselves responded to the Whittington Club's permissive policies towards them. Indeed, it is only by penetrating a little deeper into the day-to-day experience of female club members that one is able to gauge just how well the cerebral debates on the issues accorded with the reality.

Many club members maintained that women subscribed to the club purely for the purposes of socialising. One member stated, 'by far the greater portion of the ladies subscribe merely for the pleasure of the Drawing Rooms and Assemblies'.[119] However, the testimony of feminist-conscious observers, being more alert to the radical potential in the club's policies, suggests that women also responded to the more progressive opportunities which club life might offer. Certainly Douglas Jerrold, as one might expect, was keen to foster this image. He looked far beyond the socialising benefits the club provided, claiming that *all* the club's activities were enhanced by women.[120] While exaggeration often blighted Jerrold's work, his claim does appear to be corroborated by the reports of unbiased sources. Perhaps the most useful of these is a review of the club written by the American anti-slavery activist, Eliza Follen. In an article for the *Anti-Slavery Standard* (proudly reprinted in the *Whittington Club Gazette*) Follen presented a propitious picture of the full involvement in club life enjoyed by its female members.

Follen appreciated the importance of women enjoying the pleasurable, social aspects of club life and rejoiced that 'you may see a young woman . . . making herself merry and really recreating herself by a dance'. However, unlike the more conservative reports, Follen distinguished other aspects of club life from their purely socialising function, and perceived their import as liberating tools. This is evident in her sober treatment of female participation in discussions and conversation groups within the club.[121] Women's entitlement to stimulating and intellectual conversation was an important aspect of contemporary feminist thought. Great attention was paid within feminist circles to the fact that women were customarily denied access to such interaction, often being condemned to narrow, gossiping chatter.[122] Indeed, as it will be seen, in progressive plans for a society within the Whittington to promote women, conversation was cited as being, 'the most direct means for the attainment of the improvement and extension of woman's intellectual faculties'.[123] Follen was further pleased to discover that female members made good use of the educational facilities afforded by the club. She observed women taking part in the club's concerts and was pleased that one might find women 'listening to a lecture from Dr. Nichol on astronomy, or some other learned man'.

Follen was also quick to note the new code of social manners which the club sought to instil. She perceived that it encouraged social, rather than feudal protection for women: 'You may see a young woman in the reading-room, sitting at the table, reading with no other protector than the good manners and character of the club.' Taking the radical side in the influence of women debate, Follen concluded that it was through the active participation of women in the club and by making use of opportunities for further education, that women would be able to instigate a change in society. As she herself declared, 'every well-informed woman is a missionary sent out into the world'.[124]

Clearly, Follen's account of life in the club suggests that its admission of women had proved very successful. It is hard to gauge whether this experience was shared by the Whittington Club in Birmingham, although the local press did insist that its meetings were well-attended by women.[125] However, in comparison to the state of affairs in Liverpool's Roscoe Club, it would seem that the London club had succeeded brilliantly in welcoming women into club life. In a report upon the Roscoe club written by a correspondent of the *Leader*, it was stated that the club, 'combines a greater number of physical, intellectual, and moral comforts, and means for mental improvement than were enjoyed by the best of our late social institutions; with the exception that females are not received as members or allowed to attend the club'.[126] Even if the reporter may have been technically incorrect on this matter, the fact remains that evidently he did not see any women at the club, and was given the impression that they were not welcome there. A marked contrast to Follen's experience.

Although Follen thus proves an invaluable source on the club, as a casual observer she could not shed any light on the input of women behind the scenes. Nevertheless, her observation that 'Men and women are upon the same footing',[127] is evidently a key point. The fact that women were entitled to sit on the club's councils and committees and were granted full voting rights, was the most radical aspect of Whittingtonian practice. To what extent female members took advantage of these privileges is difficult to appraise. There is no mention of female participation in the meetings concerned with subscription rates and unfortunately, the *Whittington Club Gazette* did not publish figures for the membership of the society's committees. Jerrold's argument that in time at least 20 out of 50 committee members might be women, suggests that they were, at that time, very much in a minority. He nevertheless continued to maintain that it was a highly successful aspect of the club's policy: 'We understand that even in dry committees of business the work is far better done, and in less time, and with much more order and regularity, when ladies attend fully, than at other times.'[128] Certainly the club did earn a laudable reputation for the efficiency of its management. In a speech to the House of Lords, Lord Brougham referred to the Whittington as 'one of the most useful and best managed clubs in London'.[129]

However, there are more specific indications that women greatly profited from the club's policy of allowing them to sit on its councils and committees. On the club's executive council there sat a number of influential women. These included both literary feminists such as Meteyard (and possibly Cook); and those who were to make their mark on the women's rights movement – Clementia Taylor, Caroline Stansfeld and Matilda Hays for example.[130] It should also be noted that many of these women continued to support the cause of female adult education in their women's rights work during the coming decades.[131] Their participation on the council doubtlessly gave them valuable experience and confidence, in preparation for their own feminist projects in the following years. (When organising her women's rights campaigns, Barbara Leigh Smith greatly appreciated women with committee experience.)[132]

Furthermore, within the management structure of the Whittington Club there existed a caucus of radical female membership, which sought to use its position to further progressive policies towards the club's female members. In May 1849, Maria Seddon wrote to William Shaen in her capacity as chairman [*sic*] of the Management Committee. The purpose of the letter was to brief him on the committee's plans for a society, 'instituted for the Improvement and extension of woman's intellectual faculties'. This was a scheme initiated by fellow Whittingtonians, Dr and Mrs Black. In an enclosed memorandum, 'Hints for the Formation of a society to be called the Ladies Friendly Society', it transpires that at the heart of this society lay the assumption that the best means of improving woman's intellect was to engage her in various stimulating acts of conversation. Hence, 'Astronomy, Geography, History, Music, Poetry, and books are subjects to be in turn considered as suitable topics for amicable discussion and observation.' To develop the members' intellectual and social skills, individuals were to prepare topics for presentation at seminars. The club was to be well-organised; it would elect a committee of four members every six months and minutes of the proceedings were to be taken at each meeting.[133]

The organisation of this society accorded perfectly with the Whittington Club's philosophy. The club had long been amenable to the formation of clubs within its own structure, as we have seen. These internal societies (others included the parliamentary society and the society for the discussion of foreign affairs) attempted to familiarise members with the workings of parliament, and introduce them to the issues and important debates which took place within its hallowed walls. The insistence upon rigorous attention to minute-taking, elections and the workings of committees within these societies, was fundamental to the political education of the Whittington's membership. It was clearly a radical step that such education was regarded as equally important for the female members of the club.

The fact that the movement for such a women's society originated from the Management Committee is of particular interest. It has already been noted that this body had been entrusted with the duty of reinforcing a less progressive element of club life – the strict adherence to propriety. It is possible that this committee had been given a wider rubric to promote and protect the interests of female members. Certainly Meteyard had hoped that the women would deliver lectures to the Management Committee on the subject of womanly advance.[134] In any case, that a body originally established to appease the conservative members of the club should within three years have evolved into a council which actively fostered female advancement, suggests that the hopes of the club's promoters had not been entirely lost.

However, the plan for a Ladies' Friendly Society is also of wider significance. It may well be that it provided a prototype for other early feminist organisations. By the early 1850s, it was exactly this type of society, bent on self-improvement, which led the way in demands for female suffrage. The Woman's Elevation League, widely publicised at the time, is a prime example, with its objectives of promoting the social, moral, professional, pecuniary, and political elevation of women. Such societies heralded a critical moment in the history of early feminism. They represented the broad agenda of radical unitarian feminism, with its insistence that female liberation must come about not only through legislative change, but through a reformation in women's characters. The Women's Elevation League, for example, insisted upon the '*necessity* of elevating the sex to a sense of their ignoble, unmerited position in society'.[135] This was an aspect of feminist thought which was soon to be overshadowed by campaigns for specific demands, such as a change in the legal position of married women.

It is clear, therefore, that the Whittington Club continued to harbour a great variety of opinion concerning the position of women. Paradoxically, this divergence may actually have served to further the debate on feminism within the club during the club's early years. The existence of antipathetic views rubbing side by side kindled the woman question into a burning issue. During this process a gradual 'levelling up' of progressive attitudes appears to have occurred. This is manifested in such areas as the club's changing policy on women's subscriptions, and the evolving role of the management committee. The club was undoubtedly effective in demonstrating that mixed-sex socialising was beneficial for both men and women. It was also successful in providing working women with opportunities to further their education and social confidence. In addition, by encouraging women on to its councils it proved to both sexes that women had worthwhile contributions to make in spheres hitherto closed to them. This was a great success in comparison to other similar societies, such as the Roscoe Club. This may well have been due to the constant feminist support and propaganda which surrounded the London institution. This suggests that the work of the Howitts, Meteyard, Grimstone, Jerrold and the like, really did have a specific contribution to make in forming and responding to the feminist awareness of their audience.

However, on the whole, club members seemed content to adhere to a notion of common-sense justice when dealing with female members. The decision concerning female subscriptions illustrated that the majority of club members supported the concept of equal rights and responsibilities. Thus, they leaned towards a perception of woman's subordination as an essentially statutory problem. Within this narrow definition of female oppression there was little room for broader feminist visions of the need for a profound cultural evolution. While the pages of the *Whittington Club Gazette* fostered a radical, undercurrent debate on the need to encourage more dynamic images of women, in the club as a whole, enough conventional views of femininity were retained to make Jerrold's and Dawson's call for a complete reformation in social manners unworkable. Gallantry and chivalry were not allowed to die. Thus, contours were set up to limit the changes which one might expect in the reformation of the female character, and in the way women should be treated. Although, as Kent notes, some elements of the club seem to have harboured progressive notions on such issues as the bloomer costume debate, by the early 1850s the club was failing to fulfil a whole number of the club founders' original hopes – not merely their feminist principles, but also their cooperative ideals. By 1851, the club's financial crisis resulted in pushing up female subscription rates to such a level that female membership dropped by half. Consequently the club began to emerge as a 'more or less ordinary city men's club'. Thus as Walter Jerrold noted, 'it scarcely achieved the hopes of its founder'.[136]

The reception of feminist ideologies within the Whittington Club reflects their fate within the wider radical community. The visionary ideas of those such as Barmby and Meteyard sank into oblivion as feminists concentrated increasingly on formulating short-term strategies which might make headway among the general public. Grimstone's perception that the only real solution was to encourage a long-term process in which men and women re-examined their apparent differences and the way in which the sexes interacted with each other, lapsed into obscurity. It is a battle yet to be won.

6 Conclusion: The Reception, Significance and Influence of the Early Feminists

CHANGE AND CONTINUITY

Gradually, the feminist cadre began to drift apart. The tight web of personal, reforming and journalistic threads which had linked the various sections of the community together became increasingly frayed. By the late 1840s, the original South Place Circle had all but evaporated. The deaths of the Flower sisters in 1846 and 1848 had been a sore blow and the vacuum they left was compounded both by Fox's poor health and his absorption in parliamentary affairs as a Member of Parliament.[1] Horne and William Howitt demonstrated the extent to which their own commitment to British social reform was increasingly subjugated to new interests by leaving for Australia in 1852. Howitt returned in 1854, but Horne remained there for many years.[2] The Ashurst circle had been devastated by the death of Eliza Ashurst during childbirth in 1850 – her powerful personality and committed feminist objectives were a tremendous loss to the early movement – and a terrific personal shock to the intimate Muswell Hill Brigade.[3] However, equally disastrous for the early feminists was the disappearance of Mary Leman Grimstone from the scene. Grimstone, always an elusive character, appears to have also died around this date.[4] Her work had proved to be a well of constant inspiration to the radical reformers.

Meanwhile, other tensions were beginning to eat away at the cohesion of the feminist literary world. One of the old hands, Leigh Hunt, offended many with the injudicious comments which appeared in his autobiography, published in 1850.[5] Relations between those on the more left-wing of the radical unitarian network were also beginning to show signs of malaise. Linton was forced to leave the *Leader* newspaper after fierce disputes with both Holyoake and Thornton Hunt.[6] His more mainstream associates, the Howitts, had faced mounting difficulties with their radical colleagues throughout the 1840s. They had, for example fallen out with the Ashurst family over a seemingly trivial matter concerning a holiday in Germany. More damaging however, loyalties throughout London's radical publishing world were severely strained when the Howitts' dispute with their publisher, John Saunders, became public and extremely bitter. Despite reasonable circulation figures, the Howitts had always struggled desperately to make their periodicals economically viable. They seemed to allow their great sense of disappointment and frustration to boil over into their difficulties with Saunders, and many erstwhile trusted associates (such as Douglas Jerrold) felt unable to support the Howitts' uncompromising and often vindictive stance towards Saunders. Once Saunders had assumed control of the *People's Journal* it became increasingly conservative and could no longer be regarded as a platform for more experimental ideas.[7]

Similar problems beset Douglas Jerrold. His *Weekly Newspaper* and *Shilling Magazine* had fared extremely well during the first two years or so of their existence. However, increasingly, their momentum began to slow and soon both were fighting to stay in print. By 1849 they had failed, leaving Jerrold in considerable debt. Jerrold, who had never found the task of editorship an easy one, appears to have been relieved to finally have the burden and stress removed from his hands, and put his energies instead into novel-writing. He did not turn his hand to editorship again until 1852.[8]

The failure of both the Howitts' and Jerrold's publications was extremely unfortunate for the feminist cause. These journals had risen on the crest of early feminism, a remarkably rich period for the feminists' journalistic network. These years had also seen the appearance of such journals as the *People's Press*, the *Spirit of the Age* and the *Republican*. Despite the cautious tone of some of their articles (particularly in those journals run by the Howitts and Jerrold), for three years they had provided a platform for the more radical to air their views. They had given a focus for early feminist writers such as Grimstone, Meteyard and Mary Gillies, as well as giving an opportunity for the editors to articulate their progressive standpoints. The journals had also functioned as a forum whereby the public could be made aware of such issues as women's legal position, and to publicise feminist activity such as the Whittington Club and the Associate Institution.

The loss of these journals represented the end of an era. From this period a new tendency emerged within feminism. Increasingly, there was a focus not upon visions of an emancipated age, but upon specific issues and campaigns, such as the desire to change the laws relating to married women, or the need to expand women's employment opportunities. This was the fruition of a trend which had been steadily advancing throughout the 1830s and 1840s. During the 1830s, the radical unitarians' feminism was essentially a cerebral and intellectual phenomenon. However, by the late 1840s, this maelstrom of ideas was being crystallised into practical schemes to advance women's position. The feminists' campaigns to change the laws relating to women; their work with prostitutes; the launching of the Whittington Club movement; and their promotion of cooperative schemes may all be seen in this light. While their faith in the need for a long-term cultural evolution always remained intact, this desire increasingly formed but a backdrop to the greater activity in which feminists engaged. This transition was undoubtedly a product of the increasing confidence feminists were beginning to feel, aided both by their new public stature and the growing acceptability of many of their ideas.

This process may be illustrated by considering one particular example of feminist endeavour – the Ladies' Guild. As we have seen, Caroline Hill had played an important role within the feminist debates of the radical unitarians. She was closely involved with the *Monthly Repository* and the *Star in the East*, both of which demanded women's right to gainful and useful employment. By the early 1850s, however, Caroline Hill was becoming increasingly interested in translating such debates into action. This is reflected in her work for the Ladies' Guild, of which she became manager. The Guild, sponsored by E. Vansittart Neale, was a project which trained and employed women in new techniques for working with decorative glass. For Hill, this project united two of her most cherished ideals – the employment of women and the principles of cooperation. As she explained to John Stuart Mill, 'I hope the society will become a central point for the organization of the labour of all kinds of women – of all classes.'[9] The reception of the project in *Eliza Cook's Journal* (which appeared just as the other feminist mouthpieces were ceasing publication) is illustrative of the new tone which was beginning to characterise feminist thought. Extremely proud of the fact that it was a journal 'edited and conducted by women', some of its correspondents were evidently weary of the predominance of intellectual and literary debate inherent in radical unitarian feminist circles, one claiming of the Guild, 'its establishment is the recognition of a great truth, and a succession of similar experiments will do more than shelves full of books to help forward the condition and advance the social well-being of woman'.[10] Sentiments such as these were reiterated by the rising generation of feminists, who asserted the importance of 'deeds, not words'.[11] Indeed, by the early 1850s, one is struck by a sense of impatience which seems to have emerged among feminists. The sources suggest that many were beginning to feel that the intellectual arguments had been won – the time for action had come.[12]

However, this new emphasis was also testament to a more profound sea-change within the emerging feminist movement. The activists who came to light during the 1850s were nearly all women. As we have seen, in the old radical unitarian community, women played a crucial role – not only through their writing, but also through practical means: sitting on councils, editing journals, supporting cooperative meetings, circulating petitions and so on. Despite this, in numerical terms, men were in the dominant, and certainly it was men who were the public speakers and men who edited most of the journals. For this was a feminism which grew out of the male world of radical politics – it even shared its language – embracing such concepts as 'fraternity' and the 'brotherhood of mankind'.[13] It was a world which a small group of enlightened men had shared with their like-minded female associates. It was not an environment the women made their own. Indeed, for the radical unitarians of the 1830s and 1840s, feminism was but one facet of a larger ideological plan. It was that which made their radical vision of the liberal, educated and free society complete. It was a radicalism which had blended Unitarian, socialist and Romantic insights to form a holistic concept of democracy and social regeneration. By contrast, the later feminists of Langham Place pursued more circumspect objectives. They did not share the excitement of a visionary new age of democracy, but rather cohered through the agency of a more narrow, more uniquely feminist, perspective. It was the dawn of female consciousness – of the strength of sisterhood.

The old radical shibboleths wilted in the light of these new truths. The utopian dreams and grand social ideas of the radical unitarians appeared increasingly dusty and worn in a new age of social equipose and political stability. The demise of the Chartist movement and the failure of the European revolutions of 1848 triggered a subtle shift in reforming perceptions. Sensible, pragmatic politics, fuelled, in the feminists' case by a new awareness of self, was now the order of the day.

Clearly then, early Victorian feminism was an ever-evolving phenomenon. Nevertheless, its radical unitarian heritage did provide a solid basis for its growth. This was true both in terms of ideology and personnel. Historians of the women's rights movement have sometimes claimed that there was a lack of intellectual debate among the feminists of the 1850s and 1860s.[14] However, this phenomenon should be considered within the broader framework of a feminist movement which had been developing over the previous two decades. During the course of this book frequent reference has been made to the fate of radical unitarian feminist ideas among subsequent women's rights activists. It has been seen that many key concepts, such as their analysis of domestic slavery, the issue of the protection of women, and their analysis of the relationship between marriage and prostitution remained persistent themes throughout the feminist movement of the nineteenth century. It is evident, therefore, that the radical unitarians performed an invaluable service in laying the intellectual foundations of nineteenth-century feminism. Furthermore, the majority of feminists from the radical unitarian milieu went on to play leading roles in the women's rights campaigns which ensued. Yet, as we have seen, this background has been seriously overlooked in previous histories. A brief consideration of the subsequent feminist careers of some early radical unitarian feminists demonstrates their continuing importance to the movement.

Mary Howitt, for one, remained a vital source of support and inspiration to the feminists of Langham Place and became the secretary to the London committee for the married women's property campaign.[15] Matilda Hays also continued to make a substantial contribution to the women's rights movement in her capacity as editor of the *English Woman's Journal*. Those involved with this publication relied upon the expertise and experience of such figures as Howitt and Eliza Meteyard to assist them with its running. W. J. Fox also became closely involved with the project, acting as the journal's auditor.[16] Margaret Gillies and Eliza Fox combined their love of art with their desire to advance women by assisting Barbara Leigh Smith Bodichon in the establishment of a 'Society for Female Artists' in the mid-1850s.[17] Other important early feminists went on to play a significant role in the agitation for women's suffrage. Matilda Biggs, for example, kept the issue of women's right to vote before the public eye in the North of England. Her sister, Caroline, went on to assume active membership of the London Women's Suffrage Society.[18]

The campaign to repeal the Contagious Diseases Acts was one in which other members of the Ashurst clan also became closely involved. In particular, Emilie Venturi (née Ashurst) edited the movement's mouthpiece, *The Shield*. (She was also a prominent member of the Vigilance Association.) Emilie, who became a close friend of Leigh Smith Bodichon, had earlier given valuable help to the feminist projects of the Langham Place circle.[19] Her brother-in-law, James Stansfeld, put his career as a cabinet minister on the line when he too joined the campaign against the Contagious Diseases Act. Indeed, Stansfeld established a reputation as a leading figure in the movement to secure women their rights. One contemporary commentator, Ruth Fry, declared that 'he did more than any other man in Europe to promote the educational and political advancement of the female sex'. His wife Caroline played an equally important part in the battle against the Contagious Diseases Acts. Another prominent campaigner of their set, William Shaen, also continued his work for the liberation of women until his death in 1887. As well as acting as a founder member and chairperson of the National Association for the Repeal of the Contagious

Diseases Acts, he played a vital role in the battle to secure higher education, and particularly medical education, for women.[20]

The radical unitarian feminists also ensured continuity within the movement through the efforts of their offspring, many of whom became key agitators in the struggles for women's rights. This was true of Harriet Taylor's daughter, Helen, and the Howitts' daughter, Anna Mary. The latter became an important contributor to the *English Woman's Journal*.[21] The daughters of Matilda and Joseph Biggs were equally committed to the cause. Caroline Ashurst Biggs was a particularly zealous activist. Matthew Davenport Hill, who had many connections with the radical unitarian cohort and was a founding member of the Law Amendment Society, had two daughters, Rosamund and Florence, who went on to make their mark in the feminist movement.[22]

Therefore, it was not merely those directly involved in the feminist campaigns of the 1830s and 1840s who went on to play leading roles in Victorian feminism, but also those who had been close to them and were vitally influenced by them. This applied to the friends and acquaintances of radical unitarians, as much as to their children. Olive Banks has noted the importance of personal 'recruitment' in drawing men and women into the nineteenth-century feminist movement.[23] Certainly the radical unitarians performed a vital function in influencing others to join the cause. Indeed, during the late 1840s, a number of young, well-educated Unitarian women such as Elizabeth Malleson, Clementia Taylor, Bessie Rayner Parkes and Barbara Leigh Smith became increasingly involved with the radical unitarian community. These women went on to become leading figures in the women's rights campaigns of the following decades. Yet, the importance of the radical unitarian influence upon such women has been overlooked. For example, most histories of the movement mention Matilda Hays's work as a translator of George Sand, but point out that very little else is known about her. The significance of her venture to translate Sand is missed. The translation of Sand's works functioned as something of a rite of passage for those feminists wishing to launch themselves into the feminist literary coterie of the period. Certainly in Hays's case, the project, involving the support and active assistance of many other feminists from the radical unitarian community, points to the close involvement of Hays with this intellectual circle. It was from this milieu that Hays emerged as a feminist activist.[24]

Clementia Taylor had also been intimately involved with the radical unitarian circles of the 1840s, and both she and her husband were close to W. J. Fox, as well as enjoying considerable contact with such figures as William Shaen and the Ashursts. Taylor was clearly impressed by the ideologies of this set, sharing their political and social views on many key topics, and assisting with such projects as the Whittington Club. Taylor became involved in a host of women's rights organisations – perhaps most notably, serving as both the treasurer and secretary for the London National Society for Women's Suffrage. Taylor's close friend Elizabeth Malleson had been similarly involved with the radical unitarian community during the late 1840s and early 1850s, having enjoyed close contact with both the Fox set and the John Chapman entourage. Malleson came from a strong Unitarian background, which had frustrated her own needs for self-fulfilment. She had been destined to years of domestic drudgery looking after her large family, and her Unitarian education had proved intellectually frustrating. The radical unitarians appear to have provided Malleson with the liberating ideology she sought. She emerged from her acquaintance with them as an active feminist. She was a leader in the campaign to change the married women's property laws; established the Working Women's College; and was a founder-member of the London National Society for Women's Suffrage. She also acted as auditor to the Ladies' London Emancipation Society and was a trenchant campaigner in the fight to repeal the Contagious Diseases Acts.[25]

It should also be remembered that John Stuart Mill, claimed by Banks to have been the 'greatest single influence in persuading men to be feminists',[26] was also, as we have seen, vitally involved with radical unitarian feminists. As previous chapters have noted, he followed their intellectual arguments on such issues as the domestic slavery of women in his own feminist writing. A number of other male reformers who had moved within the radical unitarian orbit during the 1840s also went on to campaign for feminist causes in later years. William Shaen's brother-in-law, Henry Solly, and Lord Houghton (formerly Richard Monckton Milnes) are notable examples, both from Unitarian-inspired backgrounds.[27]

BARBARA LEIGH SMITH AND BESSIE RAYNER PARKES: A CASE STUDY

Therefore, an acquaintance with the radical unitarians demonstrates that those feminists who began campaigning in the 1850s were but the continuation of a vibrant feminist tradition. Indeed, there was no abrupt severance between the radical unitarian feminism of the 1830s and 1840s, and the women's rights campaigns which coalesced in the following decades. The feminism of the radical unitarians flowed directly into these endeavours. More importantly, some of the chief participants in the later campaigns had been drawn to feminism through their direct acquaintance with the radical unitarians. In order to illustrate the immense influence which the radical unitarians had upon the emerging feminist movement, this section takes as a case study the experiences of two of the most influential feminists of the mid-nineteenth century, Bessie Rayner Parkes and Barbara Leigh Smith.

Olive Banks has noted that Leigh Smith was 'perhaps the single most significant woman during the early days of the movement'.[28] She goes on to point to her crucial work in establishing the Langham Place circle, and its offshoot, the *English Woman's Journal*, as well as her vital role in influencing others to join the movement. Given this primary role in Victorian feminism, it is surprising that Leigh Smith's own entry into the women's rights debates has not been subject to greater scrutiny – especially as Bessie Parkes claimed that for herself and Leigh Smith, the mid-1840s and the years immediately following, were of immense importance to them both.[29] Yet, to read many standard accounts of the campaign for reform in the legal status of women, one might be forgiven for thinking that Leigh Smith's petition for a change in the law arose out of the blue. The most recent biographer of Leigh Smith, while pointing to the influence of Jameson, Mill and Caroline Norton, maintains that it is not clear when Leigh Smith decided to campaign for a change in the laws regarding women or what made her do so.[30]

However, Jane Rendall has recently used the early correspondence between Bessie Rayner Parkes and Barbara Leigh Smith to trace the emergence of their feminist consciousness. In a fascinating essay she explains that she has used their letters to trace the 'networks of friendship which underlay the slow growth' of the women's rights movement.[31] However, when this correspondence is placed within the context of the radical unitarians, the need for a reinterpretation of the origins of the women's rights movement becomes clear. Indeed, rather than using the correspondence as evidence for the friendship which existed between Leigh Smith and Parkes, it is extremely illuminating to consider the light which it sheds upon their close relationships with the radical unitarian feminists in London during the 1840s.

Both Herstein and Rendall rightly draw attention to the strong Unitarian background of both Parkes and Leigh Smith. By dint of this connection, both women were familiar with many Unitarians in London's intellectual community – including the important feminist circle which revolved around Elizabeth Jesser Reid, then in the throes of founding Bedford College.[32] While critical attention has recognised the importance of these influences upon Leigh Smith and Parkes, a similar attention has not been paid to the importance of such figures as Mary Howitt and her colleagues.

From the mid-1840s, both Parkes and Leigh Smith became drawn to the literature and personnel of the radical unitarian community. Leigh Smith's family were well-acquainted with both Anna Jameson and the Howitt family, who lived nearby.[33] At this time, both Parkes and Leigh Smith were still in their teens and appear to have been completely overawed by the personalities and ideas of the Howitts' circle (Mary Howitt, in particular, was a source of incalculable inspiration to them). Their feelings towards the Howitts seem to have amounted to hero-worship. As Parkes confessed in a letter of 1847, 'I have such an intense feeling of veneration for them.'[34] When Leigh Smith managed to arrange a meeting between Parkes and Howitt, Bessie's gratitude almost knew no bounds: 'I am so obliged to you for taking me to see her; I shall never forget it; it left a tail of hopeful light like a comet behind it.'[35]

Through their connection with the Howitts these two young women were introduced to many of the illustrious figures on the radical literary circuit. For example, they were brought into contact with another of the pivotal radical households, that of John Chapman, which, as we have seen, was an important focus for feminist intellectuals. The issues of women's rights and wrongs were a frequent subject of discussion at the Chapman's soirées, to which they were invited. (Leigh Smith became extremely close to George Eliot as a result of these meetings, and became intimate with Chapman.)[36] They were thus brought into contact with reformers who were already campaigning for changes in the laws regarding women. Eliza Lynn was a notable member of this set. Her novel, *Realities*, raised such issues in 1851, and she was soon to write an article for Dickens's *Household Words* on the importance of securing a change in the laws concerning married women.[37] Meanwhile, in Birmingham, Bessie Parkes was raving about Dawson's popular lectures, which she often attended. As seen in Chapter 4, Dawson had used these opportunities to expatiate upon the barbaric and unjust laws facing women, and his desire to join the campaign against those laws.[38] The political contacts of Leigh Smith's father also brought them into contact with W. J. Fox and his daughter, Eliza. 'Tottie', as Eliza was known, was to become a firm friend, and both she and her father assisted Leigh Smith in her attempts to organise the women's movement in Britain.[39]

Parkes's and Leigh Smith's entry into and subsequent reaction to such circles was symptomatic of their developing ideological stance. At this time, both women appear to have experienced something of a spiritual malaise with their family religion and both were to reject the Unitarianism propounded by their parents. Parkes had long felt that the Unitarians left 'too much to common sense'.[40] Thus, Leigh Smith and Parkes, while continuing to adhere to the political and intellectual values of Unitarianism, came, with many of their generation, to react against its religious basis. As Parkes admitted to Leigh Smith, 'My present faith is as yours, in *humanity*.'[41]

This attempt to redefine a new, humanistic spirituality from the old Unitarianism made these women a perfect audience for the literature and periodicals then emerging from the radical unitarian circles in the capital. Furthermore, like the radical unitarians, the two young women shared a love of nature and were immensely excited by industrialisation, while manifesting great concern with the social effects it wrought upon the working classes.[42] Of far greater importance, however, was their common political stance. Both Parkes and Leigh Smith were invigorated by issues of freedom, and joined the radical unitarian campaign to fight for the freedom of Italy.[43] Moreover, they shared an enthusiasm for what the radical unitarians perceived to be the great panacea of cooperation. Indeed, both Leigh Smith and Parkes appear to have been strongly influenced by theories of French socialism, in particular, those of Fourierism; and, it would seem, developed these ideas as they sought to forge a greater sense of female solidarity.[44] As noted in Chapter 2, such theories were much discussed and promoted in the radical unitarian press.

Furthermore, Leigh Smith's work at Portman School in the mid-1850s demonstrated that she accorded with the radical unitarians' educational views. The school was intended for the children of mechanics and artisans. It was co-educational, had no uniform and no punishments. It was concerned with the development of the individuals' intellectual skills – just as Pestalozzi had long advocated. Other radical unitarian-influenced women such as Tottie Fox, Caroline Hill's daughter, Octavia and Elizabeth Malleson helped in the school.[45] This project also testified to the fact that Leigh Smith shared with the radical unitarians a particular concern for the lower middle and upper working classes, an interest which was further reflected in her desire that these groups should have access to rational recreation.[46] This social group remained of great importance to the developing women's rights movement. The Society for the Promotion of the Employment of Women aimed to secure employment for women from the lower middle classes.[47]

Parkes's and Leigh Smith's views of marriage and the relations between the sexes also illustrate how close they were to the radical unitarian outlook at this time. As mentioned in Chapter 1 both young women were very much concerned with the narrowness of women's lives, and the desperate need for greater employment opportunities for women. Moreover, like the radical unitarians, they were dissatisfied with the existing state of marriage. In 1854 Parkes reminded her mother that she regarded marriage as a convention, 'many of whose laws and customs you are well aware I regard with no favour'. In the 1840s, Parkes had refused an offer of marriage on the these grounds.[48] Moreover, Parkes and Leigh Smith also concurred with the radical unitarians in placing little emphasis on the formal contract of marriage. They insisted that it was the personal commitment which a couple made to each other that made the relationship binding, rather than the conventions of society.[49]

Literature proved to be a vital vehicle for the growing feminist awareness of Leigh Smith and Parkes, just as the editors of journals such as *Howitt's Journal* and *Douglas Jerrold's Shilling Magazine* hoped it would be. They eagerly consumed the literature and journals which emerged from this milieu, appearing to find in it a positive outlet for their frustrations and ideas. They both received *Howitt's Journal*, of which Parkes declared, 'There is a healthy, hopeful vigorous tone in all Mary Howitt writes', and also *Eliza Cook's Journal*, in which they particularly enjoyed the work of feminist Eliza Meteyard. They were later to buy the *Leader* as well.[50]

Both young women were at pains to secure copies of these journals, and kept up with the books reviewed and praised by them. Parkes, as we have seen in Chapter 4, recommended to her friend Hurlbut's *Essays on Human Rights and their Political Guarantees*, a work which proved extremely important to the radical unitarian publicity of women's legal position, and which Leigh Smith used in her own, seminal work on women's rights. Moreover they had a particular affection for Frederika Bremer and Tennyson, both of whom were being widely discussed by the radical unitarians at this time. It has already been seen in Chapter 3, that Parkes's and Leigh Smith's reading of Tennyson's *The Princess* accorded exactly with the radical unitarian debate upon strategies for female emancipation. They also responded eagerly to the possibilities which the poem's heroine, Ida, augured for a new and powerful concept of womanhood and believed that the poem's Prince provided glimpses of what the new model of marriage might be in an era of female emancipation.[51] Their worship of Bremer (who captured brilliantly the frustrations and confusions many women felt at their position) seems to have veered almost on the fanatical, as Parkes herself admitted.[52]

The radical unitarian wish to present feminist issues through a literary medium thus struck a chord with both Leigh Smith and Parkes. They shared with the radical unitarians a fervent belief in the role of the literary intellectual in the state. Parkes explained to her mother that she considered poetry to be not an 'intellectual luxury but a very real national influence'.[53] Certainly, Parkes followed the example of her literary idols and during the late 1840s herself used literature as a means of expressing her feminist sympathies. In a novel she was working on during 1849, the story-line was used to delineate her feminist vision of the perfect marriage. Hence she admitted to Leigh Smith her reluctance to kill off the hero, John Ashton, because, 'I have been describing their plans of a happy intellectual good-diffusing life, she continuing to work, that I cannot bear to send her out on her lonely, actual life.'[54]

During the late 1840s, both women decided to try and publish some of their literary pieces in the local press. Rendall draws attention to this endeavour, and alludes to the liberal nature of the publication for which Leigh Smith wrote in Hastings.[55] However, these efforts may gain even greater significance if one places them within the context of the young women's attempts to enter more closely into the intellectual community of the radical intelligentsia. For example, Leigh Smith also attempted to have pieces published in *Eliza Cook's Journal*. Parkes, moreover, had contributions accepted by the *Birmingham Journal*, whose editor, according to W. J. Linton, was George Dawson.[56] It should be remembered that both women continued to work for such radical publications, writing later for Holyoake's *Reasoner* and also the *Leader*.[57]

Thus, the letters of Bessie Rayner Parkes and Barbara Leigh Smith not only illustrate the limitations of Unitarian womens' lives, as Chapter 1 suggested. Their correspondence indicates how the new and exciting ideas of the radical unitarian literary community provided an ideological escape route from such frustrations. Moreover, as the subsequent reforming careers of Leigh Smith and Parkes indicate, the feminism of the radical unitarians had a direct influence upon the formation of their ideas. For example, the success of the radical unitarians' feminist publicity upon these women is detected in Parkes's decision to involve herself in missionary work among the prostitutes of the Westminster slums, as noted in Chapter 4. Furthermore, the essays Leigh Smith composed in her campaign for female suffrage during the 1860s reveal the extent to which she drew upon this long-standing feminist tradition. Her article, 'Authorities and Precedents for giving the Suffrage to Qualified Women', explicitly evoked the work of the *Westminster Review*, the *Monthly Repository*, Harriet Taylor and Herbert Spencer's *Social Statics*.[58]

Therefore, the radical unitarian network provided a training ground for many of the women who were to lead the great feminist campaigns of the

1850s and 1860s. This new generation of activists drew upon the intellectual pabulum of the older writers, whom they had idolised in the 1840s, as well as depending upon their expertise and support as they sought to organise their own efforts.

RELATING TO CONTEMPORARY CULTURE

The radical unitarian heritage was not, however, wholly unproblematic. Many of the conservative tendencies inherent in the women's rights campaigns of the nineteenth century may be traced back to these roots. It could well be argued that while the early feminists made a spirited and important attack upon the sexist culture of the day, their argument that saving prostitutes, rather than engaging in direct political action was a more appropriate means of extending woman's sphere, indicates that in some fields of contemporary discourse the early feminists served to reinforce limiting ideologies. Indeed it has already been noted that the radical unitarians failed to reconcile the vexed question of gender difference. Whereas in the 1830s journals such as *Monthly Repository* devoted articles to explaining how the supposed selflessness of women was but the product of the conditioning of girls, by the late 1840s, it has been noted that writers such as Grimstone proved willing to use notions of woman's inherent goodness as a means of presenting positive images of women to a tentative audience.[59] As the movement grew during the 1850s and 1860s, feminists appear to have continued this strategy, as gender difference came to assume a vital position on their agenda.[60]

Nevertheless, while the early feminists certainly worked within the contemporary ideology of the day, this does not imply that they were necessarily completely imprisoned by it. For example, it is certainly true that many feminists actively contributed to the cultural construction of 'woman'. W. J. Linton was one who most vociferously championed the concept of 'woman'. This was made clear in his differentiation between 'female' and 'woman'. In his rhetoric, 'female' was a word devoid of the positive characteristics associated with that of 'woman'. He fumed that those who sneered at the purity of others were *'females* – call them not *women'*, he declared. Such a reverence for 'woman' indicates that for Linton, the term was no passive appellation for those of the female gender, but was laden with cultural assumption. He revered women for being more pure, more gentle and patient than their male counterparts.[61]

A number of other feminist sympathisers were equally conscious of the cultural resonance of the concept of woman. Thus John Stores Smith berated the effect which the contemporary shallow education of women wrought – it produced 'a race who are entitled to the name of "fine girl" or "elegant creature", but who can never, without mockery, bear the hallowed name of woman'. He too argued for the equality of women while professing their differences from men. Anna Jameson echoed such sentiments, declaring that without 'modesty, grace and tenderness', 'a woman is no woman, but a thing which, luckily wants a name yet'.[62]

However, the contemporary discourse on women did not prove to be an indomitable structure, inevitably definining the feminist case. Many feminists were critical of the cultural construction of women. George Dawson, for example, angrily dissented from those who heralded unique qualities for women, proclaiming that the 'nonsense which has issued about the mission of women is enough to sicken any man'.[63] Others attempted to formulate their own, progressive version of womanhood. In Eliza Lynn's *Realities*, the narrator is scathing of the way in which the heroine's mother uses the cultural convention of woman: 'Mrs de Saumarez was a Woman. By this I mean she was a person who took her stand on her womanhood, and treated it as a moral qualification. She cared not to ask herself whether her opinions and feelings were intrinsically right or no; she simply asserted that they were "womanly" according to the conventional ideal of that characteristic.' Yet, despite this cynicism, the novel also develops its own concept of woman, as it traces the maturation of the novel's heroine, Clara. When Clara discovers that she is of lowly birth (and not of the gentry as she believed) it makes her feel 'more strong and independent than I ever did. . . . 'I have only brains between me and the work house.' Indeed, Clara declares that she feels more 'womanly'.[64]

This example points to an important and more typical aspect of the feminist use of the term woman. Despite many proclamations that gender difference was the product of social conditioning and education, in practice the feminists clung to what they perceived as the positive terms associated with the word – such as gentleness, endurance, morality, and tenderness – while also seeking to expand the word's signification to include more traditional male qualities. The attempt to associate the term with an ability for hard work and independence was common. Literature proved an ideal means of developing such ideas. In Grimstone's novels, her female heroines are pure, tender-hearted, proper and gentle. Yet they are also sensible, strong, resolute and willing to act independently and unconventionally. Matilda Hays's heroine, Helen Stanley, was also in this vein, believing that action should be a woman's prerogative as well as men's. And Eliza Meteyard wrote of one of her heroines, a descendant of a soldier in the American War of Independence, 'Her masculine mind and energy were worthy of her descent.'[65]

Similarly, the feminists often urged that those qualities traditionally perceived as female should be inculcated in men. As Chapter 3 noted, in their fiction and also in their polemical essays, they posited the image of the domestic man who was caring and tender with children. Moreover, strongly influenced by the contemporary Utopian and transcendalist movements, some radical unitarians urged for a less temporal understanding of gender difference. As Goodwyn Barmby argued – as we saw in Chapter 5 – woman-power and man-power might be perceived as spiritual essences, which inhered in either sex. But, it was only once both sexes had been fully liberated and educated that the full potential inherent in humankind and the redeeming power of male and female qualities might unite to redeem industrial society.

It may well be that as the next generation of feminists sought to focus more exclusively upon women and became ever more concerned to appeal to the respectable middle classes, the need to emphasise the more conventional aspects of the feminist discourse rose ever higher on the agenda. Certainly this was a criticism often levelled at Victorian feminism – its exclusively middle-class nature.[66] While the radical unitarians actually aimed to appeal to a rather lower social group, in practice, as seen above, it was among the educated middle-class Unitarian women that they found an avid audience. Previous chapters have demonstrated that the very foundations of radical unitarian feminism shaped its appeal to this social class. The early feminists' adherence to Enlightenment concepts of equal rights led them to perceive women's slavery in the denial of employment opportunities to them, and not in their labour exploitation. Indeed, as the movement developed, the demand for female employment became one of its great shibboleths.[67] This emphasis accorded perfectly with their own middle-class concerns to relieve the *ennui* and frustrations of the lives of women, who had little to challenge them beyond the confines of their own homes.

Despite the middle-class nature of the burgeoning feminist movement, it did make some headway among the working-class-dominated Owenite movement. Owen had gone further than many of his followers could countenance when he had advocated the abolition of established marriages. Such views appear to have deterred many, especially women, from joining the movement.[68] As modern historians have pointed out, for working-class women, marriage was often an economic necessity; thus for them, a strengthening and not a weakening of marriage was preferable.[69] Consequently, radical unitarian feminism, with its emphasis on the importance

of improving marriages, may well have been far more to the taste of many
incipient socialists. Certainly, Owenite journals relied considerably upon
the feminism of the radical unitarians.[70]

It is evident that some other working-class people did have access to
the feminist works of the radical unitarians. Judy Lown, for example, has
revealed that in the educational institutes which the Courtaulds (who were
in close contact with the radical unitarians) established for their workers,
publications such as *Douglas Jerrold's Weekly Newspaper*, *Eliza Cook's
Journal* and *Howitt's Journal* were purchased regularly.[71] One is left to
wonder how the employees reacted to the feminist tenor of such journals.
For, one cannot escape the impression that the radical unitarians' proposals were based upon very little understanding of the nature of working
peoples' lives. As Lucy Aikin had admitted, 'I speak of women, but you
may say I only mean gentlewomen. In truth, I *can* speak of none else with
personal knowledge – the miserable drudges, the beaten and half-famished
wives, and a class still more miserable, are never seen, never heard of by
me in my tranquil home.'[72] Emilie Ashurst, among others, persisted in
campaigning for greater employment freedom for women through to the
1880s. During this period also, these middle-class feminists faced the
criticism that they failed to grasp the true nature of the labour of working-
class women.[73]

Indeed, among the working class at large, it is hard to believe that the
radical unitarians' feminism could have prospered. In the formulation of
their feminist agenda, the radical unitarians tended to universalise their
own middle-class experiences, rather than truly addressing themselves to
the needs of other classes. The early feminists hardly ever suggested such
measures as the creation of trades unions for working women, which
might have made a fundamental and direct contribution to the improvement of such peoples' lives.[74] Such solutions were left to a later generation of feminists to advocate. A constant *leitmotif* among the literature of
contemporary working-class women was a protest against the double burden of their lives, which work and family responsibilities created. In calling
for the establishment of associated housing projects, the most radical of
the early feminists had indicated a desire that in demanding women's right
to work they were not increasing the drudgery of many women's lives.

However, many radical unitarians appear to have been impervious to
such concerns. They suggested the foundation of evening schools for young
women which might ensure that they excelled in both the domestic and
employment spheres.[75] Thus, they demonstrated the contradictions and
ambiguities which inevitably beset a nascent ideology. Similarly, although
Margaret Hewitt maintains that unemployed factory men were expected to

contribute to the running of the home, while their wives were at work,[76] one must question whether the concept of 'domestic men', as aired by figures such as Shaen and Grimstone, would have proved widely practicable within the social mores of working-class communities.

A perhaps more significant question is to what extent the early feminists succeeded in influencing their actual target audience – the lower middle classes and upper working classes. Through the medium of their self-help culture, the radical unitarians do appear to have at least reached some of this audience. The reformers' publications and periodicals were the stock reading in the libraries of numerous adult education and self-improvement societies.[77] As Chapter 5 illustrated, in the Whittington Club at least, the feminist propaganda of these publications does appear to have met with some limited success. If club members did not embrace feminism with open arms, they were at least encouraged to discuss the issue at length and to consider more seriously women's rights to social intercourse and educational facilities.

While it is not possible to judge how members of other similar institutes responded specifically to the feminism of these journals, what is certain is that debate on the woman question was rife in such quarters. Lectures upon woman's role in society, her educational rights and influence, were commonplace in these institutions.[78] Moreover, many came to support progressive views on the issue. The Edinburgh Mechanics' Institute, for example, which maintained close contact with the editors of *Howitt's Journal*, placed its policy of female admission within the context of feminist arguments concerning the perpetuation of man's barbarity towards woman. Similarly, the secretary of the Bolton Essay and Discussion Society, D. Douglas, was happy to inform the Howitts that essays had recently been delivered on such subjects as 'Woman considered in her Physical, Intellectual, Social and Moral Relations'. This topic, he explained, 'a very important one, excited a great amount of interest. The arguments advanced tended to show the vast influence woman exerts upon society, and the benefits that would arise from her being well educated.'[79] The Co-operative League, of which many radical unitarians were honorary members, also promoted lectures – by women – on the subject of women's position.[80]

Therefore, the radical unitarians played a central role in establishing progressive views on women as a central component of the cooperative and self-help agendum. While it is true that the radicalism of their ideas may not have appealed to many, among a wide reading audience they played an important role in creating a climate of opinion which was increasingly sympathetic to more liberal treatments of women's issues.

This development must be viewed within its wider cultural context. By the 1840s, debates on women's position were not confined to radical quarters, but had infiltrated into British culture at large. As *Eliza Cook's Journal* exclaimed at the end of the decade, 'So much has been written on the subject of female improvement lately: the subject has formed the theme of novels, prize essays, poems, treatises and articles in the quarterly reviews, until the public mind seems pretty well saturated on the subject.'[81] It was during this decade that the early feminists were entering increasingly into the public and popular domain. Through their widely-read journals they were thus able to inject a radical strain into the contemporary debates, which has been largely ignored in the historiography.

The feminists' success in contributing a progressive element to contemporary discourses is evident in the gradual liberalisation of public attitudes on many pertinent issues, for which the feminists must take considerable credit. Increasingly, a liberal consensus of opinion emerged which accepted such issues as the need for better protection for battered and mistreated wives; the need for the greater availability of divorce; the importance of good education for females; and a more sympathetic treatment of prostitutes.[82] In addition, their successful publications succeeded in diffusing previously contentious ideologies of their extremist image. Thus, their widespread discussions of 'respectable' forms of communal living (associated housing, for example), encouraged a wider consideration of such schemes as boarding houses and residential homes:[83] again, a contribution which has been forgotten by historians.

However, at times, the feminists' success in championing such causes proved to be something of a Pyrrhic victory. As Chapter 4 indicated, in their endeavours to persuade the public of the need for a change in the laws relating to marriage, they raised the issue of domestic violence, and the need for greater protection to be afforded to abused wives. Tactically this was an astute move (as it broadened the acceptability of their demands) and was a strategy which feminists of the 1850s were to continue. However, when the married women's property bills were debated in Parliament, greater justice to women was granted not on the basis of women's rights, but out of sympathy for the poor women perceived as victims of brutal husbands. This served to reinforce cultural stereotypes of the defenceless, pathetic woman, in need of protection, rather than conceding the principle of the matter. Worzala notes that this ambivalence within feminist propaganda became symptomatic of the reception of feminist ideas in the coming decades.[84]

Therefore, the significance of the radical unitarian feminists should be seen at two levels. Firstly, they played a vital role in shaping public opinion on the woman question. The wide dissemination of their radical discourse helped to stimulate discussions on women into topics of the utmost importance to contemporaries and ensured the continuing vigour of the debate. Previous chapters have sought to demonstrate that the radical unitarians played a substantial role in realigning public attitudes on a number of women's issues – this is particularly true of their work on the prostitution problem, for example. Moreover, their propaganda concerning the legal position of married women proved successful in encouraging many people (many of whom held vital influence in their capacity as lawyers or members of parliament) to look upon the problem with sympathy and concern. This in turn created a climate in which a wider women's rights movement would be able to flourish.

The second, and perhaps more important, achievement of radical unitarian feminism was to lay the foundation-stones for the organised women's rights campaigns of the following decades. Twenty years before the women's rights movement is usually considered to have begun, an active and cohesive feminist movement was already campaigning for female suffrage; for reform in the legal position of women; demanding radical improvements in female education; and challenging conventional modes of domestic organisation. This vibrant group of intellectuals and reformers enjoyed both radical contacts and benefited from a Unitarian influence which led them to formulate their own, distinctive, reforming creed. Within this ideology such issues as the franchise, the cooperative principle and the central importance of the marital relationship emerged as key factors. The primacy of these debates within early Victorian feminism has often been underestimated by previous histories of the movement. This suggests the need for a re-evaluation of the ebb and flow of themes and priorities within Victorian feminism, as the movement began to mature. For the ideologies and personnel which distinguished the early feminism established the very roots from which the wider feminist movement of the Victorian age was to blossom.

Notes

Place of publication is London unless otherwise cited.

Introduction

1. See for example, Lee Holcombe, *Wives and Property. Reform of the Married Women's Property Law in Nineteenth Century England* (Toronto: Toronto University Press, 1983); Philippa Levine, *Victorian Feminism 1850–1900* (Hutchinson, 1987); Diana Mary Chase Worzala, 'The Langham Place Circle: The Beginnings of the Organized Women's Movement in England 1854–1870', (PhD thesis, University of Wisconsin-Madison, 1982).
2. The principle studies which mention the existence of these early feminists include Olive Banks, *Faces of Feminism. A Study of Feminism as a Social Movement* (Oxford: Basil Blackwell, 1981), pp. 30–1; Francis E. Mineka, *The Dissidence of Dissent. The Monthly Repository 1806–1838* (Chapel Hill: University of North Carolina, 1944), pp. 284–96; Joan Perkin, *Women and Marriage in Nineteenth Century England* (Routledge, 1989), pp. 212–13; Jane Rendall, *The Origins of Modern Feminism: Women in Britain, France and the United States 1780–1860* (Chicago: Lyceum, 1985), pp. 114–16, 247, 309–10.
3. Carl Ray Woodring, *Victorian Samplers: William and Mary Howitt* (Lawrence: University of Kansas Press, 1952), p. 115; Richard Garnett, *The Life of W. J. Fox. Public Teacher and Social Reformer, 1786–1864* (John Lane, 1909), pp. 118–19, 158–70; F. B. Smith, *Radical Artisan. William James Linton 1812–1897* (Manchester: Manchester University Press, 1973), pp. 11–17. See also Ann Blainey, *The Farthing Poet: a Biography of Richard Hengist Horne 1802–1884. A Lesser Literary Lion* (Longman, 1968), pp. 58–68 in particular. J. F. C. Harrison has examined the work of some of these radicals in *Learning and Living 1790–1960. A Study in the History of the English Adult Education Movement* (Routledge and Kegan Paul, 1961).
4. Rendall, *Origins of Modern Feminism*, passim; Banks, *Faces of Feminism*, passim.
5. E. K. Helsinger, R. L. Sheets and W. Veeder, *The Woman Question. Society and Literature in Britain and America 1837–1883* (Chicago: University of Chicago Press, 1989), p. 9. For discussions of the early feminist literary milieu see Holcombe, *Wives and Property*, Chapter 4; Sally Mitchell, *The Fallen Angel. Chastity, Class and Women's Reading, 1835–1880* (Bowling Green: University Popular Press, 1981).
6. See, for example, Leonore Davidoff and Catherine Hall, *Family Fortunes. Men and Women of the English Middle-Class 1780–1930* (Routledge and Kegan Paul, 1978), p. 454; Sheila R. Herstein, *A Mid-Victorian Feminist, Barbara Leigh Smith Bodichon* (New Haven: Yale University Press, 1985), pp. 44–7; Worzala, 'The Langham Place Circle', Chapter 1.
7. Gail Malmgreen, *Neither Bread Nor Roses: Utopian Feminists and the*

190

English Working Class, 1800–1850 (Brighton: John L. Noyce, 1978); Barbara Taylor, *Eve and the New Jerusalem. Socialism and Feminism in the Nineteenth Century* (Virago, 1983); R. K. P. Pankhurst, *William Thompson, 1775–1833, Britain's Pioneer Socialist, Feminist, and Co-operator* (Watts and Co., 1954).

8. Carol Smith-Rosenberg, 'The Female World of Love and Ritual: Relations Between Women in Nineteenth Century America', *Signs* 1 (1975), pp. 1–29; Lilian Faderman, *Surpassing the Love of Men. Friendship and Love Between Women from the Renaissance to the Present* (Women's Press, 1985).

9. Jane Rendall, 'Friendship and Politics: Barbara Leigh Smith Bodichon (1827–1891) and Bessie Raynor Parkes (1825–1925)', in Jane Rendall and Susan Mendus (eds), *Sexuality and Subordination. Interdisciplinary Studies of Gender in the Nineteenth Century* (Routledge, 1989), pp. 136 70.

10. Bertha Mason, *The Story of the Women's Suffrage Movement* (Sheratt and Hughes, 1912); Florence Balgarnie, 'The Women's Suffrage Movement in the Nineteenth Century', in B. Villiers (ed.), *The Case for Women's Suffrage* (T. Fisher Unwin, 1907), p. 12. However, Ray Strachey, *The Cause, A Short History of the Women's Movement in Great Britain* (Virago: 1988, first published 1928) does take a more balanced approach.

11. MS letter from Elisa Bardouneau-Narcy [née Ashurst] to Elizabeth Neall Gay, 6 March 1846, Sydney Howard Gay Papers, The Rare Book and Manuscript Library, Columbia University. Levine, *Victorian Feminism*, p. 21. Eliza (occasionally known as 'Elisa') Bardouneau-Narcy is referred to as Eliza Ashurst throughout, although her married name is used, when appropriate in the notes.

12. Kenneth Corfield, 'Elizabeth Heyrick: Radical Quaker', in Gail Malmgreen (ed.), *Religion in the Lives of English Women 1760–1930* (Croom Helm, 1986), pp. 41–67; F. B. Tolles (ed.), *Slavery and the 'Woman Question', Lucretia Mott's Diary of Her Visit to Great Britain to Attend the World's Anti-Slavery Convention of 1840* (Friends' Historical Society, 1952), p. 49.

13. Lee Virginia Chambers-Schiller, 'The CAB: A Trans-Atlantic Community, Aspects of Nineteenth Century Reform', (PhD thesis, University of Michigan, 1977), passim.

14. In addition to the standard works on the women's rights movement, as cited above, the following works, among others, also point to this relationship: Margaret Bryant, *The Unexpected Revolution. A Study in the History of the Education of Women and Girls in the Nineteenth Century* (University of London Institute of Education, 1979), pp. 65–6; J. A. Banks, *Victorian Values. Secularism and the Size of Families* (Routledge and Kegan Paul, 1981), p. 35.

15. Olive Banks, *Becoming a Feminist. The Social Origins of 'First Wave' Feminism* (Brighton: Wheatsheaf, 1986), p. 15; Levine, *Feminist Lives*, pp. 30–1.

16. Herstein, *Mid-Victorian Feminist*, pp. 8–16.

17. Ruth Watts, 'Knowledge is Power – Unitarians, Gender and Education in the Eighteenth and Early Nineteenth Centuries', in *Gender and Education*, Vol. 1, no. 1, 1989, pp. 42–4; John Seed, 'Theologies of Power: Unitarianism and the Social Relations of Religious Discourse, 1800–1850', in R. J. Morris (ed.), *Class, Power and Social Structure in British Nineteenth Century Towns* (Leicester: Leicester University Press, 1986), pp. 137–9.

18. See above, n.2.

19. Edward Royle, *Radical Politics 1790–1900. Religion and Unbelief* (Longman, 1971), pp. 51–3, considers the *Reasoner*, R. G. Garnett, *Co-operation and the Owenite Socialist Communities in Britain, 1825–1845* (Manchester: Manchester University Press, 1972), p. 219, refers to the *Spirit of the Age*; David Jones, *Chartism and the Chartists* (Allen Lane, 1975), p. 97, mentions the *Republican*.

20. The word 'feminism' does not appear to have entered into the English language until the 1890s. Richard J. Evans, *The Feminists. Women's Emancipation Movements in Europe, America and Australasia 1840–1920* (Croom Helm, 1977), p. 39n.

21. Banks, *Faces of Feminism*, pp. 30–1.

22. MLG, 'Sketches of Domestic Life', *Monthly Repository* (hereafter cited as *MR*), Vol. IX, 1835, p. 560. Mary Leman Grimstone married William Gillies in the late 1830s or early 1840s, thus becoming Mary Leman Gillies. She often wrote for the same publications as William Gillies's daughter, Mary Gillies. Therefore, to avoid confusion, Mary Leman Gillies will be known as Mary Leman Grimstone throughout, although her correct name will be cited in the notes.

23. 'Female Education', *MR*, Vol. VII, 1833, p. 489; 'Industrial Schools for Young Women', *Eliza Cook's Journal*, Vol. I, no. 6, 9 June 1849, pp. 81–2.

24. Helen Blackburn, *Women's Suffrage. A Record of the Women's Suffrage Movement in the British Isles* (Williams and Norgate, 1902), pp. 12–13; Mason, *The Story of the Women's Suffrage Movement*, pp. 18–22.

25. MS letter from Bessie Raynor Parkes to Barbara Leigh Smith, 20 November 1847, Girton College, Cambridge, Parkes Papers, BRP V 15. See also *Tait's Edinburgh Magazine*, Vol. XI, July 1844, p. 423; *Douglas Jerrold's Weekly Newspaper*, no. 28, 23 January 1847, p. 85.

1 Freedom and Patriarchy – The Unitarian Background

1. Henry Gow, *The Unitarians* (Methuen, 1928); H. L. Short, 'Presbyterians Under a New Name', in C. G. Bolam, *et al.*, *The English Presbyterians, From Elizabethan Puritanism to Modern Unitarianism* (George Allen and Unwin, 1968), Chapter 6; H. McLachlan, *The Unitarian Movement in the Religious Life of England. Its Contribution to Thought and Learning 1700–1900* (George Allen and Unwin, 1934).

2. Raymond V. Holt, *The Unitarian Contribution to Social Progress in England* (Butler and Tanner, 1938).

3. See, for example, R. K. Webb, 'Flying Missionaries: Unitarian Journalists in Victorian England', in J. M. W. Bean (ed.), *The Political Culture of Modern Britain, Studies in Memory of Stephen Koss* (Hamish Hamilton, 1987), pp. 10–31; D. C. Stange, *British Unitarians Against Slavery, 1833–1865* (Cranbury, New Jersey: Associated University Presses, 1984); Ruth Watts, 'The Unitarian Contribution to Education in England from the Late Eighteenth Century to 1853', (PhD thesis, University of Leicester, 1987).

4. John Seed, 'Theologies of Power: Unitarianism and the Social Relations of Religious Discourse, 1800–1850', in R. J. Morris (ed.), *Class, Power and*

Social Structure in British Nineteenth Century Towns (Leicester: Leicester University Press, 1986), pp. 108–56.

5. Ibid., p. 113.
6. Watts, 'Unitarian Contribution', p. 41.
7. Russell Lant Carpenter, *Memoirs of the Life and Work of Philip Pearsall Carpenter* (C. Kegan Paul, 1850), p. 155; John Thomas Barker (ed.), *The Life of Joseph Barker. Written by Himself* (Hodder and Stoughton, 1880), p. 281.
8. For a survey of the historiography, see Russell E. Richey, 'Did the English Presbyterians Become Unitarians?', *Church History*, Vol. 42, 1973, pp. 58–72.
9. Dennis G. Wigmore-Beddoes, *Yesterday's Radicals. A Study of the Affinity Between Unitarians and Broad Church Anglicanism in the Nineteenth Century* (James Clarke, 1971), p. 21.
10. Francis E. Mineka, *The Dissidence of Dissent, The 'Monthly Repository', 1806–1838* (Chapel Hill: University of North Carolina Press, 1944), pp. 9–17; R. K. Webb, 'The Unitarian Background', in Barbara Smith (ed.), *Truth, Liberty, Religion: Essays Celebrating Two Hundred Years of Manchester College* (Oxford: Manchester College, 1986), pp. 9–14.
11. Ibid., p. 13.
12. P. H. Le Breton (ed.), *Memoirs and Miscellanies of the Late Lucy Aikin Including Those Addressed to the Rev. Dr Channing from 1826 to 1842* (Longman, Green, Roberts, 1864), p. 237; Russell Lant Carpenter, *Memoirs of the Life of the Rev. Lant Carpenter, with Selections from his Correspondence* (Bristol: Philip and Evans, 1842), p. 25.
13. Susanna Winkworth to F. C. Maurice, 22 May 1856. Cited in Margaret Shaen (ed.), *Memorials of Two Sisters. Catherine and Susanna Winkworth* (Longmans, Green, 1908), pp. 143–9.
14. Richard Acland Armstrong, *Henry William Crosskey. His Life and Work* (Birmingham: Cornish Brothers, 1895), p. 9.
15. Mr Peacock's address to the annual dinner of the Unitarian Congregation, South Place, Finsbury. *Unitarian Chronicle*, no. XIV, March 1833, p. 84.
16. These themes are fully explored in Watts, 'The Unitarian Contribution to Education', see pp. 46–50 especially.
17. McLachlan, *Unitarian Movement*, pp. 148–50.
18. W. A. C. Stewart, *Progressives and Radicals in English Education. 1750–1870* (Macmillan, 1972), p. 66; Charles Dickens to W. C. Macready, 17 August 1845, p. 357, Kathleen Tillotson, *The Letters of Charles Dickens. Volume 4, 1844–1846* (Oxford: Clarendon Press, 1977), p. 357. The tutor was Henry Morley. J. W. T. Ley, *The Dickens Circle* (Chapman and Hall, 1918), p. 309.
19. R. K. Webb, 'The Gaskells as Unitarians', in J. Shattock (ed.), *Dickens and Other Victorians. Essays in Honour of Philip Collins* (Macmillan, 1988), Chapter 9, pp. 144–5; Webb, 'Unitarian Background', pp. 10–12.
20. John Bowring, *Autobiographical Recollections of Sir John Bowring* (Henry S. King and Co., 1877), p. 122.
21. S. Harrop, 'The Place of Education in the Genesis of the Industrial Revolution with Particular Reference to Stalybridge, Dukinfield and Hyde', MA thesis, University of Manchester, 1976, quoted in Watts, 'Unitarian Contribution to

Education', p. 18. For further examples of Unitarian manufacturers see Webb, 'Unitarian Background', pp. 16–17.

22. Letter from M. D. Hill to Mr Pare, 8 April 1871, in Rosamund and Florence Davenport Hill, *The Recorder of Birmingham. A Memoir of Matthew Davenport Hill. With Selections from his Correspondence* (Macmillan, 1878), pp. 403–4.

23. Holbrook Gaskell, John Rylands Library, Unitarian College Collection, Cupboard B, MS Sermons, Index to Sermons, Vol. I; Armstrong, *Henry William Crosskey*, p. 3.

24. R. Brook Aspland, *Memoir of the Life, Works and Correspondence of the Rev. Robert Aspland of Hackney* (Edward T. Whitfield, 1850), p. 390; Carpenter, *Memoirs of the Life of the Rev. Lant Carpenter*, p. 380.

25. Seed, 'Theologies of Power', pp. 118–19.

26. Richard W. Davis, *Dissent in Politics. 1780–1830. The Political Life of William Smith M. P.* (Epworth Press, 1971), p. 215.

27. Mr Taylor in a speech on American slavery, 1853, John Rylands Library, Unitarian College Collection, Cupboard B, MS record of the Annual Meeting of the Presbyterian and Unitarian Ministers of Lancs and Cheshire, p. 113.

28. Emily Bushrod, 'The Diary of John Gent Brooks – A Victorian Commentary on Poverty (1844–1854)', *Transactions of the Unitarian Historical Society*, Vol. 20, no. 2, April 1992, pp. 98–113.

29. Aspland, *Memoir of the Life, Works and Correspondence of the Rev. Robert Aspland*, p. 184.

30. G. M. Ditchfield, 'The Priestley Riots in Historical Perspective', *Transactions of the Unitarian Historical Society*, Vol. XX, no. 1, April 1991, pp. 3–16; Bowring, *Autobiographical Recollections*, p. 31.

31. Letter read at the Annual Meeting of the Presbyterian and Unitarian Ministers of Lancs. and Cheshire, 20 June 1822, John Ryland's Library, Unitarian College Collection, Cupboard B, MS account of proceedings, pp. 11–12.

32. Davis, *Dissent in Politics*, p. 203.

33. Short, 'Presbyterians Under a New Name', pp. 236–41.

34. R. D. Altick *The Cowden Clarkes* (Oxford University Press, 1948), p. 113.

35. Alan Ruston, 'The Non-Con Clubs and Some Other Unitarian Clubs 1783–1914', *Transactions of the Unitarian Historical Society*, Vol. XIV, no. 3, 1969, pp. 148–9; Seed, 'Theologies of Power', p. 124.

36. Bowring, *Autobiographical Recollections*, pp. 73–4; J. W. Robberds, *A Memoir of the Life and Writings of the late William Taylor of Norwich* (John Murray, 1843), passim.

37. A good picture of the Unitarian community at Stoke Newington emerges in P. J. Shirren, *Samuel Rogers, The Poet from Newington Green* (Stoke Newington Public Libraries, 1963). See also Frida Knight, *University Rebel. The Life of William Frend (1757–1841)* (Victor Gollancz, 1971), pp. 276–83.

38. George Armstrong to John Bowring, cited in Henderson, *Memoir of the Late Rev. George Armstrong*, pp. 76–9.

39. Mineka, *Dissidence of Dissent*, p. 145.

40. John Seed, 'Unitarianism, Political Economy and the Antinomies of Liberal

Culture in Manchester, 1830–1850', *Social History*, 7, 1982, p. 12; Mineka, *Dissidence of Dissent*, pp. 146–7.

41. Margaret Parnaby, 'William Johnson Fox and the "Monthly Repository" circle of 1832–1836', (PhD thesis, Australian National University, 1979), p. 37.
42. Webb, 'Unitarian Background', p. 15; Mineka, *Dissidence of Dissent*, p. 148.
43. Webb, 'Gaskells as Unitarians', p. 150.
44. Watts, 'The Unitarian Contribution to Education', p. 106.
45. Unitarians played a particularly important role in the *Sheffield Register, Cambridge Journal, Leeds Mercury* and the *Manchester Guardian*. See Donald Read, *Press and People. 1790–1850. Opinion in Three English Cities* (Edward Arnold, 1961), pp. 68–9, 76, 85.
46. R. K. Webb, 'John Hamilton Thom, Intellect and Conscience in Liverpool', in P. T. Phillips (ed.), *The View from the Pulpit, Victorian Ministers and Society* (Toronto: The Macmillan Company of Canada, 1978), p. 215; Emily Bushrod, 'The History of Unitarianism in Birmingham from the Middle of the Eighteenth Century to 1893', (MA thesis, University of Birmingham, 1954), p. 11; Lucy Aikin to Dr Channing, 23 March 1839, Le Breton (ed.), *Memoirs, Miscellanies and Letters of the Late Lucy Aikin*, p. 387.
47. Charles Wicksteed to Rev. Brook Aspland, 8 November 1849, Aspland, *Memoir of the Life, Works and Correspondence of the Rev. Robert Aspland*, pp. 559–63.
48. Elizabeth Gaskell to an unknown correspondent, [November–December] 1850, J. A. V. Chapple and Arthur Pollard (eds), *The Letters of Mrs Gaskell* (Manchester: Manchester University Press, 1966), p. 136; T. H. Ryland, *Reminiscences*, quoted in Bushrod, 'The History of Unitarianism in Birmingham', p. 10.
49. This development is considered in most histories of Unitarianism. See for example Webb, 'The Unitarian Background', pp. 20–3.
50. Ian Sellers, 'Unitarians and Social Change', *Hibbert Journal*, 61, 1963, pp. 79–80.
51. Henderson, *A Memoir of the Late Rev. George Armstrong*, p. 293.
52. Lucy Aikin to Dr Channing, 12 June 1836, Le Breton (ed.), *Memoirs, Miscellanies and Letters of the Late Lucy Aikin*, p. 342.
53. Edith Morley, *The Life and Times of Henry Crabb Robinson* (J. M. Dent and Sons, 1935), p. 14.
54. For example, in the Unitarian Manchester College, series of lectures upon German literature assumed an important part of the curriculum. MS Notes on a Course of Lectures on German Literature, 1836 by John Kenrick, Manchester College, Oxford, MSS [R] L. Carpenter. 7. See also Mineka, *The Dissidence of Dissent*, pp. 132–3.
55. E. S. Shaffer, *'Kubla Khan' and the Fall of Jerusalem. The Mythological School in Biblical Criticism and Secular Literature. 1770–1880* (Cambridge: Cambridge University Press, 1975), p. 35; Rosemary Ashton, *The German Idea. Four English Writers and the Reception of German Thought. 1800 1860* (Cambridge: Cambridge University Press, 1980), see especially pp. 12–13.
56. Henry Gow, *The Unitarians* (Methuen and Co., 1928), pp. 107–9.
57. J. Estlin Carpenter, *The Bible in the Nineteenth Century* (Longmans, Green,

1893) is an excellent source for understanding these ideas; Stephen Prickett, 'The Religious Context', in Prickett (ed.), *The Romantics* (Methuen and Co., 1981), pp. 115–63, see pp. 143–63 in particular; Shaffer, *'Kubla Khan' and the Fall of Jerusalem*, p. 26.

58. Morley, *Life of Henry Crabb Robinson*, pp. 14, 24.
59. Robert C. Solomon, *Continental Philosophy since 1750. The Rise and Fall of the Self* (Oxford: Oxford University Press, 1988), pp. 45–55.
60. Ashton, *The German Idea*, passim, provides full details of the relationship.
61. See Mineka, *Dissidence of Dissent*, pp. 123–5, for the debate on Wordsworth within the pages of the *Monthly Repository*. M. H. Abrams, *Natural Supernaturalism. Tradition and Revolution in Romantic Literature* (New York: W. W. Norton, 1973).
62. Philip F. Gura and Joel Myerson (eds), *Critical Essays on American Transcendentalism* (Boston: G. K. Hall, 1982) provides a full insight into the movement.
63. MS notes by James Martineau on a letter he received from R. H. Hutton, 18 September 1847, Manchester College, Oxford, MS J. Martineau, 7, fol. 140.
64. Ralph L. Rusk (ed.), *The Letters of Ralph Waldo Emerson* (New York: Columbia University Press, 1939), Vol. 4, pp. 5–7, 32–6, 40–5, 54–8, 85–8, 97–7, 434–5.
65. Holt, *The Unitarian Contribution*, p. 342; O. B. Frothingam, 'Some Phases of Idealism in New England', *Atlantic Monthly Magazine*, 52, July 1833, in Gura and Myerson (eds), *Critical Essays on American Transcendentalism*, pp. 197–210; Gow, *The Unitarians*, pp. 111–16.
66. Webb, 'Unitarian Background', pp. 21–2.
67. See Wigmore-Beddoes, *Yesterday's Radicals*, passim.
68. Alan Ruston, 'Radical Nonconformity in Hackney, 1805–1848', *Transactions of the Unitarian Historical Society*, Vol. 14, no. 1, 1967, pp. 1–9; Margaret Shaen, *Memorials of Two Sisters. Catherine and Susanna Winkworth* (Longmans, Green, 1908), p. 26.
69. Solomon, *Continental Philosophy*, pp. 53–4.
70. Acland, *Henry William Crosskey*, pp. 31, 80.
71. Lucy Aikin to Dr Channing, 6 August 1841, in Le Breton, *Memoirs, Miscellanies and Letters of the Late Lucy Aikin*, pp. 425–8; Henry Solly, *These Eighty Years; or, The Story of an Unfinished Life* (Simpkin, Marshall and Co., 1893), Vol. I, p. 373.
72. Deborah Gorham, 'Victorian Reform as a Family Business', in A. S. Wohl (ed.), *The Victorian Family. Structure and Stresses* (Croom Helm, 1978), see pp. 120–6.
73. J. F. C. Harrison, *Robert Owen and the Owenites in Britain and America. The Quest for the New Moral World* (Routledge and Kegan Paul, 1969), p. 6.
74. Ibid., p. 87; Harold Silver, 'Owen's Reputation as an Educationalist', in S. Pollard and J. Salt (eds), *Robert Owen. Prophet of the Poor. Essays in Honour of the Two Hundredth Anniversary of his Birth* (Macmillan, 1971), Chapter 4. See especially p. 79; *Monthly Repository*, Vol. XVII, 1823, pp. 450–7, cited in Mineka, *Dissidence of Dissent*, p. 163.
75. 'Social Calumny against Unitarians', *New Moral World* (hereafter cited as

NMW), Vol. IX, no. 23, 6 June 1841, p. 359; 'Letter to Editor', *Movement*, Vol. I, no. 12, pp. 92–3.

76. Watts, 'Unitarian Contribution to Education', p. 424; Morley, *The Life and Times of Henry Crabb Robinson*, p. 136.

77. 'Mr. Holyoake's Provincial Representation', *Reasoner*, Vol. V, no. III, 1848, p. 107.

78. Watts, 'Unitarian Contribution to Education', p. 424. Mary A. De Morgan (ed.), *Three Score Years and Ten. Reminiscences of the Late Sophia Elizabeth De Morgan* (Richard Bentley and Son, 1895), pp. 137–60.

79. Solly, *These Eighty Years*, Vol. I, p. 412.

80. 'Letters from a French Correspondent', *Unitarian Chronicle*, no. 5, June 1832, p. 92; Mineka, *Dissidence of Dissent*, pp. 213–14.

81. Mazzini, 'Thoughts upon Democracy in Europe', *People's Journal*, Vol. I, no. 5, 26 December 1846, pp. 361–4; Vol. II, no. 58, 6 February 1847, pp. 79–81.

82. George G. Iggers (ed.), *The Doctrine of Saint-Simon. An Exposition. First Year, 1828–1829* (New York: Schocken, 1972), passim; Bowring, *Autobiographical Recollections*, p. 313.

83. Barbara Taylor, *Eve and the New Jerusalem. Socialism and Feminism in the Nineteenth Century* (Virago, 1983); Gail Malmgreen, *Neither Bread nor Roses. Utopian Feminists and the English Working Class 1800–1850* (Brighton: John L. Noyce, 1978).

84. Mineka, *Dissidence of Dissent*, p. 284; Seed, 'Theologies of Power', pp. 137–9; Ruth Watts, 'Knowledge is Power   Unitarians, Gender and Education in the Eighteenth and Early Nineteenth Centuries', *Gender and Education*, Vol. 1, no. 1, 1989, pp. 47–8; she does not discuss its implications. Elizabeth Isichei has hinted that a disparity between liberal ideology and social conservatism might have spurred Quaker women to feminist awareness. Isichei, *Victorian Quakers* (Oxford: Oxford University Press, 1970), p. 252.

85. Ruth Watts, 'The Unitarian Contribution to the Development of Female Education, 1790–1850', *History of Education*, Vol. 9, no. 4, 1980, p. 275.

86. Henderson, *A Memoir of the Late Rev George Armstrong*, p. 114.

87. Shirren, *Samuel Rogers*, (n.p.); Watts, 'Unitarian Contribution to Education', pp. 71–2.

88. Knight, *University Rebel*, pp. 199–203.

89. Watts, 'Unitarian Contribution to Education', p. 76.

90. Leonore Davidoff and Catherine Hall, *Family Fortunes. Men and Women of the English Middle Class* (Hutchinson, 1987), passim.

91. Judy Lown, *Women and Industrialisation. Gender at Work in Nineteenth Century England* (Cambridge: Polity Press, 1990), e.g. pp. 97–8.

92. Catherine Hall, 'The Early Formation of Victorian Domestic Ideology', in S. Burman (ed.), *Fit Work for Women* (Croom Helm, 1979), pp. 15–32.

93. Lown, *Women and Industrialisation*, p. 176 in particular.

94. John Seed, 'Unitarianism, Political Economy and the Antinomies of Liberal Culture in Manchester, 1830–1850', *Social History*, 7, 1982, see p. 25.

95. Robberds, *A Memoir of the Life and Writings of the Late William Taylor*, p. 40; MS letter from W. J. Fox to Henry Crabb Robinson, 10 June 1832, Henry Crabb Robinson, Letters 1832–3, fol. 29, Dr Williams's Library.

96. Robberds, *A Memoir of the Life and Writings of the Late William Taylor*, Vol. 1, p. 44.
97. Elizabeth Fletcher, 'Hannah Greg née Lightbody (1766–1828)', (unpublished essay, Styal Museum); 'Obituary of William Rathbone', *Liverpool Mercury*, 6 February 1868.
98. MS letter from William Rathbone to Elizabeth Rathbone, 3 March 1833, Sidney Jones Library, Liverpool University, Rathbone Collection, VI.1.60; MS letter from Mary Howitt to Elizabeth Rathbone, 1 May 1846; MS letter from Anna Jameson to Elizabeth Rathbone, 1856, ibid., VI.1.463a, VI.1.463D.
99. F. B. Tolles (ed.), *Slavery and the 'Woman Question', Lucretia Mott's Diary of her Visit to Great Britain to Attend the World's Anti-Slavery Convention of 1840* (Friends' Historical Society, 1952), p. 76; see also pp. 15, 62.
100. MS records of the Roscoe Club, Liverpool Record Office, 920 MUS 2–45. This aspect of the Roscoe Club is discussed in Chapter 5.
101. MS letter from William Rathbone to Elizabeth Rathbone, [n.d.], Sidney Jones Library, University of Liverpool, IX. 9.9.
102. Sheila R. Herstein, *A Mid-Victorian Feminist. Barbara Leigh Smith Bodichon* (New Haven: Yale University Press, 1985), pp. 8–16.
103. MS letter from Patty Smith to Fanny Allen, 27 March 1843, Cambridge University, William Smith Papers, Add. MS 7621, MS calendar 339; MS memoirs of Julia Smith, Cambridge University, William Smith Papers, Add. MS 7621.
104. Elizabeth Gaskell to Eliza Fox, February 1853, in Chapple and Pollard (eds), *The Letters of Mrs. Gaskell*, pp. 222–3.
105. Watts, 'Unitarian Contribution to Education', in particular pp. 52 and 71–6; Watts, 'Knowledge is Power', p. 39.
106. McLachlan, *The Unitarian Movement in the Religious Life of England*, p. 106.
107. Mineka, *Dissidence of Dissent*, p. 158.
108. Hope Malleson, *Elizabeth Malleson 1828–1916, Autobiographical Notes and Letters* (Printed for Private Circulation, 1926), pp. 35–6.
109. Sarah Austin cited the correspondence in a letter to Barthélemy St Hilaire, 27 June 1860, quoted in Janet Ross, *Three Generations of English Women. Memoirs and Correspondence of Susannah Taylor, Sarah Austin and Lady Duff Gordon* (T. Fisher Unwin, 1893), pp. 363–4.
110. Sarah Austin, *Two Letters on Girls' School and on the Training of Working Women* (Chapman and Hall, 1857), p. 8; Tolles, *Slavery and the 'Woman Question'*, pp. 59–60; Bushrod, 'History of Unitarianism in Birmingham', p. 173.
111. Watts, 'Knowledge is Power', pp. 44–5.
112. Hall, 'Early Formation of Domestic Ideology'.
113. Lucy Aikin to Dr Channing, 16 May 1840, Le Breton (ed.), *Memoirs, Miscellanies and Letters of the Late Lucy Aikin*, no. 44, p. 399.
114. John Squier, *The Character and Mission of Woman. A Lecture, Applicable to the New Marriage Law* (Smallfield and Son, 1837), pp. 6–7, 11, 18–19. For a rather different interpretation of Squier's work, see Watts, 'The Unitarian Contribution to Female Education', p. 281.
115. Squier, *The Character and Mission of Woman*, pp. 24, 19–20, 6.

116. Robert Aspland, *The Beneficial Influence of Christianity on the Character and Conditions of the Female Sex. A Sermon Preached at the Rev. Dr Rees's Meeting-House* (J. Johnson, 1812), pp. 3, 27.

117. MS letter from Emma Stansfeld to Maria Stansfeld, 2 October 1840, Leeds Archives, Dixon and Stansfeld Papers, Accession 2311.

118. Stinchcombe, 'Elizabeth Malleson', p. 57; Frances Power Cobbe, *Life of Frances Power Cobbe by Herself* (Boston and New York: Riverside Press, 1894), Vol. I, p. 100; Letter from Susannah Taylor to J. Beecroft, 11 April 1785, cited in Ross, *Three Generations of English Women*, pp. 19–21.

119. Quoted in Margaret Bryant, *The Unexpected Revolution. A Study in the History of the Education of Women and Girls in the Nineteenth Century* (University of London Institute of Education, 1979), p. 39.

120. Jane Rendall, 'Friendship and Politics: Barbara Leigh Smith Bodichon (1827–91) and Bessie Raynor Parkes (1829–1925)', in Jane Rendall and Susan Mendus (eds), *Sexuality and Subordination. Interdisciplinary Studies of Gender in the Nineteenth Century* (Routledge, 1989), pp. 136–70. See p. 145.

121. MS letter from Bessie Parkes to Barbara Leigh Smith, 1847, Girton College, Parkes Papers, BRP V 2; MS letter from Barbara Leigh Smith to Bessie Parkes, [1848], Girton College, Parkes Papers, BRP 165/¹. A full analysis of the significance of this correspondence is given in Chapter 6 below. Barbara Leigh Smith Bodichon is normally referred to as Barbara Leigh Smith, although her married name is used, when appropriate, in the notes.

122. MS letter from Bessie Parkes to Barbara Leigh Smith, 5 December 1849, Girton College, Parkes Papers, BRP 39.

123. Elizabeth Gaskell to Lady Kay-Shuttleworth, 14 May 1850, Chapple and Pollard (eds), *The Letters of Mrs. Gaskell*, p. 116; Elizabeth Gaskell to Emily Shaen, 27 October 1854, ibid., p. 318; Elizabeth Gaskell to Eliza Fox, [February] 1850, ibid., pp. 106–7.

124. Elizabeth Gaskell to Emily Shaen, 27 October 1854, ibid., p. 316; Elizabeth Gaskell to Eliza Fox, [February] 1850, ibid., p. 108.

125. Elizabeth Gaskell to Eliza Fox, 26 April 1850, ibid., p. 113.

126. A point many historians of Unitarianism have noted. See for example, Mineka, *The Dissidence of Dissent*, p. 284; Watts, 'Knowledge is Power', pp. 42–3.

127. Bushrod, 'The History of Unitarianism in Birmingham', p. 61.

128. Harriet Martineau, *Autobiography* (Virago, 1983, first published 1877), Vol. II, p. 121; Elizabeth Gaskell to unknown correspondent, March 1849, Chapple and Pollard (eds), *The Letters of Mrs. Gaskell*, pp. 71–2.

129. Mary Carpenter to Dr Guillaume, 12 February 1873, J. Estlin Carpenter, *The Life and Work of Mary Carpenter* (Macmillan, 1879), p. 405; Dr P. Carpenter to Professor Henry, 4 July 1860, ibid., pp. 266–7.

130. Sarah Austin to W. E. Gladstone, 27 May 1839, cited in Ross, *Three Generations of English Women*, pp. 149–50; Sarah Austin to Dr Sciortino, 10 May 1839, pp. 147–8.

131. Geraldine Jewsbury to Jane Carlyle, 1849, Annie E. Ireland (ed.), *Selections from the Letters of Geraldine Endsor Jewsbury to Jane Welsh Carlyle* (Longmans, Green, 1892), p. 348.

2 'The Assemblage of the Just' – the Radical Unitarians

1. Richard Hengist Horne so dubbed W. J. Fox's circle, cited in Margaret Parnaby, 'William Johnson Fox and the Monthly Repository Circle of 1832 to 1836' (PhD thesis, Australian National University, 1979), p. 236.

2. Francis E. Mineka, *Dissidence of Dissent. The Monthly Repository 1806–38* (Chapel Hill: University of North Carolina, 1944), pp. 267–72; Richard Garnett, *The Life of W. J. Fox. Public Teacher and Social Reformer, 1786– 1864* (John Lane, 1909), pp. 24, 70. Fox was well-acquainted with the 'new Unitarians', J. J. Tayler and J. Martineau. For Fox's promotion of German thought and letters see Ruth Watts, 'The Unitarian Contribution to Education from the Late Eighteenth Century to 1853', (PhD thesis, University of Leicester, 1987), pp. 39–41.

3. William J. Linton, *James Watson. A Memoir* (New York: Augustus M. Kelley 1971, first published 1880), p. 58.

4. MS letter from W. J. Fox to Henry Crabb Robinson, 2 April 1832, Henry Crabb Robinson, Letters, 1832–3, fol. 19, Dr Williams's Library; Sheila R. Herstein, *A Mid-Victorian Feminist. Barbara Leigh Smith Bodichon* (New Haven: Yale University Press, 1985), p. 47; Letter to Editor from James Alexander Emerton, 'Metropolitan University', *MR*, Vol. X, 1836, p. 168; 'The *Monthly Repository*', *Crisis*, Vol. II, no. 22, 8 June 1833, p. 174.

5. MLG, 'Female Education', *MR*, Vol. IX, 1835, p. 108.

6. Junius Redivivus, 'On the Condition of Women in England', *MR*, Vol. VII, 1833, pp. 217–31, see pp. 217, 228.

7. Letter from Lant Carpenter to W. J. Fox, 2–4 [*sic*] April 1833, Letter from Lant Carpenter to Editor, 12 February 1837, both reprinted in *Christian Reformer*, Vol. IV, 1837, pp. 234–6; R. Brook Aspland, *Memoir of the Life, Works and Correspondence of the Rev. Robert Aspland of Hackney* (Edward T. Whitfield, 1850), p. 546.

8. MS letters from Eliza Flower to Harriet Taylor, British Library of Political and Economic Science, Mill-Taylor Collection, Vol. XXVII, nos 10–39; Garnett, *The Life of W. J. Fox*, pp. 159–67.

9. W. J. Fox to the members of the congregation of South Place, 15 August 1834; Resolution of the Dissenting Members of the Congregation, 4 September 1834; Resolutions of the Finsbury Congregation, passed at the Special General Meeting, held 1 September 1834, 24.86. (17, 19–20), Dr Williams's Library.

10. MS letter from Rev. S. Armstrong to James Martineau, 5 March 1835, Manchester College, Oxford, MS J. Martineau 3, 165; John Seed, 'Theologies of Power: Unitarianism and the Social Relations of Religious Discourse', in R. J. Morris (ed.), *Class Power and Social Structure in British Nineteenth Century Towns* (Leicester: Leicester University Press, 1986), p. 139; S. K. Ratcliffe, *The Story of South Place* (Watts, 1955), p. 17.

11. T. Carlyle to John A. Carlyle, 28 October 1834, C. R. Saunders (ed.), *The Collected Letters of Thomas and Jane Welsh Carlyle* (Durham, North Carolina: Duke University Press, 1977), p. 327; James Martineau's MS comments on Harriet Martineau's letters to him, 5 May 1830; letter from Harriet to James Martineau, 2 January 1834, transcribed from J. Martineau's shorthand by V. S. Coloe, Manchester College, Oxford, MS. J. Martineau

1, pp. 103, 145; P. A. Taylor's comments were quoted in South Place Congregational Resolution, 26 May 1835, South Place Ethical Society, uncatalogued material.

12. J. J. Tayler to W. J. Fox, 12 June 1835, Garnett, *The Life of W. J. Fox*, pp. 118–19; TS letter from J. B. Estlin to William Shaen, 28 August 1847 (transcribed by Shaen's daughter, M. J. Shaen), Leeds Archives, Symington Papers, Box 19.

13. John Guy, *Physician of Mankind. The Life of Thomas Southwood Smith*, forthcoming.

14. *Christian Reformer*, Vol. II, 1835, pp. 532–6; *MR*, Vol. IX, 1835, pp. 153–60.

15. 'Our Library', *People's Journal*, Vol. II, no. 28, 11 July 1846, p. 25.

16. Margaret Parnaby, 'William Johnson Fox and the *Monthly Repository* Circle of 1832–1836', (PhD thesis, Australian National University, 1979).

17. For biographical details of Fox, see Graham Wallas, *William Johnson Fox, 1786–1864. Conway Memorial Lecture* (Watts, 1924), pp. 10–27; E. F. Bridell-Fox, *Sarah Flower Adams: A Memoir and Her Hymns* (Christian Life Publishing Company, 1894), pp. 6–7; 'William Bridges Adams', *Engineering*, 26 July 1872, pp. 63–4.

18. E. Morris Miller, 'Australia's First Two Novels. Origins and Backgrounds', Tasmanian Historical Research Association *Papers and Proceedings*, Vol. 6, 1957, pp. 37–49, 54–65; Michael Roe, 'Mary Leman Grimstone (1800–1850?): For Women's Rights and Tasmanian Patriotism', Tasmanian Historical Research Association *Papers and Proceedings*, Vol. 36, no. 1, March 1989, pp. 9–32. Grimstone has received brief treatment in Jane Rendall, *The Origins of Modern Feminism: Women in Britain. France and the United States, 1780–1860* (Chicago: Lyceum, 1985), pp. 115, 116, 129, 309; Olive Banks, *Biographical Dictionary of Modern Feminists, Vol. 1: 1800–1930* (Brighton: 1985), pp. 90–1; Taylor, *Eve and the New Jerusalem*, p. 281; John Killham, *Tennyson and The Princess. Reflections of an Age* (Athlone Press, 1958), pp. 50–1. For a few examples of contemporaries' acknowledgement of Grimstone see *MR*, 1834, Vol. VIII, pp. 299–303; *Tatler*, no. 59, 6 October 1832, p. 489; *Reasoner*, Vol. III, no. 63, 1847, p. 434; *Leeds Times*, 9 November 1839, p. 6; *Tait's Edinburgh Magazine*, November 1835, p. 707.

19. Ann Blainey, *The Farthing Poet. A Biography of Richard Hengist Horne 1802–84. A Lesser Literary Lion* (Longman, 1968), pp. 2–6, 62–3; Lady Lindsay, 'Some Recollections of Miss Margaret Gillies', *Temple Bar*, Vol. 81, 1887, p. 265.

20. 'Lectures on the Morality of the Various Classes', *NMW*, Vol. II, no. 59, 12 December 1835, p. 52.

21. Hollingshead, *My Life Time* (Marston, 1895), Vol. I, p. 45; E. F. Bridell-Fox, 'Robert Browning', *Argosy*, 1890, pp. 108–4. The Mill–Taylor connection is well documented. See, for example, Alice S. Rossi (ed.), *Essays on Sex Equality* (Chicago: University of Chicago Press, 1970), pp. 19–21. Charles Dickens went to make many close contacts with these circles. As we shall see, he relied upon them when he established the *Daily News* and was also vice-president of their Whittington Club. He was particularly well-acquainted with Douglas Jerrold – a leading radical unitarian; for his relationship with the Howitts, see Carl Ray Woodring, *Victorian Samplers:*

William and Mary Howitt (Lawrence: University of Kansas Press, 1952), p. 151.

22. Hollingshead, *My Lifetime*, p. 45; R. D. Altick, *The Cowden Clarkes* (Oxford: Oxford University Press, 1948), p. 19. Mary Cowden Clarke, *My Long Life* (T. Fisher Unwin, 1896), pp. 24–5.

23. Brenda Colloms, ' "Tottie" Fox, Her Life and Background', *Gaskell Society Journal*, Vol. V, 1991, pp. 16–26; Blainey, *Farthing Poet*, pp. 66–9; MS reports for South Place Chapel for 1845, 1849, 1851, South Place Ethical Society (uncatalogued material).

24. MS letter from Harriet Taylor to John Taylor, 1847, British Library of Political and Economic Science, Mill–Taylor Collection, Vol. XXVIII, no. 163.

25. See Woodring, *Victorian Samplers* (Lawrence: University of Kansas Press, 1952), pp. 115, 119; William J. Linton, *Memories* (Lawrence and Bullen, 1895), pp. 24–6.

26. Mineka, *Dissidence of Dissent*, p. 386; Jameson enjoyed contacts with a number of mainstream Unitarian families, for example, the Rathbones and the Thoms (MS letter from Anna Jameson to Elizabeth Rathbone, 1 May 1846, Sydney Jones Library, Rathbone Collection, VI.1.463D).

27. Gillian Darley, *Octavia Hill* (London, 1990), pp. 21–7; 'Prospectus', *Star in the East*, Vol. I, no. 1, 17 September 1838.

28. Linton, *James Watson*, pp. 58–60; Linton, *Memories* is useful for the influence which the Fox circle had upon him.

29. G. J. Holyoake, *Sixty Years of an Agitator's Life* (T. Fisher Unwin, 1906), pp. 182–6; Banks, *Biographical Dictionary*, pp. 6–7.

30. MS letter from W. H. Ashurst to Wendell Phillips, 17 June 1840, MS letters from W. H. Ashurst to William Lloyd Garrison, 18 June 1840, 30 June 1840, 26 July 1840, Boston Public Library, MS.A.1.Z.v.9. The conference had a striking effect upon the views of James Stansfeld, for example. Barbara and J. L. Hammond, *James Stansfeld. A Victorian Champion of Sex Equality* (Longmans, Green, 1932), p. 286.

31. Jessie White Mario, *The Birth of Modern Italy* (T. Fisher Unwin, 1909), p. 93; MS letter from Elisa Bardouneau-Narcy, to Elizabeth Neall Gay, October 1841, Sydney Howard Gay Papers, The Rare Book and Manuscript Library, Columbia University Library, letter from Jane Welsh Carlyle to Jennie Welsh, 24 April 1847 in L. Huxley (ed.), *Jane Welsh Carlyle: Letters to her Family. 1839–1863* (John Murray, 1924), no. 129, pp. 299–300.

32. Information on the Biggs brothers may be found in A. Temple Patterson, *Radical Leicester 1780–1850* (Leicester: University College Leicester, 1954), passim.

33. Details of this group emerge in Hammond and Hammond, *James Stansfeld*; E. F. Richards, *Mazzini's Letters to an English Family 1844–1845* (John Lane, 1920). The correspondence of Eliza Ashurst is also most useful – MS letters from Elisa Bardouneau-Narcy to Elizabeth Neall Gay, Sydney Howard Gay Papers, The Rare Book and Manuscript Library, Columbia University. Shaen's life has been documented in M. J. Shaen (ed.), *William Shaen. A Brief Sketch* (Longmans, Green, 1912). Some information on the career of John Humphreys Parry emerges in Edward Royle, *Victorian Infidels. The*

Origins of the British Secularist Movement 1791–1866 (Manchester: Manchester University Press, 1974), see pp. 79–80, 85 and 146.

34. Robert Spears, *Memorable Unitarians* (British and Foreign Unitarian Association, 1906), p. 392.

35. Letter from Mazzini to his mother, 24 July 1846, in Mario, *Birth of Modern Italy*, p. 93; MS letters from Elisa Bardouneau-Narcy to Elizabeth Neall Gay, October 1841 and 6 March 1846, Sydney Howard Gay Papers, The Rare Book and Manuscript Library, Columbia University.

36. Richards, *Mazzini's Letters*, p. 40; Mrs E. Epps (ed.), *Diary of the Late John Epps, M. D., Edinburgh* (Kent and Co., 1875), pp. 376–7.

37. See Rasor's entries in J. O. S. Baylen and N. J. Gossman (eds), *Biographical Dictionary of Modern British Radicals* (Hassocks: Harvester Press, 1979); Lee Virginia Chambers-Schiller, 'The CAB: A Trans-Atlantic Community, Aspects of Nineteenth Century Reform' (PhD thesis, University of Michigan, 1977).

38. Owen Stinchcombe, 'Elizabeth Malleson (1828–1916)', and Alan Ruston, 'Clementia Taylor (1810–1908)', in *Transactions of the Unitarian Historical Society*, Vol. XX, no. 1, April 1991, pp. 56–61, 62–8. A good picture of the Chapman circle emerges in Chapman's diary, Gordon S. Haight (ed.), *George Eliot and John Chapman. With Chapman's Diaries* (Hamden, Connecticut: Archon Books, 1969, second edition).

39. Harry W. Rudman, *Italian Nationalism and English Letters* (George Allen and Unwin, 1940); Richards, *Mazzini's Letters*; Tyne and Wear Record Office, TWAS 634/ A.13, A.8, A.166.

40. The Barmbys have been well covered in the Owenite literature. For a particularly clear account see the entry in J. M. Bellamy and J. Saville (eds), *Dictionary of Labour Biography* (Macmillan, 1982). Ashurst's view of Barmby emerges in Richards, *Mazzini's Letters*, pp. 63–6.

41. Sally Mitchell, *The Fallen Angel. Chastity, Class and Women's Reading 1835–80* (Bowling Green, Kentucky: University Popular Press, 1981) provides some insight into the work of these writers. Lee Holcombe, *Wives and Property, Reform of the Married Women's Property Law in Nineteenth Century England* (Toronto: University of Toronto Press, 1983), pp. 84–5 has a useful sketch of Hays's career. See also the entries in V. Blain, P. Clements and I. Grundy (eds), *Feminist Companion to Literature in English. Women Writers from the Middle Ages to the Present* (Batsford, 1990).

42. MS letter from Mary Howitt to Eliza Meteyard [n.d.], Houghton Library, Harvard University, fMS Eng 883.1. Quoted by permission of the Houghton Library, Harvard University.

43. MS letter from Mary Howitt to Eliza Meteyard, 1848, Houghton Library, Harvard University, fMS Eng 883.1. MS letter from Eliza Meteyard to Mr Blewitt, 30 March 1868, National Library of Scotland, MS 966, ff.242–4; MS letters from Mary Leman Gillies to William James Linton, 18 May 1847 and undated, Biblioteca Archivio G. C. Feltrinelli, Milan, Archivio Linton, Vol. II-43. MS letter from Mary Leman Gillies to Leigh Hunt [n.d.], and Leigh Hunt's reply, 4 January [n.y.], Iowa University Library, MSL H94g.

44. The Bray and Hennell families are best approached through the George Eliot literature, for example, Gordon S. Haight, *The George Eliot Letters* (Oxford University Press, 1954), Vol. I, passim. See pp. 242–3 for the

impact of George Dawson. Useful information on Dawson may also be found in Emily Bushrod, 'The History of Unitarianism in Birmingham from the Middle of the Eighteenth Century to 1893', (MA thesis, University of Birmingham, 1954), pp. 10, 134; F. B. Smith, *Radical Artisan. William James Linton 1812–1897* (Manchester: Manchester University Press, 1973), p. 108.

45. J. F. C. Harrison, *Learning and Living 1790–1960. A Study in the History of the English Adult Education Movement* (Routledge and Kegan Paul, 1961), pp. 118–51. The Gaskell–Gillies relationship is indicated in MS letters from Mary Gaskell to Samuel Wilderspin, December 1846 and 1 July 1846, University College, London, Wilderspin Collection, MS 917.

46. MS letter from Mary Howitt to Eliza Meteyard [n.d.], Houghton Library, Harvard University, fMS Eng 883.1. Quoted by permission of the Houghton Library, Harvard; Chambers-Schiller, 'The CAB', p. 2.

47. Margaret Howitt (ed.), *Mary Howitt, An Autobiography* (Isbister, 1889), Vol. II, p. 38; Woodring, *Victorian Samplers*, p. 115.

48. Mazzini to George Sand, 16 January 1847, G. Lubin (ed.), *Correspondance de George Sand* (Paris: Garnier Frères, 1964), Vol. VII, p. 603; *Liberator*, 26 March 1847.

49. Holcombe, *Wives and Property*, p. 59.

50. MS letter from Bessie Raynor Parkes to her father, [1850], Girton College, Cambridge, Parkes Papers, BRP II 37; MS letter from W. H. Ashurst to William Lloyd Garrison, 30 June 1840, Boston Public Library, MS.A.1.Z.v.9.

51. E. F. Bridell-Fox, 'Memories', in *Girls Own Paper*, Vol. XI, no. 551, 19 July 1890, pp. 657–61; Harrison, *Learning and Living*, p. 32.

52. Mrs Newton Crosland, *Landmarks of a Literary Life* (Sampson Low, Marston, 1893), p. 153. Although women did not escape Jerrold's love of satire; see, for example, Walter Jerrold, *Douglas Jerrold. Dramatist and Wit* (Hodder and Stoughton, 1914), Vol. II, pp. 505–6.

53. Such views were most clearly explicated in Jerrold's 'Q' articles for *Punch*. See Bruce A. White, 'Douglas Jerrold's "Q" Papers in Punch', *Victorian Periodicals Review*, Vol. 25, no. 4, Winter 1982, pp. 131–7.

54. MS letter from R. H. Horne to Edgar Allan Poe, 16 April 1844, Boston Public Library, MS. Gris. 582; William Blanchard Jerrold, *The Life and Remains of Douglas Jerrold* (W. Kent and Co., 1859), p. 229; Letter to Garrison from Edward Search, *Liberator*, 11 June 1847.

55. Parnaby, 'William Johnson Fox', p. xx.

56. MS letter from Mary Howitt to Eliza Meteyard, 5 August 1847, Houghton Library, Harvard University, fMS Eng 883.1. Quoted by permission of Houghton Library, Harvard University; Harrison, *Learning and Living*, pp. 32–3, 140–151; Martha Vicinus, *The Industrial Muse. A Study of Nineteenth Century British Working-Class Literature* (Croom Helm, 1974), pp. 117, 161.

57. J. S. Mill to Thomas Carlyle, 17 September 1832, F. E. Mineka, *The Earlier Letters of John Stuart Mill, 1812–1848* (Toronto: University of Toronto Press, 1963), pp. 117–18; Mary A. De Morgan (ed.), *Three Score Years and Ten. Reminiscences of the Late Sophia Elizabeth De Morgan* (Richard Bentley and Son, 1895), pp. 90–1.

58. For example, W. J. Fox, 'Church Establishment', *National*, 1839, pp. 283–5; Parnaby, 'William Johnson Fox', see especially p. 158. Harrison, *Learning*

and Living, considers the influence of American transcendentalism upon English radical circles, pp. 140–4.

59. 'Letter on Unitarianism from Gloucestrensis', *Leader*, 9 November 1851, p. 783; J. S. Mill to John Pringle Nichol, 17 January 1834, Mineka (ed.), *The Earlier Letters of John Stuart Mill*, p. 209.

60. For the relationship between secularism and feminism, see J. A. Banks, *Victorian Values. Secularism and the Size of Families* (Routledge and Kegan Paul, 1981). Holyoake's contact with Unitarianism emerges in Holyoake, *Sixty Years of an Agitator's Life*, pp. 35, 47–8, 76–7; 'Letter to the Rev. Joseph Barker now a Preacher among the Unitarians', *Reasoner*, Vol. III, no. 58, 1847, pp. 359–60. For radical unitarian views of Holyoake's philosophy, see Panthea, 'Criticisms of the Reasoner', *Reasoner*, Vol. V, no. 130, 1848, pp. 408–10; MS letter from Charles Bray to G. J. Holyoake, 28 May 1848, Co-operative Union, Manchester, G. J. Holyoake Collection, no. 277 and MS letter from W. H. Ashurst to G. J. Holyoake, 20 December 1863, ibid., no. 1518.

61. MS letter from Thomas Powell to William Wordsworth, 20 July 1839, Dove Cottage, WLMS A/ Powell, Thomas /5; MS letter from William Howitt to James Hogg, 20 December 1828, National Library of Scotland, MS 2245, f.135.

62. Wordsworth, 'On the Projected Kendal and Windermere Railway', reprinted in Thomas Hutchinson (ed.), *Wordsworth's Poetical Works* (Oxford: Oxford University Press, 1978), p. 224; Dickens, *Dombey and Son* (Harmondsworth: Penguin, 1970, first published 1844–6), p. 290; William Bridges, 'The Railway', *People's Journal*, Vol. III, no. 60, 20 February 1847, p. 53. 'Modern Painters', *Douglas Jerrold's Shilling Magazine*, Vol. IV, July–December 1846, p. 11.

63. Letter to Garrison from Edward Search, *Liberator*, 25 June 1847.

64. See Adams's obituary in *Engineering*, 26 July 1872, pp. 63–4; MS letter from William Bridges Adams, 29 January 1857, National Library of Scotland, MS 51.1.15.

65. John Saunders, 'Some Points for a New People's Charter', *Illuminated Magazine*, Vol. IV, 1846, pp. 17–23. 'Rustic Townsmen', *Household Words*, 1859; H. J. Dyos, 'Railways and Housing in Victorian London', in D. Cannadine and D. Reeder (eds), *Exploring the Urban Past. Essays on Urban History by H. J. Dyos* (Cambridge: Cambridge University Press, 1982), pp. 101–18.

66. Webb, 'The Unitarian Background', p. 17.

67. W. J. Linton, 'Fair Field Festival', *People's Journal*, Vol. III, no. 76, 12 June 1847, pp. 333–4; *Reasoner*, Vol. II, 1847, no. 52, p. 53; 'Junius Redivivus on the Working Classes', *Tait's Edinburgh Magazine*, Vol. I, April 1834, pp. 179–83.

68. Mrs Leman Gillies, 'Rational Revolution', *People's Journal*, Vol. V, 1848, p. 199.

69. Taylor, *Eve and the New Jerusalem*, pp. 118–82; John Bowring, *Autobiographical Recollections of Sir John Bowring, With a Brief Memoir by Lewin B. Bowring* (Henry S. King, 1877), pp. 384–5.

70. 'The Right of Woman', *National*, 1839, pp. 135–9; 'On Female Education and Occupations', *MR*, Vol. VII, 1833, p. 491.

71. 'The Work of Today', *People's Journal*, Vol. I, no. 25, 20 June 1845, p. 341.

72. MS letter from Lady Byron to John Finch, 1831, Bodleian Library, Lovelace Byron Papers, Box 69, f.110; *NMW*, Vol. II, no. 59, 12 December 1835, p. 55.

73. *Westminster Review*, Vol. I, January 1824, cited in G. L. Nesbitt, *Benthamite Reviewing. The First Twelve Years of the Westminster Review 1824–1836* (New York: Columbia University Press, 1934), p. 42. 'Lectures on the Morality of the Various Classes, By the Rev. W. J. Fox', *NMW*, Vol. II, no. 61, 26 December 1835, p. 72.

74. Junius Redivivus, 'Housebuilding and Housekeeping', *MR*, Vol. VIII, 1834, pp. 485–94.

75. See, for example, Mary Gillies, 'Associated Homes for the Middle Classes', *Howitt's Journal*, Vol. I, no. 20, 15 May 1847, p. 271; W. Howitt, 'Observations on the Proposed Whittington Club', *People's Journal*, Vol. II, no. 43, 17 October 1846, p. 238.

76. For example, Andrew Winter, 'A Visit to the Model Lodging House, St. Giles', *People's Journal*, Vol. IV, no. 88, 4 September 1847, pp. 132–4.

77. RHH, 'The Dreamer and the Worker', *Douglas Jerrold's Shilling Magazine*, Vol. VI, July–December 1847, pp. 499–500.

78. *People*, Vol. I, no. 38, 1848; p. 303; Junius Redivivus, *The Rights of Morality* (Effingham Wilson, 1832, second edition), p. 203; 'Report of Emerson's Lectures', *Douglas Jerrold's Weekly Newspaper*, no. 101, 17 June 1848, p. 740.

79. Goodwyn Barmby, 'United Service Family Associations', *Howitt's Journals*, Vol. I, no. 25, 19 June 1847, p. 344. For the Owenite position, see Harrison, *Owen and the Owenites*, pp. 59–60.

80. William Lovett, *The Life and Struggles of William Lovett* (Trübner, 1876), p. 50.

81. 'Associated Homes', *Eliza Cook's Journal*, Vol. IV, no. 89, 11 January 1851, p. 172; Mary Gillies, 'Associated Homes for the Middle Classes', *Howitt's Journal*, Vol. I, no. 20, 15 May 1847, p. 270.

82. Lewis A. Coser, *Men of Ideas* (New York: The Free Press, 1965), see p. 47 especially; T. W. Heyck, *The Transformation of Intellectual Life in Victorian England* (Croom Helm, 1982), passim, also considers the rise of the middle-class reading audience, and to a lesser extent, the labour aristocracy.

83. G. Anderson, *Victorian Clerks* (Manchester: Manchester University Press, 1976); Geoffrey Crossick, *An Artisan Elite in Victorian Society. Kentish London 1840–1880* (Croom Helm, 1978); Robert Q. Gray, *The Labour Aristocracy in Victorian Edinburgh* (Oxford: Clarendon Press, 1976).

84. There are numerous references. The following are representative: 'Weekly Record', *Howitt's Journal*, Vol. I, no. 2, 9 January 1847, p. 3 and 'Weekly Record', Vol. II, no. 27, 3 July 1847, p. 15; 'The Co-operative League Soirée', *Douglas Jerrold's Weekly Newspaper*, no. 34, 6 March 1847, p. 285.

85. Mary Leman Gillies, 'The Commonwealth of Industry', *People's Journal*, Vol. I, no. 15, 11 April 1846, p. 200.

86. 'The Whittington Club', *Douglas Jerrold's Weekly Newspaper*, no. 1, 18 July 1846, p. 14.

87. William Linwood, Speeches Delivered at the Soirée, held at the National

Hall, Holborn, on 23 February 1848, Birmingham City Archives, MS 753 (Lovett Collection) National Association papers, p. 237.

88. 'Junius Redivivus on the Working Classes', *Tait's Edinburgh Magazine*, Vol. 1, April 1834, p. 180. See also Parnaby, 'William Johnson Fox', pp. 94ff. Barbara Leigh Smith Bodichon, 'Middle-Class Schools for Girls', *English Woman's Journal*, November 1860, reprinted in C. A. Lacey (ed.), *Barbara Leigh Smith Bodichon and the Langham Place Circle* (Routledge and Kegan Paul, 1987), p. 77.

89. Judy Lown, *Women and Industrialisation. Gender at Work in Nineteenth Century England* (Cambridge: Polity Press, 1990), pp. 159–66.

90. Barbara Bodichon, 'Middle-Class Schools for Girls', p. 77.

91. Thomas Carlyle, *On Heroes, Hero-Worship and the Heroic in History* (Chapman and Hall, 1898, first published 1841), pp. 155–6; Bridell-Fox, *Sarah Flower Adams*, p. 10.

92. MS letter from William Howitt, 10 March 1832, Boston Public Library, MS Eng. 328 (2). The desperate financial problems which such writers often faced emerge clearly in the uncatalogued correspondence between Mary Howitt and Eliza Meteyard, Houghton Library, Harvard University, fMS Eng 883.1.

93. Nesbitt, *Benthamite Reviewing*, p. 97; Vicinus, *The Industrial Muse*, p. 96.

94. *MR*, Vol. VIII, 1834, p. 300; *Douglas Jerrold's Shilling Magazine*, Vol. III, January–June 1846, p. 89.

95. Lucy Aikin to Dr Channing, 7 April 1832, Le Breton, *Memoirs, Miscellanies and Letters of the Late Lucy Aikin*, p. 259.

96. Mary Leman Grimstone, *Cleone. A Tale of Married Life* (Effingham Wilson, 1834), Vol. II, p. 276; John Stores Smith, *Social Aspects* (John Chapman, 1850), p. 102.

97. 'Wrongs of Woman – Hypocrisy of Man', *Douglas Jerrold's Weekly Newspaper*, no. 63, 23 October 1847, p. 1336; 'Memoir of Charles Fourier', *Spirit of the Age*, Vol. I, no. 2, 2 December 1848, p. 6.

98. *Tait's Edinburgh Magazine*, Vol. XI, July 1844, p. 424.

99. Kate, 'Conversations of Jane and Eliza', *NMW*, Vol. V, no. 10, 29 December 1839, p. 149.

100. Mary Leman Grimstone, *Woman's Love* (Saunders and Otley, 1832), Vol. I, pp. 75–6.

101. Anna Jameson, *Characteristics of Women. Moral, Poetical and Historical* (Saunders and Otley, 1858 first published 1832), pp. 25–6.

102. Junius Redivivus, 'Coriolanus No Aristocrat', *MR*, Vol. VIII, 1834, p. 51.

103. Dr Alexander, 'On the Duties and Rights of Woman', *Star in the East*, Vol. III, no. 161, 12 October 1839, p. 35; MLG, 'Drawing Room', *Tatler*, no. 54, 1 September 1832, p. 394.

104. MLG, 'Sketches of Domestic Life', *MR*, Vol. IX, 1835, pp. 147–53.

105. F. L., 'Wrongs of Englishwomen', *Eliza Cook's Journal*, Vol. II, no. 75, 9 October 1850, p. 354. Correspondents to the *New Moral World* often discussed these themes. E.g. John Finch, 'Ralahine Letter XII', *NMW*, Vol. IV, no. 194, 14 July 1837, pp. 298–9.

106. MLG, 'Sketches of Domestic Life – The Insipid', *MR*, Vol. IX, 1835, p. 644; Mary Leman Gillies, 'The Vanity of Wealth. A True Story', *People's Journal*, Vol. III, no. 62, p. 138.

107. A point mentioned in A. James Hammerton, *Emigrant Gentlewomen. Genteel Poverty and Female Education 1830–1914* (Croom Helm, 1979), p. 22.

108. GEJ, 'How Agnes Worral was Taught to be Respectable', *Douglas Jerrold's Shilling Magazine*, Vol. V, 1847, pp. 249, 24; Charles Dickens, *David Copperfield* (Harmondsworth: Penguin, 1986, first published 1849–50), p. 669.

109. MLG, 'Protective System of Morals', *MR*, Vol. IX, 1835, p. 686; Dickens, *David Copperfield*, p. 713.

110. Haight, *George Eliot and John Chapman*, p. 42.

111. *Tait's Edinburgh Magazine*, Vol. IX, December 1842, p. 779.

112. Howitt, *Autobiography*, Vol. II, p. 85.

113. *Tait's Edinburgh Magazine*, Vol. X, October 1843, p. 660; Frederika Bremer, *A Diary*, trans. Mary Howitt (George Bell and Sons, 1909, first published 1843), passim.

114. For a useful treatment of the translations and Sand's relationship with the Ashurst family, see Patricia Thompson, *George Sand and the Victorians. Her Influence and Reputation in Nineteenth Century England* (Macmillan, 1977).

115. *People's Press*, Vol. I, no. 5, June 1847, p. 149; *Douglas Jerrold's Weekly Newspaper*, no. 28, 23 January 1847, p. 85.

116. *Republican*, Vol. I, 1848, p. 58; *Spirit of the Age*, no. 27, 27 January 1849, p. 86.

117. W. J. Linton, 'Noble Women', *Reasoner*, Vol. IV, no. 88, 1848, p. 136.

118. MS letter from Elisa Bardouneau-Narcy to Elizabeth Neall Gay, 2 February 1842, Sydney Howard Gay Papers, The Rare Book and Manuscript Library, Columbia University.

119. The double standard was a theme which Sand was particularly concerned to develop in *Letters of a Traveller*, trans. M. M. Hays (E. Churton, 1847, first published 1837); Sand, *Simon*, trans. M. M. Hays (E. Churton, 1847, first published 1836), p. 187; Sand, *The Last Aldini*, trans. M. M. Hays (E. Churton, 1847, first published 1838), p. 117.

120. *Spirit of the Age*, no. 27, 27 January 1849, p. 86; *Douglas Jerrold's Shilling Magazine*, Vol. VI, 1847, pp. 377–8.

121. *People's Press*, Vol. I, 1847, p. 150; *Spirit of the Age*, no. 30, 17 February 1849, p. 158; *Republican*, Vol. IV, 1848, p. 59.

122. W. J. Linton, 'Noble Women', *Reasoner*, Vol. IV, no. 88. 1848, p. 136; *Republican*, Vol. I, 1848, p. 59.

123. MS letter from Elisa Bardouneau-Narcy to Elizabeth Neall Gay, 31 July 1848, Sydney Howard Gay Papers, The Rare Book and Manuscript Library, Columbia University Library.

124. *Spirit of the Age*, no. 30, 17 February 1849, p. 158.

125. Letter to Editor from Justitia, *Crisis*, Vol. III, no. 30, 30 March 1834, p. 246.

126. See for example, Rendall, *Origins of Modern Feminism*, pp. 247–54; Philippa Levine, *Victorian Feminism 1850–1900* (Hutchinson, 1987), p. 62.

127. P. Hollis, 'Anti-Slavery and British Working Class Radicalism in the Years of Reform', in C. Bolt and S. Drescher (eds), *Anti-slavery, Religion and Reform: Essays in Memory of Roger Anstey* (Kent: Dawson and Sons, 1980),

pp. 294–315; B. Fladeland, *Abolitionists and Working Class Problems in the Age of Industrialisation* (Macmillan, 1984); J. Walvin, 'The Rise of Popular Sentiment for Abolition, 1737–1832', in Bolt and Drescher (eds), *Anti-Slavery, Religion and Reform*, pp. 149–62; S. Drescher, 'Cart Whip and Billy Roller: Or, Anti-Slavery and Reform Symbolism in Industrialising Britain', *Journal of Social History*, Vol. 15, no. 1, 1981, p. 9.

128. P. Hollis, 'Anti-Slavery and British Working Class Radicalism in the Years of Reform', p. 296.

129. Letter to Editor from 'Eben', *NMW*, Vol. VI, no. 39, 20 July 1839, p. 614.

130. Abbé de Lammenais, *Modern Slavery*, trans. W. J. Linton (J. Watson, 1840), Appendix.

131. David Brion Davis, 'Slavery and Progress', in Bolt and Drescher (eds), *Anti-Slavery, Religion and Reform*, p. 358.

132. Rendall, *Origins of Modern Feminism*, pp. 20–32.

133. Adam Ferguson, *An Essay on the History of Civil Society*, ed. Duncan Forbes (Edinburgh: Edinburgh University Press, 1966, first published 1767), pp. 83, 185; Rendall, *Origins of Modern Feminism*, pp. 24–5.

134. William Alexander, *The History of Women from the Earliest Antiquity to the Present Time, Giving some account of almost every interesting particular concerning that sex, among all Nations, ancient and modern* (W. Strahan and T. Cadell, 1789), Vol. II, p. 34.

135. John Millar, 'Origin of the Distinction of Ranks', (1779) reprinted in W. C. Lehmann, *John Millar of Glasgow. 1735–1801. His Life and Thought and his Contribution to Sociological Analysis* (Cambridge: Cambridge University Press, 1960), pp. 175–322. See pp. 203, 218.

136. Rendall, *Origins of Modern Feminism*, pp. 31–2.

137. Aspland, *Memoir of the Life, Works and Correspondence of the Rev. Robert Aspland*, pp. 296–7.

138. Robert Aspland, *The Beneficial Influence of Christianity on the Character and Condition of the Female Sex* (J. Johnson, 1812), p. 5.

139. Ibid., p. 4.

140. Millar, 'Origin of the Distinction of Ranks', p. 209; Alexander, *The History of Women*, Vol. 1, p. 33, both warn against seeing the position of women too favourably in the Greek republics, but see Rendall, *Origins of Modern Feminism*, pp. 27–8.

141. Aspland, *The Beneficial Influence of Christianity*, pp. 6, 25–7, 2.

142. Lucy Aikin, *Epistles on Women, Exemplifying their Character and Condition in Various Ages and Nations, with Miscellaneous Poems* (J. Johnson, 1810), pp. 19, 36.

143. William Blake, 'Visions of the Daughters of Albion' (1793), reprinted in G. Keynes (ed.), *Blake's Complete Writings* (Oxford: Oxford University Press, 1989), pp. 189–90; Lucy Aikin to Dr Channing, 7 April 1832, Le Breton (ed.), *Memoirs, Miscellanies and Letters of the Late Lucy Aikin*, p. 259.

144. Aikin, *Epistles on Women*, pp. 17, 6, 5.

145. Ibid., pp. 80, 78–80.

146. Alan Ruston, 'Radical Nonconformity in Hackney. 1803–45', *Transactions of the Unitarian Historical Society*, Vol. XIV, no. 1, 1967, pp. 1–9; Le Breton (ed.), *Memoirs, Miscellanies and Letters of the Late Lucy Aikin*, passim.

147. 'On the Requisite Adjuncts, Social and Political of National Education', in

W. J. Fox, *Reports of Lectures Delivered at the Chapel in South Place, Finsbury* (Charles Fox, 1860), lecture 4, see p. 58.

148. Grimstone, *Cleone*, Vol. I, Preface, p. v.; MS letter from Thornton Hunt to George Combe, 21 September 1850, National Library of Scotland, MS 7309.

149. Barbara Leigh Smith Bodichon, 'A Conversation on the Enfranchisement of Female Freeholders and Householders', *Englishwoman's Review*, April 1873. Reprinted in Lacey (ed.), *Barbara Leigh Smith Bodichon and the Langham Place Group*, pp. 133–8.

150. Holcombe, *Wives and Property*, pp. 66–7.

151. Brian Harrison, *Separate Spheres. The Opposition to Woman's Suffrage in Britain* (Croom Helm, 1978), pp. 73–5; M. L. Shanley, 'Marital Slavery and Friendship. J. S. Mill's *Subjection of Women*', *Political Theory*, 9 May 1981, pp. 229–47.

152. 'National Education' in George Dawson, *Shakespeare and Other Lectures* ed. George St Clair (Kegan Paul, Trench, 1898), p. 503; 'Witness', 'Effects of Legislating Upon Love', *National*, 1839, p. 327; W. J. Fox, 'On the Requisite Adjuncts, Social and Political of National Education', pp. 58–9.

153. 'Our Library', *People's Journal*, Vol. II, no. 28, 11 July 1846, p. 25; Grimstone, *Cleone*, Vol. I, p. 200; Smith, *Social Aspects*, p. 105.

3 'The Stream of Freedom' – Democracy and Domestic Mores

1. Mary Lyndon Shanley, *Feminism, Marriage and the Law in Victorian England, 1850–95* (L. B. Tauris, 1989), p. 47.

2. Letter to Editor from Justitia, *Crisis*, Vol. III, no. 30, 11 March 1834, p. 246.

3. *Leader*, 16 November 1850, p. 809.

4. Rosamund and Florence Davenport Hill, *The Recorder of Birmingham. A Memoir of Matthew Davenport Hill. With Selections from his Correspondence* (Macmillan, 1878), p. 115; Bertha Mason, *The Story of the Women's Suffrage Movement* (Sheratt and Hughes, 1912), p. 22; Ralph E. Turner, *James Silk Buckingham 1786–1855* (Williams and Norgate, 1934), p. 329.

5. PMV, 'Woman and her Social Position', *Westminster Review*, Vol. 35, 1841, p. 37.

6. W. J. Linton, 'Universal Suffrage. The Principle of the People's Charter', *Republican*, Vol. I, 1848, p. 166.

7. MLG, 'Female Education', *MR*, Vol. 9, 1835, p. 110.

8. 'A Political and Social Anomaly', ibid., Vol. VI, 1832, p. 641. For arguments concerning the need for female qualities in the legislature see Helen Blackburn, *Women's Suffrage. A Record of the Women's Suffrage Movement in the British Isles* (Williams and Norgate, 1902), pp. 19 and 44; Susan Kingsley Kent, *Sex and Suffrage in Britain, 1860–1914* (Routledge, 1990, first published 1987), p. 58.

9. See, for example, 'A Political and Social Anomaly', *MR*, Vol. VI, 1832, pp. 637–42; *Douglas Jerrold's Weekly Newspaper*, no. 10, 19 September 1846, p. 224; Marion Reid, *A Plea for Woman* (Edinburgh: Polygon, 1988, first published 1843).

10. Brian Harrison, *Separate Spheres. The Opposition to Women's Suffrage in*

Britain (Croom Helm, 1978), p. 33; MLG, 'On Women of No Party', *MR*, Vol. X, 1836, p. 79. See also, L. D., 'Principles Before History', ibid., Vol. II, 1837, pp. 282–3; 'Study of Political Economy Made Pleasant', *Tatler*, Vol. IV, no. 435, 24 January 1832, pp. 78–9.

11. Miriam Williford, 'Bentham and the Rights of Women', *Journal of the History of Ideas*, Vol. 36, January–March 1975, pp. 167–76; Ruby J. Saywell, 'The Development of the Feminist Idea in England, 1789–1833', (MA thesis, King's College, London, 1936), p. 184. William Thompson, *Appeal of one Half of the Human Race, Women, Against the Pretensions of the Other Half, Men, to Retain them in Political and thence in Civil and Domestic Slavery* (Cork: C. P. Hyland, 1975, first published 1825); Part One considers the views of Mill and Dumont.

12. Brougham's speech to the House of Commons, 2 June 1818, cited in John Bowring (ed.), *The Works of Jeremy Bentham* (New York: Russell and Russell, 1962, first published 1843), Vol. IV, p. 568.

13. *MR*, Vol. IX, 1835, pp. 627–8.

14. Ibid., Vol. IX, 1835, pp. 408–9.

15. See for example Mrs Leman Grimstone, 'Quaker Women', ibid., p. 34.

16. MLG, 'Miss Martineau – Intellectual Women', *Tatler*, no. 59, 6 October 1832, p. 479; Mary Leman Grimstone, *Cleone, A Tale of Married Life* (Effingham Wilson, 1834), Vol. 1, p. 102; 'Whittington Club', *Douglas Jerrold's Weekly Newspaper*, no. 41, 24 April 1847, p. 506.

17. John Forster to W. J. Fox, cited in Richard Garnett, *The Life of W. J. Fox, Public Teacher and Social Reformer, 1786–1864* (John Lane, 1909), p. 288.

18. Edward Youl, 'The Breadfinder', *Howitt's Journal*, Vol. II, no. 45, 6 November 1847, p. 294.

19. *Douglas Jerrold's Weekly Newspaper*, no. 10, 19 September 1846, p. 224; *Tait's Edinburgh Magazine*, Vol. IX, July 1843, pp. 423–8.

20. D. J. Rowe (ed.), *London Radicalism 1830–43. A Selection from the Papers of Francis Place* (London Record Society, 1970), pp. 120, 220.

21. David Jones, *Chartism and the Chartists* (Allen Lane, 1975), see p. 115 especially.

22. William Lovett, *The Life and Struggles of William Lovett* (Trübner, 1976), pp. 322–3, 409, 424.

23. An excellent survey of these radical educational theories is to be found in W. A. C. Stewart, *Progressives and Radicals in English Education. 1750–1970* (Macmillan, 1972), pp. 42ff.

24. Typescript letter from William Shaen to his sister, 6 July 1841, Leeds Archives (transcribed by Shaen's daughter, Margaret) Symington Papers, Box 19.

25. See Lovett, *Life*, pp. 150–7, 273; and Jones, *Chartism and the Chartists*, p. 164.

26. MLG, 'Social Melodies', *Halfpenny Magazine*, no. 7, 16 June 1832, p. 45; no. 14, 4 August 1832, p. 105. For an example of their use, see 'Festival at Local Infant School', *Star in the East*, Vol. II, no. 72, 27 January 1838, p. 148. For Fox's role, see Margaret Parnaby, 'William Johnson Fox and the *Monthly Repository* circle of 1832 to 1836', (PhD thesis, Australian National University, 1979), p. 109; Parry's work is mentioned in J. T. Ward, *Chartism* (B. T. Batsford, 1973), p. 167; Lovett, *Life*, p. 274.

27. 'An Address to the Chartists of the United Kingdom put forth by the National Association in 1845', quoted in Lovett, *Life*, p. 309.

28. TS letter from William Shaen to his sister, 7 June 1848, Leeds Archives, Symington Papers, Box 19; F. B. Smith, *Radical Artisan. William James Linton. 1812–97* (Manchester: Manchester University Press, 1973), p. 26.

29. TS letters from William Shaen to his sister, 16 July 1846 and 13 June 1848, Leeds Archives, Symington Papers, Box 19.

30. First Annual Report of the National Association, p. 218c; MS letter from J. Goodwyn Barmby to William Lovett [1840?], Proceedings of the Working Men's Association, Part 4, p. 208a, Birmingham City Archives, MS 753 (Lovett Collection).

31. William Lovett and John Collins, *Chartism: A New Organisation of the People* (Leicester: Leicester University Press, 1969, first published 1840), p. 61.

32. Lovett, *Life*, p. 259.

33. MS letter from Elisa Bardouneau-Narcy to Elizabeth Neall Gay, 2 February 1842, Sydney Howard Gay Papers, The Rare Book and Manuscript Library, Columbia University.

34. Lovett, *Life*, pp. 287, 333.

35. I. J. Prothero, 'Chartism in London', *Past and Present*, no. 44, 1969, pp. 76–105; F. Goodway, *London Chartism 1838–1848* (Cambridge: Cambridge University Press, 1982), pp. 40–2. See also Ward, *Chartism*, p. 150.

36. Jutta Schwarzkopf, *Women in the Chartist Movement* (Macmillan, 1991), pp. 61–2. For the role of women in radical movements see, for example, Malcolm I. Thomis and Jennifer Grimmett, *Women in Protest, 1800–1850* (Croom Helm, 1982), see especially pp. 113, 132–4; Jane Rendall, *The Origins of Modern Feminism: Women in Britain, France and the United States 1780–1860* (Chicago: Lyceum, 1985), pp. 238–43.

37. Gail Malmgreen, *Neither Bread Nor Roses. Utopian Feminists and the English Working Class, 1800–1850* (Brighton: John L. Noyce, 1978), p. 31; Dorothy Thompson, *The Early Chartists* (Temple Smith, 1984), Ch. 7.

38. *Northern Star*, 3 March 1849; 11 February 1843; 20 October 1838; 1 July 1843, cited in D. Jones, 'Women and the Chartists', *History*, Vol. 68, 1983, pp. 1–21, see pp. 2, 8–9.

39. Malmgreen, *Neither Bread Nor Roses*, pp. 19–20, 31.

40. Thomis and Grimmett, *Women in Protest*, p. 134.

41. MS letter from Harriet Taylor to Algernon Taylor, n.d., British Library of Political and Economic Science, Mill-Taylor Papers, Vol. 27, no. 101; H. Taylor, 'Enfranchisement of Women', *Westminster Review*, Vol. 55, July 1851, p. 152.

42. 'The Rights and Wrongs of Women', *Star in the East*, Vol. III, no. 145, 22 June 1839, p. 341.

43. 'Address by Goodwyn Barmby in the "Cheltenham Free Press"'. Reprinted in Barbara Taylor, *Eve and the New Jerusalem. Socialism and Feminism in the Nineteenth Century* (Virago, 1983); Ruth Watts, 'The Unitarian Contribution to Education in England from the Late Eighteenth Century to 1853' (PhD thesis, Leicester University, 1987), p. 440.

44. MS letter from W. J. Linton to Thornton Hunt, 10 October 1849, Linton

Collection, Beinecke Rare Book and Manuscript Library, Yale University, MS Vault Shelves Linton; *Reasoner*, Vol. IV, no. 100, 1848, p. 308.

45. See the *Northern Star*, 20 October 1848, a point noted by Malmgreen, *Neither Bread Nor Roses*, p. 31.

46. See for example the reference in 'The Unitarians and Chartism', *People*, Vol. I, no. 1, 27 May 1848, p. 7.

47. Abbé de Lamennais, *Modern Slavery* trans. W. J. Linton (J. Watson, 1840), appendix. See *Spirit of the Age*, no. 32, 3 March 1849, p. 206; *NMW*, Vol. VII, no. 78, 18 April 1840, pp. 1247–8; *National Association Gazette*, no. 6, 5 February 1842, pp. 43–4.

48. W. J. Linton, 'Universal Suffrage: The Principles of the People's Charter', *Republican*, Vol. I, 1848, pp. 165–8.

49. 'One of the People', 'Political Suggestions', *National*, 1839, p. 359.

50. Joseph Barker, *The Life of Joseph Barker, Written by Himself*, edited by John Thomas Barker (Hodder and Stoughton, 1880), p. 281; Mary Howitt, *An Autobiography* edited by her daughter, Margaret Howitt (Isbister Ltd, 1889), Vol. II, p. 38.

51. See for example, 'What I would do if I had the Power', *People*, Vol. 1, no. 22, 1848, p. 173.

52. Betty Fladeland, *Abolitionists and Working Class Problems in the Age of Industrialisation* (Macmillan, 1984), p. 144.

53. 'Letter from J. Haughton', *People*, Vol. I. no. 17, 1848, p. 136; 'Rights of Women', ibid., Vol. III, no. 146, 1851, p. 331.

54. Taylor, *Eve and the New Jerusalem*, p. 180; 'The People's Charter, and Communization of Electoral and Societarian Reform', *Promethean*, Vol. I, no. 2, February 1842, p. 48.

55. Gail Malmgreen, 'Anne Knight and the Radical Subculture', *Quaker History*, Vol. 71, 1982, p. 108.

56. See Schwarzkopf, *Women and the Chartist Movement*, pp. 248ff.

57. Letter quoted in Blackburn, *Women's Suffrage*, p. 19; 'The Rights of Women', *People*, Vol. II, no. 92, 1850, p. 315.

58. *Birmingham Journal*, 5 February 1848.

59. 'Report of Conference at Birmingham', *Northern Star*, 7 January 1843, p. 6; Editorial Letter, ibid., 1 July 1843.

60. *Reasoner*, Vol. I, no. 9, 29 July 1846, p. 138.

61. For example, 'Duty of Women', *National Association Gazette*, no. 6, 5 February 1842, pp. 43–4; Letter to Editor from Sarah Fuller, ibid., no. 19, 7 May 1842, p. 148.

62. 'Report of Frances Wright's Lectures', *Reasoner*, Vol. III, no. 53, 1847, p. 297.

63. John Stuart Mill to Harriet Taylor, 22 March 1849, quoted in F. A. Hayek, *John Stuart Mill and Harriet Taylor: Their Correspondence and Subsequent Marriage* (Chicago: University of Chicago Press, 1951), p. 141; Graham Wallas, *William Johnson Fox. Conway Memorial Lecture* (Watts, 1924), pp. 29–30.

64. 'Class Legislation and Competition; Electoral Reform and Community', *Promethean; or, Communitarian Apostle*, Vol. I, no. 1, 1 January 1842, p. 13.

65. Schwarzkopf, *Women in the Chartist Movement*, p. 238.

66. For details of the Whittington Club, see Chapter 5 below. For the Friends of Italy and its policy towards women, see J. O. S. Baylen and N. J. Gossman (eds), *Biographical Dictionary of Modern Radicals* (Hassocks: Harvester Press, 1979), pp. 60–1.

67. Mary Howitt, for example, sat at the guest table at meetings at the National Hall, *First Annual Report of the National Association*, p. 237, Birmingham City Library, MS 753 (Lovett Papers). But, for women's usual role at such events see *Reasoner*, Vol. I, no. 9, 29 July 1846, p. 138; ibid., Vol. III, no. 70, 1847, p. 535.

68. 'Whittington Club and Metropolitan Athenaeum', *Douglas Jerrold's Weekly Newspaper*, no. 16, 31 October 1846, p. 371.

69. Uncatalogued correspondence between Mary Howitt and Eliza Meteyard, Houghton Collection, Harvard University, fMS Eng 883.1.

70. Jones, 'Women and the Chartists', pp. 2–3.

71. GJH, 'Hints to the Advocates of the Rights of Women', *People's Press*, Vol. I, no. 4, May 1847, pp. 117–21; no. 5, June 1847, pp. 154–8. The article was reprinted in the *Reasoner*, Vol. III, no. 63, 1847, pp. 429–37.

72. John Finch, 'Ralahine Letter XII', *NMW*, Vol. IV, no. 194, 14 July 1838, p. 299; Catherine Barmby, 'New Tracts for the Times', Vol. I, no. 3, reprinted in Taylor, *Eve and the New Jerusalem*. Similar views were occasionally aired in the more mainstream feminist press, for example, 'Improvement of the Social Condition of Women', *Howitt's Journal*, Vol. I, no. 20, 15 May 1847, p. 40.

73. Sally Alexander, *Women's Work in Nineteenth Century London* (Journeyman Press, 1976), p. 31; Rendall, *Origins of Modern Feminism*, p. 161.

74. Ida, 'Female Education', *People's Press*, Vol. II, no. 16, March 1848, p. 61; A. K., 'The Rights of Women', ibid., no. 17, April 1848, p. 55; Anne Knight, 'The Rights of Women', ibid., Vol. I, no. 9, October 1847, pp. 269–71.

75. MS letter from Harriet Taylor to Mr Fox, 10 May 1848, British Library of Political and Economic Science, Mill-Taylor Collection, Vol. 28, no. 40.

76. A. Wheeler, 'The Pretended Moral Incapacity of Women', *British Co-operator*, no. 2, May 1830, p. 35.

77. *MR*, Vol. VIII, 1834, p. 596; MLG, 'Female Education', ibid., Vol. IX, 1835, p. 108; 'Extract from No. 5 of the Phalange', *NMW*, Vol. III, no. 107, 12 November 1836, p. 31.

78. W. J. Linton, 'Universal Suffrage. The Principles of the People's Charter', *Republican*, Vol. I, 1848, pp. 165–8; Lee Holcombe, *Wives and Property. Reform of the Married Women's Property Law in Nineteenth Century England* (Toronto: University of Toronto Press, 1983), p. 163.

79. Paul Bell, 'Heads and Tales of Families', *Douglas Jerrold's Shilling Magazine*, Vol. V, January–June, 1847, p. 40; Kate, 'Conversations of Jane and Eliza', *NMW*, Vol. V, no. 10, 29 December 1839, p. 149.

80. MLG, 'Drawing Room', *Tatler*, no. 54, 1 September 1832, p. 394; Ida, 'Female Education', *People's Press*, Vol. I, no. 11, December 1847, p. 342.

81. 'The Mosiac Masters', *Douglas Jerrold's Weekly Newspaper*, no. 42, 1 May 1847; 'Noble Sentiments on the Influence of Women', *Howitt's Journal*, Vol. I, no. 11, 13 March 1847, p. 21.

82. MLG, 'Self Dependence', *MR*, Vol. IX, 1835, p. 602; GEJ, 'How Agnes

Worral was Taught to be Respectable', *Douglas Jerrold's Shilling Magazine*, Vol. V, January–June 1847, p. 258.

83. Garnett, *Life of W. J. Fox*, p. 324; see also *Unitarian Social Reformers* No. 4 – Rt. Hon. James Stansfeld (Lindsey Press, [n.d.]), p. 5.

84. MS letter from W. H. Ashurst to Sydney Howard Gay, 17 October 1853, Sydney Howard Gay Papers, The Rare Book and Manuscript Library, Columbia University Library.

85. Mrs Leman Grimstone, *Character; or, Jew and Gentile* (Charles Fox, 1833), Vol. I, p. 91; MLG, 'Servants', *Tatler*, no. 52, 18 August 1832, p. 364.

86. Carl Woodring, *Victorian Samplers: William and Mary Howitt* (Lawrence: University of Kansas Press, 1952), pp. 107–8. For examples of the poem's reception in the radical press, see 'Alfred Tennyson and His Poems', *Eliza Cook's Journal*, Vol. IV, no. 196, 10 May 1852, pp. 20–1; Panthea, 'Tennyson's Princess', *Reasoner*, Vol. IV, no. 91, 1848, pp. 175–6; E. T., 'Tennyson's Poems', *Truth-Seeker and Present Age*, 1849, p. 58; MS letter from Bessie Raynor Parkes to Barbara Leigh Smith, 28 January 1848, Girton College, Cambridge, Parkes Papers, BRP V 20.

87. Meeting at the Institution, Charlotte Street, *Crisis*, Vol. III, no. 16, 14 December 1834, p. 124.

88. Judy Lown, *Women and Industrialisation. Gender at Work in Nineteenth Century England* (Cambridge: Polity Press, 1990), see esp. Chapter 12, Angela V. John, *By the Sweat of Their Brow. Women Workers at Victorian Coal Mines* (Routledge and Kegan Paul, 1984, second edition), p. 24 in particular.

89. Schwarzkopf, *Women in the Chartist Movement*, p. 40.

90. *Northern Star*, 26 February 1848.

91. Lovett, *Life*, op.cit., p. 170; *National Association Gazette*, no. 2, 8 January 1842, pp. 9–10.

92. Lovett, *Life*, p. 430; William Lovett, *Woman's Mission* (Simpkin and Marshall, 1856), see pp. 14, 16, 19.

93. Lovett and Collins, *Chartism*, pp. 77 n, 41, 105.

94. 'National Hall, Holborn', *Reasoner*, Vol. I, no. 9, 29 July 1846, p. 138.

95. See, for example, 'Military Morality', in W. J. Fox, *Reports of Lectures Delivered at the Chapel in South Place, Finsbury* (Charles Fox, 1835), no. 4, pp. 15–17; Junius Redivivus, *The Rights of Morality* (Effingham Wilson, 1832), pp. 37–8.

96. 'Relations of Great Men to Women', in George Dawson, *Shakespeare and Other Lectures*, ed. George St Clair (Kegan Paul, Trench, 1888), p. 301. This was an important theme, see also Mrs Phillips, 'On the Importance of Female Educational Establishments', *People's Press*, Vol. II, no. 19, June 1848, p. 85; MLG, 'Acephala', *MR*, Vol. 8, 1834, p. 771.

97. Thomis and Grimmett, *Women in Protest*, p. 134.

98. 'Extract from "The Rights of Woman" by R. J. Richardson', reprinted in Dorothy Thompson (ed.), *The Early Chartists* (Macmillan, 1971), p. 122.

99. P. N. Backström, *Christian Socialism and Co-operation in Victorian England. Edward Vansittart Neale and the Co-operative Movement* (Croom Helm, 1974), p. 148; *Leader*, 16 November 1850, pp. 809–10.

100. Pat Thane, 'Women and the Poor Law in Victorian and Edwardian England', *History Workshop*, Vol. 5, Autumn 1978, pp. 29–51; Lown, *Women*

and Industrialisation, pp. 180–1; Margaret Hewitt, *Wives and Mothers in Victorian Industry* (Rockliff, 1958), see pp. 31, 49.

101. 'Mill Labour', *Manchester Guardian*, 25 January 1833, p. 5.
102. See, for example, 'On the Spirit and Purpose with which the Establishment of a National Education Should be Attempted', in W. J. Fox, *Reports of Lectures Delivered at the Chapel in South Place, Finsbury* (Charles Fox, 1860) Lecture 1, p. 9; FL, 'Wrongs of Englishwomen', *Eliza Cook's Journal*, Vol. III, no. 75, 9 October 1850, p. 353.
103. Mrs Percy Sinnett, 'The Rights and Wrongs of Women', *People's Journal*, Vol. IV, no. 83, 31 July 1847, p. 60.
104. W. J. Fox, 'Lectures on the Morality of the Various Classes', quoted in *NMW*, Vol. II, no. 55, 14 November 1835, p. 24; S. Smiles, 'The Condition of Factory Women – What is Doing for Them [*sic*]?', *People's Journal*, Vol. II, no. 45, 7 November 1846, pp. 258–60, and Vol. III, no. 56, 23 January 1847, pp. 50–2; G. L. Lewes, *Dr Southwood Smith. A Retrospect* (William Blackwood and Sons, 1891), p. 153.
105. 'The Relations of Great Men to Women', in Dawson, *Shakespeare and Other Lectures*, p. 301; Catherine Barmby, 'The Organisation of Labour for Women', *People's Press*, Vol. II, no. 19, June 1848, p. 122. See also the review of R. H. Horne in *Westminster Review*, Vol. 41, 1844, pp. 379–80.
106. Shanley, *Feminism, Marriage and the Law in Victorian England*, p. 99.
107. See E. K. Helsinger, R. L. Sheets, and W. Veeder, *The Woman Question. Society and Literature in Britain and America 1837–1883. Volume 2, Social Issues* (Chicago: University of Chicago Press, 1983), pp. 120–33; Ruth Watts, 'Knowledge is Power – Unitarians, Gender and Education in the Eighteenth and Early Nineteenth Centuries', *Gender and Education*, Vol. I, no. 1, 1989, pp. 44–5.
108. *Daily News* 2 July 1846, cited in Lown, *Women and Industrialisation*, p. 42. For useful insights into Dickens's *Daily News*, see Garnett, *Life of W. J. Fox*, pp. 278–84; 'The Employment of Young Women', *Eliza Cook's Journal*, Vol. II, no. 36, 5 January 1850, p. 145.
109. Mary Gillies, 'Associated Homes for the Middle Classes', *Howitt's Journal*, Vol. I, no. 20, 15 May 1847, p. 270; Alexander, *Women's Work in Nineteenth Century London*, p. 14.
110. B. Taylor, '"The Men are as Bad as their Masters": Socialism, Feminism, and Sexual Antagonism in the London Tailoring Trade in the early 1830s', *Feminist Studies*, Vol. V, Part 1, Spring 1979, pp. 8–40. For the broader picture, see Leonore Davidoff and Catherine Hall, *Family Fortunes. Men and Women of the English Middle Class 1780–1850* (Hutchinson, 1987), pp. 312–13.
111. Lown, *Women and Industrialisation*, p. 29.
112. 'On the Influence of Women on Society and of Society on Women', *Star in the East*, Vol. I, no. 1, 17 September 1836, p. 2; *Westminster Review*, Vol. 49, 1848, p. 305.
113. Mary Leman Grimstone, *Character; or Jew and Gentile*, Vol. 1, pp. 32–3; *MR*, Vol. VII, 1833, p. 548. Some of the most notable articles on the ubiquitous theme of female employment include 'The Vocations of Women', *Eliza Cook's Journal*, Vol. III, no. 56, 25 May 1850, pp. 59–61; Mrs Leman Grimstone, 'Quaker Women', *MR*, Vol. IX, 1835, pp. 34–5; Catherine

Barmby, 'Employment for Women', *People's Press*, Vol. II, no. 24, 24 September 1848, pp. 165–7; 'On Female Education and Occupations', *MR*, Vol. VII, 1833, pp. 489–98.

114. 'Campbell's *Life of Mrs Siddons*', *MR*, Vol. VIII, 1834, pp. 548–9; *Tait's Edinburgh Magazine*, Vol. IX, July 1844, pp. 424–5.

115. Examples abound; see, for example, 'A National Gallery', *MR*, Vol. VIII, 1834, p. 842; 'Women and Wood Engraving', *National Association Gazette*, no. 33, 4 June 1842, p. 186; 'Woman's Mission and Woman's Position', in Anna Jameson, *Memoirs and Essays. Illustrative of Art, Literature and Social Morals* (Richard Bentley, 1846), p. 236.

116. MS letter from Mary Howitt to Eliza Meteyard [n.d.], Houghton Library, Harvard University, fMS Eng. 883.1. See also Caroline Smith Hill's work for the *Ladies Guild*, discussed in Chapter 6.

117. Anna Jameson, 'Woman's Mission and Woman's Position', pp. 213, 230.

118. TT, 'Women in Germany', *Douglas Jerrold's Shilling Magazine*, Vol. V, January–June 1847, p. 27; 'On the Necessity of Female Education', *National Association Gazette*, no. 7, 12 February 1842, p. 71.

119. Mrs Percy Sinnett, 'The Rights and Wrongs of Women', *People's Journal*, Vol. IV, no. 83, 31 July 1847, p. 60; Mrs Phillips, 'On the Importance of Female Educational Establishments', *People's Press*, Vol. II, no. 19, June 1848, p. 85.

120. Camilla Toulmin, 'The Orphan Milliners', *Illuminated Magazine*, Vol. II, 1846, pp. 278–85.

121. M. L. G., *Douglas Jerrold's Shilling Magazine*, Vol. IV, July–December 1846, pp. 440–57; Mary Leman Gillies, 'The First and Second Marriage', *People's Journal*, Vol. IV, no. 83, 31 July 1847, pp. 63–76.

122. Jonathan Beecher, *Charles Fourier. The Visionary and His World* (Berkeley: University of California Press, 1986), see p. 209 in particular.

123. See for example, MLG, 'Sketches of Domestic Life – The Insipid', *MR*, Vol. IX, 1835, pp. 643–53; 'A Political and Social Anomaly', ibid., Vol. VI, 1832, pp. 640–1; 'Campbell's *Life of Mrs. Siddons*', ibid., Vol. VIII, 1834, pp. 548–9.

124. Barbara Leigh Smith Bodichon, 'Women and Work' (1857), reprinted in Candida Ann Lacey, *Barbara Leigh Smith Bodichon and the Langham Place Group* (Routledge and Kegan Paul, 1987), pp. 36–73, see p. 41.

125. 'Campbell's Life of Mrs Siddons', *MR*, Vol. VIII, 1834, p. 549.

126. 'Memoir of Charles Fourier', *Spirit of the Age*, no. 2, 2 December 1848, p. 6.

127. Ida, 'Female Education', *People's Press*, Vol. I, no. 12, 13 December 1847, p. 372.

128. SY, 'The Luxembourg', *MR*, Vol. VIII, 1834, p. 61.

129. Mrs Epps (ed.), *Diary of the Late John Epps* (Kent, 1875), p. 377.

130. GEJ, 'How Agnes Worral was Taught to be Respectable', *Douglas Jerrold's Shilling Magazine*, Vol. V, January–June 1847, p. 250.

131. Frederika Bremer, *The Home or Life in Sweden*, trans. Mary Howitt (G. Bell and Sons, 1913, first published 1843), pp. 330, 94, 96.

132. MLG, 'Sketches of Domestic Life', *MR*, Vol. IX, 1835, pp. 554–62, 225–34.

133. See Junius Redivivus, 'On the Condition of Women in England', *MR*, Vol.

VII, 1835, pp. 217–31; for other ambivalent declarations compare Mrs Leman Grimstone, 'Quaker Women', ibid., Vol. 9, 1835, pp. 30–7; with MLG, 'Female Education', ibid., Vol. 9, 1835, pp. 106–12.

134. Solly, *These Eighty Years*, Vol. II, pp. 198–9.

135. MS letter from Eliza Cook, 17 August 1849, National Library of Scotland, MS 584, no. 965. Compare, for example, 'Governesses', *Eliza Cook's Journal*, Vol. I, no. 20, 16 September 1849, pp. 305–7 with 'The "Young Idea" – Female Education', ibid., Vol. V, no. 146, 14 February 1851, pp. 270–1.

136. These issues emerge in the Howitt–Meteyard correspondence. For example, MS letter from Mary Howitt to Eliza Meteyard, 5 August 1847, Houghton Library, Harvard University, fMS Eng. 883.1. For an instance of Meteyard's more conventional work, see Silverpen, 'The "Works" of John Ironshaft', *Douglas Jerrold's Shilling Magazine*, Vol. 6, July–December 1847, pp. 453–70.

137. For the breadth of Grimstone's approach, consider her 'Men and Women', *Tait's Edinburgh Magazine*, Vol. I, March 1834, pp. 101–3, alongside her 'Passage of Domestic History in Van Dieman's Land', *People's Journal*, Vol. 1, 23 May 1846, pp. 289–92.

138. Compare Catherine Barmby's essays, 'Woman and Domestics', *People's Journal*, Vol. III, no. 55, 16 January 1847, pp. 37–8; 'The Organisation of Labour for Women', *People's Press*, Vol. II, no. 19, June 1848, pp. 121–3; 'Women's Industrial Independence', *Apostle and Chronicle of the Communist Church 1*, no. 1, 1 August 1848, repr. in J. Saville and J. M. Bellamy (eds), *Dictionary of Labour Biography* (Macmillan, 1982), Vol. VI, pp. 16–17.

139. Ida, 'Female Education', *People's Press*, Vol. I, no. 12, 13 December 1847, pp. 371–2; ibid., Vol. I, no. 11, December 1847, pp. 341–2; ibid., Vol. II, no. 16, March 1848, pp. 60–1.

140. R. H. Horne, *A New Spirit of the Age* (Smith, Elder, 1844), p. 198.

141. Harriet Martineau, *Autobiography* (Virago, 1983, originally published 1877), Vol. II, p. 225.

142. Silverpen, 'Lucy Dean; the Noble Needlewoman', *Eliza Cook's Journal*, Vol. II, no. 48, 30 March 1850, pp. 340–4.

143. Reid, *A Plea for Woman*, Chapter 3; Jameson, 'Woman's Mission and Woman's Position'; Mary Leman Grimstone, *Woman's Love* (Saunders and Otley, 1832), postscript.

144. Mary Leman Gillies, 'Associated Homes', *People's Journal*, Vol. I, no. 2, 10 January 1846, p. 26.

145. See R. G. Garnett, *Co-operation and the Owenite Socialist Communities in Britain, 1825–1845* (Manchester: Manchester University Press, 1972), p. 47; see also Chapter 1 above.

146. JR, 'Domestic Arrangements of the Working Classes', *Westminster Review*, Vol. 25, 1836, p. 465.

147. Mary Gillies, 'Associated Homes for the Middle Classes', *Howitt's Journal*, Vol. I, no. 20, 15 May 1847, p. 272.

148. Mary Leman Gillies, 'A Happy New Year to the People', *People's Journal*, Vol. I, no. 3, 17 January 1846, p. 39.

149. Mary Gillies, 'Associated Homes for the Middle Classes', *Howitt's Journal*,

Vol. I, no. 20, 15 May 1847, p. 273; Mary Leman Grimstone, 'Homes for the People', *People's Journal*, Vol. I, no. 5, 31 January 1846, p. 68.

150. Anna Wheeler, 'The Pretended Moral Incapacity of Women', *British Co-Operator*, no. 2, May 1830, p. 36; Catherine Barmby, 'Women's Industrial Independence', *Apostle and Chronicle of the Communist Church 1*, no. 1, 1 August 1848; Selma B. Kanner, 'Victorian Institutional Patronage: Angela Burdett-Coutts, Charles Dickens and Urania Cottage, Reformatory for Women, 1846–58' (PhD thesis, University of California, 1972), p. 307; JR, 'Domestic Arrangements of the Working Classes', *Westminster Review*, Vol. 25, 1836, p. 466.

151. MLG, 'Sketches of Domestic Life – The Insipid', *MR* Vol. IX, 1835, p. 647.

152. Mary Leman Gillies, 'An Appeal to the Better Order of Men in Behalf of the Women of the Factory Districts', *People's Journal*, Vol. II, no. 36, 5 September 1846, pp. 131–4.

153. Shanley, *Feminism, Marriage and the Law in Victorian England*, p. 13; J. A. Banks, *Victorian Values. Secularism and the Size of Families* (Routledge and Kegan Paul, 1981), p. 35.

154. Patricia Branca, *Silent Sisterhood. Middle-Class Women in the Victorian Home* (Croom Helm, 1975), see p. 133.

155. For a recent discussion of the relationship between secularism, family planning and the motives behind contraceptive propaganda, see Banks, *Victorian Values*.

156. See for example, Robert Dale Owen, *Moral Physiology, or, a Brief and Plain Treatise on the Population Question* (E. Truelove, 1831), especially p. 50 and appendix.

157. 'The Weekly Record', *Howitt's Journal*, Vol. I, no. 11, 13 March 1847, p. 21.

158. Mary Gillies, 'Associated Homes for the Middle Classes', *Howitt's Journal*, Vol. I, no. 20, 15 May 1847, p. 270; Shaen's words are cited in Frances Power Cobbe, *Life of Frances Power Cobbe by Herself* (Boston and New York: Riverside Press, 1894), Vol. I, pp. 548–9.

159. Branca, *Silent Sisterhood*, pp. 22–3, 46.

160. MLG, 'A Coat from Flower Seeds', *Halfpenny Magazine*, no. 3, 19 May 1832, pp. 18–19; MLG, 'Kate of Kildare', *People's Journal*, Vol. II, no. 45, 7 November 1846, pp. 255–6; Silverpen, 'The Xmas Angels', *Eliza Cook's Journal*, Vol. 1, no. 34, 22 December 1849, pp. 116–21; Ruth Watts, '"Knowledge is Power" – Unitarians, Gender and Education in the Eighteenth and Early Nineteenth Centuries', *Gender and Education*, Vol. 1, no. 1, 1989, pp. 35–50; Margaret Parnaby, 'William Johnson Fox and the *Monthly Repository*', pp. 439–40.

161. 'Industrial Schools for Young Women', *Eliza Cook's Journal*, Vol. I, no. 6, 9 June 1849, pp. 81–2.

162. 'The Dreamer and the Worker. By the author of *Orion*', *Douglas Jerrold's Shilling Magazine*, Vol. 6, July–December 1847, pp. 1–20. In practice, in addition to domestic instruction, the schemes provided basic instruction in the three 'Rs'; see Davidoff and Hall, *Family Fortunes*, p. 188.

163. 'Physical Education; or the Nurture and Management of Children', *Star in the East*, Vol. II, no. 76, 24 February 1838, p. 188.

164. See Thomas Southwood Smith, *The Philosophy of Health* (Charles Knight,

1835), Vol. I, pp. 7–8 and *MR*, Vol. IX, 1835, p. 157; *Christian Reformer*, Vol. II, January–December 1835, p. 533.

165. Catherine Hall, 'The Early Formation of Victorian Domestic Ideology', in Burman (ed.), *Fit Work for Women*, pp. 15–32.

166. Grimstone, *Cleone*, Vol. I, pp. 215–17; Caroline Southwood Smith, 'Memoranda of Observations and Experiments in Education', *MR*, Vol. VIII, 1834, pp. 477–84, 551–61, 687–91, 855–68. The articles were reprinted in the *Star in the East* (1837) and later publicised by S. D. Collet in the *Reasoner* Vol. VI, no. 155, 1849, pp. 312–24.

167. MS letter from M. L. Gillies, 31 July 1846, University College, London, Wilderspin Collection, MS 917; MS letters from Mary Leman Gillies to W. J. Linton [n.d.], Biblioteca Archivio G. G. Feltrinelli, Archivio Linton, Vol. 2–43. Parnaby, 'William Johnson Fox', pp. 375–436. See also P. McCann and F. A. Young, *Samuel Wilderspin and the Infant School Movement* (Croom Helm, 1982).

168. For example, MLG, 'Pestalozzi', *MR*, Vol. 7, 1833, pp. 839–40; 'Fragments of Pestalozzi', *National*, 1839, pp. 304–5. The *Star in the East*, Vol. III (1838), ran a series of 'Pestalozzian Recollections'.

169. For a fine treatment of the mainstream Unitarian position, see R. Watts, 'The Unitarian Contribution to the Development of Female Education, 1790–1850', *History of Education*, Vol. 9, no. 4, 1980, pp. 273–86.

170. TS letter from William Shaen to his sister, 10 October 1848, Leeds Archives, Symington Papers, Box 19.

171. Bremer, *The Home*, p. 285.

172. TS letter from William Shaen to his sister, 26 February 1848, Leeds Archives, Symington Papers, Box 19.

173. 'The Rights and Wrongs of Woman', *Star in the East*, Vol. III, no. 145, 22 June 1839, p. 341.

174. W. J. Linton, 'Mr. Cooper and the French Divorce Bill', *Reasoner*, Vol. V, no. 121, 1848, p. 267; W. J. Linton, 'Universal Suffrage. The Principle of the People's Charter', *Republican*, Vol. I, 1848, p. 167.

175. 'Woman and Society', *Eliza Cook's Journal*, Vol. IV, no. 103, 19 April 1851, p. 397.

176. 'Declaration', *Promethean*, Vol. I, no. 1, January 1842; H. Spencer, *Social Statics* (New York: Augustus M. Kelley, 1969, first published London 1851), p. 161; Holcombe, *Wives and Property*, p. 155.

177. *Report of a Public Meeting . . . , November 15, 1847, 'To Explain the Principles and Objects of the People's International League'*, Tyne and Wear Archives, TWAS 634/A13, p. 15; MS letter from W. J. Linton to Thornton Hunt, 10 October 1849, Beinecke Library, Yale University Library, MS Vault Shelves Linton; Panthea, 'A Woman's Plea for Italian Liberty', *Reasoner*, Vol. XIII, no. 14, 1852, p. 215.

178. Hall, 'The Early Formation of Victorian Domestic Ideology'.

179. Ian Bradley, *The Call to Seriousness* (Jonathan Cape, 1976), Introduction.

180. 'Things Unseen' in Dawson, *Shakespeare and Other Lectures*, p. 419.

181. Marriage address, Dr and Mrs Rigby, 1 January 1851, in Bound Volume of Addresses at Marriages, Christenings, Adult Baptisms and Burials, 1822–67, Manchester College, Oxford, MSS Tayler, MS 20.

182. Angela John, for example, notes that 'for many, the reassertion of traditional

family values was seen as an essential means of restoring harmony to a country threatened by Chartism'. John, *By the Sweat of their Brow*, p. 43.

183. Mary Leman Gillies, 'A Happy New Year to the People', *People's Journal*, Vol. I, no. 3, 17 January 1846, pp. 38–9.

4 'Merely a Question of Bargain and Sale': Law Reform and the Union of the Sexes

1. *People*, Vol. I, no. 1, 27 May 1848, p. 1.
2. Silverpen, 'The Whittington Club and the Ladies', *Douglas Jerrold's Weekly Newspaper*, 24 October 1846, p. 343; R. H. Horne, *A New Spirit of the Age* (Smith, Elder, 1844), p. 75.
3. Allen Horstman, *Victorian Divorce* (Croom Helm, 1985), p. 41.
4. Mary Lyndon Shanley, *Feminism, Marriage and the Law in Victorian England, 1850–1895* (L. B. Tauris, 1989), p. 29.
5. P. Mallet, 'Woman and Marriage in Victorian Society', in E. M. Craik (ed.), *Marriage and Property* (Aberdeen: Aberdeen University Press, 1984), p. 163.
6. Olive Banks, *Faces of Feminism. A Study of Feminism as a Social Movement* (Oxford: Basil Blackwell, 1981), p. 16; Mallet, 'Woman and Marriage', p. 180.
7. Witness, 'Effects of Legislating upon Love, or, Some Reasons Against Lawful Wedlock', *National*, 1839, p. 328.
8. See the entries in J. O. S. Baylen and N. J. Gossman (eds), *Biographical Dictionary of Modern British Radicals* (Hassocks: Harvester Press, 1979).
9. Robert Owen, 'The Sexual Law', *National*, 1839, pp. 145–6.
10. Christopher Hill, *Milton and the English Revolution* (Faber and Faber, 1977), pp. 119, 123–4. References to Milton's views on divorce amongst nineteenth-century radicals are ubiquitous. See for example, 'Milton on Divorce', *National*, 1839, pp. 133–4; 'Milton on Divorce', *NMW*, Vol. V, no. 33, 8 June 1839, pp. 295–6.
11. R. Acland Armstrong, *Henry William Crosskey, His Life and Work* (Birmingham: Cornish Brothers, 1895), p. 31.
12. *MR*, Vol. X, 1836, p. 746.
13. G. S., 'The Rights and Wrongs of Woman. Part II, Marriage Laws and Prostitution', *Star in the East*, Vol. III, no. 148, 13 July 1839, p. 365; Witness, 'Effects of Legislating upon Love, or, Some Reasons against Lawful Wedlock', *National*, 1839, p. 327.
14. WJF, 'Politics of the Common Pleas', *MR*, Vol. X, 1836, p. 398.
15. Robert Owen, 'The Sexual Law', *National*, pp. 145–6. For a full explanation of the difficulties in obtaining divorce in this period, see Lee Holcombe, *Wives and Property. Reform of the Married Women's Property Law in Nineteenth Century England* (Toronto: University of Toronto Press, 1983), pp. 93–6.
16. 'Slavery', *National*, 1839, p. 71.
17. 'The Dissenting Marriage Question', *MR*, Vol. VII, 1833, p. 142.
18. See, for example, Fraser Harrison, *The Dark Angel* (Sheldon Press, 1977), p. 218. A rare, albeit cursory acknowledgement of the radicalism of this

work may be found in Patricia Thompson, *George Sand and the Victorians. Her Influence and Reputation in Nineteenth Century England* (Macmillan, 1977), p. 147.

19. E. Lynn Linton, *My Literary Life* (Hodder and Stoughton, 1899), see esp. pp. 11–26.
20. *Daily News*, quoted in Kent, *Sex and Suffrage*, p. 178.
21. Gordon S. Haight, *George Eliot and John Chapman, with Chapman's Diaries* (Hamden, Conn., Archon Books, 1969, second edition), p. 174; Susanne Howe, *Geraldine Jewsbury, her Life and Errors* (Aberdeen: Aberdeen University Press, 1935), p. 125.
22. Junius Redivivus, 'On the Condition of Women in England', *MR*, Vol. VII, 1833, see pp. 217–19.
23. Eliza Lynn, *Realities. A Tale* (Saunders and Otley, 1851), Vol. I, see pp. 149, 154, 178–9, 103.
24. *Tait's Edinburgh Magazine*, Vol. XII, January 1845, p. 61.
25. Meteyard and the Ashurst sisters were in favour of delayed marriages (Silverpen, 'Protection to Women', *Douglas Jerrold's Weekly Newspaper*, no. 4, 6 August 1846, pp. 78–9; MS letter from Eliza Bardouneau-Narcy to Elizabeth Neall Gay, October 1841, Sidney Howard Gay Papers, The Rare Book and Manuscript Library, Columbia University Library; but more typically William Shaen detailed his objections to Malthus in a letter to his sister, 13 June 1848, Leeds Archives, Symington Papers, Box 19.
26. Charles Dickens to Fanny Burnett, 6 December 1844, Dickens House Museum, Burnett Notebooks, XA524; Francis E. Mineka, *The Dissidence of Dissent. The 'Monthly Repository' 1806–1838* (Chapel Hill: University of North Carolina Press, 1944), p. 267.
27. 'Hints on Marriage', *People's Press*, Vol. I, no. I, January 1847, pp. 14–15; 'Time Versus Malthus: the Last Verdict', *Douglas Jerrold's Shilling Magazine*, Vol. III, January–June 1846, pp. 445, 448.
28. W. J. Linton (and possibly James Hill too), it seems, had married his wife's sister, technically an illegal move. F. B. Smith, *Radical Artisan. William James Linton. 1812–1897* (Manchester: Manchester University Press, 1973), p. 36. For the relationships of W. J. Fox, Eliza Flower, Thomas Southwood Smith and Margaret Gillies, see Chapter 2. For the relationship between J. S. Mill and Harriet Taylor, see Alice S. Rossi, *Essays on Sexual Equality* (Chicago: University of Chicago Press, 1970), esp. pp. 28–9.
29. Lynn Linton, *My Literary Life*, pp. 22–3; Thompson also makes such a claim in *George Sand and the Victorians*, pp. 42–3. For a more circumspect approach see Hock Guan Tjoa, *George Henry Lewes. A Victorian Mind* (Cambridge, Mass.: Harvard University Press, 1977), p. 16.
30. Their relationship was so dubbed by Elizabeth Barrett Browning. Holcombe, *Wives and Property*, p. 85; MS letter from Eliza Cook to unidentified correspondent, 25 October 1844, Boston Public Library, MS. Gris, 204.
31. Letter to a correspondent, *Crisis*, Vol. III, no. 13, 23 November 1834, p. 100.
32. Witness, 'Effects of Legislating upon Love, or, Some Reasons against Lawful Wedlock', *National*, 1839, p. 327; Letter from Francis Worsley, 'Love and Marriage', *Leader*, 18 May 1850, p. 180.
33. MS letter from Elisa Bardouneau-Narcy to Elizabeth Neall Gay, 6 March

1846, Sydney Howard Gay Papers, The Rare Book and Manuscript Library, Columbia University Library.

34. Mary Leman Grimstone, *Cleone. A Tale of Married Life* (Effingham Wilson, 1834, Vol. I, pp. 107–8.

35. 'Light out of the Cloud, A Tale', *Eliza Cook's Journal*, Vol. II, no. 72, 14 September 1850, pp. 315–16.

36. Ruth Watts, 'Knowledge is Power – Unitarians, Gender and Education in the Eighteenth and Early Nineteenth Centuries', *Gender and Education*, Vol. I, no. 1. 1989, pp. 41–2; 'Marriage and Protest', *Christian Reformer*, Vol. II, 1835, p. 60; Richard W. Davis, *Dissent in Politics 1780–1830. The Life of William Smith, M.P.* (Epworth Press, 1971), p. 210.

37. Emily Bushrod, 'The History of Unitarianism in Birmingham from the Middle of the Eighteenth Century to 1893' (MA thesis, University of Birmingham, 1954), p. 35.

38. TS letter from William Shaen to his sister, 13 July 1844, Leeds Archives, Symington Papers, Box 19.

39. Harriet Martineau, *Society in America*, ed. M. Lupset, (Gloucester, Mass.: Peter Smith, 1968, first published 1837), p. 296; Jutta Schwarzkopf, *Women in the Chartist Movement* (Macmillan, 1991), p. 51.

40. Mrs Leman Grimstone, *Woman's Love* (Saunders and Otley, 1832), Vol. III, p. 354; Hope Malleson, *Elizabeth Malleson, 1828–1916. Autobiographical Notes and Letters* (Printed for Private Circulation, 1926), p. 36, p. 81.

41. Letter to Editor from Anna Wheeler in *Crisis*, Vol. II, no. 23, 15 June 1833, p. 182.

42. Rossi, *Essays on Sex Equality*, pp. 145–6, Henry Solly, *These Eighty Years, or, the Story of an Unfinished Life* (Simpkin, Marshall, 1893), Vol. II, p. 46. See also Harriet Martineau, 'The Conciencious [*sic*]', *National*, 1839, pp. 342–3; Shanley, *Feminism, Marriage and the Law*, p. 18.

43. John Halkett, *Milton and the Idea of Matrimony* (New Haven, Conn.: Yale University Press, 1970), p. 8; Matilda M. Hays, *Helen Stanley. A Tale* (E. Churton, 1846), Letter to Reader, p. 333.

44. Judith R. Walkowitz, *Prostitution and Victorian Society. Women, Class and the State* (Cambridge: Cambridge University Press, 1980), p. 33.

45. G. S., 'The Rights and Wrongs of Woman, II, Marriage Laws and Prostitution', *Star in the East*, Vol. III, no. 148, 13 July 1839, p. 365; John Stores Smith, *Social Aspects* (John Chapman, 1850), pp. 243–4.

46. 'Chastity and Celibacy', *National*, 1839, p. 156; Schwarzkopf, *Women in the Chartist Movement*, p. 48, notes that some Chartist novels from this period also used the metaphor. However, as will become apparent, the feminists used the metaphor in the context of a sophisticated feminist ideology, an angle completely missing from Chartist accounts, as Schwarzkopf acknowledges.

47. Barbara Taylor, *Eve and the New Jerusalem. Socialism and Feminism in the Nineteenth Century* (Virago, 1983), p. 211.

48. Charles Dickens, *Dombey and Son* (Harmondsworth: Penguin, 1988, first published 1846–8), pp. 473, 856.

49. Junius Redivivus, 'On the Condition of Women in England', *MR*. Vol. VII, 1833, p. 218.

50. Dickens, *Dombey and Son*, pp. 847, 662, 847.

51. Sally Mitchell, *The Fallen Angel. Chastity, Class and Women's Reading, 1835–80* (Bowling Green: University Popular Press, 1981), pp. 57–8; R. D. Sell, 'Dickens and the New Historicism: the Polyvocal Audience and the Discourse of *Dombey and Son*', in J. Hawthorn (ed.), *The Nineteenth Century British Novel* (Edward Arnold, 1986), pp. 71–2.
52. Dickens, *Dombey and Son*, p. 579.
53. See Hays, *Helen Stanley*; 'George Sand', *Howitt's Journal*, Vol. I, no. 10, 6 March 1847, pp. 128–30.
54. 'The Rights of Men and Wrongs of Women. Coutts v. Dun', *Douglas Jerrold's Weekly Newspaper*, no. 34, 6 March 1847, p. 280.
55. MS letter from Sarah K. Hennell to G. J. Holyoake, 19 May 1854, Co-operative Union, Manchester, George Jacob Holyoake Collection, no. 667; 'Marriage with a Deceased Wife's Sister', *Douglas Jerrold's Weekly Newspaper*, no. 25, 2 January 1847, p. 17.
56. 'Plan of a Practical Moral Union of the Women of Great Britain and Ireland', *Crisis*, Vol. II, no. 33, 17 August 1833, p. 263; B. Warden, 'Union of Women Only', *Crisis*, Vol. II, no. 34, 24 August 1833, p. 268.
57. Concordia, 'The Fancied Freedom of Women!', *Crisis*, Vol. IV, no. 9, 7 June 1834, p. 67 and 'Letter to Editor', ibid., Vol. IV, no. 10, 14 June 1834, p. 75.
58. 'Education and Capacities of Women', *NMW*, Vol. VI, no. 39, 20 July 1839, pp. 612–14; A. Wheeler, 'Rights of Women', *British Co-operator*, no. 1, April 1830, pp. 12–15.
59. Anna Jameson to Ottilie van Goethe, quoted in Clara Thomas, *Love and Work Enough. The Life of Anna Jameson* (Macdonald, 1967), p. 127; *Tait's Edinburgh Magazine*, Vol. VI, February 1839, pp. 69–81.
60. *MR*, Vol. X, 1836, p. 202. It was reprinted, for example, in *NMW*, II, no. 91, pp. 309–10; *National*, pp. 62–3.
61. *MR*, Vol. VIII, 1834, pp. 548–9; Graham Wallas, *William Johnson Fox 1786–1864. Conway Memorial Lecture* (Watts, 1924), p. 28.
62. See, for example, 'Critical Notice of Reports of Lectures. Delivered at the Chapel, South Place, Finsbury, by W. J. Fox', *National* 1839, pp. 56–7.
63. 'The Right of Woman', *National*, 1839, p. 135; Witness, 'Effects of Legislating upon Love or, Some Reasons Against Lawful Wedlock', *National*, p. 327; see also, 'Slavery', *National*, 1839, pp. 71–2.
64. MS letter from Leigh Hunt to W. J. Linton, 31 January 1839, Iowa University Library, Leigh Hunt Correspondence, MSL, H.
65. 'Treatment of Women', *Eliza Cook's Journal*, Vol. V, no. 119, 9 August 1851, pp. 226–7.
66. Kent, *Sex and Suffrage*, p. 141.
67. Junius Redivivus, 'On the Condition of Women in England', *MR*, Vol. VII, 1833, p. 230; 'Marriage as it is', *NMW*, Vol. IV, no. 182, 21 April 1838, pp. 202–4.
68. 'What I would do if I had the Power', *People*, Vol. I, no. 21, 1848, p. 161; 'Our Admirable Constitution in Church and State', ibid., Vol. I, no. 22, 1848, p. 173.
69. H. T. Mill, 'Enfranchisement of Women', *Westminster Review*, Vol. 55, July 1851, p. 152.

70. Witness, 'Effects of Legislating upon Love', *National*, 1839, p. 328. For further arguments concerning the need to establish women's independent existence through reforming the marriage laws, see 'Revelations of Truth. Chapter IX', *National*, 1839, pp. 126–8; 'Slavery', ibid., p. 71.

71. 'On Social Reformation', *People and Howitt's Journal*, Vol. II, no. 5, 1850, p. 24.

72. A view held by Catherine Barmby in her Owenite days, see Kate, 'Condition of Women', *NMW*, Vol. V, no. 24, 6 April 1839, pp. 372–3.

73. Mrs Leman Grimstone, 'Rich and Poor', *NMW*, Vol. I, no. 30, 23 May 1835, p. 238.

74. 'A Victim', *MR*, Vol. VII, 1833, p. 177; WJL, 'Love and Marriage', *Reasoner*, Vol. I, no. 7, 15 July 1846, pp. 99–100.

75. '"Rights" of Men and Wrongs of Women. – Coutts v. Dun', *Douglas Jerrold's Weekly Newspaper*, no. 34, 6 March 1847, p. 280; 'Wrongs of Woman – Hypocrisy of Man', ibid., no. 67, 23 October 1847, p. 1337.

76. 'He's Too Much the Gentleman', *Wade's London Review*, Vol. II, no. 2, August 1845, p. 156.

77. 'Treatment of Women', *Eliza Cook's Journal*, Vol. V, no. 119, 9 August 1851, pp. 225–7.

78. *Spirit of the Age*, Vol. II, no. 30, 17 February 1849, p. 158; 'Memoir of Charles Fourier', *Spirit of the Age*, Vol. I, Supplement no. 2, 2 December 1848, p. 6.

79. 'Political Maxims', *People*, Vol. 1, no. 35, 1848, p. 276; 'What I would do if I had the Power', ibid., Vol. I, no. 21, 1848, p. 161.

80. MS transcription of Harriet Martineau's letter to James Martineau, January 1844, transcribed from Martineau's shorthand by William S. Coloe, July 1958, Manchester College, Oxford, MS J. Martineau (1), p. 195; *Tait's Edinburgh Magazine*, Vol. XI, July 1844, p. 427.

81. *Douglas Jerrold's Weekly Newspaper*, no. 10, 19 September 1846, p. 224.

82. E. P. Hurlbut, *Essays on Human Rights and their Political Guarantees* (Edinburgh: Maclachlan, Stewart, 1847), p. 57; *Douglas Jerrold's Weekly Newspaper*, no. 46, 29 May 1847, p. 660.

83. MS letter from Bessie Raynor Parkes to Barbara Leigh Smith, 21 April 1847, Girton College, Cambridge, Parkes Papers, BRP V 8; B. Leigh Smith Bodichon, *A Brief Summary, in Plain Language, of the Most Important Laws Concerning Women: Together with a Few Observations Thereon* (1854), repr. in C. A. Lacey (ed.), *Barbara Leigh Smith Bodichon and the Langham Place Group* (Routledge and Kegan Paul, 1987), p. 34.

84. 'Women's Rights', *Leader*, 17 May 1851, p. 465; 'Marriage in America', *Douglas Jerrold's Weekly Newspaper*, no. 98, 27 May 1848, p. 676.

85. 'Wrongs of Woman – Hypocrisy of Man', ibid., no. 67, 23 October 1847, p. 1337.

86. Quoted in C. E. Robinson, 'Leigh Hunt's Dramatic Success; A Legend of Florence', in R. A. McCowen (ed.), *The Life and Times of Leigh Hunt* (Iowa: Friends of the University of Iowa Libraries, 1985), p. 551.

87. CW, 'My Opposite Neighbours – A Tale of the Tally System', *Douglas Jerrold's Shilling Magazine*, Vol. II, July–December 1845, pp. 513–20; W. Howitt, 'English Scenes and Characters', ibid., Vol. III, January–June 1846, pp. 38–44.

88. See 'The Laws Relating to Women', *Law Review*, Vol. 20, no. 39, 1854, p. 22.
89. Goodwyn Barmby, 'Mine is Thine', *Douglas Jerrold's Weekly Newspaper*, Vol. IV, July–December, 1846, p. 119; Charles Dickens to Rev. W. J. Fox, [6 February 1846], Kathleen Tillotson, *The Letters of Charles Dickens. Vol. 4, 1844–6* (Oxford: Clarendon Press, 1977), p. 491.
90. Herstein, *A Mid-Victorian Feminist*, p. 80.
91. 'He's too much the Gentleman', *Wade's London Review,* Vol. II, no. II, August, 1845, p. 156; 'Rights of Women', ibid., p. 171; the *Examiner*'s treatment of the issue (the article was by J. S. Mill) is given in the *Crisis*, Vol. II, no. 13, 31 March 1833, p. 102.
92. PMV, 'Woman and her Social Position', *Westminster Review*, Vol. 35, 1841, p. 25; '*Woman's Mission*', ibid., Vol. 52, 1850, p. 368. For the *Leader*'s position see 'The Morality of Easy Divorce', *Leader*, 11 May 1850, pp. 156–7; 'Women's Rights', ibid., 17 May 1851, p. 465; 'The History of Women', ibid., 16 November 1850, pp. 809–10.
93. Roy and his work were greatly admired among the Unitarian community at large – who found his ideas very akin to their own. For example, 'Death of Rammohun Roy', *Manchester Guardian*, 5 October 1832, p. 2. S. D. Collet wrote a biography of Roy, published in 1913. For an example of the reception of his ideas on women among Unitarians, see L. Aikin to Dr Channing, 23 October 1833 in P. H. Le Breton (ed.), *Memoirs, Miscellanies and Letters of the Late Lucy Aikin including those addressed to the Rev. Dr Channing from 1826 to 1842* (Longman, Green, Roberts, 1864), pp. 288–95.
94. Quoted in Thomas, *Love and Work Enough* (Macdonald, 1967), p. 139.
95. Harriet Martineau to W. J. Fox, 13 May 1837, Valerie Saunders (ed.), *Harriet Martineau. Selected Letters* (Oxford: Clarendon Press, 1990), pp. 44–5; Martineau, *Society in America*, p. 297.
96. MS transcript by James Martineau of a letter from Harriet Martineau, 6 March 1838, transcribed from Martineau's shorthand by William S. Coloe, July 1958, Manchester College, Oxford, MS J. Martineau (1)., p. 154; Harriet Martineau, *Autobiography* (Virago, 1983, first published 1877), Vol. II, p. 104.
97. Margaret Forster, *Significant Sisters. The Grassroots of Active Feminism 1839–1939* (Harmondsworth: Penguin, 1984), Ch. 1; Holcombe, *Wives and Property*, pp. 53–4.
98. Quoted in Harriet Martineau, *A History of the Thirty Years Peace 1816–1846* (George Bell and Sons, 1877), p. 17.
99. Charles Dickens to John Forster [24 and 25 August 1846], Tillotson (ed.), *Letters of Charles Dickens*, Vol. 4, p. 609.
100. Charles Dickens to John Forster, 1846. Quoted in John Forster, *The Life of Charles Dickens* (ed. J. W. T. Ley) (Whitefriars Press, 1928), p. 412; MS letter from John Chapman to Harriet Martineau, 22 October 1855, Birmingham University Library, HM, no. 192.
101. Mary Lyndon Shanley, *Feminism, Marriage and the Law in Victorian England, 1850–1895* (L. B. Tauris, 1989), p. 79.
102. '"Rights" of Men and Wrongs of Women – Coutts v. Dun', *Douglas Jerrold's Weekly Newspaper*, no. 34, 6 March 1847, p. 280.

103. Rossi, *Essays on Sex Equality*, p. 22; Holcombe, *Wives and Property*, pp. 53, 64; Shanley, *Feminism, Marriage and the Law*, pp. 31, 34.

104. Dorothy M. Stetson, *A Woman's Issue. The Politics of Family Law Reform in England* (Greenwood, Connecticut: Greenwood Press, 1982), p. 25. Regarding the society prior to the 1850s, Shanley notes simply that in 1848 the society asked for changes in the divorce law. Stetson argues that its position on this matter was conservative.

105. B. and J. L. Hammond, *James Stansfeld. A Victorian Champion of Sex Equality* (Longmans, Green, 1932), pp. 9–10.

106. MS letter from J. H. Parry to Bessie Raynor Parkes, 15 May 1846, Girton College, Cambridge, Parkes Papers, BRP. VI. 49; Diana M. Chase Worzala, 'The Langham Place Circle. The Beginnings of the Organised Women's Movement in England. 1854–1870', (PhD thesis, University of Wisconsin–Madison, 1982), pp. 373 and 375.

107. Details of the collaboration between Chadwick and Adams emerge in MS letters from Edwin Chadwick to William Bridges Adams, University College, London, Chadwick papers, Copybook IV, pp. 96–7, 154. For Smith's reform work see G. L. Lewes, *Dr Southwood Smith. A Retrospect* (William Blackwood and Sons, 1891).

108. Stetson, *A Woman's Issue*, p. 23; Holcombe, *Wives and Property*, p. 17.

109. *Westminster Review*, Vol. 41, 1844, p. 380.

110. Shanley, *Feminism, Marriage and the Law*, p. 117; Jane Grey Perkins, *Life of Mrs Norton* (John Murray, 1909), p. 154.

111. See the society's publication, the *Law Review*, passim.

112. See, for example, 'Reports of the Society for Promoting the Amendment of the Law, Ecclesiastical Committee – Divorce', *Law Review*, Vol. 8, no. 16, 1848, pp. 347–52, which suggested that divorce should not be granted as readily to women as to men. However, this view was not consistently promoted by the society. See below, note 115.

113. 'Papers of Society for Promoting the Amendment of the Law', *Law Review*, Vol. 22, no. 43, 1855, p. 124; 'Proceedings', ibid., Vol. 9, no. 18, 1848, p. 444; E. V. Neale was on the society's Committee of Management, 'Annual Meeting, 16 June 1847', ibid., Vol. 6, no. 12, 1847, p. 413; 'Proceedings', ibid., Vol. 8, no. 15, 1848, p. 222; 'Proceedings', *Law Review*, Vol. 9, no. 17, 1848, p. 215.

114. 'Proceedings', *Law Review*, Vol. 9, no. 18, 1848, p. 444. The society wished to ensure married women's consent for out-of-court settlements, for example, 'The Humble Memorial of the Metropolitan and Provincial Law Association', ibid., Vol. 8, no. 16, 1848, p. 407.

115. 'Divorce', ibid., Vol. I, no. II, 1845, p. 370; 'Wife's Reversionary Interest in Choses in Action', ibid., Vol. 4, no. 8, 1846, p. 429.

116. Ibid., Vol. 10, no. 20, 1849, pp. 424–5.

117. 'On Social Reformation', *People and Howitt's Journal*, Vol. II, no. 5, p. 24.

118. PMV, 'Woman and her Social Position', *Westminster Review*, Vol. 35, 1841, p. 24.

119. Shanley, *Feminism, Marriage and the Law*, p. 33.

120. Stetson, *A Woman's Issue*, p. 38.

121. For Stansfeld's contribution to the later cause, see J. O. S. Baylen and

N. J. Gossman (eds), *Biographical Dictionary of Modern British Radicals* (Hassocks: Harvester Press), 1979, p. 480.

122. MS notes by William Smith on a bill concerning women's rights. Cambridge University Library, William Smith Papers, Add. MS. 7621, no. 145; letter from Lucy Aikin to Dr Channing, 18 April 1838, Le Breton, *Memoirs, Miscellanies and Letters of the Late Lucy Aikin*, pp. 367–74.

123. 'Marriage System of Socialism', *NMW*, Vol. VII, no. 72, 7 March 1840, p. 1156.

124. E. M. Sigsworth and T. J. Wyke, 'A Study of Victorian Prostitution and Venereal Disease', in Martha Vicinus (ed.), *Suffer and Be Still* (Bloomington: Indiana University Press, 1972), p. 80; Judith R. Walkowitz, *Prostitution and Victorian Society. Women, Class and the State* (Cambridge: Cambridge University Press, 1980), pp. 35–7.

125. See, for example, Silverpen, 'Protection to Women', *Douglas Jerrold's Weekly Newspaper*, no. 4, 8 August 1846, p. 78.

126. Eric Bristow, *Vice and Vigilance* (Dublin: Gill and Macmillan, 1977), p. 71.

127. Harrison, *The Dark Angel*, p. 254.

128. Selma B. Kanner, 'Victorian Institutional Patronage: Angela Burdett-Coutts, Charles Dickens and Urania Cottage; Reformatory for Women, 1846–58', (PhD thesis, University of California, Los Angeles, 1972), passim; John P. Frazee, 'Dickens and Unitarianism', *Dickens Studies Annual*, 18, 1989, pp. 116–43.

129. MS letter from Eliza Ashurst to H. C. Wright, 24 September 1846, Houghton Library, Harvard University, MS Eng 501 Vol. 1; 'House for Penitent Females in Leicester', *Leicestershire Mercury*, 12 September 1846; 'Lincoln Penitent Females' Home', *Leader*, 20 September 1851, p. 890.

130. Bristow, *Vice and Vigilance*, pp. 60–1.

131. The sources for the Associate Institution are as follows: the *Female's Friend* (its official mouthpiece), see in particular, 'The Origin, Object and Operations of the Associate Institution', *Female's Friend*, no. 7, 21 July 1846, pp. 17–18; 'Concluding Appeal', no. 1, January 1846, p. 23; 'Address to the Queen', ibid., pp. 18–19. *Remedies for the Wrongs of Women* (Hatchard and Son, 1844), see pp. 7, 41–2. The history of the Institution may also be found in *Associate Institution, The First Report* (Brewster and West, 1846), see pp. 14, 16.

132. Bristow, *Vice and Vigilance* p. 61; Mitchell, *The Fallen Angel*, p. 26.

133. Walkowitz, *Prostitution and Victorian Society*, p. 39.

134. 'Address', *Female's Friend*, no. 1, January 1846, p. 1; *Remedies for the Wrongs of Women*, p. 40; 'Operations of the Associate Institution', *Female's Friend*, no. 4, April 1846, p. 93.

135. TS letter from William Shaen to his sister, 5 March 1846, Leeds Archives, Symington Papers, Box 19.

136. Silverpen, 'Protection to Women', *Douglas Jerrold's Weekly Newspaper*, no. 4, 8 August 1846, p. 78; TS letter from William Shaen to his sister, 5 March 1846, Leeds Archives, Symington Papers, Box 19.

137. 'The Present State of the Law, by a Barrister', *Female's Friend*, no. 4, April 1846, pp. 73–6. Stansfeld is identified as the author in TS letter from William Shaen to his sister, 5 March 1846, Leeds Archives, Symington Papers, Box 19.

138. See for example, Letter to Editor from William Biggs, *Leicestershire Mercury*, 23 May 1846; and Meeting of the Town Council, ibid., 6 June 1846.

139. *Associate Institution, The First Report*, 21 July 1846; 'The Week', *People's Journal*, Vol. II, no. 31, 18 July 1846, p. 9.

140. 'Operations of the Associate Institution', *Female's Friend*, no. 4, April 1846, p. 96; *Associate Institution. The First Report*, p. 34.

141. See 'The Woman Question in England', *Liberator*, 31 July 1840.

142. MB, 'Prevention', *Female's Friend*, no. 3, March 1846, pp. 53–4.

143. For example, *Leicestershire Mercury*, 6 June 1846.

144. MLG, 'The Protective System of Morals', *MR*, Vol. IX, 1835, p. 685; Kate, 'Man's Legislation', *NMW*, Vol. V, no. 31, 25 May 1839, p. 480.

145. 'Edinburgh Mechanics' Institution Soirée', *People's Journal*, Vol. IV, no. 79, 3 July 1847, p. 1; 'Early Essays on Marriage and Divorce', Rossi, *Essays on Sex Equality*, see p. 85.

146. 'The Mental and Moral Dignity of Woman', *Female's Friend*, no. 1, January 1846, pp. 6–8.

147. An Observer of Life as It Is, 'Protection of Females', *Leicestershire Mercury*, 30 May 1846; Meeting of Town Council, ibid., 6 June 1846. Lynn's novel, *Realities* had provoked just such a discussion in radical unitarian circles, Haight, *George Eliot and John Chapman*, p. 174.

148. See the case reported in *Douglas Jerrold's Weekly Newspaper*, no. 67, 23 October 1847, pp. 1336–7.

149. Walkowitz, *Prostitution and Victorian Society*, esp. pp. 18–20.

150. P. T. Cominos, 'Late Victorian Sexual Respectability and the Social System', *International Review of Social History*, Vol. 8, 1963, pp. 18–48, 216–50.

151. See, for example, 'The Outcast', *National*, 1839, p. 129, Geraldine Jewsbury, *Zoe* (1845).

152. *Reasoner*, Vol. IV, no. 103, p. 30; Edward Search, 'The Late Emma Martin', *Reasoner*, Vol. XII, no. 4, 1852, p. 59.

153. Joan Perkin, *Women and Marriage in Nineteenth Century England* (Routledge, 1989), p. 18.

154. See, for example, 'Aristocratical and Political Morality' in W. J. Fox, *Finsbury Lectures. Reports of Lectures. . . .* (Charles Fox, 1835), no. 2, p. 21; Catherine Barmby, 'Employment for Women', *People's Press*, Vol. II, no. 24, September 1848, pp. 165–7; *MR*, Vol. IX, 1835, pp. 627–8.

155. Barmby, 'The Outlines of Communism, Associality, and Communization', *Promethean*, Vol. I, no. 2, February 1842, p. 24.

156. MS letter from W. J. Linton to Thornton Hunt, 11 October 1849, Beinecke Library, Yale University, MS Vault Shelves Linton.

157. W. J. Fox, for example, delivered a long series of lectures on the subject at South Place Chapel. *Reports of Lectures Delivered at the Chapel in South Place, Finsbury, by W. J. Fox* (Charles Fox, 1840), nos 22 to 25.

158. For a full consideration of women's attraction to the anti-slavery cause, see L. and R. Billington, '"A Burning Zeal for Righteousness": Women in the British Anti-Slavery Movement, 1820–1860', in J. Rendall (ed.), *Equal or Different. Women's Politics 1800–1914* (Oxford: Basil Blackwell, 1987), pp. 82–111.

159. *Remedies for the Wrongs of Women*, pp. 41–2; 'The Week', *People's Journal*, Vol. II, no. 31, 1 August 1846, p. 9; see 'Address', *Female's Friend*, no. 1, January 1846, p. 2.

160. 'The Week', *People's Journal*, Vol. II, no. 31, 1 August 1846, p. 9.

161. *Remedies for the Wrongs of Women*, pp. 41–2, 45, 47.

162. F. K. Prochaska, *Women and Philanthropy in Nineteenth Century England* (Oxford: Oxford University Press, 1980); Ann Summers, 'A Home from Home – Women's Philanthropic Work in the Nineteenth Century', in Sandra Burman (ed.), *Fit Work for Women* (Croom Helm, 1979), pp. 33–63.

163. Jane Rendall, *Origins of Modern Feminism: Women in Britain, France and the United States 1780–1860* (Chicago: Lyceum, 1986), pp. 254–75; Banks, *Faces of Feminism*, p. 16.

164. Prochaska, *Women and Philanthropy*, p. 186; W. R. Greg, 'Prostitution', *Westminster Review*, no. 53, 1850, cited in Bristow, *Vice and Vigilance*, p. 62.

165. Banks, *Faces of Feminism*, pp. 16–17.

166. 'The Present State of the Law, by a Barrister', *Female's Friend*, no. 4, April 1846, p. 73.

167. See Lynn, *Realities*, Vol. II, esp. p. 277.

168. TS letter from William Shaen to his sister, 5 March 1846, Leeds Archives, Symington Papers, Box 19.

169. MS letter from Bessie Raynor Parkes to Samuel Blackwell, Girton College, Cambridge, Parkes Papers, Vol. IX/16. Also cited in Jane Rendall, 'Friendship and Politics: Barbara Leigh Smith Bodichon (1827–1892) and Bessie Raynor Parkes (1829–1925)', in J. Rendall and Susan Mendus (eds), *Sexuality and Subordination. Interdisciplinary Studies of Gender in the Nineteenth Century* (Routledge, 1989), p. 156.

170. A good account of such perceptions of early feminism is to be found in Ruby Saywell, 'The Development of the Feminist Idea in England 1789–1833', (MA thesis, King's College, London, 1936), p. 78.

171. Two writers greatly influenced by the radical unitarians, Charles Dickens and Elizabeth Gaskell, proved instrumental in effecting such a shift. Geoffrey Watts, *The Fallen Woman in the Nineteenth Century English Novel* (Croom Helm, 1984), p. 9; Eric Trudgill, *Madonnas and Magdalenes. The Origins and Development of Victorian Sexual Attitudes* (New York: Holmes and Meier, 1976), p. 289.

5   The Whittington Clubs

1. R. K. Webb, *Harriet Martineau. A Radical Victorian* (Heineman, 1960), p. 17.

2. Mary Leman Grimstone, 'Men and Women', *Tait's Edinburgh Magazine*, Vol. 1, March 1834, p. 103; MS letter from Lady Byron to Sophia de Morgan, 4 November 1849. Bodleian Library, Dep. Lovelace Byron papers, Box 67, f.134.

3. In particular, Reid engaged the assistance of Barbara Leigh Smith and the Howitts' daughter, Anna Mary. Leigh Smith's aunt, Julia Smith, also became actively involved at this point. See Shelia R. Herstein, *A Mid-Victorian*

Feminist, Barbara Leigh Smith Bodichon (New Haven: Yale University Press, 1985), pp. 19–21.

4. See ibid; and also Margaret J. Tuke, *A History of Bedford College for Women 1849–1937* (Oxford: Oxford University Press, 1939).

5. June Purvis, *Hard Lessons. The Lives and Education of Working Women in Nineteenth Century England* (Cambridge: Polity Press, 1989), see pp. 153, 156, 171–2 for her allusions to the women's rights movement.

6. For the material comforts the club was to provide see the series, 'Club Crotchets and Cheap Comforts: Being Contributions to the Whittington Fund', *Douglas Jerrold's Shilling Magazine*, Vol. VI, July–December 1847, pp. 1–20, 132–40, 343–50.

7. 'Vegetarian Supper Party at Whittington Club', *Douglas Jerrold's Weekly Newspaper*, no. 124, 25 November 1848, p. 1525.

8. Printed advertisement for the Whittington Club, Leeds Archives, Symington Papers, Box 19.

9. Christopher Kent, 'The Whittington Club: A Bohemian Experiment in Middle-Class Social Reform', *Victorian Studies*, Vol. 18, 1974, pp. 31–56.

10. For the fate of the clubs, see Kent, 'A Bohemian Experiment', p. 56; 'Birmingham Whittington Club', *Birmingham Journal*, 29 April 1848, p. 3; 'From the Athenæum', *Whittington Club and Metropolitan Athenæum Gazette*, new series, 12 October 1850, no. 40, p. 301. *Howitt's Journal* often provided a useful forum where these institutions might communicate with one another.

11. See for example, MLG, 'Amusement', *Monthly Repository*, Vol. X, 1836, pp. 747–55; Francis E. Mineka, *The Dissidence of Dissent* (Chapel Hill: University of North Carolina Press, 1944), p. 342.

12. Thomas Kelly, *A History of Adult Education in Great Britain* (Liverpool: Liverpool University Press, 1962), p. 108, 117; Raymond V. Holt, *The Unitarian Contribution to Social Progress in England* (Butler and Tanner, 1938), p. 267.

13. Eileen Yeo, 'Culture and Constraint in Working-Class Movements, 1830–55', in E. and S. Yeo (eds), *Popular Culture and Class Conflict 1590–1914* (Brighton: Harvester Press, 1981), pp. 154–86; Barbara Taylor, *Eve and the New Jerusalem: Socialism and Feminism in the Nineteenth Century* (Virago, 1983), pp. 232–3.

14. Jutta Schwarzkopf, *Women in the Chartist Movement* (Macmillan, 1991), p. 181; William Lovett and John Collins, *Chartism: A New Organisation of the People* (Leicester: Leicester University Press, 1969, first published 1840), pp. 41, 77, 105.

15. WT, 'To the Members and Managers of Mechanics' Institutions in Great Britain and Ireland', *Co-operative Magazine and Monthly Herald*, no. 2, February 1826, pp. 46–8.

16. MLG, 'The Poor Woman's Appeal to her Husband', *Tatler*, Vol. IV, no. 485, 22 March 1832, p. 279.

17. MS letter from Mary Leman Grimstone to Charles Cowden Clarke, 26 March 1832, Brotherton Collection, Leeds University, Novello-Cowden-Clarke Collection.

18. For example, in the *Halfpenny Magazine*, no. 15, 11 August 1832, p. 112 and *National Association Gazette*, no. 3, 15 January 1842, p. 24.

19. 'Ladies in Coffee Houses', *Tatler*, no. 1, 2–4 [*sic*] April, p. 3.
20. Mary Leman Gillies, 'The Mechanic's Wife', *People's Journal*, Vol. 1, no. 26, 27 June 1846, pp. 356–9.
21. Herstein, *Mid-Victorian Feminist*, p. 55.
22. Purvis, *Hard Lessons*, pp. 103, 106; J. W. Hudson, *The History of Adult Education* (Woburn Press, 1969. First published 1851), pp. 88 and 152.
23. Ida, 'Female Education', *People's Press*, Vol. I, no. 11, December 1847, p. 342.
24. 'Bolton Essay and Discussion Class', *People's Journal*, Vol. III, no. 77, 19 June 1847, p. 50; 'Edinburgh Mechanics' Institution Soirée', ibid., Vol. IV, no. 79, 3 July 1847, p. 1; 'The Winlaton Literary and Mechanics' Institution', *People*, Vol. II, no. 53, 1849, p. 6; Kentish Town Literary Institution', *People and Howitt's Journal*, Vol. II, no. 5, 1847, p. 5.
25. John Killham, *Tennyson and the Princess. Reflections of an Age* (Athlone Press, 1958), p. 130; R. and F. Davenport Hill, *The Recorder of Birmingham. A Memoir of Matthew Davenport Hill with Selections from his Correspondence* (Macmillan, 1878), p. 250; Edgar Johnson, *Charles Dickens: His Tragedy and Triumph* (Harmondsworth: Penguin, 1980), p. 254; 'Soirée of the Mechanics' Institution: Leeds', 1 December 1847, in K. J. Fielding (ed.), *The Speeches of Charles Dickens* (Oxford: Clarendon Press, 1960), pp. 81–5.
26. 'First Annual Soirée of the Athenæum Glasgow', 28 December 1847, in Fielding, *Speeches of Charles Dickens*, pp. 85–92; 'Address of Charles Dickens', 5 October 1843, *Manchester Athenæum. Addresses* (Manchester: 1888), pp. 6–7.
27. 'Address of Mr Disraeli', 3 October 1844, *Manchester Athenæum. Addresses*, p. 10.
28. 'Address of Lord Morpeth', 1846, ibid., p. 62. Worthington made bids to allow women to attend lectures at the Royal Manchester Institution, 4 August 1836, Manchester City Archives, Royal Manchester Institution, M6.
29. 'To the People of Birmingham! The Whittington Club', 30 June 1847, printed circular, Birmingham City Archives, MS 1412/9; 'Edinburgh Mechanics' Institute', *Howitt's Journal*, Vol. II, no. 34, 21 August 1847, pp. 127–8.
30. Printed circular of the Roscoe Club, Liverpool Record Office, 920 MUS. 2–45; MS minutes of a meeting held at the Office of Mr Charles Redish on 6 April 1847, ibid; 'The Liverpool Roscoe Club', *Leader*, 13 April 1850, p. 52.
31. Letter to editor, *Whittington Club and Metropolis Athenæum Gazette* (hereafter cited as *Club Gazette*), no. 49, 14 December 1850, pp. 374–5.
32. Hudson, *History of Adult Education*, pp. 136–7; see also Yeo, 'Culture and Constraint', p. 175; Peter Bailey, *Leisure and Class in Victorian England. Rational Recreation and the Contest for Control, 1830–1885* (Routledge and Kegan Paul, 1978), pp. 36, 54.
33. Letter to Editor, *Birmingham Journal*, 7 August 1847, p. 3.
34. J. F. C. Harrison, *Learning and Living 1790–1960. A Study in the History of the English Adult Education Movement* (Routledge and Kegan Paul, 1961), p. 67; Hudson, *History of Adult Education*, pp. 52, 130.
35. G. Anderson, *Victorian Clerks* (Manchester: University of Manchester Press, 1976), pp. 41–2.

36. The Calton Mechanics' Institute, for example; see Hudson, *History of Adult Education*, p. 88; Purvis, *Hard Lessons*, pp. 111, 126–7.

37. Hudson, *History of Adult Education*, p. 135. Purvis suggests that such instruction may have had practical value for young women, as it would prepare them to be governesses, *Hard Lessons*, pp. 134–6.

38. Alan Ruston, 'The Non-Con Clubs and Some other Unitarian Clubs. 1783–1914', *Transactions of the Unitarian Historical Society*, Vol. XIV, no. 3, 1969, p. 149.

39. *Report of the Proceedings of the Public Meeting, held 28 October 1835 for the Purpose of Establishing The ATHENÆUM* (Manchester: Taylor and Garnett, 1835), p. 20.

40. Alexander Ireland was familiar with many radical circles, for example he was close to John Chapman, with whom he shared discussions on the position of women. See Gordon S. Haight, *George Eliot and John Chapman, with Chapman's Diaries* (Hamden, Conn.: Archon Books, 1969, second edition), p. 210.

41. Hudson, *The History of Adult Education*, p. 83; 'Address of Mr Disraeli', 3 October 1844, in *Manchester Athenæum. Addresses*, p. 10.

42. Rule Book, 1844, in *Manchester Athenæum, Report of the Provisional Directors* (Manchester, 1844), pp. 18, 16; Rule Book, 1848, ibid., p. 20 and Rule Book, 1844, ibid., p. 8.

43. 'The Whittington Club', *Douglas Jerrold's Weekly Newspaper* no. 2, 25 July 1846, p. 29.

44. 'Whittington Club', ibid., no. 41, 24 April 1847, p. 506.

45. Purvis, *Hard Lessons*, pp. 118, 122.

46. A fact acknowledged by Kent, 'A Bohemian Experiment', p. 41.

47. 'Whittington Club', *Douglas Jerrold's Weekly Newspaper*, no. 68, 30 October 1847, p. 1365; 'Halls of the People', *Star in the East*, Vol. II, no. 94, 30 June 1838, p. 321.

48. Letter to Editor from Kate, *New Moral World*, Vol. VII, no. 79, 25 April 1840, pp. 1263–4; W. H. G. Armytage, *Heavens Below. Utopian Experiments in England 1560–1960* (Routledge and Kegan Paul, 1960), p. 198.

49. J. T. Ward, *Chartism* (B. T. Batsford, 1973), p. 150.

50. Despite Lovett's proclamations concerning the status of women within the National Association, the Association's records suggest that women did not play a significant role within it. Birmingham City Archives, MS 753 (Lovett Collection), First Annual Report of the National Association, p. 218c.

51. MS letter from W. Potter to Robert Martineau, 1847, Birmingham City Archives, MS 1412/9; 'Is the Adoption of the People's Charter Desirable?', *Club Gazette*, new series, no. 14, 13 April 1850, p. 111.

52. ABR, 'The Whittington Club', *Douglas Jerrold's Weekly Newspaper*, no. 3, 1 August 1846, p. 53.

53. 'The Whittington Club', ibid., no. 1, 18 July 1846, p. 14.

54. 'Whittington Club', *Birmingham Journal*, 21 August 1847, p. 6.

55. TS letter from William Shaen to his sister, 24 August 1848, Leeds Archives, Symington Papers, Box 19; 'London Clubs', *Spirit of the Age*, Vol. 1, no. 8, 16 September 1848, p. 125.

56. Harrison, *Living and Learning*, pp. 149–51.

57. The policy is clearly enunciated in 'Whittington Club', *Douglas Jerrold's Weekly Newspaper*, no. 14, 24 April 1847, p. 506.

58. 'Introductory Address', *Club Gazette*, no. 1. 16 December 1848; 'Prosperity of the Co-operative Cause', *Howitt's Journal*, Vol. I, no. 2, 9 January 1847, p. 3.

59. This was a prominent message in the printed circular of the Birmingham Whittington Club, 30 June 1847, Birmingham City Archives, MS 1412/9.

60. 'Club Crotchets and Cheap Comforts: Being Contributions to the Whittington Fund', *Douglas Jerrold's Shilling Magazine*, Vol. VI, July–December 1847, pp. 22–31.

61. 'The Whittington Club', *Douglas Jerrold's Weekly Newspaper*, no. 14, 17 October 1846, p. 314.

62. 'Club Crotchets and Cheap Comforts: Being Contributions to the Whittington Fund', *Douglas Jerrold's Shilling Magazine*, Vol. VI, July–December 1847, pp. 29–30.

63. 'The Whittington Club', *Douglas Jerrold's Weekly Newspaper*, no. 1, 18 July 1846, p. 14; 'Whittington Club', *Birmingham Journal*, 10 July 1847, p. 6.

64. 'Whittington Club', *Birmingham Journal*, 21 August 1847, p. 6; 'The Whittington Club', *Douglas Jerrold's Weekly Newspaper*, no. 1, 18 July 1846, p. 14.

65. See, for example, ibid.

66. 'Whittington Club and Metropolitan Athenæum', ibid., no. 13, 10 October 1846, p. 302. William Howitt, who often presided at such meetings, was unable to attend on this occasion.

67. W. Howitt, 'Observations of the Proposed Whittington Club', *People's Journal*, Vol. II, no. 43, 29 October 1846, pp. 236–8.

68. Silverpen, 'The Manchester Early Closing Demonstration', *Douglas Jerrold's Weekly Newspaper*, no. 17, 7 November 1846, p. 391; 'Whittington Club and Metropolitan Athenæum', ibid., no. 13, 10 October 1846, p. 302.

69. 'Whittington Club and Metropolitan Athenæum', ibid., no. 13, 10 October 1846, p. 302; 'Whittington Club and Metropolitan Athenæum', ibid., no. 16, 31 October 1846, p. 371.

70. See below, note 73.

71. W. Howitt, 'Observations on the Proposed Whittington Club', *People's Journal*, Vol. II, no. 43, 24 October 1846, p. 238; 'The Whittington Club', ibid., Vol. II, no. 42, 17 October 1846, p. 32.

72. 'The Whittington Club', *Douglas Jerrold's Weekly Newspaper*, no. 14, 17 October 1846, p. 314.

73. MS letter from Mary Howitt to Eliza Meteyard, 23 September 1846, Houghton Library, Harvard University, fMS Eng 883.1. Vol. 1. Quoted by permission of the Houghton Library, Harvard University; 'Our Lady Members', *Club Gazette*, no. 49, 14 December 1850.

74. 'Whittington Club', *Douglas Jerrold's Weekly Newspaper*, no. 68, 30 October 1847, p. 1365.

75. Rosemary Billington, 'The Dominant Values of Victorian Feminism', in E. M. Sigsworth (ed.), *In Search of Victorian Values* (Manchester: Manchester University Press, 1988), pp. 116–30.

76. See, for example, Philippa Levine, *Victorian Feminism 1850–1900* (Hutchinson, 1987), pp. 63 and 13.
77. Kate, 'An Appeal to Woman', *NMW*, Vol. I, no. 42, 15 August 1835, p. 335.
78. See, for example, the ideas aired at the 'Whittington Club Soirée', *Douglas Jerrold's Weekly Newspaper*, no. 84, 19 February 1848, p. 244.
79. Ida, 'Female Education', *People's Press*, Vol. I, no. 11, December 1847, p. 342.
80. 'Aristocratical and Political Morality', in W. J. Fox, *Finsbury Lectures. Reports of Lectures Delivered at South Place, Finsbury* (Charles and Fox, 1835), pp. 20–1.
81. This was a criticism which the *Monthly Repository* levelled at Mrs Trollope, 'Domestic Manners of the Americans', *MR*, Vol. VI, 1832, p. 408. Grimstone was also critical of Mrs Jameson for the way in which she overvalued the beauty of woman, 'Quaker Women', *MR*, Vol. IX, 1835, p. 35.
82. SY, 'The Three Visits', *MR*, Vol. VIII, 1834, p. 724.
83. Harriet Martineau to unidentified correspondent, 25 May 1833, Valerie Sanders (ed.), *Harriet Martineau. Selected Letters* (Oxford: Clarendon Press, 1990), pp. 40–1.
84. 'The Vocations of Women', *Eliza Cook's Journal*, Vol. II, no. 56, 25 May 1850, pp. 59–61.
85. Silverpen, 'Protection to Women', *Douglas Jerrold's Weekly Newspaper*, no. 4, 8 August 1846, p. 79; *Female's Friend*, January 1846, p. 24.
86. Silverpen, 'The Whittington Club and the Ladies', ibid., no. 15, 24 October 1846, p. 343.
87. W. Howitt, 'Observations on the Proposed Whittington Club', *People's Journal*, Vol. II, no. 43, 24 October 1846, pp. 236–8.
88. 'Clubs', *Eliza Cook's Journal*, Vol. I, no. 3, May 1849, pp. 44–5.
89. Silverpen, 'The Whittington Club and the Ladies', *Douglas Jerrold's Weekly Newspaper*, no. 15, 24 October 1846, p. 343.
90. Goodwyn Barmby, 'United Service Family Associations', *Howitt's Journal*, Vol. I, no. 25, 19 June 1847, pp. 344–5; J. Goodwyn Barmby, 'The Man-Power, The Woman-Power, and the Woman–Man Power', *NMW*, Vol. IX, no. 18, 1 May 1841, pp. 268–9.
91. Letter to Editor from Kate, *NMW*, Vol. VII, no. 79, 25 April 1840, pp. 1263–4; Silverpen, 'The Whittington Club and the Ladies', *Douglas Jerrold's Weekly Newspaper*, no. 15, 24 October 1846, p. 343.
92. 'Objects', *National Association Gazette*, no. 3, 15 January 1842, p. 23.
93. 'Club Crotchets and Cheap Comforts, Being Contributions to the Whittington Fund: Our Behaviour', *Douglas Jerrold's Shilling Magazine*, Vol. 6, July–December 1847, p. 349.
94. W. Howitt, 'Observation on the Proposed Whittington Club', *People's Journal*, Vol. II, no. 43, 24 October 1846, p. 236.
95. 'The Birmingham Whittington Club', *Douglas Jerrold's Weekly Newspaper*, no. 52, 10 July 1847, p. 862; 'Club Crotchets and Cheap Comforts: Being Contributions to the Whittington Fund. The Guests', *Douglas Jerrold's Shilling Magazine*, Vol. VI, July–December 1847, p. 139.
96. Eliza Lynn, *Realities, A Tale* (Saunders and Otley, 1851), Vol. I, pp. 272–3.
97. Ibid., Vol. II, p. 172; Vol. III, pp. 263–4.

98. Letter to Editor from J. Guthrie, *Club Gazette*, new series, no. 32, 17 August 1850, p. 240.
99. 'Parallel of the Sexes', ibid., no. 22, 8 June 1850, p. 164; 'Courage in Women', ibid., no. 37, 21 September 1850, p. 283.
100. AWJM, 'Mary Wollstonecraft', ibid., no. 36, 14 September 1850, pp. 270–2; 'Letter to Editor from Homo', ibid., no. 37, 21 September 1850, p. 282; 'Letter to Editor from Anna H', ibid., no. 39, 5 October 1850, pp. 297–8.
101. Printed advertisement for the Whittington Club, 1 January 1848, Leeds Archives, Symington Papers, Box 19.
102. 'Letter to Editor', 'Letter to Editor from S. W.', *Club Gazette*, Vol. I, no. 2, 30 December 1848.
103. 'Quarterly General Meeting', ibid., no. 27, 13 July 1850, pp. 202–3.
104. 'Alteration in the rules', Report of the Provisional Directors of the Athenæum, 1844, *Manchester Athenæum, Reports*, p. 18. Purvis's research suggests that this was a common policy, Purvis, *Hard Lessons*, p. 111.
105. 'Roscoe Club and Liverpool Athenæum', *Howitt's Journal*, Vol. I, no. 15, 10 April 1847, p. 29; Printed Circular of the Roscoe Club, Liverpool Record Office, 920 MUS. 2–45.
106. MS minutes of meeting of the Council; General Meeting, 7 September 1847, p. 13, Liverpool Roscoe Club, Liverpool Record Office, 920 MUS. 2–45.
107. 'Letter to Editor from EPR', *Club Gazette*, new series, no. 47, 30 November 1850, p. 361; Shenstone Short, 'Another Scene from an Unpublished Drama', ibid., no. 49, 14 December 1850, p. 377.
108. 'Whittington Club', *Douglas Jerrold's Weekly Newspaper*, no. 41, 24 April 1847, p. 506.
109. Letter to Editor from Timbuctoo, *Club Gazette*, new series, no. 48, 7 December 1850, p. 369; Letter to Editor from W. Batley, ibid., no. 49, 14 December 1850, p. 374.
110. 'Report of Anniversary Dinner', ibid., no. 16, 27 April 1850, p. 115; List of subscriptions from 29 December 1849–23 March 1850, ibid., no. 15, 20 April 1850, p. 109.
111. Purvis, *Hard Lessons*, p. 129.
112. Letter to Editor from Adolphus Quiet, *Club Gazette*, new series, no. 22, 8 June 1850, p. 165; Letter to Editor from LN, ibid., no. 48, 7 December 1850, p. 369.
113. 'The Institution', ibid., no. 17, 4 May 1850, p. 123.
114. Letter to Editor from A Lady Member, ibid., no. 49, 14 December 1850, p. 375.
115. Letter to Editor from Timbuctoo, ibid., no. 48, 7 December 1850, p. 369; 'Whittington Club', *Birmingham Journal*, 21 August 1847, p. 6.
116. 'Extract from an Unpublished Drama by "14"', *Club Gazette* new series, no. 48, 7 December 1850, pp. 370–1.
117. 'Our Lady Members', ibid., no. 49, 14 December 1850.
118. Shaen's words are quoted in MS letter from Douglas Jerrold to Charles Cowden Clarke, 12 February 1852, Brotherton Collection, Leeds University Library, Novello-Cowden-Clarke Collection; Letter from William Shaen, *Public Good*, 19 June 1850, p. 14.

119. Letter to Editor from 'A Member and Well-wisher of the Whittington Club', *Club Gazette*, Vol. I, no. 2, 30 December 1848, p. 6.

120. 'Report of the Whittington Club's First Soirée', *Douglas Jerrold's Weekly Newspaper*, no. 32, 20 February 1847, p. 218.

121. Mrs Follen, 'An American Lady on the Whittington Club', *Club Gazette*, new series, no. 17, 4 May 1850, p. 128.

122. See for example, Ida, 'Female Education', *People's Press*. Vol. I, no. 11, December 1847, p. 342.

123. TS notes on 'Hints for the Formation of a Society to be Called the Ladies' Friendly Society for the Improvement and Extension of Woman's Intellectual Faculties', included in a TS letter from Maria Seddon to William Shaen, 3 May 1849, Leeds Archives, Symington Papers, Box 19.

124. Mrs Follen, 'An American Lady on the Whittington Club', *Club Gazette*, new series, no. 17, 4 May 1850, p. 128.

125. 'Whittington Club', *Birmingham Journal*, 21 August 1847, p. 6.

126. 'The Liverpool Roscoe Club', *Leader*, 13 April 1850, p. 52.

127. Mrs Follen, 'An American Lady on the Whittington Club', *Club Gazette*, new series, no. 17, 4 May 1850, p. 128.

128. 'Whittington Club', *Douglas Jerrold's Weekly Newspaper*, no. 41, 24 April 1847, p. 506.

129. Editorial, *Club Gazette*, new series, no. 12, 30 March 1850, p. 84.

130. Printed advertisement for the Whittington Club, 1 January 1848, Leeds Archives, Symington Papers, Box 19.

131. Clementia Taylor, for example, played a leading role. See Alan Ruston, 'Clementia Taylor', *Transactions of the Unitarian Historical Society*, Vol. 20, no. 1, April 1991, pp. 64–5; see also Purvis, *Hard Lessons*, p. 189. The club movement remained important to the feminist movement. See MS letter from Emilie Ashurst Venturi to Helen Taylor [n.d.], British Library of Political and Economic Science, Mill-Taylor Collection, Vol. XIV, ff.218–36; Martha Vicinus, *Independent Women. Work and Community for Single Women, 1850–1900* (Virago, 1985), pp. 297–9.

132. D. M. Chase Worzala, 'The Langham Place Circle: The Beginnings of the Organized Women's Movement in England 1854–1870', (PhD thesis, University of Wisconsin–Madison, 1982), p. 290.

133. TS letter from Maria Seddon to William Shaen, 3 May 1849, Leeds Archives, Symington Papers, Box 19.

134. Silverpen, 'The Whittington Club and the Ladies', *Douglas Jerrold's Weekly Newspaper*, no. 15, 24 October 1846, p. 343.

135. 'The Woman's Elevation League', *Northern Star*, 8 May 1852, p. 5; see also Jutta Schwarzkopf, *Women in the Chartist Movement* (Macmillan, 1991), pp. 251–5.

136. Kent, 'The Whittington Club', pp. 45, 49–50; Walter Jerrold, *Douglas Jerrold. Dramatist and Wit* (Hodder and Stoughton, 1914), Vol. II, p. 474.

6 Conclusion: The Reception, Significance and Influence of the Early Feminists

1. Brenda Colloms, ' "Tottie" Fox, Her Life and Background', *Gaskell Society Journal*, Vol. V. 1991, pp. 19–20.

2. Mary Howitt, *An Autobiography*, edited by her daughter, Margaret Howitt (Isbister, 1889), p. 211.

3. E. F. Richards (ed.), *Mazzini's Letters to an English Family 1844–1854* (John Lane, 1920), pp. 175–7.

4. Michael Roe, 'Mary Leman Grimstone (1880–1850?). For Women's Rights and Patriotism', in *Papers and Proceedings, Tasmanian Historical Research Association*, Vol. 6, no. 1, March 1989, p. 24.

5. Walter Jerrold, *Douglas Jerrold. Dramatist and Wit* (Hodder and Stoughton, 1914), Vol. II, p. 543.

6. F. B. Smith, *Radical Artisan. William James Linton, 1812–1897* (Manchester: Manchester University Press, 1973), pp. 95–8.

7. Carl Ray Woodring, *Victorian Samplers: William and Mary Howitt* (Lawrence: University of Kansas Press, 1952), pp. 86, 138; MS letters from Mary Howitt to Eliza Meteyard, March 1847 and n.d., Houghton Library, Harvard University, fMS Eng 883.1.

8. Jerrold, *Douglas Jerrold*, pp. 481–2, 491–2.

9. MS letter from Caroline Hill to John Stuart Mill [n.d.], British Library of Political and Economic Science, Mill–Taylor Collection, Vol. II, item 291, fols. 656–7; C. E. Maurice (ed.), *Life of Octavia Hill, as Told in Her Letters* (Macmillan, 1913), pp. 13, 255.

10. Silverpen, 'Early Closing Movement', *Eliza Cook's Journal*, Vol. I, no. 10, 7 July 1849, p. 155; 'The Ladies Guild', ibid., Vol. V, no. 122, 30 August 1851, p. 277.

11. Bessie Raynor Parkes, 'Remarks', cited in D. M. Chase Worzala, 'The Langham Place Circle, The Beginnings of the Organized Women's Movement in England, 1854–1870', (PhD thesis, University of Wisconsin–Madison, 1982), p. 82.

12. This was certainly the view of G. J. Holyoake, see GHJ, 'Hints to the Advocates on the Rights of Women', *Reasoner*, Vol. III, no. 63, pp. 429–37.

13. See Chapter 3.

14. Worzala, 'The Langham Place Circle', p. viii.

15. Jane Rendall, *The Origins of Modern Feminism: Women in Britain, France and the United States, 1780–1860* (Chicago: Lyceum Books, 1985), p. 228.

16. Lee Holcombe, *Wives and Property. Reform of the Married Women's Property Law in Nineteenth Century England* (Toronto: University of Toronto Press, 1983), p. 85; Woodring, *Victorian Samplers*, p. 180; Jane Rendall, ' "A Moral Engine?" Feminism, Liberalism and the *English Woman's Journal*', in Jane Rendall (ed.), *Equal or Different. Women's Politics 1800–1914* (Oxford: Basil Blackwell, 1987), p. 119.

17. Colloms, ' "Tottie" Fox', p. 23.

18. J. O. S. Baylen and N. J. Gossman (eds), *Biographical Dictionary of Modern British Radicals* (Hassocks: Harvester Press, 1979), pp. 60–1, 478–9.

19. Ibid., pp. 512–15; Worzala, 'The Langham Place Circle', p. 375.

20. MS notice of the death of Sir James Stansfeld, by Ruth Fry, Leeds Archives, Dixon and Stansfeld Papers, Accession 2311, Box 2, no. 3; Baylen and Gossman, *Biographical Dictionary*, pp. 478–82, 450–4.

21. Philippa Levine, *Victorian Feminism 1850–1900* (Hutchinson, 1987), p. 21; Rendall, *Origins of Modern Feminism*, p. 314.

22. Helen Blackburn, *Women's Suffrage. A Record of the Women's Suffrage Movement in the British Isles* (Williams and Norgate, 1902), p. 64; Levine, *Victorian Feminism*, pp. 66, 141.

23. Olive Banks, *Becoming a Feminist. The Social Origins of 'First Wave' Feminism* (Brighton: Wheatsheaf, 1986), p. 133.

24. Mary Gillies and Anna Blackwell, for example, had also translated Sand during the 1840s. *Howitt's Journal*, Vol. I, no. 2, 9 January, 1847, pp. 22–6; Holcombe, *Wives and Property*, p. 85; Worzala, 'The Langham Place Circle', p. 79; see also Chapter 2 above.

25. Alan Ruston, 'Clementia Taylor', *Transactions of the Unitarian Historical Society*, Vol. XX, no. 1, April 1991, pp. 62–8; Olive Stinchcombe, 'Elizabeth Malleson', ibid., pp. 56–61; Hope Malleson, *Elizabeth Malleson 1828–1916, Autobiographical Notes and Letters* (Printed for Private Circulation, 1926), see pp. 36–41, 45, 58, 94, in particular.

26. Banks, *Becoming a Feminist*, p. 134.

27. Henry Solly, *These Eighty Years, or Story of an Unfinished Life* (Simpkin, Marshall and Co., 1893), Vol. II, pp. 421–2; T. Wemyss Reid, *The Life and Letters and Friendships of Richard Monckton Milnes. First Lord Houghton* (Cassell, 1890, second edition), Vol. II, p. 178. Houghton's relationship with the radical unitarian community emerges passim, in the largely uncatalogued Houghton Collection, Trinity College, Cambridge; see, for example, MS letters Cullum P.91[1]; Houghton 26/162; Houghton 222[19].

28. Banks, *Becoming a Feminist*, p. 133.

29. Blackburn, *Women's Suffrage*, p. 48.

30. Sheila R. Herstein, *A Mid-Victorian Feminist, Barbara Leigh Smith Bodichon* (New Haven: Yale University Press, 1985), p. 70.

31. Jane Rendall, 'Friendship and Politics: Barbara Leigh Smith Bodichon (1827–91) and Bessie Raynor Parkes (1829–1925)', in Jane Rendall and Susan Mendus (eds), *Sexuality and Subordination. Interdisciplinary Studies of Gender in the Nineteenth Century* (Routledge, 1989), pp. 136–70, p. 163.

32. Ibid., pp. 137–9; Herstein, *Mid-Victorian Feminist*, pp. 16–19.

33. Leigh Smith's lifelong friendship with Anna-Mary Howitt was also forged at this time. Worzala, 'Langham Place Circle', p. 67.

34. MS letter from Bessie Parkes to Barbara Leigh Smith, [1847], Girton College, Cambridge, Parkes Papers [hereafter cited as BRP], BRP V 2.

35. MS letter from Bessie Parkes to Barbara Leigh Smith, 19 November 1848, BRP V 28[2].

36. MS letter from Bessie Raynor Parkes to her mother, 16 October 1851, BRP II 3/31; Gordon S. Haight (ed.), *George Eliot and John Chapman. With Chapman's Diaries* (Hamden, Conn: Archon Books, 1969, second edn), p. 88.

37. See Mary Lyndon Shanley, *Feminism, Marriage and the Law in Victorian England, 1850–1895* (L. B. Tauris, 1989), p. 29; see also Chapter 4 above.

38. MS letter from Bessie Raynor Parkes to Barbara Leigh Smith, [1848], BRP V 27[1].

39. Colloms, ' "Tottie" Fox', p. 20; see also nn. 16 and 17 above.

40. TS letter from Bessie Raynor Parkes to Kate Jeavons, 11 November 1847, BRP VI 51.

41. MS letter from Bessie Raynor Parkes to Barbara Leigh Smith, 10 May 1849, BRP V 29.

42. MS letters from Bessie Raynor Parkes to Barbara Leigh Smith, 25 June 1847, BRP V 10^2; 30 April 1848, BRP V 23^1; 5 December 1849, BRP 39; 'A Scene of Every Day', ERP, *Birmingham Journal*, 8 July 1848, p. 3.

43. MS letter from Bessie Raynor Parkes to Barbara Leigh Smith, June 1849, BRP V 31.

44. Rendall, *Origins of Modern Feminism*, p. 318; Worzala, 'The Langham Place Circle', p. 329.

45. Herstein, *Mid-Victorian Feminist*, pp. 58ff.

46. Parkes' interest in rational recreation is indicated in Rendall, 'Friendship and Politics', p. 150.

47. Worzala, 'The Langham Place Circle', p. 215; Smith's concern for the reformation of these strata has also been noted above, Chapter 2.

48. MS letter from Bessie Raynor Parkes to her mother, 15 December 1854, BRP II 41^1; MS letter from Bessie Raynor Parkes to a suitor, November 1849, BRP IX 109.

49. MS letter from Bessie Raynor Parkes to Barbara Leigh Smith, 3 August 1849, BRP V 34.

50. MS letters from Bessie Raynor Parkes to Barbara Leigh Smith, 19 November 1848, BRP V 28^2; 20 September 1849, BRP V 37; 23 April 1850, BRP V 46.

51. MS letters from Bessie Raynor Parkes to Barbara Leigh Smith, [1848], BRP V 19; 28 January 1848, BRP V 20.

52. MS letter from Bessie Raynor Parkes to Barbara Leigh Smith, 27 May 1847, BRP V 9; MS letter from Bessie Raynor Parkes to her mother, 16 October 1851, BRP II 3/3.

53. MS letter from Bessie Raynor Parkes to her mother, [1855], BRP II 4*1.

54. MS letter from Bessie Raynor Parkes to Barbara Leigh Smith, 3 August 1849, BRP V 34.

55. Rendall, 'Friendship and Politics', p. 150.

56. MS letter from Bessie Raynor Parkes to Barbara Leigh Smith, 20 September 1849, BRP V 37; see 'Progression' and 'A Scene of Every Day', *Birmingham Journal*, 22 April 1848, p. 3, and 8 July 1848, p. 3. W. J. Linton, *Memories* (Lawrence and Bullen, 1895), p. 159.

57. Worzala, 'Langham Place Circle', pp. 321–2.

58. Barbara Leigh Smith Bodichon, 'Authorities and Precedents for Giving the Suffrage to Qualified Women' (1867), in C. A. Lacey (ed.), *Barbara Leigh Smith Bodichon and the Langham Place Group* (Routledge and Kegan Paul, 1986), pp. 118–32.

59. These themes are discussed in Chapter 3. Good examples of the arguments concerning gender conditioning include 'D', 'Devotion and Self-Sacrifice', *MR*, X, 1836, pp. 424–33; AW, 'On Ideas', *Star in the East*, Vol. III, no. 137, 27 April 1839, p. 278.

60. Worzala, 'Langham Place Circle', passim, provides an excellent analysis of the development of feminist ideologies in the subsequent years.

61. 'The Outcast', *National* (1839), p. 132; see also 'The Right of Woman', ibid., p. 135.

62. John Stores Smith, *Social Aspects* (John Chapman, 1850), pp. 82–3; Anna Jameson, *Characteristics of Women. Moral, Poetical and Historical* (Saunders and Otley, 1858), p. 256.

63. 'On Social Reformation', *People and Howitt's Journal*, Vol. II, no. 5, p. 24.

64. Eliza Lynn, *Realities. A Tale* (Saunders and Otley, 1851), Vol. I, pp. 8–9; Vol. II, p. 74.

65. For a personification of Grimstone's ideal heroine, see Ida in *Woman's Love* (Saunders and Otley, 1832); Matilda M. Hays, *Helen Stanley. A Tale* (E. Churton, 1846), p. 244; Eliza Meteyard, *Struggles For Fame* (T. C. Newby, 1845), Vol. III, p. 5.

66. Levine, *Victorian Feminism*, provides an account of this controversy, and the consequent tendency of many historians to divide the women's rights movement into 'bourgeois' and 'socialist' feminism, pp. 15–18.

67. Banks, *Becoming a Feminist*, p. 66, notes that the campaign for employment was one of the most stable features of 'first wave' feminism.

68. J. F. C. Harrison, *Robert Owen and the Owenites in Britain and America. The Quest for the New Moral World* (Routledge and Kegan Paul, 1969), pp. 59–60; 'Female Influence and Training', *NMW*, Vol. V, no. 2, 3 November 1838, p. 23.

69. See Jeffrey Weeks, *Sex. Politics and Society. The Regulation of Sexuality since 1800* (Longman, 1989), p. 68.

70. The *Crisis* occasionally published extracts from the *Monthly Repository*, e.g. 'The *Monthly Repository*', Vol. II, no. 22, 8 June 1833, p. 174; however, the *New Moral World* was even more dependent. It printed numerous articles from the *Monthly Repository*, as well as faithfully reporting Fox's Finsbury lectures. See, for example, Mrs Leman Grimstone, 'Female Education', *NMW*, Vol. I, no. 17, 21 February 1835, pp. 132–5; 'Lectures on the Morality of the Various Classes by the Rev. W. J. Fox', *NMW*, Vol. II, no. 59, 12 December 1835, pp. 52–3; 'Women in England', *NMW*, Vol. IV, no. 186, 19 May 1838, p. 240.

71. Judy Lown, *Women and Industrialisation. Gender at Work in Nineteenth Century England* (Cambridge: Polity Press), pp. 152, 98.

72. Lucy Aikin to Dr Channing, 18 April 1838, P. H. Le Breton (ed.), *Memoirs, Miscellanies, and Letters of the Late Lucy Aikin including those addressed to the Rev. Dr. Channing from 1826 to 1842* (Longman, Green, Roberts, 1864), p. 369.

73. Angela John, *By the Sweat of Their Brow. Women Workers at Victorian Coal Mines* (Routledge and Kegan Paul, 1984, second edn), pp. 148–9.

74. One rare exception is Lynn, *Realities*, Vol. I, pp. 186–7.

75. These themes were discussed in Chapter 3.

76. Margaret Hewitt, *Wives and Mothers in Victorian Industry* (Rockliff, 1958), p. 66.

77. See, for example, 'The Winlaton Literary and Mechanics Institution', *People*, Vol. I, no. 53, 1849, p. 6; 'Weekly Record', *Howitt's Journal*, Vol. II, no. 49, 4 December 1846, p. 367; J. F. C. Harrison, *Learning and Living. 1790–1960. A Study in the History of the English Adult Education Movement* (Routledge and Kegan Paul, 1961), p. 148.

78. See June Purvis, *Hard Lessons. The Lives and Education of Working Women in Nineteenth Century England* (Cambridge: Polity Press, 1989), pp. 153–6.

79. 'The Weekly Record', *Howitt's Journal*, Vol. I, no. 11, 13 March 1847, p. 21; 'The Week', *People's Journal*, Vol. III, no. 77, 19 June 1847, p. 50.

80. 'The Co-operative League', *Douglas Jerrold's Weekly Newspaper*, no. 32, 20 February 1847, p. 223.
81. 'Men and Women – Education of the Sexes', *Eliza Cook's Journal*, Vol. IV, 14 December 1850, p. 97.
82. Shanley, *Feminism, Marriage and the Law*, see pp. 60, 67, 77, 159–60 especially; George Watt, *The Fallen Woman in the Nineteenth Century Novel* (Croom Helm, 1984), pp. 9ff; Herstein, *A Mid-Victorian Feminist*, p. 53.
83. See Martha Vicinus, *Independent Women. Work and Community for Single Women. 1850–1920* (Virago, 1985), for a consideration of the application of these ideas to single women – see esp. Chapter 6 and pp. 295–7.
84. Worzala, 'The Langham Place Circle', pp. 92, 233; Shanley, *Feminism, Marriage and the Law*, p. 77.

Bibliography

MANUSCRIPT SOURCES

Beinecke Rare Book and Manuscript Library, Yale University
William James Linton Collection

Birmingham City Archives
Lovett Collection, MS 753
Robert Martineau Papers, MS 1412/9

Birmingham University Library
Harriet Martineau Collection

Bodleian Library
Lovelace Byron Papers, Boxes 69, 75

Boston Public Library
MS A.1.z. vols 9, 23, 25
MS Gris. 204, 582, 584
MS Eng. 328

British Library of Political and Economic Science
Mill and Taylor Collection, Vols 2, 14, 27–9

Cambridge University Library
William Smith Papers, CUL Add, MS 7621

Columbia University Library, New York
Sidney Howard Gay Papers

Co-operative Union, Manchester
George Jacob Holyoake Collection

Dickens House Museum
Burnett Notebook
Carlton, Peyrouton and Suzannet Collections

Dr. Williams's Library
Finsbury Congregation Papers
Henry Crabb Robinson, Letters 1832–33

Fondazione Giangiacomo Feltrinelli, Milan
Archivio Linton, Vol. 2/43

Girton College, Cambridge
Parkes Papers, Vols 2–9

Houghton Library, Harvard University
fMS Eng. 883.1 Vol. 1
MS Eng. 501 Vol. 1

Iowa University Library
Leigh Hunt Papers

John Rylands Library, Manchester
Unitarian College Collection:
Holbrook Gaskell, MS Sermons, Cupboard B
Proceedings of the Annual Meetings of the Presbyterian and Unitarian Ministers
of Lancashire and Cheshire, Cupboard B

Leeds District Archives
Dixon Stansfeld Papers, Accession 2311
Symington Papers, Box 19

Leeds University Library, Brotherton Collection
Novello-Cowden Clarke Collection

Liverpool Record Office
Roscoe Club Papers, 920 MUS 2–45

Manchester Public Library
George Wilson Papers, M20 (1844–45)
National Public Schools Association, M136 (1849–50)
Royal Manchester Institution, M6 (1836)

Manchester College, Oxford
MS J. Martineau, Vols 1, 2, 7
MS L. C. 1, fols., 153–67
MSS [R] L. C. 7
MSS Tayler, Vol. 20

National Library of Australia
William James Linton Papers, MS 1698, MS 1776

National Library of Scotland
Miscellaneous MS letters, nos. 51.1.15, 551, 581–4, 604, 665, 966, 2245, 2622, 3823, (3915), 4040, 4675, 7309, 7331, 7334, 7346, 7391, 7392, 9392

Sidney Jones Library, University of Liverpool
Rathbone Collection, Vols 5–9

South Place Ethical Society
Uncatalogued documents relating to South Place Chapel, 1835–53

Trinity College, Cambridge
Cullum Papers
Houghton Collection

Tyne and Wear Archives
Cowan Papers, TWAS 634/A8, A13, A53, A166, A176, A179

University College, London
Chadwick Papers, Copy Books 4, 17–20
Wilderspin Collection, MS 917

Wordsworth Trust, Dove Cottage, Grasmere
WLMS A / Powell, Thomas /5; A / Gillies, M / 1–2

NEWSPAPERS AND PERIODICALS

The years indicated are those studied for this book.

The Birmingham Journal and General Advertiser 1847–8
The British Co-operator or Record and Review of Co-operative and Entertaining Knowledge 1830
The Christian Reformer or Unitarian Magazine and Review 1835–7
Common Sense 1841
The Co-operative Magazine and Monthly Herald 1826–9; continued as *London Co-operative Magazine* 1830
The Crisis, or the Change from Error and Misery to Truth and Happiness. Organ of the National Association of Industry, Humanity and Knowledge 1832–3; continued as *The Crisis and National Co-operative Trades Union Gazette* 1833–4
Douglas Jerrold's Shilling Magazine 1845–8
Douglas Jerrold's Weekly Newspaper 1846–8
Eliza Cook's Journal 1849–54
The Female's Friend 1846
The Half-Penny Magazine. A Miscellany of Original Articles 1832
Howitt's Journal of Literature and Popular Progress 1847–8
The Illuminated Magazine 1843–5
La Belle Assemblée or Bell's Court and Fashionable Magazine; continued as *The Court Magazine and Belle Assemblée* 1832
Law Review and Quarterly Review of British and Foreign Jurisprudence 1846–56
The Leader 1850–1
The Leicestershire Mercury and General Advertiser for the Midland Counties 1845–6
The Liberator 1840, 1847
Manchester Guardian 1833–4
The Monthly Repository and Review of Theology 1831–8
The Movement. Anti-Persecution Gazette and Register of Progress 1843–5
The National. A Library for the People 1839
The National Association Gazette. The Rights of Man and the Rights of Woman 1842
The New Monthly Magazine and Literary Journal 1832
The New Moral World ... Developing the Principles of the Rational System of Society 1834–5; continued as *The New Moral World, or Millenium* 1835–6; continued as *The New Moral World and Manual of Science* 1836–8; continued as *The New Moral World* 1838–9; continued as *The New Moral World or Gazette of the Universal Community Society of Rational Religionists* 1839–41
The Northern Star and Leeds General Advertiser 1838–44; continued as *The Northern Star and National Trades' Journal* 1846–8, 1852
The People – Their Rights and Liberties 1848–52
The People's Journal 1846–9; continued with *Howitt's Journal* as *The People's and Howitt's Journal* 1849–51
The People's Press and Monthly Historical Newspaper 1847–8
The Promethean or Communitarian Apostle 1842
The Public Good 1850–1
The Reasoner and Herald of Progress 1846; continued as *The Reasoner and Utilitarian Record* 1847; continued as *The Reasoner. A Weekly Journal. Utilitarian. Republican and Communist* 1848–50; continued as *The Reasoner and Theological Register* 1850–4
The Republican. A Magazine Advocating the Sovereignty of the People 1848

The Spirit of the Age 1848–9
The Star in the East 1836–40
Tait's Edinburgh Magazine 1832–53
The Tatler. A Daily Journal of Literature and the Stage 1830–2
The Truth Seeker, in Literature, Philosophy and Religion 1846–8; continued as *The Truth Seeker and Present Age: a Catholic Review of Literature, Philosophy and Religion* 1849–50
The Unitarian Chronicle and Companion to the Monthly Repository 1832–3; continued as *The Unitarian Magazine and Chronicle* 1834–5
Wade's London Review 1845–6
The Westminster Review 1831–6; continued as *The London and Westminster Review* 1836–40; continued as *The Westminster Review* 1840–6; continued as *The Westminster Review and Foreign Quarterly Review* 1846–51
The Whittington Club and Metropolitan Athenæum Gazette 1848–51 [imperfect series only available]

PUBLISHED WORKS

Place of publication is London, unless otherwise stated.

Abrams, M. H., *Natural Supernaturalism. Tradition and Revolution in Romantic Literature* (W. W. Norton, 1973)
Adams, William Bridges [Junius Redivivus], *The Rights of Morality* (Effingham Wilson, 1832)
Adams, William Bridges, Obituary of, *Engineering*, 26 June 1872, pp. 63–4
Aikin, Lucy, *Epistles on Women, Exemplifying Their Character and Condition in Various Ages and Nations. With Miscellaneous Poems* (J. Johnson, 1810)
Alexander, Sally, *Women's Work in Nineteenth Century London* (Journeyman Press, 1976)
Alexander, William, *The History of Women from the Earliest Antiquity to the Present Time, Giving Some Account of Almost Every Particular Concerning that Sex, Among All Nations Ancient and Modern* (W. Stachan and T. Cadell, 1779)
Altick, Richard Daniel, *The Cowden Clarkes* (Oxford: Oxford University Press, 1948)
Anderson, G., *Victorian Clerks* (Manchester: Manchester University Press, 1976)
Anon., By a Foreigner, *Hints to Mothers, on the Cultivation of the Minds of Children, in the Spirit of Pestalozzi's Methods* (Longman, Hurst, Rees, Orme and Browne, 1823)
Armstrong, Richard Acland, *Henry William Crosskey. His Life and Work* (Birmingham: Cornish Brothers, 1895)
Armytage, W. H. G., *Heavens Below. Utopian Experiments in England 1560–1960* (Routledge and Kegan Paul, 1961)
Ashton, Rosemary, *The German Idea. Four English Writers and the Reception of German Thought 1800–1860* (Cambridge: Cambridge University Press, 1980)
Aspland, Robert, *The Beneficial Influence of Christianity on the Character and*

Condition of the Female Sex. A Sermon Preached at the Rev. Dr Rees's Meeting House, Jewin Street, Aldersgate Street on Wednesday, April 8, 1812, in Behalf of the Society for the Relief of the Necessitous Widows and the Fatherless Children of Protestant Dissenting Ministers (J. Johnson, 1812)

Aspland, R. Brook, *Memoirs of the Life, Works and Correspondence of the Rev. Robert Aspland of Hackney* (Edward T. Whitfield, 1850)

Associate Institution for Improving and Enforcing the Laws for the Protection of Women, *Remedies for the Wrongs of Women* (Hatchard and Son, 1844)

Associate Institution for Improving and Enforcing the Laws for the Protection of Women, *First Report* (Brewster and West, 1846)

Austin, Sarah, *Two Letters on Girls' Schools and on the Training of Working Women* (Chapman and Hall, 1857)

Backström, Philip N., *Christian Socialism and Co-operation in Victorian England. Edward Vansittart Neale and the Co-operative Movement* (Croom Helm, 1974)

Bailey, Peter, *Leisure and Class in Victorian England. Rational Recreation and the Contest for Control 1830–1885* (Routledge and Kegan Paul, 1978)

Banks, J. A., *Victorian Values. Secularism and the Size of Families* (Routledge and Kegan Paul, 1981)

Banks, Olive, *Faces of Feminism. A Study of Feminism as a Social Movement* (Oxford: Basil Blackwell, 1981)

Banks, Olive, *Biographical Dictionary of Modern British Feminists. Vol. I, 1800–1900* (Brighton: Wheatsheaf, 1985)

Banks, Olive, *Becoming a Feminist. The Social Origins of 'First Wave' Feminism* (Brighton: Wheatsheaf, 1986)

Barker, Joseph, *The Life of Joseph Barker. Written by Himself*, edited by his nephew, John Thomas Barker (Hodder and Stoughton, 1880)

Baylen, Joseph Oscar and Norbert Joseph Gossman (eds), *Biographical Dictionary of Modern British Radicals* (Hassocks: Harvester Press, 1979)

Beecher, Jonathan, *Charles Fourier. The Visionary and His World* (Berkeley: University of California Press, 1986)

Bellamy, Joyce M. and John Saville (eds), *Dictionary of Labour Biography* (Macmillan, 1982)

Billington, L. and R. Billington, ' "A Burning Zeal for Righteousness": Women in the British Anti-Slavery Movement 1820–1860', in Jane Rendall (ed.), *Equal or Different. Women's Politics, 1800–1914* (Oxford: Basil Blackwell, 1987), pp. 82–111

Billington, Rosamund, 'The Dominant Values of Victorian Feminism', in E. M. Sigsworth (ed.), *In Search of Victorian Values* (Manchester: Manchester University Press, 1988), pp. 118–30

Blackburn, Helen, *Women's Suffrage. A Record of the Women's Suffrage Movement in the British Isles* (Williams and Norgate, 1902)

Blain, Virginia, Patricia Clements and Isobel Grundy (eds), *Feminist Companion to Literature in English. Women Writers from the Middle Ages to the Present* (B. T. Batsford, 1990)

Blainey, Ann, *The Farthing Poet. A Biography of Richard Hengist Horne 1802–1884. A Lesser Literary Lion* (Longman, 1968)

Blake, William, *Complete Writings*, ed. Geoffrey Keynes (Oxford: Oxford University Press, 1989)

Bolt, C., and S. Drescher (eds), *Anti-Slavery, Religion and Reform: Essays in Memory of Roger Anstey* (Kent: Dawson and Sons, 1980)

Bowring, John, *The Works of Jeremy Bentham* (New York: Russell and Russell, 1962, first published 1843), Vols 3–4, 9

Bowring, John, *Autobiographical Recollections of Sir John Bowring. With a Brief Memoir by Lewin B. Bowring* (Henry S. King, 1877)

Bradley, Ian, *The Call to Seriousness* (Jonathan Cape, 1976)

Branca, Patricia, *Silent Sisterhood. Middle-Class Women in the Victorian Home* (Croom Helm, 1975)

Bremer, Frederika, *A Diary* translated by Mary Howitt (George Bell and Sons, 1909, first published 1843)

Bremer, Frederika, *The Home; or Life in Sweden* translated by Mary Howitt (George Bell and Sons, 1913, first published 1843)

Bridell-Fox, E. F., 'Robert Browning', *Argosy*, 1890, pp. 108–14

Bridell-Fox, E. F., 'Memories', *Girls' Own Paper*, 19 July 1890, Vol. 11, no. 551, pp. 657–61

Bridell-Fox, E. F., *Sarah Flower Adams; A Memoir and Her Hymns. Also 'The Flock at the Fountain'* (Christian Life, 1894)

Bristow, E. J., *Vice and Vigilance* (Dublin: Gill and Macmillan, 1977)

Bryant, Margaret, *The Unexpected Revolution. A Study in the History of the Education of Women and Girls in the Nineteenth Century* (University of London Institute of Education, 1979)

Bushrod, Emily, 'The Diary of John Gent Brooks – A Victorian Commentary on Poverty (1844–1854)', *Transactions of the Unitarian Historical Society*, Vol. 20, no. 2, April 1992, pp. 98–113

Cannadine, D. and D. Reeder, (eds), *Exploring the Urban Past: Essays in Urban History by H. J. Dyos* (Cambridge: Cambridge University Press, 1982)

Carlyle, Thomas, *On Heroes, Hero-Worship and the Heroic in History* (Chapman and Hall, 1898, first published 1841)

Carpenter, J. Estlin, *The Life and Work of Mary Carpenter* (Macmillan, 1879)

Carpenter, J. Estlin, *The Bible in the Nineteenth Century* (Longmans, Green, 1903)

Carpenter, Russell Lant (ed.), *Memoirs of the Life of the Rev. Lant Carpenter. With Selections from his Correspondence* (Bristol: Philip and Evans, 1841)

Carpenter, Russell Lant (ed.), *Memoirs of the Life and Work of Philip Pearsall Carpenter. Chiefly Derived from his Letters* (Kegan Paul, 1880)

Chapple, J. A. V. and Pollard, Arthur (eds), *The Letters of Mrs Gaskell* (Manchester: Manchester University Press, 1966)

Clarke, Mary Cowden, *My Long Life* (T. Fisher Unwin, 1896)

Clayden, P. W., *Rogers and His Contemporaries* (Smith, Elder, 1889)

Cobbe, Francis Power, *Life of Francis Power Cobbe by Herself* (Boston and New York: Riverside Press, 1894)

Colloms, Brenda, '"Tottie" Fox, Her Life and Background', *Gaskell Society Journal*, Vol. V, 1991, pp. 16–26

Cominos, Peter T., 'Late Victorian Sexual Respectability in the Social System', *International Review of Social History*, Vol. 8, 1963, pp. 18–48, 216–50

Corfield, Kenneth, 'Elizabeth Heyrick: Radical Quaker', in Gail Malmgreen (ed.), *Religion in the Lives of English Women 1760–1930* (Croom Helm, 1986), pp. 41–67

Coser, Lewis A., *Men of Ideas* (New York: The Free Press, 1965)

Crosland, Mrs Newton (Camilla Toulmin) *Landmarks of a Literary Life* (Sampson, Low, Marston, 1983)

Crossick, Geoffrey, *An Artisan Elite in Victorian Society. Kentish London 1840–1880* (Croom Helm, 1978)

Darley, Gillian, *Octavia Hill* (Constable, 1990)

Davidoff, Leonore and Catherine Hall, *Family Fortunes. Men and Women of the English Middle Class 1780–1850* (Hutchinson, 1987)

Davis, Richard W., *Dissent in Politics 1780–1830. The Political Life of William Smith, M.P.* (Epworth Press, 1971)

Dawson, George, *Shakespeare and Other Lectures*, ed. George St Clair (Kegan Paul, Trench, 1888)

De Morgan, Mary A (ed.), *Three Score Years and Ten. Reminiscences of the Late Sophia Elizabeth De Morgan. To which are added Letters to and from Her Husband, the Late Augustus De Morgan and Others*, edited by her daughter (Richard Bentley and Son, 1895)

Dickens, Charles, *The Old Curiosity Shop* (Harmondsworth: Penguin, 1972, first published 1841)

Dickens, Charles, *Dombey and Son* (Harmondsworth: Penguin, 1970, first published 1846–8)

Dickens, Charles, *David Copperfield* (Harmondsworth: Penguin, 1966, first published 1849–50)

Ditchfield, G. M., 'Priestley Riots in Historical Perspective', *Transactions of the Unitarian Historical Society*, Vol. 20, no. 1, April 1991, pp. 3–16

Drescher, Seymour, 'Cart Whip and Billy Roller: Or Anti-Slavery and Reform Symbolism in Industrialising Britain', in *Journal of Social History*, Vol. 15, no. 1, Fall 1981, pp. 3–25

Epps, Mrs E. (ed.), *Diary of the Late John Epps, M. D.*, Edinburgh (Kent, 1875)

Erskine, Mrs Steuart (ed.), *Anna Jameson. Letters and Friendships (1812–1860)* (T. Fisher Unwin, 1915)

Evans, Richard J., *The Feminists. Women's Emancipation Movements in Europe, America and Australasia 1840–1920* (Croom Helm, 1977)

Faderman, Lilian, *Surpassing the Love of Men. Friendship and Love Between Women from the Renaissance to the Present* (Women's Press, 1985)

Ferguson, Adam, *An Essay on the History of Civil Society*, ed. Duncan Forbes (Edinburgh: Edinburgh University Press, 1966, first published 1767)

Fielding, K. J. (ed.), *The Speeches of Charles Dickens* (Oxford: Clarendon Press, 1960)

Fladeland, Betty, *Abolitionists and Working Class Problems in the Age of Industrialisation* (Macmillan, 1984)

Forster, John, *The Life of Charles Dickens*, ed. J. M. T. Ley (Whitefriars Press, 1928, first published 1874)

Forster, Margaret, *Significant Sisters. The Grassroots of Active Feminism 1839–1939* (Harmondsworth: Penguin, 1984)

Fox, Franklin (ed.), *Memoir of Mrs Eliza Fox. To Which Extracts are Added from the Journals and Letters of Her Husband, the Late W. J. Fox* (N. Trübner, 1860)

Fox, William Johnson, *Reports of the Lectures Delivered at the Chapel in South Place, Finsbury* (Charles Fox, 1835)

Fox, William Johnson, *Reports of the Lectures Delivered in South Place, Finsbury* (Charles Fox, 1840)

Fox, William Johnson, *Memorial Edition of Collected Works of W. J. Fox. Reports of Lectures at South Place Chapel, Finsbury, Supplementary to the Course of Religious Ideas* (Charles Fox, 1866)

Frazee, John P., 'Dickens and Unitarianism', *Dickens Studies Annual*, 18, 1989, pp. 116–43

Frow, Edmund and Ruth Frow, 'Women in the Early Radical and Labour Movement', *Marxism Today*, Vol. 12, no. 4. April 1968, pp. 105–12

Garnett, Richard, *The Life of W. J. Fox. Public Teacher and Social Reformer, 1786–1864* (John Lane, 1909)

Garnett, R. G., *Co-operation and the Owenite Socialist Communities in Britain, 1825–45* (Manchester: Manchester University Press, 1972)

Goodway, F., *London Chartism 1838–1848* (Cambridge: Cambridge University Press, 1982)

Gorham, Deborah, 'Victorian Reform as a Family Business', in A. S. Wohl (ed.), *The Victorian Family. Structure and Stresses* (Croom Helm, 1978), Chapter 7.

Gow, Henry, *The Unitarians* (Methuen, 1928).

Gray, Robert Q., *The Labour Aristocracy in Victorian Edinburgh* (Oxford: Clarendon Press, 1976)

Grimstone, Mary Leman, *Woman's Love* (Saunders and Otley, 1832)

Grimstone, Mary Leman, *Character; or Jew and Gentile* (Charles Fox, 1833)

Grimstone, Mary Leman, *Cleone. A Tale of Married Life* (Effingham Wilson, 1834)

Gura, Philip F. and Joel Myerson (eds), *Critical Essays on American Transcendentalism* (Boston: G. K. Hall, 1982)

Haight, Gordon S. (ed.), *The George Eliot Letters* (Oxford University Press, 1954), Vol. 1

Haight, Gordon S. (ed.), *George Eliot and John Chapman. With Chapman's Diaries* (Hamden, Conn: Archon Books, 1969, second edn)

Hall, Catherine, 'The Early Formation of Victorian Domestic Ideology', in Sandra Burman (ed.), *Fit Work for Women* (Croom Helm, 1979), pp. 15–33

Hammond J. L. and Barbara Hammond, *James Stansfeld. A Victorian Champion of Sex Equality* (Longmans, Green, 1932)

Hammerton, A. James, *Emigrant Gentlewomen. Genteel Poverty and Female Education 1830–1914* (Croom Helm, 1979)

Harrison, Brian, *Separate Spheres. The Opposition to Women's Suffrage in Britain* (Croom Helm, 1978)

Harrison, Fraser, *The Dark Angel* (Sheldon Press, 1977)

Harrison, J. F. C., *Learning and Living 1790–1960. A Study in the History of the English Adult Education Movement* (Routledge and Kegan Paul, 1961)

Harrison, J. F. C., *Robert Owen and the Owenites in Britain and America. The Quest for the New Moral World* (Routledge and Kegan Paul, 1969)

Hayek, F. A. (ed.), *John Stuart Mill and Harriet Taylor: Their Correspondence and Subsequent Marriage* (Chicago: University of Chicago Press, 1951)

Hays, Matilda M., *Helen Stanley. A Tale* (E. Churton, 1846)

Helsinger, Elizabeth K., R. L. Sheets, W. Veeder, *The Woman Question. Society and Literature in Britain and America 1837–1883* (Chicago: University of Chicago Press, 1989, second edn)

Henderson, Robert, *Memoir of the Late Rev. George Armstrong* (Edward T. Whitfield, 1859)

Herstein, Sheila R., *A Mid-Victorian Feminist, Barbara Leigh Smith Bodichon* (New Haven: Yale University Press, 1985)

Hewitt, Margaret, *Wives and Mothers in Victorian Industry* (Rockliff, 1958)

Heyck, T. W., *The Transformation of Intellectual Life in Victorian England* (Croom Helm, 1982)

Hill, Christopher, *Milton and the English Revolution* (Faber and Faber, 1977)

Hill, Rosamund and Florence Davenport, *The Recorder of Birmingham. A Memoir of Matthew Davenport Hill. With Selections from his Correspondence* (Macmillan, 1878)

Hock, Guan Tjoa, *George Henry Lewes. A Victorian Mind* (Harvard University Press, 1977)

Holcombe, Lee, *Wives and Property. Reform of the Married Women's Property Law in Nineteenth Century England* (Toronto: University of Toronto Press, 1983)

Holt, Raymond V., *The Unitarian Contribution to Social Progress in England* (Butler and Tanner, 1938)

Holyoake, George Jacob, *A History of Co-operation* (T. Fisher Unwin, 1906)

Holyoake, George Jacob, *Sixty Years of an Agitator's Life* (T. Fisher Unwin, 1906)

Horne, Richard Hengist, *A New Spirit of the Age* (Smith, Elder, 1844)

Horstman, Allen, *Victorian Divorce* (Croom Helm, 1975)

Howe, Susanne, *Geraldine Jewsbury, Her Life and Errors* (Aberdeen: Aberdeen University Press, 1935)

Howitt, Mary, *An Autobiography* edited by her daughter, Margaret Howitt (Isbister, 1889)

Hudson, J. W., *The History of Adult Education* (Woburn Press, 1969, first published 1851)

Hurlbut, E. P., *Essays on Human Rights and Their Political Guarantees* with a preface and notes by George Combe (Edinburgh: MacLachlan, Stewart, 1847)

Huxley, Leonard (ed.), *Jane Welsh Carlyle: Letters to Her Family, 1839–1863* (John Murray, 1924)

Ireland, Annie E. (ed.), *Selections from the Letters of Geraldine Endsor Jewsbury to Jane Welsh Carlyle* (Longmans, Green, 1892)

Isichei, Elizabeth, *Victorian Quakers* (Oxford: Oxford University Press, 1970)

Jameson, Anna, *Winter Studies and Summer Rambles* (Saunders and Otley, 1838, first published 1833)

Jameson, Anna, *Memoirs and Essays Illustrative of Art, Literature and Social Morals* (Richard Bentley, 1846)

Jameson, Anna, *Characteristics of Women. Moral, Poetical and Historical* (Saunders and Otley, 1858)

Jerrold, William Blanchard, *The Life and Remains of Douglas Jerrold* (W. Kent, 1859)

Jerrold, Walter, *Douglas Jerrold. Dramatist and Wit* (Hodder and Stoughton, 1914)

Jewsbury, Geraldine, *Zoe: The History of Two Lives* (Virago, 1989, first published 1845)

John, Angela V., *By the Sweat of their Brow. Women Workers at Victorian Coal mines* (Routledge and Kegan Paul, 1984, second edn)

Jones, David, *Chartism and the Chartists* (Allen Lane, 1975)

Jones, David, 'Women and Chartism', *History*, Vol. 68, 1983, pp. 1–21

Kelly, Thomas, *A History of Adult Education in Great Britain* (Liverpool: Liverpool University Press, 1962)

Kent, Christopher, 'The Whittington Club: A Bohemian Experiment in Middle Class Social Reform', in *Victorian Studies*, Vol. 18, 1974, pp. 31–56

Kent, Susan Kingsley, *Sex and Suffrage in Britain 1860–1914* (Princeton: Princeton University Press, 1987)

Killham, John, *Tennyson and The Princess. Reflections of an Age* (Athlone Press, 1958)

Knight, Frida, *University Rebel. The Life of William Frend 1757–1841* (Victor Gollancz, 1971)

Lacey, Candida Ann (ed.), *Barbara Leigh Smith Bodichon and the Langham Place Circle* (Routledge and Kegan Paul, 1987)

Lammenais, Abbé de, *Modern Slavery* translated by W. J. Linton (J. Watson, 1840)

Le Breton, Philip Hemery (ed.), *Memoirs, Miscellanies and Letters of the Late Lucy Aikin, including those addressed to the Rev. Dr Channing from 1826–1842* (Longman, Green, Roberts, 1864)

Lee, Amice, *Laurels and Rosemary. The Life of William and Mary Howitt* (Oxford University Press, 1955)

Levine, Philippa, *Victorian Feminism 1850–1900* (Hutchinson, 1987)

Levine, Philippa, *Feminist Lives in Victorian England. Private Roles and Public Commitment* (Oxford: Basil Blackwell, 1990)

Lewes, G. L., *Dr Southwood Smith. A Retrospect* (William Blackwood and Sons, 1898)

Lindsay, Lady, 'Some Recollections of Miss Margaret Gillies', *Temple Bar*, Vol. LXXXI, pp. 265–73

Linton, Eliza Lynn, *Realities. A Tale* (Saunders and Otley, 1851)

Linton, Eliza Lynn, *My Literary Life* (Hodder and Stoughton, 1899)

Linton, William James, *James Watson. A Memoir* (New York: Augustus M. Kelley, 1971, first published 1880)

Linton, W. J., *Memories* (Lawrence and Bullen, 1895)

Lovett, William and John Collins, *Chartism, A New Social Organisation of the People* (Leicester: Leicester University Press, 1969, first published 1840)

Lovett, William, *Woman's Mission* (Simpkin, Marshall, 1856)

Lovett, William, *The Life and Struggles of William Lovett* (Trübner, 1876)

Lown, Judy, *Women and Industrialisation. Gender at Work in Nineteenth Century England* (Cambridge: Polity Press, 1990)

Lubin, Georges (ed.), *Correspondance de George Sand* (Paris: Garnier Frères, 1964), Vol. VII

Malleson, Hope, *Elizabeth Malleson 1828–1916. Autobiographical Notes and Letters* (Printed for Private Circulation, 1926)

Mallet, Phillip, 'Woman and Marriage in Victorian Society', in E. M. Craik (ed.), *Marriage and Property* (Aberdeen: Aberdeen University Press, 1984), pp. 159–89

Malmgreen, Gail, *Neither Bread Nor Roses: Utopian Feminists and the English Working Class, 1800–1850* (Brighton: John L. Noyce, 1978)

Malmgreen, Gail, 'Ann Knight and the Radical Subculture', *Quaker History*, Vol. 71, 1982, pp. 100–13

Manchester Athenæum, *Report of the Proceedings of the Public Meeting, Held 28 October, 1835, for the Purpose of Establishing the Athenæum* (Manchester: 1835)

Manchester Athenæum, *Report of the Provisional Directors of the Athenæum* (Manchester: 1836–48)

Manchester Athenæum, *Addresses 1835–1885* (Manchester: Taylor and Garnett, 1888)

Mario, Jessie White, *The Birth of Modern Italy* (T. Fisher Unwin, 1909)

Martineau, Harriet, *Society in America*, ed. Martin Lupset (Gloucester, Mass., Peter Smith, 1968, first published 1837)

Martineau, Harriet, *A History of the Thirty Years' Peace, 1816–1846* (George Bell and Son, 1877)

Martineau, Harriet, *Autobiography* (Virago, 1983, first published 1877)

Mason, Bertha, *The Story of the Women's Suffrage Movement* (Sheratt and Hughes, 1912)

Maurice, C. Edmund (ed.), *Life of Octavia Hill, as Told in Her Letters* (Macmillan, 1913)

McCann, Philip and Francis A. Young, *Samuel Wilderspin and the Infant School Movement* (Croom Helm, 1982)

McCown, Robert A. (ed.), *The Life and Times of Leigh Hunt. Papers Delivered at a Symposium at the University of Iowa, 13 April 1984* (Iowa: Friends of the University of Iowa Libraries, 1985)

McLachlan, H., *The Unitarian Movement in the Religious Life of England. Its Contribution to Thought and Learning. 1700–1900* (George Allen and Unwin, 1934)

Meteyard, Eliza, *Struggles for Fame* (T. C. Newby, 1845)

Millar, John, *Origin of the Distinction of Ranks* (Edinburgh: 1779), repr. in William C. Lehmann, *John Millar of Glasgow, 1735–1801. His Life and Thought and His Contributions to Sociological Analysis* (Cambridge: Cambridge University Press, 1960), pp. 175–322

Miller, E. Morris, 'Australia's First Two Novels. Origins and Backgrounds', *Papers and Proceedings, Tasmanian Historical Research Association*, Vol. 6, no. 2, 1957, pp. 37–49, 54–65

Mineka, Francis E., *The Dissidence of Dissent. The 'Monthly Repository' 1806–1838* (Chapel Hill: University of North Carolina, 1944)

Mineka, Francis E. (ed.), *The Earlier Letters of John Stuart Mill 1812–1848* (Toronto: University of Toronto Press, 1963)

Mitchell, Sally, *The Fallen Angel. Chastity, Class and Women's Reading 1835–1880* (Bowling Green, Kentucky: University Popular Press, 1981)

Morley, Edith, *The Life and Times of Henry Crabb Robinson* (J. M. Dent and Sons, 1935)

Nesbitt, George L., *Benthamite Reviewing. The First Twelve Years of the 'Westminster Review' 1824–1836* (New York: Columbia University Press, 1934)

Owen, Robert Dale, *Moral Physiology; Or a Brief and Plain Treatise on the Population Question* (E. Truelove, 1831)

Pankhurst, R. K. P., *William Thompson. Britain's Pioneer Socialist, Feminist and Co-operator* (Watts, 1954)

Patterson, A. Temple, *Radical Leicester. 1780–1850* (Leicester: University College, Leicester, 1954)

Perkin, Joan, *Women and Marriage in Nineteenth Century England* (Routledge, 1989)

Perkins, Jane Grey, *The Life of Mrs Norton* (John Murray, 1909)

Pollard, Sidney and John Salt (eds), *Robert Owen. Prophet of the Poor. Essays in Honour of the Two Hundredth Anniversary of His Birth* (Macmillan, 1971)

Prickett, Stephen (ed.), *The Romantics* (Methuen, 1981)

Prochaska, F. K., *Women and Philanthropy in Nineteenth Century England* (Oxford: Oxford University Press, 1980)

Prothero, I. J., 'Chartism in London', in *Past and Present*, no. 44, 1969, pp. 76–105

Purvis, June, *Hard Lessons. The Lives and Education of Working Women in Nineteenth Century England* (Cambridge: Polity Press, 1989)

Ratcliffe, S. K., *The Story of South Place* (Watts, 1955)

Read, Donald, *Press and People 1790–1850. Opinion in Three English Cities* (Edward Arnold, 1961)

Reid, Marion, *A Plea for Woman* (Edinburgh: Polygon, 1988, first published 1843)

Reid, T. Wemyss, *The Life, Letters and Friendships of Richard Monckton Milnes, First Lord Houghton* (Cassell, 1898)

Rendall, Jane, *The Origins of Modern Feminism: Women in Britain, France and the United States 1780–1860* (Chicago: Lyceum, 1985)

Rendall, Jane, '"A Moral Engine?" Feminism, Liberalism and the *English Woman's Journal*', in Jane Rendall, *Equal or Different. Women's Politics 1800–1914* (Oxford: Basil Blackwell, 1987), pp. 112–38

Rendall, Jane, 'Friendship and Politics: Barbara Leigh Smith Bodichon (1827–91) and Bessie Raynor Parkes (1829–1925)', in Jane Rendall and Susan Mendus (eds), *Sexuality and Subordination. Interdisciplinary Studies of Gender in the Nineteenth Century* (Routledge, 1989), pp. 136–70

Richards, E. F. (ed.), *Mazzini's Letters to an English Family, 1844–1854* (John Lane, 1920)

Richey, Russell E., 'Did the English Presbyterians Become Unitarian?' *Church History*, Vol. 42, 1973, pp. 58–72

Robberds, J. W., *A Memoir of the Life and Writings of the Late William Taylor of Norwich* (John Murray, 1843)

Roe, Michael, 'Mary Leman Grimstone (1800–1850?) For Women's Rights and Tasmanian Patriotism', *Papers and Proceedings, Tasmanian Historical Research Association*, Vol. 6, no. 1, March 1989, pp. 8–32

Rossi, Alice S. (ed.), *Essays on Sex Equality* (Chicago: University of Chicago Press, 1970)

Rowe, D. J. (ed.), *London Radicalism 1830–1843. A Selection from the Papers of Francis Place* (London Records Society, 1970)

Roy, Rammohun, *The English Works of Raj Rammohun Roy*, ed. Jogendra Chundra Ghose (Calcutta: Oriental Press, 1885)

Royle, Edward, *Radical Politics 1790–1900. Religion and Unbelief* (Longman, 1971)

Royle, Edward, *Victorian Infidels. The Origins of the British Secularist Movement 1791–1866* (Manchester: Manchester University Press, 1974)

Rudman, Harry W., *Italian Nationalism and English Letters* (George Allen and Unwin, 1940)

Rusk, Ralph (ed.), *The Letters of Ralph Waldo Emerson* (New York: Columbia University Press, 1939), Vols 3–4

Ruston, Alan, 'Radical Nonconformity in Hackney. 1805–1845', *Transactions of the Unitarian Historical Society*, Vol. 14, no. 1, 1967, pp. 1–9

Ruston, Alan, 'The Non-Con Clubs and Some Other Unitarian Clubs', *Transactions of the Unitarian Historical Society*, Vol. 14, no. 3, 1969, pp. 147–62

Ruston, Alan, 'Clementia Taylor', *Transactions of the Unitarian Historical Society*, Vol. 20, no. 1, April 1991, pp. 62–8

Saint-Simon, Comte de, *The Doctrine of Saint-Simon; An Exposition. First Year, 1828–1829* trans. with notes and an introduction by Georg G. Iggers (New York: Schocken, 1972)

Sand, George, *The Works of George Sand*, trans. Eliza A. Ashurst, Matilda M. Hays and Rev. Edmund R. Larken (E. Churton, 1847)

Sanders, C. R. (ed.), *The Collected Letters of Thomas and Jane Welsh Carlyle* (Durham, North Carolina: Duke University Press, 1977), Vols 6–7, 13

Sanders, Valerie (ed.), *Harriet Martineau. Selected Letters* (Oxford: Clarendon Press, 1990)

Shirren, A. J., *Samuel Rogers, the Poet from Newington Green* (Stoke Newington Public Libraries Committee, 1963)

Schwarzkopf, Jutta, *Women in the Chartist Movement* (Macmillan, 1991)

Seed, John, 'Unitarianism, Political Economy and the Antinomies of Liberal Culture in Manchester, 1830–50', *Social History*, Vol. 7, 1982, pp. 1–25

Seed, John, 'Theologies of Power: Unitarianism and the Social Relations of Religious Discourse', in R. J. Morris (ed.), *Class, Power and Social Structure in British Nineteenth Century Towns* (Leicester: Leicester University Press, 1986), pp. 108–56

Sell, Roger D., 'Dickens and the New Historicism: the Polyvocal Audience and Discourse of *Dombey and Son*', in Jeremy Hawthorn (ed.), *The Nineteenth Century British Novel* (Edward Arnold, 1986), pp. 63–79

Sellers, Ian, 'Unitarians and Social Change', *Hibbert Journal*, Vol. 61, 1963, pp. 16–22, 78–80, 122–8

Shaffer, E. S., *'Kubla Khan' and the Fall of Jerusalem. The Mythological School in Biblical Criticism and Secular Literature. 1770–1880* (Cambridge: Cambridge University Press, 1975)

Shanley, Mary Lyndon, 'Marital Slavery and Friendship: J. S. Mill's *Subjection of Women*', *Political Theory*, May 1981, pp. 229–47

Shanley, Mary Lyndon, *Feminism, Marriage and the Law in Victorian England, 1850–1895* (L. B. Tauris, 1989)

Short, H. L., 'Presbyterians Under a New Name', in C. G. Bolam *et al.*, *The English Presbyterians, from Elizabethan Puritanism to Modern Unitarianism* (George Allen and Unwin, 1968), Chapter 6

Sigsworth, E. M. and T. J. Wyke, 'A Study of Victorian Prostitution and Venereal Disease', in Martha Vicinus (ed.), *Suffer and Be Still* (Bloomington: Indiana University Press, 1972)

Smith, Barbara (ed.), *Truth, Liberty, Religion. Essays Celebrating Two Hundred Years of Manchester College* (Oxford: Manchester College, 1986)

Smith, F. B., *Radical Artisan. William James Linton, 1812–1897* (Manchester: Manchester University Press, 1973)

Smith, John Stores, *Social Aspects* (John Chapman, 1850)

Smith, Thomas Southwood, *The Philosophy of Health* (Charles Knight, 1835)

Solomon, Robert C., *Continental Philosophy since 1750. The Rise and Fall of the Self* (Oxford: Oxford University Press, 1988)

Spears, Robert, *Memorable Unitarians* (British and Foreign Unitarian Association, 1906)

Spencer, Herbert, *Social Statics, or the Conditions Essential to Human Happiness Specified, and the First of them Developed* (New York: Augustus M. Kelley, 1969, first published 1851)

Squier, John Omer, *The Character and Mission of Woman: A Lecture Applicable to the New Marriage Law* (Smallfield and Son, 1837)

Stange, Douglas C., *British Unitarians Against Slavery. 1833–1865* (Cranbury, New Jersey: Associated University Presses, 1977)

Stetson, Dorothy M., *A Woman's Issue. The Politics of Family Law Reform in England* (Greenwood, Connecticut: Greenwood Press, 1982)

Stewart, W. A. C., *Progressives and Radicals in English Education 1750–1970* (Macmillan, 1972)

Stinchcombe, Owen, 'Elizabeth Malleson', *Transactions of the Unitarian Historical Society*, Vol. 20, no. 1, April 1991, pp. 56–61

Storey, Graham and K. J. Fielding (eds), *The Letters of Charles Dickens* (Oxford: Clarendon Press, 1981), Vol. 5

Summers, Anne, 'Home from Home – Women's Philanthropic Work in the Nineteenth Century', in Sandra Burman (ed.), *Fit Work for Women* (Croom Helm, 1979), pp. 33–63

Taylor, Barbara, *Eve and the New Jerusalem. Socialism and Feminism in the Nineteenth Century* (Virago, 1983)

Taylor, Barbara, '"The men are as bad as their masters . . .": Socialism, Feminism and Sexual Antagonism in the London Tailoring Trade in the Early 1830s', *Feminist Studies*, Vol. 5, no. 1, Spring 1979, pp. 7–40

Thomas, Clara, *Love and Work Enough. The Life of Anna Jameson* (Macdonald, 1967)

Thomis, Malcolm I., and Jennifer Grimmett, *Women in Protest 1800–1850* (Croom Helm, 1989)

Thompson, Dorothy (ed.), *The Early Chartists* (Macmillan, 1971)

Thompson, Dorothy, *The Chartists* (Temple Smith, 1984)

Thompson, Patricia, *George Sand and the Victorians. Her Influence and Reputation in Nineteenth Century England* (Macmillan, 1977)

Thompson, William, *Appeal of One Half of the Human Race, Women, Against the Pretensions of the Other Half, Men, To Retain them in Political, and thence in Civil and Domestic Slavery* (Cork: Eagle Printing, 1975, first published 1825)

Tillotson, Kathleen (ed.), *The Letters of Charles Dickens* (Oxford: Clarendon Press, 1977), Vol. 4

Tolles, F. B. (ed.), *'Slavery and the Woman Question': Lucretia Mott's Diary of Her Visit to Great Britain to Attend the World Anti-Slavery Convention of 1840* (Friends' Historical Association, 1852)

Trudghill, Eric, *Madonnas and Magdalenes. The Origins and Development of Victorian Sexual Attitudes* (New York: Holmes and Meier, 1976)

Tuke, Margaret J., *A History of Bedford College for Women. 1849–1937* (Oxford University Press, 1939)

Turner, Ralph E., *James Silk Buckingham 1786–1855* (Williams and Norgate, 1934)

Unitarian Social Reformers, Number 4. Right Honourable James Stansfeld (Lindsey Press, n.d.)

Vicinus, Martha, *The Industrial Muse. A Study of Nineteenth Century British Working Class Literature* (Croom Helm, 1974)

Vicinus, Martha, *Independent Women. Work and Community for Single Women. 1850–1920* (Virago, 1985)

Villiers, Brougham, *The Case for Women's Suffrage* (T. Fisher Unwin, 1907)

Walkowitz, Judith R., *Prostitution and Victorian Society. Women, Class and the State* (Cambridge: Cambridge University Press, 1980)

Wallas, Graham, *William Johnson Fox. 1786–1864, Conway Memorial Lecture* (Watts, 1924)

Walvin, James (ed.), *Slavery and British Society 1776–1846* (Macmillan, 1982)

Ward, J. T., *Chartism* (B. T. Batsford, 1973)

Watt, George, *The Fallen Woman in the Nineteenth Century English Novel* (Croom Helm, 1984)

Watts, Ruth, 'The Unitarian Contribution to the Development of Female Education, 1790–1850', *History of Education*, Vol. 9, no. 4, 1980, pp. 273–86

Watts, Ruth, 'Knowledge is Power – Unitarians, Gender and Education in the Eighteenth and Early Nineteenth Centuries', *Gender and Education*, Vol. 1, no. 1, 1989, pp. 35–50

Webb, R. K., *Harriet Martineau. A Radical Victorian* (Heinemann, 1960)

Webb, R. K., 'John Hamilton Thom: Intellect and Conscience in Liverpool', in P. T. Phillips (ed.), *The View from the Pulpit: Victorian Ministers and Society* (Toronto: Macmillan Company of Canada, 1978), pp. 210–43

Webb, R. K., 'Flying Missionaries: Unitarian Journalists in Victorian England', in J. M. W. Bean (ed.), *The Political Culture of Modern Britain: Studies in Memory of Stephen Koss* (Hamish Hamilton, 1987), pp. 11–31

Webb, R. K., 'The Gaskells as Unitarians', in J. Shattock (ed.), *Dickens and Other Victorians. Essays in Honour of Philip Collins* (Macmillan, 1988), pp. 144–71

Weeks, Jeffrey, *Sex, Politics and Society. The Regulation of Sexuality since 1800* (Longman, 1989)

White, Bruce A., 'Douglas Jerrold's "Q" Papers', *Victorian Periodicals Review*, Vol. 25, no. 4, Winter 1982, pp. 131–7

Wigmore-Beddoes, Dennis, G., *Yesterday's Radicals. A Study of the Affinity Between Unitarianism and Broad Church Anglicanism in the Nineteenth Century* (James Clarke, 1971)

Williford, Miriam, 'Bentham and the Rights of Women', *Journal of the History of Ideas*, 36, January–March 1975, pp. 167–76

Woodring, Carl Ray, *Victorian Samplers: William and Mary Howitt* (Lawrence: University of Kansas Press, 1952)

Wordsworth, William, *Wordsworth. Poetical Works*, ed. Thomas Hutchinson, revised by Ernest de Selincourt (Oxford: Oxford University Press, 1978)

Yeo, Eileen, 'Culture and Constraint in Working Class Movements, 1830–1855', in Eileen and Stephen Yeo (eds), *Popular Culture and Class Conflict 1590–1914: Explorations in the History of Labour and Leisure* (Brighton: Harvester Press, 1981), pp. 154–86

UNPUBLISHED WORKS

Bushrod, Emily, 'The History of Unitarianism in Birmingham from the Middle of the Eighteenth Century to 1893', (MA thesis, University of Birmingham, 1954)

Chambers-Schiller, Lee Virginia, 'The CAB: A Trans-Atlantic Community, Aspects of Nineteenth Century Reform', (PhD thesis, University of Michigan, 1977)

Kanner, Selma Barbara, 'Victorian Institutional Patronage: Angela Burdett-Coutts, Charles Dickens and Urania Cottage; Reformatory for Women, 1846–1858', (PhD thesis, University of California, 1972)

Parnaby, Margaret, 'William Johnson Fox and the *Monthly Repository* Circle of 1832–1836', (PhD thesis, Australian National University, 1979)

Saywell, Ruby J., 'The Development of the Feminist Idea in England 1789–1833', (MA thesis, King's College, London, 1936)

Watts, Ruth, 'The Unitarian Contribution to Education in England from the Late Eighteenth Century to 1853', (PhD thesis, University of Leicester, 1987)

Worzala, Diana Mary Chase, 'The Langham Place Circle: The Beginnings of the Organized Women's Movement in England 1854–1870', (PhD thesis, University of Wisconsin–Madison, 1982)

Index